THE
SECRET
SIX

Other books by Otto Scott:

James I: The Fool As King
Robespierre: The Fool As Revolutionary
The Professional: A Biography Of JB Saunders
The Creative Ordeal: The Story Of Raytheon
The Exception: The Story Of Ashland Oil
The Other End of the Lifeboat

Cover Designs/Artwork: Stephen W. Platts.

Typography: Continental Typographics, Inc.

THE SECRET SIX:
THE FOOL
AS MARTYR

Volume Three of the
Sacred Fool Quartet

Otto Scott

Foundation for American Education
Distributed by Southron Press
Box 11708
Columbia, S.C. 29211

First printing 1979 by Times Books,
a division of Quadrangle/The New York Times Book Co., Inc.
Second Printing 1987 Foundation for American Education

Library of Congress Cataloguing in Publication Data

Scott, Otto J.
  The secret six

  Bibliography; p. 355
  1. John Brown, 1800–1859. 2. Harpers Ferry, W. Va.–John Brown Raid, 1859.
3. Kansas–History–1854–1861. 4. Abolitionists–United States–Biography.
I. Title. E451.S36 973.6'8'0924 78-53310 ISBN O-8129-0777-9

"Lilies that fester smell far worse than weeds."

Shakespeare: *Sonnets*

INTRODUCTION

This is the third of a quartet of books about fools made sacred by fame. "Sacred," because modern man, like his pagan predecessors, considers fame an attribute that elevates an individual beyond the ordinary; that expands his dimensions and conveys a form of immortality.

Fame that lasts a lifetime is considered a great achievement; fame that extends into the foreseeable future, as in historic personages, is regarded as lifting the individual to the height of a demi-god, wreathed in myth.

A number of such personages arose in Europe during the 19th century, whose names still glitter: Napoleon I, Queen Victoria, Karl Marx, Darwin. These were personages associated with either high position or unforgettable contributions. In contrast the United States presented only two remarkable figures: Abraham Lincoln, its President during a great sectional war–and John Brown, the Abolitionist. Lincoln was murdered at the close of the war and Brown was hanged at Harper's Ferry in December, 1859, before the war started. Both men were hailed by 19th century Americans not only as martyrs, but also as great contributors to world history.

That this seemed a provincial exaggeration to most of the world is understandable. Less generally understood is that of the two, it was John Brown who did the most to change history–though he did so unintentionally, by sowing an example that remains to darken our lives to this day. For John Brown was one of the fathers of modern political terror.

That is not to say that the world was not acquainted with political crime before Brown. Assassins and killers have plagued every society; every social order, every nation and all peoples throughout history. Political murderers have always claimed some sort of logic; some rationale. Shakespeare's Brutus claimed to assist the murderers of his benefactor in the name of Roman freedom. Murders have also been committed in the name of religion, and in the name of virtue.

Brown's accidental importance comes from the fact that although he claimed a noble political motive, his victims were innocent private citizens, selected at random. Even then; if he had simply acted alone, his behavior might have been dismissed as aberrant and unimportant. But Brown did not act alone. He acted as the instrument of a small group of men, who secretly determined that they would change the society of half their country, using illegal force and condoning unchristian murders in the name of freedom, Christianity and a Higher Law.

How the Committee of Six, as they called themselves, hired John Brown and encouraged his activities has long been known to American historians. But the historical establishment long ago decided to approve the Secret Six, as they are now known, on the grounds that the Six believed that John Brown's bloodthirsty rhetoric was mere rodomontade.

That rationale is destroyed, however, by evidence that the Six provided Brown with guns and ammunition. Guns are not instruments of persuasion. There also exists evidence that at least one of the Six knew that Brown had murdered five innocent men in the Kansas Territory, before he was hired by the Committee. It is clear, therefore, that the Committee of Six intended that Brown continue.

Why did six well-educated, well-placed New Englanders, totally remote by background and habit from any sort of criminal activity, finance random political murders? They told each other–and later the world–that they wanted to abolish chattel slavery in the American South.

They believed that purpose to be so noble that it sanctioned any means– including the murder of non-slave holders and even bystanders. This was, and is, a very strange position for well-educated men to adopt.

Abolition was not, in the 1850s, a new idea. Britain had emancipated all its slaves in the West Indies by 1833. And all the slaves in all its colonies by 1834–without finding it necessary to murder anyone. Spain ended slavery even earlier, in 1817. France earlier yet, in 1794.

All the nations of western Europe were, by the 1850s, moving toward industrialization and against slavery–which had proven uneconomic in the new industrial world. Of course, Europeans would later discover that only force would stop black Africans from enslaving one another, but colonialism is seldom praised for that achievement. In any event, the theory that murder at random is the way to improve a society was not even held by the most cruel of the colonial overlords.

How was it, then, that the Secret Six agreed with John Brown that random murders could lead to brotherhood and equality? Certainly Christianity did not advocate force: Christianity specifically condemns murder, i.e., the cold-blooded taking of a human life in order to clear the way toward some desired goal.

To understand the rationale of the Six, it is necessary to look into the denial of Christianity that arose–paradoxically, in the name of Christianity–in the 1830s in New England. Alexis de Toqueville, whose tour of the country was between 1831 and 1832, provides part of the answer in *Democracy in America*. In this examination, he noted that "Here and there in the midst of the American society you meet with men full of a fanatical and almost wild spiritualism... From time to time strange sects arise which endeavor to strike out extraordinary paths..."

Some of these paths were anachronistically called "crusades." They started out against tobacco, dancing, travel on the Sabbath, against tea and coffee, against eating meat, against liquor, in favor of vegetarianism and cold baths. Their adherents formed communes, colonies and cults; fellow travelers appeared in evangelical circles.

More intellectual paths were traversed by the Reverend Ralph Waldo Emerson, and the Reverend William Ellery Channing who established the American form of anti-Christian Unitarianism. This was called "The New England religion" and was a central force in the Abolitionist movement.

The Six represented the dark side of this movement. Yet even the light side took the position that Christianity was insufficiently virtuous, and moved too slowly.

Two of the Six were, astonishingly, ordained Christian ministers. But the Reverend Theodore Parker, for all his fame, had to deliver his famous sermons in a theater. And the Reverend Thomas Wentworth Higginson found the duties of a pastor boring and confining. Two—Gerrit Smith and George Luther Stearns—were wealthy businessmen, but both were considered eccentric even by their friends. One, Franklin Benjamin Sanford, was the tutor of the Emerson children, but at a time when the Concord sky was dominated by Transcendental clouds. And the sixth, Dr. Samuel Gridley Howe, although a famous physician, operated within the closed and esoteric world of the blind, deaf and mute—a setting almost guaranteed to create a sense of omnipotence.

But the Six were not out of step in New England. They were respected friends of both Emerson and Thoreau, who approved—and shared—their support of John Brown. They had fashionable intellectual encouragement from the violent rhetoric of William Lloyd Garrison, the living megaphone of Abolition, as well as the Northern press. They were heartened by the advocates of the Higher Law theory, (whose arguments, fashioned from Emerson, were the models for Nietszche's *Übermensch*).

When their murderous activities were finally exposed, the Six—and Brown—were hailed by the North as heroes in a great Cause. Until this third book of the Sacred Fool Quartet, the Six have remained on a pedestal, maintained by American historians, repeatedly described in admiring biographies as men of virtue and compassion—murders notwithstanding.

Yet by every ethic of civilization, they suborned crime, and left an evil legacy. It is one of the great ironies of history that their formula of murder at random in the name of a noble cause has now traveled around the world—and seems likely, in the near future, to return to the land of its origin to threaten us all.

That the South was unable, in the 1850s, to analyze and expose the arguments used by the Six is no surprise. The South was taken aback at being labelled unchristian, and by a torrent of self-righteous abuse.

Those enlightened by the clarity of hindsight who might wonder why Southerners could not properly analyze the tactics of the Abolitionists should ask why our entire historical Establishment has not been able to penetrate such arguments in all the years since. If this third volume of the Sacred Fool Quartet manages to provoke a belated examination, it will have been well worth the effort.

But it is my hope that deeper reflections will also be inspired. The role of the Reverend Ralph Waldo Emerson and others long honored in the American Pantheon need, in my opinion, to be reassessed. For unless we learn to recognize and acknowledge folly even when it wears the masks of fame, we will hardly be able to leave this world better than it was when we entered. And to fail in that task is to prove unworthy of our heritage.

OTTO SCOTT
1987

Contents

Part I
THE CURTAIN RISES

Chapter 1

Near sundown James Blood saw a large man on a pony, riding alongside a wagonload of men being drawn by a team of horses. When Blood neared the wagon an old man suddenly rose upright and shouted, "Halt!"

Blood stopped. The men in the wagon were armed with revolvers and knives in their belts, rifles in one hand, and heavy artillery sabers in the other. Blood was not alarmed; he knew the old man as a Northern settler in the Kansas region. Even the sabers didn't surprise him; the old man had a stock of them and had given one to Blood, in the town of Lawrence, the previous autumn. But he was immediately aware that something unusual was underway.

He listened while the old man denounced the Free State leaders as "cowards" for having surrendered Lawrence without firing a shot. Years later Blood could still recall his vehemence in the twilight. "His manner," he wrote, "was wild and frenzied, and the whole party watched with excited eagerness every word or motion of the old man. Finally, as I left them, he requested me not to mention the fact that I had met them, as they were on a secret mission and did not want anyone to know . . ."[1]

Blood nodded and the driver picked up the reins; the wagon, with its seven men, trundled on toward Pottawatomie Creek, the large man on the pony trotting alongside. That was Friday, May 23, 1856.

As darkness fell the wagonload of men and the man on the pony neared the edge of the woods between two deep ravines. The driver forced the team down the bank, and in that pocket they made their camp for the night. They were about one mile north of Dutch Henry's Crossing.

They spent the entire next day, Saturday, stretched on the ground, waiting for nightfall. The moon was scheduled to rise that night at 11:58, and they knew—or the old man had told them—that they had to move before that reflected light appeared, for their plan needed the cover of darkness. At the same time they did not want to move too early; they preferred to make their visit after the settlers were in bed and asleep.

The old man watched the stars, by which he could tell time. At ten o'clock, he arose. The others rose with him, gripping their sabers.

They left the team unhitched near some bushes, the wagon hidden, and waded through the shallow waters of Mosquito Creek, heading north. Not far from the opposite bank they reached a cabin and one of them knocked heavily on the door. There was no reply, but a few minutes later they heard the sound of a rifle barrel being jammed through the chinks of the cabin wall.

"At that we all scattered. We did not disturb that man. With some candle wicking soaked in coal oil to throw some light inside, so that we could see inside while he could not see outside, we would have managed it. *It was a method much used later.*" (Italics added.)[2]

The night was hot and humid; the river was not far away. The Doyle family was asleep as the men approached their cabin. Two bulldogs rushed out, barking. Two of the men stopped and slashed one to death with their sabers. The other dog fled, howling, and the family awoke.

The men knocked heavily on the door and James Doyle swung out of bed. "What is it?" he called.

"What way to the Wilkinson place?" a man's voice answered.

Doyle opened the door, saying he would tell them, and was almost knocked off his feet when several men rushed in, shouting, "We're the Northern Army! Surrender!"

Mahala Doyle clutched her youngest, a girl, and began to stammer. "Hush, Mother, hush," said James Doyle. His three sons moved beside him: William, twenty-two, Drury, twenty, and John, fourteen. The men pushed Doyle, and then the two eldest sons, out the door. Mahala Doyle began to weep, but when they reached for the fourteen-year-old she sprang out of bed and clutched him. "Not him; Oh, God, not him."[3]

The old man in the light jacket, leather tie, and farmer's straw hat, his face as thin and stern as an ax, pushed the boy back and the men left, slamming the door.

Mahala Doyle clutched John and listened, her eyes wide.

The men stopped their prisoners about two hundred yards from the Doyle cabin. The leader placed his revolver against Doyle's forehead and pulled the trigger,[4] as coolly as a man shooting a lame horse.

That set them off. One, in a frenzy, stabbed Doyle's corpse with his saber. William Doyle was stabbed in the face, slashed over the head, and shot in the side. Drury broke and ran in the darkness, was pursued, and overtaken near a ravine. He put his arms up to ward off their blows, but the men, bearded, burly, and in a near frenzy, hacked at him with their sabers. His fingers and then his arms were cut off; his head was cut open, and he was stabbed in the chest. They continued to hack after he fell—and after he was dead. He had frightened them; he might have escaped.

The Wilkinson cabin was next. Mrs. Wilkinson had measles and had trouble sleeping. She heard the dogs bark and she woke her husband. He grunted, said it only was someone passing, and went back to sleep. But the dogs grew louder; Mrs. Wilkinson heard footsteps, and saw a man pass by the window. Then she heard loud knocks on the door.

"Who is that?" she called, and there was no reply. That was strange, and she awoke her husband. He called, "Who is that?" and a man answered, "I want you to tell me the way to Dutch Henry's."

Wilkinson began to give directions and the voice said, "Come out and show us."

His wife clutched at him, intuitively aware something was wrong. Wilkinson said he couldn't find his clothes but he could tell them the way without coming out, and there was the sound of footsteps retreating and men whispering.

Then another voice asked Wilkinson, "Are you a Northern *armist?*" Wilkinson replied, "I am!"

At that, the voice said, "You are our prisoner. Do you surrender?"

"Gentlemen," said Wilkinson, "I do."

"Open the door," said several voices, and Wilkinson asked for time while he found a light. "If you don't open it, we will open it for you," a voice shouted and Wilkinson—ignoring his wife's cries against it—opened the door.

Four men rushed in and told Wilkinson to get dressed. Heavily armed, they searched the small house to see if any others were present, found a gun—the only weapon the Wilkinsons possessed—and a powder flask and took them. Mrs. Wilkinson sat up in bed, clutching the covers, and begged them to leave her husband, saying that she was sick and helpless. The old man in the light coat and leather cravat looked at her, and then at their small children.

"You have neighbors," he said.

"So I have," she replied, "but they are not here, and I cannot go for them."

"It matters not," he answered, and turned away. The others urged Wilkinson to hurry; when he started to put on his boots they couldn't wait any longer, and pushed him out the door.

Mrs. Wilkinson was still in bed when two of the men returned. They came through the doorway as though the property no longer belonged to anyone, and picked up two saddles. Mrs. Wilkinson ventured to ask what they planned to do with her husband and one of them—youthful beneath his beard—said, "Take him a prisoner to the camp."

That was reassuring, and she asked if one of them could stay with her and the children. One said he'd like to, "but they wouldn't let me." Then they left again.[5] After a few minutes Mrs. Wilkinson got out of bed shakily and listened, but there was nothing to be heard but the chirping of insects and soft wind shaking the trees. She wept, trying not to make any noise.

Outside in the dark they cut Wilkinson's throat, stabbed him in the side, and over the head. The murder was quick and silent—except for the chopping sound of the sabers.

Then they rushed toward the James Harris cabin. Harris worked for Dutch Henry, of Dutch Henry's Crossing. Harris had three men staying overnight at his cabin: John S. Wightman, Jerome Glanville, who had come to buy a cow, and Dutch Henry's brother William: "Dutch Bill."

This time there was no knock on the door, but the door was unlocked; until this particular night the region had been safe and peaceful. The sleepers awakened to find sabers at their throats, and eyes glaring at them.

"The Northern army is upon you," said one of the invaders, "It will be useless to resist."

Nobody dared; the men were heavily armed, laboring under great excitement, and obviously dangerous. Harris, who recognized two of them as nearby settlers, was astonished. The men took Wightman outside and questioned him about his political sympathies, learned he was a Northerner and brought him back. Then they took Glanville and —in time—returned him also. Others, meanwhile, ransacked the room, grabbing two rifles and a bowie knife that were in plain sight, and then searched diligently for ammunition.

They asked all three about Dutch Henry; they wanted him badly. But Dutch Henry was out searching for some cattle missing from his fine herd and had camped somewhere on the limitless prairie.

Intermingled with questions about his Northern sympathies and convictions, they asked Harris why he worked for Dutch Henry. Harris replied that the rancher paid him higher wages than he could receive from anyone else, but he knew that there was more behind the question. Dutch Henry used the open prairie to feed his cattle, replenished his herd by trades with travelers passing through the Kansas Territory and toward California, and maintained an oasis of prosperity amid the "dirt-poor" settlers pouring into the region. His hospitality to these newcomers, his assistance to them and their families did not check a flood of jealousy and resentment. Harris sweated in the night in the hands of the "Northern Army."

When they asked about bridles and saddles a new element was added: the Army was interested in loot. Harris told them there was only one saddle available, belonging to Dutch Henry. They marched him to the stable and waited while he saddled Dutch Henry's fine grey horse. Then they marched him back to the cabin.[6]

Inside the cabin, Glanville noticed the old man's hands were "caked with blood."[7] That was something a farmer, accustomed to butchering, would recognize. Meanwhile the old man, his dark blue eyes glinting, beckoned to Dutch Bill, whose previous days in strictly ordered Prussia or in the serene Kansas Territory, before the settlers arrived, had not prepared him for such a summons.

He was murdered beside the Pottawatomie with sabers. One blow severed his left hand, except for a strand of flesh, as he raised it in self-defense. His skull was opened in two places; and he fell headlong into the shallows. After his murderers washed their sabers and walked away, the chilly waters of the river gradually carried away part of his brain.[8]

Inside the Harris cabin the captives heard a shot. The guards, recognizing the signal, departed. They had all arrived on foot but several were on horses when they left Dutch Henry's, with the old man in the lead, astride the rancher's prize grey. The arms they had collected were distributed among them. Left behind were five mutilated dead men, two widows, and a number of fatherless children. And the peace of the region was in a shambles.

Five of the seven men whom fifty-six-year-old John Brown led in murder along the banks of the Pottawatomie were members of his own family. Four were sons: Owen, thirty-one, Frederick, twenty-five, Salmon, nineteen, and Oliver, seventeen. One was a son-in-law: Henry Thompson. The other two men were James Townsley, thirty-six, who had the team and wagon Brown needed to reach the scene, and Theodore Wiener, thirty-six, a storekeeper. Neither Townsley nor Wiener had ever before been involved in violence, let alone crime. Neither— for that matter—had any of Brown's sons or his son-in-law.

That is not too unusual. Although murder is the most serious of all crimes, it is often committed by those who have never before broken a major law. What was far more unusual about the Pottawatomie murderers, beyond their familial relationship, was that although their names were soon known, none of them was ever brought to justice for the crimes.

Chapter 2

Two years before the Pottawatomie murders but, by coincidence, on the same calendar month and day, May 24, three slave hunters from Virginia, searching the city of Boston, followed one of their quarry— Anthony Burns—as he stopped to look into a jewelry store window.

The bounty hunters could not legally make an arrest, but they had Deputy U.S. Marshal Asa O. Butman along. They pointed to their man and Butman went into Peter Brent Brigham's nearby saloon and called for help. Men came boiling out and Burns, who was six feet tall, with a deformed hand and a scarred cheek, was carried off to the Boston Court House and into the jury room of the United States Court.[1]

There he was confronted by Colonel Suttler, who took off his hat, made a bow, and said, "How do you do, *Mr.* Burns?" Then he added, "Why did you run away from me?"

"I fell asleep on board of the vessel where I worked and before I woke up she set sail and carried me off."[2]

The colonel laughed, clapped his hat back on and turned away. The marshal was satisfied that a proper identification had been made, and the fugitive was locked up. The next morning Richard Henry Dana, Jr., thirty-nine, famous for his *Two Years Before the Mast* and in 1854 a practicing attorney in Boston, learned of the capture. He offered his services and Burns refused, fearing matters would go harder for him in Virginia if he resisted the law. But Dana spread the news that another fugitive was in custody.

The vigilance committee, formed to prevent the provisions of the Fugitive Slave Law from being carried out, was alerted and its leaders swung into action at once. These included the Reverend Theodore Parker, forty-four, the city's best-known Unitarian firebrand and orator, Dr. Samuel Gridley Howe, fifty-three, world famous for his work among the deaf, blind, and mute, Wendell Phillips, forty-two, the elegant agitator and cohort of William Lloyd Garrison, and others. Among these others was the tall, athletic Reverend Thomas Wentworth Higginson, thirty, pastor of a "free" church in Worcester and organizer of a Vigilance Committee in that town; he had received a message from the Reverend Samuel J. May, fifty-seven, still another Unitarian divine, to come to Boston at once—with his forces. Meanwhile, Dana managed to delay the hearing in the courthouse.

On Friday morning, May 26, 1854, Higginson met with other members of the vigilance committee in Boston. As usual the windows were closed, curtains drawn, and lookouts posted. There were sixty men at the gathering and many spoke passionately but not to any particular purpose. Higginson was exasperated: he proposed that the courthouse be assailed and the prisoner released by force. A protest meeting had already been scheduled at Faneuil Hall that evening, at which Reverend Parker and Wendell Phillips would speak. Higginson wanted them to incite the crowd to attack the courthouse, but when that plan was put to a vote, the vote was three to one against it. During these arguments some lookouts ran in to announce that Colonel Suttler was passing by, surrounded by a volunteer guard of Southern students from Harvard. The meeting broke up while most men ran outside to "point the finger of scorn" at the colonel.[3]

Higginson later insisted that it was during this interlude that an "executive committee" consisting of Parker, Higginson, Wendell Phillips, Dr. Samuel Gridley Howe, Captain Austin Bearse, and William Kemp was formed, which agreed to rally the crowd at Faneuil Hall and storm the courthouse that night. When Martin Stowell arrived from Worcester with fifty more men at 6:00 P.M., Higginson told him of this plan, and added his name to the executive committee.[4]

Considering the high positions and lofty intellectual reputations of the conspirators, it might have been expected that they would evolve a plan of using forged documents, or men impersonating soldiers, or some other clever means of getting Burns free of the authorities. But the leaders of the Vigilance Committee were not simply intent upon breaking a law with which they disagreed: they wanted to flout it in so spectacular and popular a manner that the law would not only be thwarted, but deeply injured.

Reverend Higginson's plan, therefore, fell into the classic pattern of political agitation. Speakers at Faneuil Hall would inflame the crowd from the rostrum, abetted by agents in the audience who would help inspire a fevered response. Other agents would appear in the doors shouting that the people were marching on the courthouse; the leaders —overcome with indignation—would jump from the rostrum, lead the march down the aisles and against the courthouse. The surging mob so created would assist Higginson, Stowell, and their handful to break down the doors, overpower the guards, and free the fugitive slave.

While men were pouring into Faneuil Hall, Reverend Higginson, went to the establishment of Gardener & Thayer, Importers & Dealers in Foreign & Domestic Hardware & Cutlery. There he bought a dozen axes, paying cash. He gave his name as Higgins—surely one of the most transparent aliases ever adopted. Then the minister carried the axes to the law offices of Henry Bowditch, another abolitionist, across the street from the Boston Court House. Stowell, meanwhile, loaded a small pistol and put it in his pocket. Then both men went to Faneuil Hall.[5]

They arrived in the anteroom just as the meeting had started. Phillips was already on his way to the rostrum, Captain Bearse of the "executive committee" objected to the plan and Dr. Howe and Parker later said they were confused. But Higginson persuaded a few men to assist him, and these scattered about the hall and stationed themselves near the doors, to create excitement later.

Phillips, immaculate, tall, and impassive, worked the crowd to fever pitch with his usual skill. He could dominate through the sheer aristocracy of his presence, the modulated accents of his voice, and the quiet manner in which he would coldly utter the most remarkable extravagances. On the evening of May 26, he described the capture of the fugitive Burns in terms that stressed its stealth and brutality, and then said, ". . . The question is . . . whether Virginia conquers Massachusetts." No question could have seemed more remote, but shouts arose, and he continued. "Try to behave," he told the excited listeners, ". . . so that no kidnapper will dare to show his face in the city of Boston . . ."[6]

Finally he stepped back and Parker sprang forward. "Fellow subjects of Virginia!" he shouted, and cries of, "No!" "Never!" were heard. Then, after some further remarks, Parker suggested that the crowd adjourn, and collect again for a demonstration outside the court-house at nine o'clock the following morning. Some in the crowd bellowed, "No! Now!" but the suggestion took much of the urgency out of the meeting, even though one man—anxious to get matters into motion, dramatically rushed off the platform calling, "Come On!" Nobody followed.[7] Finally a man in the doorway shouted that a mob of negroes was in Court Square attempting a rescue. At that there was a move toward the doors and to the courthouse, with the eager running ahead but the rest following from curiosity.

At the steps of the courthouse, Higginson was flanked by Stowell and a burly black man named Lewis Hayden, who had previously led a violent and successful rescue of a fugitive named Shadrack. Both Stowell and Hayden had pistols, Higginson held a wooden beam to use as a battering ram, and a small group of whites and blacks held axes. When they heard the sound of the approaching crowd, Higginson picked up the wooden beam, the others began to attack the door with their axes, and a black man shinnied up the lamppost and put out its light. Others began to throw bricks against the courthouse windows.

The door collapsed, and Higginson, Stowell, Hayden, and a few others rushed inside to run headlong into fifty guards armed with clubs and cutlasses. A disheveled melee ensued, in which Higginson was slashed on the chin by a sword—and a shot rang out. One of the guards, James Batchelder, collapsed as the invaders were pushed out of the courthouse and down the steps. Meanwhile the crowd from Faneuil Hall, far from coming to their rescue, watched like spectators at a play. The police arrived and began making arrests, the crowd began to melt into the night, and Higginson, in despair, bellowed, "You cowards, will you desert us now?"[8]

Only Bronson Alcott, stately and dramatic at fifty-five, emerged. He climbed the steps slowly, using his cane. He paused at the top and a shot rang out from inside the courthouse, and he slowly descended. That gesture earned him great acclaim later, just as Higginson's bleeding chin later left a scar that thrilled abolitionist ranks. But it was not all opéra bouffe. The guard Batchelder, shot in the belly at close quarters, was in critical condition—and Martin Stowell was in custody.

There was confusion in Boston for the rest of the evening. U.S. Marshal Sherman swore in an extra 124 men as special deputies, placed an order for federal troops, and wired an explanation to the White House. President Pierce sent a swift response: "Your conduct is approved. The Law must be executed." Crowds wandered aimlessly, looking for more excitement and rumors flew. Reverend Parker ran to the house of Wendell Phillips, and told Mrs. Phillips—a bedridden invalid—that she would have to leave in ten minutes to elude a mob coming to sack the residence. He was, fortunately, wrong.[9]

Meanwhile a sense that events had moved beyond previous bounds floated over the city. Dana marveled in his journal at Higginson's conduct: "I hardly expected a married man, a clergyman, and a man of education to lead the mob." The mayor ordered two companies of the Massachusetts Artillery; federal troops were alerted as far away as New York.

A couple of days later Higginson appeared in public in Worcester, his chin bandaged, and was applauded. Both Northern and Southern newspapers had carried dense accounts of the Boston events, and he was a hero—at least to some. He announced a fund drive to assist the defense of Martin Stowell—the guard Batchelder had died. The authorities said it was murder.

On Monday, May 29, Higginson led a contingent of nearly nine hundred men back to Boston to demonstrate again outside the Boston Court House, where the fugitive Burns and Colonel Suttler were appearing before U.S. Commissioner Edward G. Loring. This time there was no thought of storming the building: it was ringed by police and federal and state troops; the doors, hallways and even the stairs inside were guarded.

Early in June, court proceedings ended and Burns was taken out to be escorted to a vessel that would carry him south. Troops from Rhode Island and New Hampshire as well as Massachusetts acted as guards; a detachment of mounted National Lancers appeared, as well as a company of artillery with a cannon. A huge crowd, estimated at twenty thousand, lined the streets.

Meanwhile Martin Stowell was in jail, accused of being one of the men who used an ax against the courthouse door. The authorities did not know that he had been armed with a pistol, and his own explanation for his arrest was ingenuous. He had been imprisoned, he said, "for no other offense than loving your neighbor as yourself, and doing as you would be done by."[10] That rationale sailed loftily over such mundane details as axes and pistols, and was reprinted in Garrison's *Liberator* together with other noble sentiments.

Thomas Drew, once a pacifist but converted to violence in the antislavery cause, visited Stowell, carrying a hollowed-out Bible. The jailors, impressed by the aura of sanctity that Drew exuded, left him alone to pray with the prisoner. When Drew left, he carried Stowell's pistol away in the Bible.[11] The Vigilance Committee was mute about that exchange.

Dana and others accused the U.S. marshal of having enlisted criminals in the courthouse to serve on that fatal occasion. Parker was scathing. "Marshal Freeman," he said, "raked the bowels of Boston . . . dispossessed the stews . . . gathered the spoils of brothels, prodigals not penitent who upon harlots wasted their substance on riotous living; pimps, gamblers, the succubus of Slavery . . ."[12] Having blackened the special deputies, Parker then passed a pitiless judgement upon the slain James Batchelder, a trucker who had sought to earn some extra money. "He was a volunteer in this service," Parker said. "He liked the business of enslaving a man, and has gone to render an account to God for his gratuitous work."[13]

Higginson delivered an inflamed sermon in Worcester on the same subject, which he called "Massachusetts in Mourning." It was so well received that he allowed copies to be printed. He was disappointed that his wife, the arthritic Mary Channing Higginson, refused to have a special daguerreotype made to illustrate this opus: he had planned to run her likeness with a special legend: "Mrs. Thomas Wentworth Higginson, wife of the Martyr."[14]

Six days later Higginson was arrested for "riot," and was greatly relieved. He had anticipated a charge of murder, a not unreasonable fear under the circumstances. His supporters rallied to his defense and bail was posted at once. And although the abolitionists denied that they favored violence, they also created still another secret organization whose members purchased blackjacks.

Their hardened mood was dramatically proven when Deputy Marshal Butman, Burns' captor, came to Worcester after another fugitive. The Worcester Vigilance Committee stoned the hotel that housed the marshal, ringed it with demonstrators, and acquired a warrant for his arrest, for carrying a concealed weapon. That charge landed Butman in jail. Later, in court, he was taunted by an overflow—and hostile—crowd. At one point during an adjournment a group of negroes rushed at him and beat him. Crowds outside roared imprecations and threats; some shouts were heard demanding a lynching and others for tar and feathers.

When Butman was acquitted, Judge George F. Hoar so feared for the marshal's safety that he personally escorted him out of the courthouse. The gesture was not entirely successful: a crowd ringed them as they walked. Butman was pelted with eggs and tobacco-chewers spat freely upon him. Thomas Drew—the former pacifist—would kick him from time to time and then appeal to the crowd not to kill the marshal. At the depot Butman was locked, for his own safety, in the privy. Finally he was shoved aboard the train to Boston, bruised, bespattered, and stained, while the immaculate Higginson sat beside him to lecture him on the evils of his ways.

The Worcester *Spy*, an ardent antislavery newspaper, lauded the crowd for its restraint in the face of nearly unbearable provocation, and especially praised those who voluntarily guarded Butman from death for their noble spirit. Meanwhile Higginson's trial approached. Lucy Stone, a gentle leader in the struggle for women's rights, asked Higginson if he did not agree that it would be "best for the 'cause' if they should hang you?"[15] His response to that is, unfortunately, unrecorded.

Parker, who also awaited trial together with Wendell Phillips might have known how to answer Lucy Stone, for he seldom lacked words. One of his sermons, made after the fugitive Burns had been taken away, was headed "The New Crime Against Humanity," and succeeded in imbedding a new phrase into the language. In its course, the most famous ministerial orator in the nation said, "I well know the responsibility of the place I occupy . . . tomorrow's sun shall carry my words to all America. They will be read on both sides of the continent. They will cross the ocean."[16] They did.

After all this, and amid a great flurry of pretrial preparations, the grand jury refused to indict. A second grand jury was called; it indicted, but federal judge George F. Curtis quashed the indictment on technical grounds. Parker was so piqued at losing his day in court—where he had planned to address the jury himself—that he published his defense, or the defense he would have made had he been forced to defend himself.

It ran to 221 printed pages, and made curious reading. It contained long pages of instructions to the jury on its duties, attacked Daniel Webster and the judge—and even the judge's family. "When Webster prostituted himself to the Slave Power," wrote Parker, "his family went out and pimped for him in the streets . . ."[17]

A month later Burns, by then returned to Virginia, had his freedom purchased for him by some modest and quiet citizens, who paid to send him to Oberlin College. In due course he would emerge a Baptist minister.

But Higginson, who had hired John A. Andrew, William Burt, and Henry Durant as lawyers in his defense, was pleased to be free, clear, and a hero. He never again referred to the death of James Batchelder, nor did it appear to trouble him. Some of his associates were similarly cool. Reverend William Henry Channing, whose addiction for causes had led him to abandon the pulpit, was sombre. "The next thing," he said, "is guerrilla war . . . at every chance."[18]

Chapter 3

Three years earlier, the city of Boston had been similarly agitated over a fugitive slave, and Parker, Higginson, and others had been similarly involved. But time had reduced the agitation over that incident, and time would have reduced the excitement over the fugitive Burns, had it not been that the Kansas-Nebraska Act, which repealed the Missouri Compromise, was made law just when the Burns rioting was underway: May 26, 1854.

The abolitionists had hated the Compromise of 1850, for it upheld slavery below the Mason-Dixon line, and included the Fugitive-Slave law as one of its provisions. Another provision—little noticed at the time—allowed settlers in a new region to determine for themselves whether it would be slave or free, when it was admitted as a new state.

That provision suddenly became important when Senator Stephen A. Douglas of Illinois, chairman of the important Senate Committee on Territories, was informed that Thomas Hart Benton—"Old Bullion"—a leader of antislavery forces in Missouri, had combined with Senator A.C. Dodge of Iowa to introduce a bill to establish a territorial government for the vast area called Nebraska. That was the first step toward statehood, and meant land would be opened to settlers. Since the territory was next to the slave state of Missouri, it brought Missouri Senator David R. Atchison and his forces for the South into immediate opposition.[1]

Senator Atchison, who was president of the Senate, was publicly sworn to break the Missouri Compromise and extend slavery north of the 36° 30′ Parallel. Benton's move had created a crisis, and Senator Douglas—who had ambitions for the presidency, was in a bad spot. A decision for one group would lose the other—one half the country would doom his chances to be president.

Much had been said about the small and brilliant Douglas and his ability to move decisively. In this quandary, he plucked the provision about settlers being able to resolve the issue of free or slaveholding from the provisions of the compromise of 1850, and split the Nebraska territory into two possible new states. He persuaded the antagonists to accept these two on the basis that one would be free, one slaveholding. Atchison was pleased because the Kansas Territory, closest to Missouri, would be a slaveholding state.

At first the White House, Senator Douglas, and most lawyers and politicians—the terms were already growing nearly synonymous—were pleased. The Kansas-Nebraska Act maintained the balance between North and South, and also focused on local elections as a means of avoiding future conflicts over slavery.

But howls of outrage mounted from the abolitionists. They focused on one central point: that slavery was previously held below the 36° 30′ line, and under the Douglas formula could expand north of that line. They derided popular sovereignty as "squatter sovereignty" and rained invectives on the Kansas-Nebraska Act.

One farsighted New Englander, however, saw what was coming next sooner than his fellows. Eli M. Thayer, combining altruistic appeal with a chance for profits, organized a stock company that he called The Massachusetts Emigrant Aid Society.[2] The idea was probably inevitable, but Thayer gave it a body and a goal. If enough Northerners could be persuaded to settle Kansas, that territory could vote itself—according to the Douglas formula—a free state. Southerners were sent into flames. They thought the idea of two new states—one slave and one free—which followed the lines of two historic compromises, had already settled the matter.

But Calhoun, Clay, and Webster were dead—and with them the spirit of the Union. The abolitionists had gone beyond the legalities of the situation. Theodore Parker had already linked antislavery with the "law of God," and said "the Constitution was not morally binding,"[3] but pulpit hyperbole had attained an informal license to be loose. Many men deplored slavery, but most thought it an institution that would collapse with changes in time, and looked toward the new lands in the West with far different eyes than those of abolitionists.

New territories opened meant a land rush. Such rushes had been part of the nation's life since Jefferson had expanded the thirteen colonies by 140 percent with the purchase of the huge Louisiana Territory. The opening of two possible new states at once doubled the usual rush, and doubled all the opportunities. Some thought of new political offices. Land developers smiled and plotted investments and advertisements; farmers thought of new virgin land, businessmen of sawmills and a vast array of ventures, miners of new ore bodies: a host of possibilities beckoned in which the destinies of blacks played little, if any, role.

Many thousands, locked into difficult situations, began to assess their ability to relocate. Among these—and among the poorer and more mediocre of these—was the Brown family in Ohio. The "boys" were all grown men: John, Jr. and Jason were married and fathers. Both of these elder sons owned small farms they had bought with their wives' money. Their father was working three farms on shares, with his other five sons. The summer of 1854 was dry and hot, but the drought that hurt many farmers that year did not greatly affect the Browns. Even then, however, they did not prosper to any great extent. They seldom prospered at anything, and though they knew little else, none of them appears to have been very good at farming.

Old John Brown—and even at the age of fifty-four the term "old" appeared in everyone's mind on seeing him—was not at first interested in Kansas, because he had a place left to which he could retreat. It was an odd location in upstate New York, near Lake Placid, on land that Gerrit Smith, a multimillionaire landowner—lord of more land than any other individual in the state—had given away some years before to landless, impoverished negroes.

Smith's land-grant project was astonishing—but no more astonishing than Gerrit Smith himself. Son of a partner of John Jacob Astor, he had inherited vast estates which he expanded by shrewd purchases and sharp practice.[4] Smith was best known, however, for his philanthropies and the amazing number of special causes that attracted his support. He wrote, printed and distributed a series of tracts against what he considered the evils of society. These included liquor in any form, meat, spices, tea, coffee, tobacco, fish, gravy, and butter. All had demonic significance in his eyes. The use of anything on Smith's forbidden list was, in his view, a sin that would lead directly to perdition.

In 1846 Smith decided to liquidate some outstanding business debts by selling 750,000 acres of land at public auction. The sales were conducted over several years. The tracts that Smith chose were scattered through forty-five of New York's forty-nine counties. He planned fifteen auctions so no single buyer could dominate the purchases— having strong opinions against any one person acquiring his own swollen possessions. Part of this land was in the Adirondacks, in Franklin and Essex counties. Unsurveyed and unoccupied, the region was chosen by Smith for worthy blacks.

He set about its distribution in the manner of a skilled and experienced philanthropist. Four committees were appointed to select

poor blacks on welfare throughout the state. The committees came up
with three thousand, all between the ages of twenty-one and sixty, all
with no property. Smith's purpose was to give blacks property so they
could vote, and he made it clear to his agents that no drunkards were
to be included. While these screenings were under way, Smith toyed
with the idea of distributing the land through a lottery, and conducted
a vast correspondence on the various aspects of the scheme.

He was somewhat chagrined to discover that he would have to drop
his teetotaler's demand, because most of the blacks were discovered
to be "addicted to drink." Nevertheless, he held to his purpose, and
in October, 1848 the National Convention of Colored People at Troy,
N.Y. thanked him for his gift of 140,000 acres. By that time about
twenty or thirty black families were settled on farms. Smith sent them
each a letter telling them to "turn your backs upon American Christianity and American politics, as upon the Devil himself, for he is their
author."[5] He was bitter against the churches for differing with him on
various theological points, and on a political issue.

Smith's land gift created a mountain of publicity—as his charities
were apt to do. Among those attracted was John Brown, who went to
Peterboro in the fall of 1848 and met the magnate. Smith was not hard
to meet if anyone took the trouble. He often put people up at his
mansion—Peterboro—for days or even weeks. He would also, it was
true, lose patience with some and pray in a loud voice before them,
asking God to take them out of his sight.

Brown and Smith were a study in contrasts. Brown was weather-
beaten, leathery, sinewy but slender, with grizzled hair and keen eyes.
He was nearly six feet tall but his head was oddly small; his features
were sharp. He spoke in biblical terms, but that was a fashion to which
Gerrit Smith was accustomed. Brown told Smith that he was a former
pioneer—which was true though not especially unusual—and that he
wanted to settle among the blacks in northern New York, on the lands
that Smith was giving away, to be a father to those people, and to help
show them how to get settled. That was a new approach, and Smith
was charmed.

Not long after that Brown showed up in the black Timbuctoo Colony
near North Elba, where he found about ten families, each with forty
acres, living in crude huts and having a hard time. His manner toward
blacks was always that of an equal, which made some of them uncomfortable, although they were skilled at masking their reactions. Not
long after that visit Brown sent some barrels of pork and flour to the
colony, and followed up with a number of letters giving advice.[6]

Meanwhile, a wool business that Brown managed in Ohio was col-
lapsing. He was costing his partner, Colonel Simon Perkins, a great
deal of money—and would cost him more. By 1849 the dissolution of
the firm of Perkins & Brown was imminent, and Brown's foresight in
calling on Gerrit Smith and planting his gifts among the blacks at
North Elba began to pay off. He could, of course, have moved his large
brood to Springfield, Ohio, where he was known and had previously

lived, and where Colonel Perkins could help him. But he seemed to feel it would be cheaper and safer—for he was hounded by numerous creditors—to go to North Elba.

He rented a farm in the remote and desolate region from a man named Cone Flanders, for $50 a year, and in mid-May, 1849, used a two-wheeled wagon and an ox to move his household goods, wife, and his younger children from Ohio to Westport, Connecticut. There he added two horses and a black named Thomas Jefferson, also headed for North Elba, to drive the rest of the way. The trip from Connecticut through to Keene, New Hampshire, from which they crossed to North Elba, was filled with mountain marvels. ". . . Father kept our spirits up by pointing out something new and interesting all the way," his daughter Ruth wrote years later. "We never tired of looking at the mountain scenery, which seemed awfully grand. Father wanted us to notice how fragrant the air was, filled with the perfume of spruce, hemlock, and balsams . . ."[7]

His sons Owen, Watson, and Salmon drove a small herd of cattle to the location and arrived first. The Flanders house had a large ground-floor room and two bedrooms, with space on the second floor for two more beds. John Brown bustled about this new residence for a few weeks, setting things in order. One of the neighbors noticed that he always wore "fine clean linen shirts and a brown frock coat, never descending to the usual flannel shirt."[8] That was natural; Brown was still a partner in Perkins & Brown, wool merchants, and he was preparing against the future more than establishing a homestead. He hired some help for his wife, who was "poorly" but assumed the airs of a community leader.

He had been there only a month when Richard Henry Dana and two of his friends from Boston, who had been walking the region and had lost their way in the woods, arrived at the Brown house in a state of exhaustion. Dana's journal for June 27, 1849, recorded his impressions.

> The place belonged (Dana wrote, unaware it had just been rented for a paltry sum) to a man named Brown, originally from Berkshire in Massachusetts (which was not true) a tall, sinewy, hard-favored, clear-headed, honest-minded man.
>
> On conversing with him we found him well-informed on most subjects, especially the natural sciences . . . Having acquired some property, he was able to keep a good farm, and had confessedly the best cattle and best farming utensils for miles around. His wife looked superior to the poor place they lived in, which was a cabin with only four rooms. She appeared to be out of health. He seemed to have an unlimited family of children. . . .
>
> June 29, Friday—After breakfast we started for home . . . We stopped at the Browns' cabin on the way . . . We found them at breakfast, in the patriarchal style. Mr. and Mrs. Brown and their large family of children, including three negroes all at the table together. Their meal was neat, substantial and wholesome . . .[9]

The entry went into the history books and created an image of John Brown, the leading and settled farmer of North Elba, playing the role he had promised Gerrit Smith. He had managed to make that impression when he had barely arrived. And he made it on one of the key men of Boston, acquainted with all those with whom he would later deal. Brown was remarkably able to impress people on short acquaintance. But the coincidence is uncanny.

Chapter 4

Brown kept his family on the Flanders farm at North Elba for two years, during which time he was usually away. The wool business was active, and Brown's methods were so obstinately against its traditions, rules, and standards that he met with increasing difficulties.

By 1851 an avalanche of lawsuits had fallen on Brown and his partner, Colonel Perkins, and Brown had to move his family back to Akron, Ohio, where he remained dependent upon his partner's kindness and support. Perkins was his only defense against an army of creditors. For the next several years Brown was either in court or preparing to appear, making depositions or listening to them, traveling to one judicial arena or another, arguing or hearing arguments. How he escaped punishment for his incredibly inept commercial dealings, his numerous violations of contract, and his cavalier handling of other men's money and goods remains a mystery.[1] In many respects John Brown's life was charmed.

By 1854 the painful experience of dealing with John Brown finally exhausted Colonel Perkins' patience. It was time for Brown to move on. He had, in reality, been moving on for a long time; it had become the way he lived. But now Brown was tired, his resources were depleted, and he had even become reconciled to the departure of his sons—over whom he had exercised a long and despotic rule. In August, 1854 he wrote John, Jr., "If you or any of my family are disposed to go to Kansas or Nebraska with a view to help defeat Satan and his legions in that direction, I have not a word to say, but I feel committed to work in another part of the field. If I were not so committed I would be on my way this fall."[2]

That was bravado. The fact was that he was exhausted and old before his time. He looked toward North Elba, where he had—with the help of his sons Jason and Owen—been able to scrape together $244 for as many acres,[3] and where he had briefly established a presence.

It was not that the location was good so much as that it was connected —however remotely—with the immensely wealthy Gerrit Smith, and with Smith's world. But Brown was so reduced financially he could not even manage the expenses of moving without selling his cattle. His daughter Ruth, however, had married Henry Thompson, a young North Elba farmer, and Thompson said he would build a house on his own land for the remnant of the Brown clan.

John Brown, Jr. was a tall, heavy man who had received the best education of all the old man's sons. He had served as chief clerk for Perkins & Brown, though not with outstanding ability, and had studied phrenology with Fowler & Wells in New York City for a period. That gave him the air of an expert; phrenology—which provided a physical explanation for the mysteries of personality and behavior—was immensely popular among those who were turning away from formal religion.

John junior had many thousands of fellow believers in phrenology. It was eagerly embraced in Boston where Ralph Waldo Emerson, Dr. Samuel Gridley Howe, Senator Charles Sumner, Charles A. Dana, and others were devotees. That he had some training in this new science, as well as experience in New York City, and had worked as his father's chief clerk combined with his being the eldest, gave John junior much of his father's mantle of leadership.

The next three sons: Jason, Owen, and Frederick resembled John junior, for they all had the same mother: Dianthe Lusk Brown, Brown's first wife. They were—as she had been—large, heavy, and quiet. Unfortunately, the first Mrs. Brown was intermittently insane for several years before her death in labor, and many of her relatives and forebears had been similarly afflicted. John junior was subject to fluctuating moods of sometimes frightening intensity, Frederick even more so. "Frederick has been very wild again," his father wrote.[4] Shortly before he and his brothers pooled their slender resources to go to Kansas, Frederick had tried to emasculate himself.[5]

Jason, the second brother, was tall, thin, and a tinkerer. Like John junior, he had married and had two children. Like all the Brown sons, his life, both early and later, was so shaded by his father's that details of his marriage are scanty, although his wife's maiden name was Ellen Sherbondy. John junior did not initially share Jason's admiration for her, but she seems to have been a good wife. John junior married Wealthy Hotchkiss, daughter of a substantial farmer.

Owen, the third son, was 30 years old in 1854 and was the first to wear a beard. He was quiet and in any other setting would have been considered somewhat peculiar; his brothers called him "Old eccentricity." In the Brown family he seemed prosaic. Salmon, a son of Brown's second wife, was eighteen, a calm youth. Watson, in his nineteenth year, had elected to go to North Elba.

The Brown boys' plan to leave Ohio was part of the larger national enthusiasm toward new lands in the West, and was also flavored with antislavery sentiment, which was being whipped to a fine bead by the literature the Browns favored: the New York *Tribune, Liberator*, and other abolitionist publications. All the Browns were ardent against slavery though most of them had never been to the South and knew only the propaganda—and only one side of that. But the Emigrant Aid Society and other efforts in 1854 made moving to Kansas a noble act in itself. The combination of opportunity and idealism was alluring; the Browns were only unique in being more fervent than most other settlers.

The brothers had a destination in Kansas, which put them in better position than most who made the trip. Their uncle, the Reverend Samuel L. Adair, who had married one of John Brown's half-sisters, had already made the move and settled near a tiny hamlet called Osawatomie. Osawatomie, by another of the coincidences that hovered over John Brown, was established by a man named O. C. Brown, who had a sawmill. He was, inevitably, called Osawatomie Brown—and his efforts and his nickname were later fastened to John Brown.

The three younger brothers—Owen, Frederick, and Salmon, being unencumbered with wives or children—chose to drive the cattle which all the brothers owned in common across Ohio, Illinois, and Iowa to the Kansas Territory. Since this could not be done in winter, they planned to drive their eleven head of cattle and three horses as far as possible, then winter, and continue the journey in the spring. The trio left Ohio in October, 1854, traveled by water to Chicago, and then drove the cattle overland to Meridosia, Illinois. They resumed their journey months later, and entered the Kansas Territory on April 20, 1855. John Brown, Jr. and Jason, with their wives and children, did not start until that same spring of 1855.

During the preparation period John Brown wrote endless letters—a habit of his life—and visibly wavered. He longed to go to Kansas but it seems that his sons did not urge his companionship. He still had the responsibility for his wife and other children. And he talked—as he had been intermittently talking for years—about helping blacks.

He floated letters to Gerrit Smith, to Frederick Douglass—whom he plagued for years—to Dr. McCune Smith, a black physician, and others, pleading for their advice. It was fairly clear he hoped for a commission from these well-known and prosperous people, but none appeared.

"Dear Children," he wrote in September, 1854. "After being hard pressed to go with my family to Kansas as more likely to benefit the colored people *on the whole* than to return with them to North Elba; I have consented to ask your *advice and feelings* in the matter; and also to ask you to learn from Mr. Epps and all the colored people . . . how they would wish and advise me to act . . ."[6]

That went to North Elba, where—at least in his own mind—he was a leader helping an oppressed race. It is noteworthy that he also reported: "We have a new daughter now five days old. Mother and child are doing well."

By February, 1855 the old man was so anxious to escape North Elba and virtual retirement that he wrote a friend, John E. Cook, of Wolcott-ville, Conn.: "Since I saw you I have undertaken to direct the opera-tions of a Surveying, & exploring party, to be employed in Kansas for a considerable time perhaps for some Two or Three years, & I lack for time to make all my arrangements, & get on the ground in season."[7]

That monumental lie drew no recorded response, however, and Gerrit Smith wrote that Brown would be well advised to return to North Elba. In other words, the situation in Kansas might alarm many, but not to the extent of sending John Brown to Kansas. That was galling; the newspapers were trumpeting calls for all good men to go to the aid of the territory.

Chapter 5

Eli Thayer had organized his Emigrant Aid Society, with Dr. Samuel Gridley Howe and A. A. Lawrence on the board; Theodore Parker called ministers together to explain how the South could be thwarted by New England settlers in Kansas. Horace Greeley swung the New York *Tribune* behind the plan, as did the *Daily Advertiser* in Boston. All the members of the vigilance committee climbed aboard the venture, including Higginson and his Worcester contingent; Gerrit Smith was enlisted, as well as lead-pipe manufacturer George Luther Stearns. Mass rallies were organized; settlers would be provided with goods and supplies and credit. That was far better than taking a chance with one's own resources, to sink or swim alone. The reaction was enthusi-astic—and impressive.

Emigrant Aid societies not connected with Thayer's stock company sprang into life all across the Northern states. Emigrant trains were formed—and cheered—in towns and cities; there was more than a hint of sectional war in the climate created. Yet the intellectual leadership remained centered in New England: It was there that the arguments were issued, and the rhetoric coined, and the fires blazed highest.

The Brown boys, headed for Osawatomie, probably did not even know that the townsite was created by O. C. Brown, William Ward, and S. C. Pomeroy as trustees for the Emigrant Aid Company in return for O. C. Brown's sawmill and other equipment. Other "free-state" towns such as Topeka were similarly created; Lawrence, named after Amos Adams Lawrence, was to become, for a period, the most famous.[1]

All these moves, made during the fall of 1854 and the spring of

1855, alarmed the South and especially the slaveholders of Missouri. Senator Atchison, who saw his bargain with Douglas, the White House, and Congress being openly subverted, was leader of the reaction.

Many Missourians had already staked claims in Kansas, and Senator Atchison's stake was as high as possible. If his bargain collapsed, so did his prestige—and Thomas Hart Benton, the paradoxical slaveholder against slavery (not an unusual type in the Border states) would triumph.

Atchison's next move was to organize a Missourian invasion of Kansas, to ensure that the votes of the first settlers would establish the control of the territorial legislature and the territorial government. That intention was no secret, and was greeted with predictable outrage in Boston, New York, Cleveland, and other northern centers. Neither side appeared to have any sense of fair play; neither side was willing to see the issue naturally resolved. Both sides wanted to force through their ideas of victory with no scruples whatever. But the Southerners made the mistake of being blunt and the Northern leader took high ground—very high ground indeed—in terms of rhetoric. Meanwhile ordinary settlers, both Southern and Northern, began to trickle into a region where the possibility of violence grew steadily more evident, and more ominous.

In Ohio Brown, stooped and greying, finally sold his remaining cattle and took his wife and four young children on the railroad to Cleveland. There were several routes from there to North Elba: One involved a large number of trains and the other lake and canal boats. No record remains of how they traveled; probably by the cheapest route since the old man was strapped and time was of little significance. The family arrived about June 20, 1855, at the house that Henry Thompson had built for them of unpainted yellow sawmill lumber. It was tiny, with two rooms, an open attic, and a cellar. As far as the eye could see they were ringed with mountains. To old Brown, it must have looked like the end of the road.

Toward the end of April, 1855, John Brown, Jr. and Jason, with their wives and children, were in St. Louis, and at the end of the railroad lines. In that city they bought two tents, a plow, and a handmill for grinding corn and booked passage on the *New Lucy,* a paddlewheel steamer. John Brown, Jr., who wrote long letters—a habit of the family and the times—described the Southerners aboard the vessel with distaste. He was alarmed at their open display of weapons, unaware this was customary all through the South, and thought it meant they were all villains.

The trip was nightmarish: cholera struck and Jason's eldest son, Austin, died. The steamer laid up at Waverly, Missouri, to repair a broken rudder and the Browns went ashore with the dead child. They buried him at night on the outskirts of the little town in the midst of a thunderstorm, with their labors "illuminated only by the lightning . . ."[2]

When they finished their task and started back to the ship they were shocked to see the steamer pull away from the dock without them. John Brown, Jr. was sure they were abandoned because they were Northerners; he did not realize the captain was accustomed more to herding than to counting passengers and had simply cast off when ready. But John Brown, Jr.'s suspicions reflected the times and the Brown upbringing, in which everything Southern was held to be tainted, evil and malevolent.

The travelers now made their way by stagecoach to Kansas City, and were turned away at various places when they asked for food. Again, John Brown, Jr. was sure it was because of their Northern accents; it might as plausibly have been that the hospitality of the region had already been exhausted.

The Kansas Territory, when John Brown, Jr. saw it, impressed him. "Here in prospect we saw our cattle increased to hundreds, and possibly thousands, fields of corn, orchards and vineyards. At once we set about the work. . . . Our tents would suffice . . . until we could plough our land, plant corn and other crops, fruit trees and vines, cure and secure as hay enough of the waving grass to supply our stock the coming winter . . ."[3]

Unfortunately the three younger boys staked claims between the Pottawatomie and Osage rivers, ten miles west of Osawatomie and the Adairs—on lands that still belonged to Indians. They did not know that, and it is doubtful if they ever fully realized it, because they never filed the claims.[4]

The Brown boys came together in Kansas only a month after elections in the territory had been overwhelmed by an illegal infusion of Southerners. The Eastern and Northern press howled in anger, because Southern contingents had openly lined up and marched into the territory for the event.[5] The Southerners, in fact, treated the matter as a romp, complete with rallies, buckboards, costumes, whiskey, shooting matches, and organization parades. In the process the thousands that poured across the border whooped and shouted the yells later made famous in the Civil War, and defied Andrew H. Reeder, the territorial governor, to undo the election results.[6]

Under the circumstances it was remarkable that seven legislators were elected who were not pro-Southern; Senator Atchison himself appeared on the scene with eighty Missourians from Platte County. The governor considered throwing all the the results out as illegal, but later settled for discarding the results in six districts.

Although the North howled in anger, the fact remains that even without the Missouri invasion the Southerners would have won overall, for they—being nearer—had settled the region first. Furthermore the Washington bargain to have Kansas a proslavery state and Nebraska an antislavery state was still holding. Therefore to President Pierce, Senator Douglas, and other lawyers, the election results were satisfactory and were allowed to stand.

The newspapers took a different view. While the Southern newspapers crowed, the abolitionist press foamed. The description of all Southerners in Missouri as "Border Ruffians" circulated to such good effect that the term remains today to slander everyone who entered Kansas from the South, and scathing descriptions of the sort Theodore Parker attached to the marshal's office in Boston became part of the language. It would have seemed that poverty in a Southerner was a vice, while poverty in a Northerner was a sign of virtue—a paradox that has proved a permanent American contradiction.

To the average Northerner the Southern victory over the first territorial government was presented as a triumph for slavery, but in reality it was a victory for Southern entrepreneurs over their Northern counterparts. The territorial legislature would draw up the territorial constitution. It would be in charge of territorial offices, taxes, charters for businesses, contracts for internal improvements, and similar matters that were of prime importance in organizing the region.

The South had pulled off a coup, and Southerners in Washington pressed Congress and the White House to solidify the victory. Governor Reeder, a Northerner, was afraid to cancel the election results for fear of bloodshed. The Northern newspapers screamed in outrage. Yet neither section could be proud of its behavior; the South had been reckless to make a mockery of elections and the North was hypocritical in its indignation over stacked polls when it openly promoted a stacked territory.

The greatest damage was done by extremists on both sides who persistently misrepresented both the issues and the sentiments of the settlers. Most of the Southern settlers had no slaves, and no special sympathy with slavery. The Northerners had no slaves either, and though some were vocal in their antislavery, many were indifferent. The most ignored aspect of settler attitudes was that the majority—from North or South—was overwhelmingly hostile toward blacks, either free or slave. To depict the issue as pro- or antislavery was to create and perpetuate a myth.[7]

The *Herald of Freedom* in Lawrence, operating with a press sent from Massachusetts by the Emigrant Aid Society and edited—another coincidence—by a man named G. W. Brown, thundered daily against the newly elected "bogus" legislature. The same ragings came from Boston and New York newspapers and across the abolitionist belt, and a movement to overthrow the fraudulent elections was discussed. Governor Reeder, realizing he had been bullied, left for the East and a talk with President Pierce.

Chapter 6

The numerous antislavery societies that mushroomed across the Northern landscape since the 1830's held their conventions in Boston and New York in May, 1855. The New York *Daily News* called one of these conventions "a kraal of howling maniacs" and "a Bedlamite Congress." But the *Christian Inquirer* observed, "It is only within three years that a hall could be procured anywhere in the city for the meeting of the society. Now, the only difficulty is to find one large enough . . ."[1]

Thanks to the Kansas-Nebraska Act and the events in Kansas, the movement had suddenly rocketed into the limelight. In Boston Parker, to whom the subject of slavery had become a burning obsession, spoke on "The Nebraska Question." His subsequent brochure, as usual, began with a long and pedantic historical background, in which the famed Unitarian attacked the Spaniards, whom he blamed for bringing "greed and the institutions of theocracy, monarchy, aristocracy and despotism" to the American continent.[2]

Having disposed of the evil Spaniards, Parker then accused his countrymen of being obsessed by greed. "Covetousness," he declaimed, "is the American passion." All this—and a great deal more—led to the charge that the South wanted to control Nebraska, and the South, "I must say it, is the enemy of the North." He went on for several thousand words castigating the South, and finally declared it had to be stopped *"even at the price of Union."*[3] (Italics added.)

As if this and similar orations were not enough, Reeder, the territorial governor of Kansas, spent the months of April and May touring the East under the guise of seeing the President. He made speeches at every stop about the election outrages of the Southerners who had invaded Kansas. He saw Pierce daily for almost two weeks and was sent away with soothing words while Northern newspapers raged. Then he made speeches all the way back to the territory.[4]

All this helped create high fever, but the fact was that only a trickle of abolitionists had reached Kansas. The Emigrant Aid Society had sent less than eight hundred in 1854 and no more than nine hundred would be sent in 1855. Fewer were to remain.[5] The largest flow was from Kentucky, Tennessee, North Carolina and western Virginia, Ohio, Pennsylvania, and New Jersey—and these were people disgusted with orations who simply wanted to settle and be let alone.

By June, 1855 that simple desire appeared doomed. Spells were being woven by men of words and politics that obscured the realities of the territory, which were far from easy even in ordinary circumstances. Fierce winds blew across the plains. Waves of typhoid and malaria

attacked the settlers. Wolves prowled the prairie. Survival meant planting corn, potatoes, pumpkins, beans—and creating a shelter.

The Brown boys took some of these steps: They planted ten acres
of corn on the prairie and put some more serious efforts into what they
called their "garden." That was a one-acre plot in which they planted
onions, cabbages, potatoes, peas, squash, and lettuce. But they had
little money and could not afford lumber from Osawatomie Brown's
sawmill. Surprisingly, though they were between the rivers and the
woods—the location considered best by all settlers—they made no
effort toward permanent shelters. Since they had no stoves, their wives
had to cook over open fires.

But the men were intent upon large matters and great events. In his
May 20–24 letter to his father, John Brown, Jr.—after a rambling
description of their circumstances—plunged into what most interested
them.

> And now I come to the matter, that more than all else I intended should
> be the principal subject of this letter. I tell you the truth when I say that
> while the interest of despotism has secured to its cause hundreds and
> thousands of the meanest and most desperate of men, armed to the teeth
> with Revolvers, Bowie Knives, Rifles & Cannon,—while they are not only
> thoroughly organized, but under pay from Slave-holders—the friends of
> freedom *are not one fourth* of them *half-armed,* and as to *Military Organiza-
> tion* among them it *no where exists in this territory. . . .* The result of this is
> that the people here exhibit the most abject and cowardly spirit.

After a few more comments along the same general line, John
Brown, Jr. enclosed a clipping from the St. Louis *Republican* as an
illustration of how entrenched the Southerners had become in the
territory. Then he resumed:

> Now the remedy we propose is, that the Anti slavery portion of the
> inhabitants should *immediately, thoroughly arm and organize themselves in
> military companies.* In order to effect this, some persons must begin and
> lead in the matter. There are five of us here who are not only anxious
> to fully prepare, but are thoroughly determined to fight . . .
>
> The General Government may be petitioned until the people here are
> grey, and no redress will be had so long as it makes slavery its paramount
> interest.—We have among us 5, 1 Revolver, 1 Bowie Knife, 1 middling
> good Rifle, 1 poor Rifle, 1 small pocket pistol and 2 slung shots. What
> we need in order to be thoroughly armed for each man, is 1 Colts large
> sized Revolver, 1 *Allen & Thurber*'s large sized Revolver manufactured at
> Worcester, Mass. or Connecticut (Mr. Paine of Springfield would proba-
> bly know) and 1 heavy Bowie Knife—I think the Minnie Rifles are made
> so that a sword bayonet may be attached. With these we could compete
> with men who even possessed Cannon. The real Minnie Rifle has a
> killing range almost equal to Cannon and of course is more easily han-
> dled, perhaps enough so to make up the difference. Now we want you
> to get these arms. We need them more than we do bread. Would not
> Gerrit Smith or someone, furnish the money and loan it to us for one,

two or three years, for the purpose, until we can raise enough to refund it from the *Free* soil of Kansas? . . .⁶

That letter must have evoked prayerful thanks from old John Brown; it fit inside the rising tempest like an ark. Apparently he dashed off an immediate reply, which did not reveal his intentions, but asked a series of sharp questions about prices, goods, and the needs of the boys. John Brown, Jr. sent back a long list, and included a crude map of their claims, inaccurate but clear enough to serve as a guide. There is no hint in his letter that he expected his father to appear—but he should have known what a plea for help could evoke.

A meeting of persons billing themselves as "Radical Political Abolitionists" was held in Syracuse, New York, with Gerrit Smith presiding. That was an honor the millionaire was often offered and often accepted: it was the best means of obtaining his highly valued presence. Frederick Douglass, Lewis Tappan, and Reverend Samuel J. May were also listed as speakers and attendance was—as in the larger meetings in Boston and New York—excellent.

All such meetings were packed with people intent upon some special purpose or another within the larger agenda. Lewis Tappan, one of two wealthy New York City merchants who were virtually a philanthropic holding company in themselves, hoped that the Syracuse convention would mark the beginning of a vast antislavery campaign with speakers sent all over the country to deliver lectures, with mountains of brochures printed, and the like. He was—and he was soon to realize it—falling behind the times. Those were earlier tactics; the situation was changing fast. But Mr. Tappan did—and is apparently the only man who ever did—suggest to Gerrit Smith that he *give away* his entire vast fortune, retaining only a modest amount for himself and his family to get such an enterprise launched. Mr. Smith's reply was, unfortunately, not recorded.⁷

Old Brown appeared, to lope around the hall and pursue Frederick Douglass whose position virtually forced him into courteous attention. He also found, somewhere in the crush and bustle of the proceedings, Gerrit Smith. Since the convention had been called to organize resistance to the Fugitive Slave Law, Brown was—though uninvited—in tune with the mood of the gathering. He wanted money, he said, to send guns and various other weapons to his sons in Kansas, who were resisting slave owners. In pressing this argument the old man appeared blunt and homespun, but he was effectively deceptive: he had charmed money from many a man who never saw it again.

On June 28, 1855, the third day of the convention, Gerrit Smith read aloud both the letters from John junior to such effect that tears came to many.⁸ It was a tearful age. Some rose to object to such warlike appeals, but Frederick Douglass—whose very appearance shrieked of suppressed rage—made a stirring speech on the young Brown's behalf. Then Brown himself appeared on the podium adding his peculiar eloquence. It was finally decided that a collection would be allowed. The old man humbly thanked the audience for the results: sixty dollars.

Gerrit Smith had given twenty of this sum, and five more had come from retired British Army officer Charles Stuart—a bizarre figure in a tartan cape who had been the mentor of Theodore Weld, and who was world famous for his abolitionist tracts. The audience had dredged up the balance in lesser coin, but at a time when land could still be sold for one dollar an acre, the sum was handsome. It was more than Brown had earned for many months and though some might have seen it as begging, he saw it as part of his leadership role in the great antislavery crusade.

The money—and the attention—was like a tonic. Brown threw off the lassitude of the last few years as if he had been rejuvenated, which was not far from the truth. His travels became, and were ever after to remain, somewhat obscure from that moment. Apparently he solicited funds in Springfield, Massachusetts, and ordered five "Fire arms" from I. W. Carter, agent of the Massachusetts Arms Company.[9] Then his trail vanished, until he surfaced again in Akron, Ohio on August 13, 1855.

He was known in Akron, where he read his son's letters aloud to former neighbors, business acquaintances, and others who flocked around. Committees were organized to donate clothing, weapons, and ammunition. The mayor of Akron, Lucius V. Bierce, together with a candidate for sheriff helped organize a mass meeting in a rented hall. Bierce donated a number of artillery sabers that had once been part of the armory of the Order of Grand Eagles, organized to invade Canada—a venture in which Bierce had once been a general.[10]

The communities of Akron and Tallmadge were so enthused that they turned over to Brown arms that had once been used by disbanded militia companies, and Brown wrote to his family in North Elba that he had received "Guns, Revolvers, Swords, Powder, Caps, & money." He was succeeding remarkably: in two days he raised two hundred dollars[11]—a large sum at a time when a top lecturer like Ralph Waldo Emerson was proud of being paid fifty dollars for an appearance.

Amos Adams Lawrence, in the meantime, had stepped in and taken control of Eli Thayer's wonderful instrument for making a profit from politics: the Emigrant Aid Society. Lawrence was in a peculiar position for an abolitionist: his mills relied on Southern cotton. At the same time he had contributed to the Emigrant Aid Society, and as a practical businessman he preferred to control the use of his money. Therefore he recapitalized and reorganized Thayer's venture, changing its name from the Massachusetts Emigrant Aid Society to the New England Emigrant Aid Society.

Lawrence might have been forgiven for his self-confidence. He was wealthy and important, and connected either by birth or business, with virtually all the New England elite. His name was prestigious and his presence commanding, and he had a sharp competence in collections and disbursements. But a businessman in politics, like an Eskimo in the tropics, is soon confronted with steaming conditions for which he is, by nature, unsuited.

In April, 1855, just before John Brown emerged in upstate New York and Ohio, Lawrence received a long letter from his cousin, Dr. Charles Robinson—a bearded, impassive man in his middle thirties who was one of the Emigrant Aid agents in Kansas. The letter brought up some formidable problems.

"Our people have now formed themselves into four military companies," wrote Robinson, "and will meet to drill until they have perfected themselves in this art. Also, companies are being formed in other places, and we want *arms*. Give us the weapons and every man from the North will be a soldier and die in his tracks if necessary to protect and defend our rights."[12]

Like many businessmen, Lawrence had a gift for reducing all implications to the mundane, and he relayed Robinson's request to other Aid Society leaders. His listeners, like Dr. Samuel Cabot, were content with Lawrence's interpretation. But one burly, businessman whose face was nearly completely enveloped in a huge beard that descended in ripples down to his chest, radiated more warlike perception. His name was George Luther Stearns, and he was a member of Reverend Theodore Parker's vigilance committee in Boston.

With Lawrence's somewhat reluctant permission, Stearns and the others launched a subscription fund and bought some of the new breech-loading Sharp's rifles, which could fire ten shots a minute and had a longer range than any the Missourians were likely to possess in Kansas. These were shipped but the long crates marked "books" aroused suspicions in St. Louis, and were opened. The rifles were discovered and confiscated.

Lawrence used that mischance, which he regarded as providential, to attempt to cool matters. He proposed—having had second thoughts —that such shipments not be attempted again, saying he "did not believe in saving Kansas by revolutionary methods." George Luther Stearns disagreed sharply. Stearns, in fact, said, "A revolution was what the country needed."[13]

That would have been startling enough if Stearns had been alone, but he spoke for many of the emigrant company leaders. When Lawrence demurred, Stearns rushed out, drew a subscription list of his own, and regular shipments of Sharp's rifles, routed through Iowa, began to trickle to Robinson, S. C. Pomeroy, and their "military companies" in Kansas.

That turn of the road carried the Emigrant Aid Society into new and more dangerous channels. Lawrence's control diminished as he found himself borne into waters deeper than commerce contains—and the situation in Kansas moved closer to flashpoint.

By mid-August, 1855, Brown had coursed through Detroit, Cleveland, and a number of smaller places, and was in Chicago with his son-in-law

Henry Thompson. No doubt much of the money he collected flowed, not to Kansas, but to his family in North Elba. But there was enough left over to buy "a fine young horse" and wagon, and to load it so heavily that it was all the horse could do to pull it. Then, accompanied by his youngest son Oliver, sixteen, and Henry Thompson, he headed for Kansas.

Their progress was slow and antique, with the men forced to walk beside the straining horse and heavy wagon most of the time. They made about six or eight miles a day, stopping overnight in small towns or sleeping in the open. The sun hung hot in a blazing sky as they plodded along. Brown was an odd mixture of patience and eagerness, but it is hard not to believe that he was happy away from the troubling cares of domesticity, the endless chores of farming, the boredom of sheepherding, the vexations of lawsuits, and all the other aggravations of recent years. Both his young companions were completely under his domination, and looked to him for every decision—and that was always his greatest pleasure.

Chapter 7

The newspapers shrieked. In Kansas the Southerners elected to the legislature had convened near the Missouri line and enacted a constitution based on Missouri's, including its slave code. Provisions of that code forbade any efforts—even conversational—against the peculiar institution on pain of imprisonment. Then the legislators whooped through dozens of bills chartering ventures and creating offices—setting the terms for the latter at six years.

The South crowed, the North wailed, and Governor Reeder sought to stem the avalanche in vain. His vetoes were overridden with insulting ease and contemptuous speeches. Readers in other parts of the country followed these events in some confusion, because newspapers then relied on both the telegraph and the mails. One result was that fresh bulletins appeared next to long, but outdated, dispatches written as breathlessly as the new. Correspondents used pseudonyms, which added to the confusion, because some worked for several different papers at once. Virtually all the journalists were addicted to coloring their dispatches with false interviews, imaginary encounters, fictional events, and rumors, mixed with whatever facts fit the editorial policy of a paper and their own personal prejudices. All these practices are, of course, endemic to newspapers, but in 1855 the disease was virulent. As a result, reading the papers provided both fuel for indignation and cause for despair.[1]

Informed observers, however, were in no better condition. The President was told Kansas was a powder keg, and that the South insisted that the bargain bringing it into the union as a slave state and Nebraska as a free state had to be kept. Southerners insisted that Reeder had to go, and he was dismissed on a charge of trading with Indians for land.[2] The charge was true enough, but everyone knew the real reasons were political. Reeder immediately lined up with the Free State forces, and remained in the Territory.

The President did not help matters by appointing a pro-Southern Cincinnati lawyer, Wilson Shannon, to replace Reeder. He then added more coals to Northern fires by selecting Sterling G. Cato of Alabama and S. D. Lecompte of Maryland to be federal judges in the territory. It was a period when judges did not dispute the law, holding, in the main, the English practice of applying whatever it said. Federal judges in territories had to apply both federal and territorial laws. But charges were raised in the North that neither man could possibly be fair, since both came from Southern slave states.

The nature of that protest worsened the situation. If men were to be judged unsuitable because they came from one section or the other, room for the sort of cooperative effort needed to retain the nation was drastically reduced. The North, by charging that Cato and Lecompte were unfit to be federal judges by reason of their backgrounds—before they even made a decision on the bench—succumbed to the same prejudice against which it protested.

The Southerners in charge of the territorial legislature and the various offices it controlled were crude, outraged men, determined to force the pattern of the Deep South upon the territory. But they were also open in this determination. The tactics of Robinson and Pomeroy, on the other hand, were both shrewd and more devious, and couched in the classic language of liberty.

Both men were paid agents of the Emigrant Aid Society who posed as ordinary settlers. The fact that they staked claims and that Robinson was an ambitious land developer lent credence to their positions, but their purposes were beyond those of other settlers. Both men were graduates of Amherst and better educated than the average; both were difficult to track.

Because the traditional way to control a territory was through a political party, Robinson and Pomeroy called a convention of Free-Staters in Big Springs in 1855. One of the men they selected to join an executive committee to organize that Free State convention was John Brown, Jr. No position could have more clearly marked his difference from his father.

Old John Brown was never a member of a committee for any purpose, at any time. He was incapable of cooperating with a group—or even a partner—unless he gave all the orders. But John Brown, Jr. was tall, well-spoken—he had lectured on phrenology—and agreeable. No doubt he met Robinson and Pomeroy in Lawrence—a Mecca to which Free-Staters made frequent pilgrimages.

The fact that he and his brothers were still living in tents did not bar John Brown, Jr. from high level councils. Settlers were living in hard conditions all over the territory. Both the Southerners and the Northerners found things especially difficult. Westerners and those from the Midwest were more accustomed to the winds and the prairie, the wolves and the lack of woods, the sight of Indians, and the lack of civilized comforts. Newly arrived people were forced to make shelters out of straw or "shakes," pieces of wood that provided virtually no protection from the elements; they burned "buffalo chips" for fuel, crowded together for comfort, and then suffered from vermin or were attacked by waves of typhus, cholera, and a host of other diseases.[3]

There is no question that John Brown, Jr. was a fervent abolitionist, but it was also true that with the Southerners in control of all territorial offices and all federal funds, that the only source of bounty available to free-staters was the Emigrant Aid Society, and whatever organization Robinson, Pomeroy, and other leaders could create. John Brown, Jr. was, therefore, moving into the only group that could—without violating his principles—assist him in Kansas.

The Big Springs convention mirrored all the mixed factions and diverse opinions collected under the Free-State banner, and the abolitionists—who were the noisiest—were dismayed to discover they were also the least numerous among the hundred men collected.

Both Robinson and Pomeroy—ambitious and experienced, as well as educated—were dismayed to have the control of their convention taken out of their hands by an unschooled but dynamic force named Jim Lane.

Lane was later described as "a strange magnetic man in his middle forties, six feet tall, slender, wiry, nervous, tremendously alive. He burst with vitality—his voice was hypnotic. His hair was long and reckless, and above his ears black locks curled like horns. There was always a hint of Mephistopheles about him."[4]

His background was as unconventional as his appearance: he had been a lieutenant governor of Indiana and a congressman who voted for the Kansas-Nebraska Act. He had come to Kansas thirsting for higher office, for money, for power—and for adventure. Unschooled in the conventional sense, he had developed his powers of speaking through every conceivable, and some incredible, efforts. He was a product of countless revival meetings in which he would spring up to announce himself converted, and then capture the audience from the minister.[5] He told Southerners he was from Kentucky and Northerners he was from Indiana. A type familiar to American politics—then and now—he would say whatever moved an audience. He had no more ethics than a lynx, or any other hungry animal.

As soon as he spoke he reduced Robinson and Pomeroy to part of the scenery. Plucking the sentiment of the delegates out of the air as skillfully as a magician, Lane denounced abolitionists, blacks, and "nigger stealing" alike. The delegates roared to their feet and Lane pushed through a platform that barred blacks—of any condition—from the territory. Another provision separated "free-soilers" from abolitionists, and thereby cut the ground out of the sectional argument. His last stroke was to persuade the delegates to resolve to uphold the Fugitive Slave Law.

These actions distorted Robinson's purpose, and dismayed Pomeroy, John Brown, Jr., and other fervent supporters of the Emigrant Aid Society. They struggled to keep from being swept away by forces they had themselves evoked, but with only partial success. They managed to have Reeder nominated as candidate for territorial delegate, but the arrangements were disheveled. The Free-Staters would hold their own nominations for Congress, and also hold their own constitutional convention in Topeka two weeks later.[6]

That meant that the Northern settlers—or at least one hundred men initially acting in their name—would create a new territorial government. In the heat of the oratory at Big Springs—"a hamlet of shake-cabins and log huts not far from Lawrence"—that plan sounded creative and constructive. But the federal government had already recognized a territorial government of Kansas. What Lane, Robinson and Pomeroy had hatched and then scrambled was a rump government with no legal standing; a movement that was, if not treasonable, at least rebellious. Northern newspapers, however, masked that with the argument that Washington had recognized a territorial government that had attained unrepresentative power. Shouts about "Border Ruffians" made the Free-State moves seem respectable by contrast, and the sacred antislavery cause covered a variety of less noble purposes.

Chapter 8

The Brown boys had put in a fairly good summer on their claims, and their letters—and those of their wives—were typical of that Kansas frontier. The families had been frightened by a large, whooping band of Sacs and Fixes in warpaint who circled their tents, but the Browns stood their ground. The Indians, seeing the whites had passed that customary test, became friendly. Later John Brown, Jr. visited the Sacs, and had one memorable exchange when he asked the tribe's old chief why he and his people did not build schools and churches like the Delawares and Shawnees.

"We want no houses and barns," the chief replied. "We want no schools and churches. We want no preachers and teachers. We bad enough now."[1]

Two weeks after the Big Springs convention the Free-Staters met at Topeka, with the formidable Lane as president. A constitution was drawn up, and plans made to hold elections in December, 1855, both on the constitution and for various territorial offices and officers. The legality of these proceedings was as questionable as the Southern invasion and the illegal elections earlier in the year, but the leaders said it could all be regarded as a way of "petitioning" the federal government and creating an alternative to the territorial government. That was fairly thin as rationalizations went, but the larger accomplishment was the addition of Jim Lane to the abolitionist-Emigrant Aid forces.

In moving from the majority to the well-financed minority Lane obeyed his instincts for immediate survival against greater chances on a higher level over a longer period. It is possible that he himself never realized that he had, however briefly, held the allegiance of the majority of settlers in Kansas. For there is little doubt that the majority favored neither slavery nor abolition—nor was interested in the fate of the blacks, however hard that may sound to later generations. They were settlers in a harsh frontier, anxious to establish the foundations of a new existence, and not to reform society. Had Lane led them he would have pleased Senator Douglas—whom rumor credited with sending him to the territory in the first place—and helped to heal a widening breach in the Democratic party, which stretched both North and South. That alone would have delayed, and perhaps averted, a great national crisis.

Instead, Lane succumbed to the people who offered the most immediate lures: arms, money, and comradeship. The Emigrant Aid agents, Robinson and Pomeroy, had worked speedily and well behind the scenes. Their price—which seemed small to the pragmatic Lane, was a constitution that came out against slavery in the Territory. Beside that agreement, the fact that only white males would be permitted to vote seemed relatively unimportant—though it was clearly a sop to the settlers.

Another interesting sop was offered to those who supported the Territorial government for commercial or business reasons, in the form of a clause that promised "no suits, prosecutions, claims or contracts" issued by the new constitution would change the tangible contracts issued by the territorial government. That was a huge political concession which convinced many that the Free-State leaders were selfless and idealistic.

The entire North broke into peals of praise for the Free-State constitution, and contrasted its freedoms with the savageries of the Territorial slave code. These drums rolled to great effect through the North and the Border states, and muffled to the casual listener several deeper meanings of the situation being developed. A sizeable vote for the new constitution and the slate of officers it proposed—with Robinson as governor—would convert the movement for a shadow government in the Territory into a tangible organization.

Little Austin Brown had died of cholera on the steamboat *New Lucy* when the Brown boys and their wives were enroute to Kansas. Letters from John Jr. to Ohio and North Elba had, several times, mentioned that Austin's parents still grieved—especially his mother. Enroute to Kansas, old Brown detoured, therefore, to Waverly, Missouri where he stopped to dig up the small, crude coffin.[2] How he found the site remains one of the many minor mysteries of his strange career and activities.

With this additional, macabre offering in the back of the wagon the old man, his son Oliver and Henry Thompson crossed the line into the Kansas Territory on October 4, 1855. Their long trip had turned, toward its close, into an ordeal, and they had only sixty cents among them.[3] That was another mystery, and the old man added to it by saying he was tired and would spend the night in Osawatomie, when they reached that hamlet—sending the younger men ahead 10 miles to his sons' claims.[4] No doubt that was an excuse; old Brown spent the night with his brother-in-law, the Rev. Adair and his half-sister. It is plausible to assume that he pumped them for information and also borrowed some money. Mr. Brown's way with money often impelled him into loans.

The next day he arrived at his sons' claims, reined his horse and regarded their sad situation. The Brown boys had not tended their crops nor built any permanent shelters for their families. Their condition resembled the grasshopper of fable: they had fiddled with politics all summer long, and held heady conferences with various leaders. Now the leaders had retired to the comforts of the fortress-like Free State Hotel in Lawrence, and followers like the Browns had to return to their claims.

Between the end of September and early October the climate changed with an abrupt brutality for which they were completely unprepared. The wind howled, bringing an Arctic chill; the cold was worse—far worse—than Ohio, or even North Elba. It was, in fact, to be one of the most severe winters on record in Kansas.

Meanwhile, on Brown's arrival, the old man found all his kin shaking with "ague"—malaria—and huddled over open fires which, stocked with damp, green wood, burned poorly and set aloft dense clouds of grey smoke into the chill air. Their wives despaired of getting them to move; all of them were sick except Wealthy, John Brown, Jr.'s wife and their retarded son Johnny. They had no meat, little sugar, their livestock had wandered off on the prairie, and they had nothing with which to make bread except some corn—and the nearest handmill was two miles away.

Old Brown climbed down from the wagon, his eyes icy. He took charge as though the others were children and he towered above them. The wagon, with its load of guns, ammunition, sabers, and goods, was

unloaded. Work was launched at once to build shelters, the families of
John junior and Jason taking precedence. The results were primitive:
Wealthy watched the erection of an open shed with four poles supporting a shingle roof, with three sides protected only by long sheaves of
prairie grass pressed between stakes. Jason's wife, Ellen, received four
walls, three logs high, chinked with mud, and covered by the cotton
sheeting of one of the tents. But it had a chimney, and she wrote her
mother-in-law in North Elba that she could, at last, "cook a meal
without smoking my eyes almost out of my head."[5]

In the midst of these efforts, on the first Tuesday after Brown's
arrival, he and all his sons except Jason—who was still too ill—went to
Osawatomie, ten miles away, to vote in the Free State election. All were
heavily armed but the occasion was peaceful; no doubt Adair introduced his brother-in-law around the hamlet, where his sons were already known. Apparently no questions were asked about the new-
comer's right to vote: the Northern settlers were as careless of legalities
as the Southerners and both factions seemed unaware that they were
making a mockery out of rights their forebears had died to obtain.[6]

The Free-State election had no legal standing but went off without
incident, as had the legal elections of the territorial government earlier
in the month of October, 1855. The fact that the Browns would halt
their essential labors to attend what amounted to a demonstration,
however, was indication, if any was needed, of their intense political
ardor. But not even old Brown's sharp and suspicious eyes could see
any signs of actual trouble in the Osawatomie region. "I believe," he
wrote to North Elba, "that Missouri is fast becoming discouraged
about making Kansas a slave state."[7]

But that was a brief respite. The old man and his boys went back to
their camp labors, and he soon wrote of icy rains and bone-chilling
nights; on October 25 of "the hardest freezing" he had ever seen south
of North Elba. He told his family in North Elba (". . . that miserable
frosty region") they should know that "those here are not altogether
in Paradise."[8]

Chapter 9

New England winters were also severe, but that long-settled and prosperous region did not suffer. In the comfortable and cozy home of
George Luther Stearns "two boys came down to breakfast and found
a thin, spare-looking gentleman warming his hands before the fire; and

he said to them with a very pleasant smile, 'I lectured in your town last evening and your father brought me here to spend the night. My name is Emerson.' "

The visitor extended himself, and called their attention to an atlas on the sofa. "Do you know Sirius and Aldeberan?" he asked. "Do you know that the star in the west which they call Vega is moving steadily northward, and in a great many thousand years will become the polar star?"[1]

Mr. Emerson could be charming. Stearns was very proud of his friendship with him; the two men often discussed the situation in Kansas and agreed that strong measures were necessary to keep the territory from expanding Southern power and what they called "slavocracy." To have Emerson's approval was reassuring, for Stearns' efforts had grown quite serious, as had those of the New England Emigrant Aid Society.

These efforts were conducted on several levels. The newspapers made much of the political struggle and the Free-State movement, and of emigrant trains and Northern settlers. But another, more subterranean level, remained shadowed, and light penetrated its activities only obliquely and accidentally. One such insight was provided by Patrick Laughlin, a native of Ireland and former resident of Kentucky, who settled in the Kansas Territory in June, 1855. The Southern invasion and mockery of the first territorial elections had disgusted him, and he became ardent for the Free-State cause. Laughlin was elected—together with a neighbor named Samuel Collins—a delegate to the Big Springs convention, where he served on several committees. His duties were to "supervise free-state mail, arbitrate between members and . . . gather information against the pro-slavery party."[2]

The last duty was the most interesting. Information—whether factual or not—was an important part of the Free-State effort, for it was immediately carried in the dispatches of the Northern correspondents to their newspapers in New England and the East. The Southern party may have done much the same, but in a far less organized and deliberate way. The South had its newspapers, of course, but these had no audiences to compare with the millions spreading across the North; nor had the South's leaders who seemed to grasp that propaganda was the heaviest instrument in the, as yet muffled, regional warfare underway.

Laughlin discovered one such undercurrent at the Big Springs convention. It was called the Kansas Legion—a group whose very existence was a secret, and which never appeared in the miles of copy the newspaper correspondents filed. Laughlin was initiated into the Legion, took an oath to keep its activities and even its name a secret. He left the convention early to carry two sealed books of the Legion to men at Grasshopper Falls. A chapter was organized there, and Laughlin was given a letter to take to G. W. Brown, the Lawrence editor of the *Herald of Freedom*—a newspaper whose dispatches were received in New England abolitionist circles as coming straight from Sinai itself.

The editor took Laughlin into tow, showing him stores of Sharp's rifles, blue jackets and white trousers, and talking eloquently of freedom. Then he gave Laughlin—who must have impressed the leaders as an eager convert—two more sealed books, told him to organize a Legion chapter in Doniphan County, and then carry the books to still another destination. Laughlin carried out part of these instructions, organizing a Legion chapter among his neighbors. But curiosity finally, and inevitably, overwhelmed him, and he sat down and broke the seals of the books.

What he read disillusioned him. Perhaps he did not know that many in abolitionist circles in New England and New York were deeply antiforeign and especially anti-Irish. Many had, in fact, been active in the "Know-Nothing," or American Party before they concentrated their energies on antislavery. At any rate, Laughlin learned that antiforeign elements were dominant in the Kansas Legion. Deeply angered and embittered, he felt that he had been played for a fool.

He went home, broke with the Kansas Legion, and broke his vow of perpetual silence. That created a great stir in the territory, and Samuel Collins, his neighbor and fellow delegate to Big Springs, and also a member of the Legion, threatened to stop his talk. The argument began in a doctor's office in Atchison, Kansas, and resumed in the street the following day. A melee ensued, in which a third man named Lynch became involved. In the end Collins was killed and Laughlin wounded. He was rushed across the border to Missouri for safety's sake.[3]

A shriek of anger rose from the Free-State ranks, which the newspapers of the North managed, with remarkable skill, to muffle and misdirect. Attention was focused on the dead Collins, whom Robinson— with truly impressive effrontery—described as a martyr to the antislavery cause.[4] Laughlin was described as a proslaver, and his revelations about the Kansas Legion as exaggerations designed to injure the Free-State, antislavery cause.

That this impudent propaganda succeeded in large measure can be credited to the fact that newspapers were really important mainly in the North. The facts of the case were, of course, opposite to what the Free-Staters claimed. Collins appears to have been assigned the task of silencing Laughlin. To that extent he might, by some stretch of the truth, be termed a martyr to the Free-State cause, since he lost his life in the effort. But as far as the editor of the *Herald of Freedom* was concerned, there seems little doubt that he was a leader of the Kansas Legion and a liar about it later. Much the same can be said of Robinson, the Free-State "governor."

The Southerners supporting the territorial government had reason to be alarmed. Dr. A. J. Francis, who had tried, and failed, to organize a Free White State party, had met with Reeder, Robinson, Lane, and John Hutchinson in Lawrence only weeks before the Laughlin-Collins shootout, and had been initiated into still another secret organization called the Kansas Regulars, armed and mobilized by the Free-Staters. Dr. Francis was better educated than Laughlin, and recoiled from the nature of the oath he was asked to take. He pointed out that it would obligate him to defy the lawful government of the territory, and walked out of the meeting.[5]

Dr. Francis did not keep his experience or his observation to himself, but was too prominent and respected a citizen to be treated like Laughlin.[6] The two events, however, sent rumors coursing through the territory and alarmed the supporters of the territorial government. Their reaction was natural but shortsighted.

Had they rested on their now virtually unassailable legal position, as guaranteed by the White House, they could have let the Free-State leaders organize, arm, and introduce violence—and rely on federal troops to maintain the peace. But that sort of Fabian patience was beyond the control of Southerners reared from childhood to prove their manhood by rising in defense of their personal rights.

Alarmed at the prospect of resistance where they had assumed control, the Southerners rushed to a "law and order" convention of their own at Leavenworth in mid-November. There they swore to organize "military companies" to support the territorial legislature and to see that its laws were enforced. That open proceeding—in contrast to the carefully cloaked and secret organizing of the Free-Staters—was used by the Northern newspapers as reason to shriek that massacres were being plotted, and that free settlers were imperiled by rising forces of evil.

The Southerners—as they were to tardily realized—had been goaded into a trap. Moderates were left without a party. Men who were neutral on the subject of slavery had no chance of maintaining that dispassionate serenity, for the only two territorial parties in the winter of 1855 were in the control of extremists.

Proof was not long in coming. Charles Dow, a Free-Stater, cut wood on the claim of Franklin Coleman, a Southerner, and a dispute took place. Shots were fired and Dow fell dead. Coleman claimed self-defense and surrendered to the authorities, a step that lent credence to his claim.

The Northern press shrieked that the killing was political. Coleman's house was burned, as were those of "one or two" other Southerners.[7] Coleman's wife fled to Missouri and Coleman himself went to the territorial authorities at Shawnee Mission. There, he apparently convinced the officials that the shooting was not a criminal act on his part. He was returned to the scene by Sheriff Samuel J. Jones and a posse. En route they were met by a party of Free-Staters who told them that Coleman was no longer safe in the region. Sheriff Jones disregarded this. When the sheriff left, however, he took with him a man named Branson, with whom Coleman had been staying, on a minor charge. Branson was a Free-Stater, and a rumor was floated charging that Branson was to be punished for Coleman's crime.

When the sheriff reached a place called Blanton's Bridge a large party of Free-Staters headed by a man named S. N. Wood appeared and took his prisoner away from him. The sheriff then proceeded to Shawnee Mission and made his report. The freed prisoner Branson was taken to Lawrence. There a public meeting was held, a committee of public safety appointed, and plans made to defy the territorial government.[8] One result was that Governor Shannon wrote in alarm to President Pierce:

Executive Office, Shawnee Mission
November 28, 1855

Sir:

Affairs in this Territory are daily assuming a shape of great danger to the peace and good order of society. I am well satisfied that there exists in this Territory a secret military organization which has for its object, among other things, resistance to the laws by force. Until within a few days past I have looked upon the threats of leading men and public papers . . . as not intended to be carried into execution. I am now satisfied of the existence of this secret military organization, and that those engaged in it have been secretly supplied with arms and the munitions of war, and that . . . the strength of the organization is variously estimated at one to two thousand . . . they are said to be supplied the Sharpe's rifles and revolvers . . . and they are bound with an oath . . .[9]

If the governor expected President Pierce to do anything he was one of the few men in politics with such an expectation: Franklin Pierce appeared incapable of independent action. In fact, the only men on the landscape who seemed nerveless, adroit, and aware of every implication were the Emigrant Aid Society agents, Robinson and Pomeroy. Lane, predictably, was stalking about Lawrence claiming to be a military expert, and breathing fire.

The agents put several companies at drill, and sent out a call for Free-Staters to rally to the town. One such message reached Osawatomie, dated December 5, 1855. It read, "We want every true Free State man in Kansas at Lawrence immediately."[10]

John Brown, Jr., who was on his way on foot to Lawrence for news, met the messenger and read the message. When he returned to the camp with the news his father mobilized his sons. With John Brown, Jr., Frederick, Owen, and Salmon, he loaded the wagon with arms and sabers, harnessed the horse and set out for Lawrence at five o'clock on the evening of December 6, 1855.

The Browns were hardy, but the march must have been difficult. It was already dark when they left and they only stopped once to rest on the chilly plains. They reached Lawrence during the morning of December 7, while the town was becoming filled with men, and while several of Robinson's military companies were drilling. The *Herald of Freedom* left a description of their arrival.

As they drove up in front of the Free State Hotel they were all standing in a small lumber wagon. To each of their persons was strapped a short heavy broad sword. Each was supplied with a goodly number of fire arms, and navy revolvers, and poles were standing endwise around the wagon box with fixed bayonets pointing upwards. They looked really formidable and were received with great eclat. A small military company was organized at once, and the command was given to Old Brown. From that hour he commenced fomenting difficulties in camp, disregarding the commands of superior officers, and trying to induce the men to go down to Franklin and make an attack on the pro-slavery forces encamped there . . .[11]

Meanwhile a huge untidy force of Missourians and Southerners had collected and was marching on the town. Governor Shannon, who had organized some territorial militia, was embarrassed by the numbers that appeared—especially because they were disorganized and untidy, both in appearance and purpose.

Somewhere along their line of march they fell upon a hapless Free-Stater named John Barber, who was shot and killed. That, at least, was the version of the faction inside Lawrence, which carried the body to the Free State Hotel and spread rumors of martyrdom, massacres, and war to come.

Earthen walls were thrown up; Robinson was named "commander-in-chief," Jim Lane second in command; and rifles were distributed. The Browns gave away some swords, and the old man gloried in the rank of Captain of the Fifth Regiment, First Brigade of Kansas Volunteers. The regiment was somewhat scanty, consisting of twenty men, of whom four were officers, four sergeants, and four corporals, leaving only eight privates.[12]

The Wakarusa War—an ironic title—was also far beneath such lofty nomenclature. The facts of the incident were brief: Governor Shannon appeared with a small escort, was courteously received, and guided into the Free State Hotel, while the Southern and territorial forces camped a few miles away. Shannon was escorted past the ghastly, pallid corpse of Barber, stretched out on a bench at the top of the stairs leading to the council room, and was also exposed to the wails of Barber's widow.

After that psychological shock Shannon was plied with liquor and assured of everyone's peaceful intentions. He abandoned his demand that all arms be surrendered and settled for the ammunition. Nobody believed all of that would be surrendered, but Shannon's gesture was better than defiance.

After reaching an amicable agreement, the governor, accompanied by Robinson and Lane, rode to Franklin and spoke to the territorial militia captains, persuading them to lead their forces home. That was the Wakarusa War, in which old John Brown won his spurs as a captain —a title that clung to him like a burr forever after.

At least one of the remaining details had similar comic overtones. The Browns, together with the other volunteers, were credited with travel pay, with the use of their horses, and with sixteen days' service. These padded expenses were a minor windfall to the family, and the padding was part of a far greater padding by all the Free-Staters involved.

Senator Atchison of Missouri sought to extract some comfort from the Southern retreat, and said, "If you attack Lawrence now, you attack as a mob and what would be the result? You would cause the election of an abolition President and the ruin of the Democratic party. Wait a little. You cannot destroy these people without losing more than you would gain."[13]

Senator Atchison was right, but the newspapers of the North crowed as though an engagement had been fought and won. They stressed the efficiency of the Lawrence defenders and wrote as though all Southerners and supporters of the territorial government were drunken and cowardly men, continuing a theme of abuse that had plagued the South for nearly a generation.

Had the press taken a different tone, there seems little reason to believe that peace would not have spread through the region. Few of the settlers had traveled to Kansas to engage in a war. Even John Brown was only a farmer and a broken businessman addicted to hard language; his life had never included a single violent encounter. But propaganda has a way of warping the common vision of reality, and the propaganda that flowed from the huge and slightly comic feinting known as the Wakarusa War gradually made it seem as real as a bloody collison.

Winter settled in deadly earnest to put an end to political posturing for a while. From time to time the old man made wagon trips to Missouri, twenty-four miles away, to buy pork, flour, and other supplies. His letters to North Elba indicated straitened circumstances. He received some money from his own elderly father in Ohio, and sent some of this on to North Elba, where his wife and children had not been replenished for months. Luckily Brown's brother-in-law, Orson Day, wrote that he would pay to have a claim made in his name, and a cabin built for a later arrival. That was providential; the old man had seven adults and a child to feed at a time when the snow lay ten inches deep and the temperature lurked anywhere from ten to twenty-eight degrees below zero.

On January 8, 1856, the horse and wagon was sold in Missouri to repay money owed the Adairs; the oxen were loaded for the return trip, which must have been excruciating for the old man and Salmon, who accompanied him.

A few days before, however, the old man had been elected chairman of a small nominating convention in Osawatomie, where the Free-State settlers, a relative handful, also nominated John junior for the Free-State legislature. That was an honor for John Brown, Jr., and historian James C. Malin notes that it was curious that old Brown, who had no claim and was not a settler, should have acted as one, while being indignant that Missourians behaved with the same freedom in the southern part of the territory.

In February, 1856, Pierce finally made his choice. The President recognized the territorial government and ordered all armed bands to disperse, giving Governor Shannon the right to call federal troops if necessary. Even the more determined abolitionists recognized these moves as difficult to oppose legally.

The President's position had, in fact, been all that the South could have dreamed of, and Northern newspapers and leaders rose in protest. The state of Ohio, under Governor Salmon P. Chase, made its displeasure known, and others soon followed.

But the President had chosen: Shannon was authorized to use troops, and the Free-Staters could no longer claim the territorial government was illegal. Robinson, who had been called "governor" by the Free-Staters in their special election, was warned by Reeder that there was a limit beyond which it would not be wise to press the issue.

Deep snows delayed the mails and the Free-Staters did not learn of the new state of affairs at once; in the interim the Free-State legislature met in Topeka, with John Brown, Jr. among the seated delegates. On the third day of the session a message arrived from Governor Shannon. Robinson and the other leaders had to climb down considerably; they did this by a resolution calling themselves a gathering to petition the federal government. There was only one vote against this attempt to cling to at least some semblance of legality—and it was cast by John Brown, Jr.[14]

Not long afterward the elder Brown wrote a letter to Congressman Joshua Giddings of Ohio wondering if Free-State men could safely resist "the constituted authorities of the Territory of Kansas?" It was clear he thought all was lost.

Similar questions were rising in other minds as well. General Whitfield, the territorial delegate to Congress, wrote reassuringly to Major George E. Clark, the U.S. Indian agent in the territory about what it all meant. "One thing certain, Clark," he ended, "if they attempt to fight Uncle Sam's boys, the ball is open and civil war is certain."[15]

But Congressman Giddings, already established in the national mind as an extremist, put the same thought from a radically different perspective, in a letter to Brown:

Hall of Representatives, U.S.,
March 17, 1856

My Dear Sir:

We shall do all we can, but we are in a minority, and are dependent on the "Know-Nothings" for aid to effect anything, and they are in a very doubtful position; we know not how they will act. All I can say is, we shall try to relieve you. In the meantime, you need have no fear of the troops.

The President will never *dare* to employ the troops of the United States to shoot the citizens of Kansas. The death of the first man by the troops will involve every free State in our fate. *It will light up the fires of civil war throughout the North, and we shall stand or fall with you.* Such an act will also bring the President so deep in infamy that the hand of political resurrection will never reach him. Your safety depends on the supply of men and arms and money which will move forward to your relief next winter. I am confident there will be as many people in Kansas next winter as can be supplied with provisions. I may be mistaken, but I feel confident there will be no war in Kansas.

Yours respectfully,
J.R. Giddings[16]

John Brown, Esq.

Two congressmen, one pro-Southern, the other Northern and abolitionist, spelled the situation's two sides very neatly in these letters. If the Northern settlers, armed and directed by the Emigrant Aid Society and the New England abolitionists, forcefully defied federal troops, said Whitfield, a civil war would erupt. Congressman Giddings, a smooth-faced, carefully dressed man whose calm expression gave no hint of his fanaticism, agreed—but with a crucial difference. He thought the Free-Staters could do as they pleased; if the troops dared to repress them, the North would rebel. The two views, separately expressed without either man's knowledge of the other's, reversed the eventual course of events, but they indicate that the North was as close to the South to seceding. Perhaps closer, for the North did not have the same provocations on its own soil.

Before Congressman Giddings' letter reached him, John Brown wrote his wife in North Elba a letter on April 7, 1856, hinting that he might leave Kansas. "We are doing off a house for Orson Day," he said in part, "which we hope to get through with soon; after which we shall probably soon leave this neighborhood, but will advise you further when we do leave. It may be that Watson [in North Elba] can manage to get a little money for shearing sheep if you do not get any from Connecticut. I still hope you will get help from that source. We have no wars as yet, but we still have abundance of 'rumors.' We still have frosty nights, but the grass starts a little . . ." He enclosed thirty dollars, with no explanation of the source. Perhaps he had quietly been selling the "Guns, Revolvers" that he had been given by the citizens of Ohio and upstate New York a year before and carried to the territory in his now-vanished wagon.

Then, apparently, Giddings' letter arrived and Brown's attitude underwent a deep—and as it would prove—permanent change. A letter from a congressman to a man in his position was an honor—and this was no ordinary letter. It may have seemed to Brown an official promise that money and goods would be poured into the territory for some time to come, and also may have made clear that he and other Free-

Staters had no reason to pay serious attention to the federal troops—
to say nothing of the territorial government.

From that moment, the old man changed. No longer merely irascible
and spoiling for trouble, he became an oddly grim, sure figure. He
appeared in this new role at a settlers' meeting at Osawatomie on April
16, 1856, and made a deeply disturbing, if not ominous, impression.

Chapter 10

Later accounts of the meeting stressed its political nature, but to the
settlers in Osawatomie the more immediate issues were the practical
matters of taxes and surveys. John Brown, Jr., who had learned much
in his attendance as a delegate at various Free-State gatherings, later
wrote a letter to the *Herald of Freedom* saying that the settlers in the
southeastern part of the territory had received word that the assessor
would call upon them to evaluate their property for tax purposes. Soon
after that a deputy marshal appeared and served notice on settlers to
appear for jury duty.[1]

These were matters for the territorial government to conduct, and
in the wake of the news that the President had recognized the territorial government as legal, it had the effect of letting the air out of the
balloon of a great deal of inflated rhetoric about Free-Staters and
defiance. There was also another matter that would soon be decided:
boundaries on claims. Surveying teams were making their way toward
the region, and those with expanded claims could expect to see them
redrawn.

The Browns, whether they knew it or not, or recognized it or not,
were in very equivocal positions on the latter point.[2] Each of the boys
—including Salmon, who was underage and had no right to a claim at
all—had occupied lands that still belonged to Indians. Furthermore,
they were not Osawatomie settlers at all, being located ten miles away.
Their claims were near the settlement of Dutch Henry's Crossing.

Dutch Henry Sherman, who had been in the region longer than
anyone except trader Ottawa Jones, operated as a cattleman and had
assisted the first settlers—who were Southerners. Several of these had
staked claims in his region, built cabins, and started their farms. They
comprised a community. It was a community with its own internal
stresses, like all others, but distinct from Osawatomie.[3]

The Browns, however, attended settlers' meetings in Osawatomie
because they had a relative—the Reverend Samuel Adair—there, and

because that community of Free-Staters was more congenial and receptive than the settlement at Dutch Henry's. It speaks volumes for the
unpretentious but innate courtesy of the Osawatomie settlement that
the presence of the Browns was never questioned at their meetings,
and that John Brown, Jr., was actually elected as their delegate and
representative to the Free-State legislature. At a time when rules
seemed unimportant this was an easily overlooked technicality.

But by April, 1855 the President's declaration brought home the
reality of rules. Other indications of order, in the form of surveys,
assessments, and taxes made it necessary to face up to realities.

Richard Mendenhall chaired the April 16 Osawatomie meeting, with
Oscar V. Dayton as secretary. Mendenhall had been a Quaker mission-
ary to the Indians and Dayton was a commander of one of the Free-
State military companies in the region. Others in attendance included
Reverend Adair and Martin White, who had been an Illinois state
legislator. The record is incomplete on all others who attended—or all
who remained during the entire meeting—but the original call was
signed by twenty-three names, a small number, even in the territory.
Especially small considering the loud and continuing noise created
around the gathering.

On the surface the settlers did not seem to have much choice: a
government was in power and conducting its constituted activities.
Reverend Adair, however, was for nonresistance—but against paying
taxes. Martin White, who was a justice of the peace under the territorial
government but who had also been active in the Free-State movement,
disagreed. It was White's position that settlers should not defy the law
or the authorities, and should pay their taxes. He said any other course
would constitute rebellion and treason.[4]

At that old Brown, seated among his huge sons, erupted like a
volcano. White later said the old man identified himself as "an Abolitionist of the old stock—was dyed in the wool and that negroes were
his brothers and equals—that he would rather see this Union dissolved
and the country drenched with blood than to pay taxes to the amount
of one-hundredth part of a mill!"

That tore the meeting apart. Voices were raised, but Brown's soared
higher than any. At one point he denounced Osawatomie Brown, the
founder of the settlement, for "backing down." At another, according
to White, he said he would, "kill any officer of the Territory or Federal
government who attempted to enforce the laws against him."[5]

Some settlers finally left in disgust. The number of those who remained is unknown, but they proceeded to draw up a series of resolutions in the name of all the settlers. These repudiated the authority of
the territorial government, pledged "forcible" resistance and warned
those "appointed by the office of Assessor or Sheriff" that "any attempt to levy or collect taxes . . . will do so at the peril of such
consequences as may be necessary."[6]

It is noteworthy that slavery was not mentioned. The settlers' stand
was against paying taxes—and even that came from "a committee of

five." Nevertheless, the propaganda value of the resolutions was heavy, and evidence that this was realized was provided by the fact that the final resolution called for the statement to be "furnished the several papers of Kansas . . ."

While that fiery statement circulated, the more law-abiding settlers held another meeting at Stanton, and denounced "the lawless spirit exhibited at the Osawatomie meeting."[7] But John Brown, Jr. was also at the Stanton meeting, and spoke against the majority, saying that, "England was ready to help the abolitionists of Kansas." His basis for that was never explored, but it is clear he was very busy—organizing a "military company" called the Pottawatomie Rifles, with himself as captain.

Chapter 11

The split between the settlers reflected, in microcosm, a far larger and greater split across the Kansas Territory and the nation. Congress erupted over the initial legality of the election of the territorial government and the seating of General Whitfield as territorial delegate was contested by Reeder and the Free-Staters. On March 19, three congressmen were appointed to investigate the trouble in Kansas. These were William A. Howard of Michigan, John Sherman of Ohio—both dedicated to the antislavery cause—and Mordecai Oliver of Missouri, who was proslavery. In other words, the House of Representatives, which was Northern-dominated, was going to prepare a case to overturn President Pierce's ruling in favor of the territorial government. Whitfield, who had sat in Congress in the previous session, was forced to retreat to the sidelines alongside Reeder, and await the outcome of the investigation which—in view of the partisan climate and the nature of the committee—was as predictable as the seasons.

Senator Douglas was outraged. He had been absent, ill for two months, but now returned to denounce the Emigrant Aid Society as "a movement for the purpose of producing a collision, with the hope that a civil war may be the result . . ."[1]

He was disputed by Senators Charles Sumner and William H. Seward, who led an attack that gradually embroiled virtually the entire Senate for the months of March and April, and later. Bills were introduced, debated, shredded, tossed aside, and redrafted. Charges became increasingly bitter and tempers grew short. But toward the end of April, 1856, the possibility that the Kansas issues could be resolved in Washington so cheered A. A. Lawrence that he wrote, in a letter to an uncle, that Kansas was nearly saved for the North, "against all risks of being a slave state." The "free state men," he continued, "will have some tribulation this summer: but after that, it is not possible that they should be seriously damaged."[2]

But Lawrence was far from the actual scene, where collisions—being subject to interpretations from afar—were disproportionately important. The actual territorial government, aware that its fate depended to a great extent upon its mastery of the local situation, moved to apply its powers as soon as it was sure of the President's backing. The question of law was crucial to that effort, and Sheriff Jones, who had lost a prisoner to the Lawrence Free-Staters—and whose warrants had been ignored in the settlement of the Wakarusa War—moved at once.

He was aware, as were all others, that the Free-State party had sent a number of men east during the winter to lecture, raise funds, and claim the Free-State legislature was the "true" government of Kansas. One such lecturer and fundraiser was S. N. Wood, who had taken the prisoner Branson away from Sheriff Jones and his posse at Blanton's Bridge.

On April 19, 1856, three days after the settlers' meeting at Osawatomie, Jones rode into Lawrence to arrest Wood, who had just returned at the head of a large party of emigrants. He had two warrants for the rebel, whom he found with no difficulty. But Wood resisted arrest, and a menacing crowd surrounded the sheriff, who retreated. The next day he named four civilians as a posse and returned, and was threatened with death if he persisted.[3] He withdrew again and called for federal troops. They responded, and a detachment was assigned to Jones under Lieutenant McIntosh.[4]

By the time Jones and the troops arrived, Wood had vanished, but the sheriff made six other arrests—all of men who had threatened him earlier. But even the presence of troops did not stop hostile remarks. Jones prepared to spend the night, and was shot at by an unknown sniper when he went with Lieutenant McIntosh for a drink. Later, on the night of April 23, 1856, while seated in a tent whose light cast his shadow upon the canvas, he was shot in the back from someone outside.[5]

While these events were taking place in Lawrence, the northern stronghold of freedom, Federal Judge Sterling G. Cato arrived at Dutch Henry's Crossing for the regularly scheduled spring court hearing. He stayed and held his hearings at Dutch Henry's house—for which the cattleman was paid. Officially, the site was known as Shermansville, in Franklin County. Cato was one of three judges in the three districts of the territory; they made this circuit twice a year. The cases awaiting trial in Shermansville were minor, and Cato—who had to hold, in effect, two courts, one federal and one territorial—scheduled only two days for this location, before moving on to the next county.

Among those on Judge Cato's fifteen-man grand jury (which included six Free-Staters) were James Harris, who worked for Dutch Henry, and James Doyle, whose son also served as bailiff. Allen Wilkinson, Shermansville's postmaster, was district attorney pro tem. The grand jury sat and heard cases for one day, followed by a petit jury on the next.[6]

Cato arrived at a time when the Osawatomie region was afloat in a sea of rumors, one of which was that the Browns would be arrested. That rumor, logical under the circumstances, greatly alarmed the clan and filled its patriarch with passion. He sent Henry Thompson and young Salmon ahead to the court at Dutch Henry's Crossing "to see," said Salmon later, "if Cato would arrest us. We went ten miles afoot and stood around to see if they would carry out their threat. I did not like it. I did not want to be in the middle of a rescue. That's a risky situation. I thought father was wild to send us, but he wanted to *hurry up the fight*—always."[7]

Henry Thompson was apparently the one whom the Browns expected to be arrested, for he had told a tale of arguing with the elder Doyle on the issue of slavery. According to Thompson, his remarks were caustic and overwhelming. He claimed to have told the settler that "he had seen colored men who were as much smarter than Doyle as he was smarter than his dog." Then, said Thompson, Doyle used "incendiary language" and implied that Thompson could get into trouble.[8] That was translated by the clan as possible arrest for speaking against slavery. No such arrests had ever been made in the territory—but the offense was in the territorial slave code, and subject to much agitation in abolitionist literature.

But Henry Thompson and Salmon were ignored by Judge Cato, whose cases consisted of one faulty indictment for the killing of two hogs, another equally faulty, for selling liquor to Indians, and one for assault with intent to kill. The defendant on that matter was prudently absent. For the rest the judge levied fines against absent jurors.

While this small-change of frontier life was being shuffled, the rest of the Browns appeared—as well as members of the Pottawatomie Rifle Company headed by John Brown, Jr. The members of this force left their rifles stacked in a nearby cabin while their captain entered the court.

About a week later a long letter appeared in the *Herald of Freedom* signed "J. B., Jr.," saying that at one point in the proceeding "one of the Rifle Company" rose, said he had a question for the court, and passed along a slip of paper on which was written "Does this Court intend to enforce the enactments of the Territorial Legislature, so-called? MANY CITIZENS."

Brown, Jr.'s letter continued: "The Judge said the Court could not be interrupted, but that when he had finished giving his charge 'if the question was of any consequence, he could answer it.' When he had done with the jury, he took up the paper, and after looking at it, laid it down near the clerk in a rather contemptuous manner . . . The Clerk then did the same thing, and also the Marshall. After waiting a while longer the Captain of the Company then left, and after getting out of the door, called to the members of his Company to meet on their parade ground . . ."

According to the letter, John Jr. and his company now swore allegiance to the resolutions defying the territorial laws and officers, and appointed a committee of three to wait until the court session ended, and to hand it to Judge Cato. The letter ended by saying the court left early the next day.[9]

Old Brown also wrote a letter, on April 22, 1856, to Reverend Adair, describing the same episode more excitedly, and ended by saying, "You will see that matters are in a fair way of coming to a head."[10]

Both events in which the Browns were involved—the "resolutions" at Osawatomie and the attempt to overawe Judge Cato's court—seemed frail foundations upon which to base any coherent program or claims to leadership. But it was clear that John Brown, Jr. was doing his best, and that his father—who until the Giddings letter had played no political role in the territory—had become eager for action. For the first time the Brown clan had two leaders instead of one. And Old Brown was never known to have endured such a situation long.

It was assumed at first that Sheriff Jones would die (although in fact he was only slightly wounded). Southern newspapers appeared in heavy headlines and shrieked for revenge. The Emigrant Aid agents in Lawrence—Robinson, Pomeroy, and Conway—were appalled. Their moralizing had been undone by a reckless young man from New York—though none then knew his identity.[11] The leaders hastened to call a mass rally denouncing Jones' shooting and dissociating themselves from it. Their speeches rang hollowly, for the crowd was by no means displeased with what had happened to Jones.

The *Herald of Freedom* charged that Jones had only himself to blame for sitting in a lighted tent. It hinted that he had arranged to have himself shot, insinuated a personal enemy had fired the weapon, and ended by saying that the event was "a lesson to the unfortunate tool of Oppression."

In the East the papers struggled with the incident, but in such a manner that it appeared simply one of a series of unending Kansas outrages. Readers could hardly have been blamed for considering the territory awash in blood, though in reality it was hardly more turbulent than any other newly settled land. The danger was in the exaggerations of the press, and the shooting of Sheriff Jones inflamed the South, where citizens were repeatedly told that he had died.

Governor Shannon, in his report on April 27, 1856, gave a dry, factual account of the assassination attempt, and analyzed the Free-State resistance strategy. "The plan," he wrote, "is this: whenever an officer, whether United States Marshal, sheriff or constable, shall attempt to execute a writ or process issued under Territorial law, aided

. . . by a posse of United States troops, he is to be evaded but not openly resisted. Should an attempt be made . . . unaided by a posse of United States troops, he is to be resisted by force at all hazards."[12] Shannon went on to observe that this policy would lay such a burden on the use of troops that the processes of the territorial government would be "practically nullified. It will be impossible to collect the taxes assessed for county and Territorial purposes if this plan of resistance is successful."

The stand of the Browns at the settlers' meeting at Osawatomie, therefore, fell into place as part of a larger strategy devised by Free-State leaders. John Brown, Jr. was in touch with these, for he had been elected a Free-State legislator. His activities as captain and organizer of the Pottawatomie Rifle Company fit neatly inside the "oath-bound military company" described to a grand jury by Dr. A. J. Francis and revealed by Patrick Laughlin as the Kansas Legion. It was clear that while the senators were arguing principles and approaches in the Capitol, and A.A. Lawrence sent anxious letters from Massachusetts pleading for patience, others, while using antislavery as a cloak to defy the authorities, were in reality fomenting revolution.

Robinson, Pomeroy, Conway, and John Hutchinson and other Free-State leaders had no hand in the shooting of the sheriff, but there was no way the South could know that—nor, if Southern leaders knew it, would they have regarded that detail as important. Lawrence was the font of Free-State power, which had deliberately made itself a fortress.

The fiery speeches of Emigrant Aid leaders and the arming of Northern emigrant trains with Sharp's rifles—copiously reported in the Southern press—inflamed that region. Colonel Jefferson Buford of Alabama spent $20,000 and advertised for three hundred recruits, offering twenty acres and guarantees of support for a year to go to Kansas. On April 7, 1856, equipped with Bibles, the recruits left Montgomery by boat for the territory. In other Southern cities similar efforts were mounted; Southern emigrant aid societies sprang into life, women donated jewels, and other recruits were raised. But these efforts were small compared to New England, where organization was conducted along lines of efficiency the South could not match. In New York, on April 9, three thousand crowded to hear the elite of the city orate in favor of free Kansas.[13]

In tiny Concord, Massachusetts, where Kansas events were closely monitored, the Sage encouraged his children's tutor, Franklin B. Sanborn, to become secretary of the Concord committee of the New England Kansas Aid Society—and to launch efforts that would become the most important in Sanborn's life.[14]

Chapter 12

Early in May, 1856, the supporters of emigrants of one section or another were sent into even higher paroxysms by the actions of Federal Judge S. D. Lecompte, whom journalist James Redpath later described as "a human skin distended by whiskey," and who, says historian Allen Nevins was "jovial in ordinary aspect but fierce when aroused."[1]

Judge Lecompte instructed a Grand Jury in Lecompton, Kansas, to indict the Free-State leaders. His charge was that all the Free-State organization, from "men who are dubbed governors . . . men who are dubbed all the other dubs" were resisters to territorial authority, which derived from the federal government. Even if indirect, such resistance, he said, was "constructive treason."[2]

Lecompte was quoting prevailing legal opinion, which President Pierce had emphasized in his special Kansas message earlier that year, referring to the Topeka Free-State movement as being of "revolutionary character." The President had warned that if resistance reached the "length of organized resistance" it would become "treasonous insurrection."[3]

The judge made this so clear that the grand jury—without hearing any witnesses—immediately indicted Reeder, Robinson, Jim Lane, G. W. Brown, Samuel N. Wood, George Dietzler, Gaius Jenkins, and George W. Smith. The North was indignant.

Robinson, who was called "governor" by Free-Staters, had already left the territory on a fundraising trip east, but was taken from a steamboat at Lexington, Missouri, held until papers arrived, and shipped back to Leavenworth. Reeder, who was appearing before the three-man congressional investigating committee, defied a subpoena and fled the territory in disguise. Jim Lane was, to his good fortune and the later misfortune of a number of settlers, out of the territory and in Indiana.[4]

But the grand jury did not stop with indictments. It issued orders to abate, as public nuisances, the *Herald of Freedom* and the *Free Press*—the two Lawrence newspapers whose fulminations, reportage, and editorials had inflamed animosities and infuriated the territorial government and Southerners for many months.

"We are on the eve of great events," wrote the St. Louis correspondent of the New York *Tribune*. For once, the hyperbole seemed appropriate.

Over the next fortnight some angry men began to move. The first of these was U.S. Marshal J. B. Donaldson. The immediate cause of Donaldson's rage was the defiance, by former territorial Governor Reeder, of a federal subpoena. That defiance, assisted by other Free-

54

Staters in Lawrence, cost the marshal an important prisoner, and he knew it. He also accepted the situation as one where federal laws were openly scorned, and his own post dismissed as beneath contempt. Donaldson's long-simmering resentment broke into rage, and, disdaining territorial Governor Shannon, he issued an open appeal to citizens of the territory to appear at Lecompton to serve as a posse. Being Southern in his sympathies and aware such an appeal directed to Free-Staters would be considered comic, he sent flyers to all territorial strongholds and into Missouri as well.[5]

Colonel Buford of Alabama and a force of several hundred hurried to Lecompton; General David A. Atchison led the Platte County Riflemen from Missouri; the Kickapoo Rangers appeared; Southern settlers in Kansas were not slow to join them. Tents blossomed around Lecompton, drills were conducted, and cavalry units rehearsed charges to the sounds of bugles.

The Free-Staters in Lawrence began to hear rumors of an invasion. The more timorous left town and the remaining leaders began to hold hasty conferences. A committee of safety was appointed, and plans made to answer the threat of force with humble words and pledges of cooperations with all laws—territorial as well as federal. That was a tactic that had worked before, during the Wakarusa episode; many believed it would work again. In that, as in so many of other attitudes, the Northerners betrayed a lack of sensitivity to the impact of goading, which, if repeated too often, does not so much deter as invite attack.

Chapter 13

Senator Charles Sumner of Massachusetts was about to learn the same lesson in the nation's capitol. A great figure in New England abolitionist circles, where he was a close friend of Dr. Samuel Gridley Howe, Wendell Phillips, Theodore Parker, George Luther Stearns, Henry Longfellow, John Greenleaf Whittier, and Emerson, the Senator was, nevertheless, a "psychic puzzle" to many of his contemporaries.

His father had been a sheriff who acted as his own hangman because, he said, hanging was too unpleasant a task to assign to underlings. Sumner inherited the same blend of the callous and the lofty. Six feet two inches tall—nearly as tall as Lincoln—with curly hair and distinguished, though petulant, features he was an ideologue in the Robespierre mold: austere, aloof, warm only toward those who agreed with him, cold as ice to everyone else.

Sumner prided himself on his oratory. His speeches were highly regarded by abolitionists and widely circulated. They were, in fact, remarkable in many respects, but they fell short of the first demand of eloquence because they failed to persuade the uncommitted. They were, however, masterpieces of denunciation, for Sumner's habitual stance was one of indignation. In that mood, he spent the early part of May 1856 preparing a speech on Kansas.

Senator Stephen Douglas, more than a foot shorter physically but a much larger man in every other sense, later said that Sumner had prepared his speech, "committed it to memory, practiced every night before the glass with a Negro boy to hold the candle and watch the gestures, and annoying the boarders in the neighboring rooms until they were forced to quit the house."[1] But that may just have been Douglas' sense of humor, which was apt to convulse his listeners, even in serious moments.

On May 19, 1856, Sumner rose to deliver—as he had written Theodore Parker two days before—"the most philippic ever uttered in a legislative body."[2] He called it "The Crime Against Kansas." It took the better part of two days to deliver, and succeeded in stunning all who heard it.

Sumner's thesis, stripped of classical allusions, quotations, and paraphrases of Cicero and Demosthenes, was that the Kansas-Nebraska Act was replete with "the meanness and wickedness of the cheat" and a sin, a sacrilege, a crime, a horror—all that was evil. He attacked Senator Andrew P. Butler of South Carolina, one of the best-loved men in the chamber, as a Don Quixote, and Senator Douglas—with an obvious reference to his short stature—as Sancho Panza. He accused them both of chasing "the harlot, Slavery," characterized the Missourians as "hirelings, picked from the drunken spew and vomit of an uneasy civilization," and continued in that vein for many hours.

Douglas listened in amazement. "Is it his object," he asked, "to provoke some of us to kick him as we would a dog in the street, that he may get sympathy upon the just chastisement?"[3] That was shrewd.

By the time Sumner finished, on May 20, he could not be ignored. Senator Lewis Cass of Michigan, a highly respected figure, rebuked him, and Douglas leaped to his feet to answer what amounted to personal abuse—not only of himself but of Senator Butler, who was absent.

Douglas spoke with some heat, which was natural, and Sumner of all people, accused him of being intemperate. He added that he would brand some of the Illinois Senator's charges as "false."

"I also say to the Senator," Sumner continued, "and I wish him to bear it in mind, that no person with the upright form of man can be allowed . . ." He hesitated.

"Say it," said Douglas.

"I will say it. No person with the upright form of man can be allowed, without violation of all decency, to switch out from his tongue the perpetual stench of offensive personality. Sir, this is not a proper weapon of debate at least, on this floor. The noisome, squat, and nameless animal, to which I now refer, is not a proper model for a United States Senator. Will the Senator from Illinois take notice?"

"I will not imitate the Senator in that regard," said Douglas, and Sumner then compounded his insult.

"Mr. President," he said, turning his back on Douglas and looking toward the chair, "again the Senator has switched his tongue, and again he fills the Senate with its offensive odor."[4]

Though the Senators did not know it, a similar dialogue was being conducted in Kansas at the same time, while U.S. Marshal Donaldson's motley army was collecting outside Lawrence. Their numbers vary with the sympathies of the observers, and no completely accurate account exists, but there were at least five hundred men. They had a vast collection of small arms and at least four small cannon, variegated banners, and a considerable number of leaders giving conflicting orders.

A committee sallied forth from Lawrence to attempt to placate this force, and to pledge future obedience to all laws and to cooperate with the serving of court orders. They also proposed that all hostilities be suspended—a natural desire—and that federal troops be called to supervise the serving of writs. From some distance these troops had watched events with misgivings. Lieutenant McIntosh, who had grown familiar with the disorderly proceedings and personalities in the territory, sent a memo to his superior, Colonel Sumner, saying he feared the huge Southern posse would escape the marshal's control.

But the troops could not intervene unless they were called upon—and Governor Shannon did not want to interfere with the marshal, who was charged with enforcing the orders of a federal court. The governor, therefore, had no power to interfere with the marshal.

On the morning of May 21, 1856, Deputy Marshal W. P. Fain entered Lawrence with an unarmed escort of eight men, called on five Free-Staters to help him and arrested George Dietzler, G. W. Smith, and Gaius Jenkins for treason, as ordered by Judge Lecompte and the federal grand jury. Fain met with no resistance. The leaders of the town repeated their willingness to comply with all laws—territorial as well as federal. They were grimly told that Sheriff Jones had some unserved warrants and would also appear.

In due course Jones clattered into Lawrence and hundreds of assembled Southerners came with him, dragging their cannon, whooping, and spoiling for action. The Free-Staters, however, had no intention of creating any provocations; their famed military companies had vanished. Sheriff Jones, who had inherited the posse, watched while three cannons were trained on the Free State Hotel and shots poured into it. These failed to destroy the structure—built of stone, with turrets and sentry-walks—so it was first ransacked and then set on fire. Colonel Buford protested that he had not agreed to any destruction of property, but the sheriff insisted the fort was being "abated." The *Herald of Freedom* and the *Free Press* offices were invaded, the presses destroyed, and their type thrown in the river. A number of liquor stores were looted and many of the Southerners got drunk, staggered around, and created a considerable din, but none of the citizens were attacked or harmed, though one man was killed in an accident.[5]

Few of these activities reflected the orders of any court: the newspapers had not been legally directed to shut down; the Free State Hotel destruction had not been ordered—and arson, looting, and robbery are hardly legal. General Atchison, Colonel Buford, and other Southern leaders were aware matters had escaped control. The news of the assaults in Lawrence sped toward Governor Shannon and the federal troops, and hummed over the nation's telegraph wires. By the time the posse began to leave, in as disorderly a manner as it had arrived, the Southerners had—like a henpecked man who punches his wife—lost their moral position and fundamentally altered the grounds of the situation.

Unaware of these events, Senator Sumner in the capitol had finished his speech—which was to plant his name in the history books in a manner he had not foreseen. Throughout the evening of May 21, 1856, a young representative from South Carolina, Preston S. Brooks, had tossed all night over the insults the orator from Massachusetts had rained upon his uncle, Senator Butler.

Retribution for insults to family honor was an obligation Southerners took very seriously. Ordinarily a gentleman would be challenged, but Brooks did not consider Sumner a gentleman. He was an inferior, to be punished accordingly. Brooks wavered between using a horsewhip and a cowhide. He had to consider that Sumner was a huge man. He might seize the whip and Brooks might, in that event, have to kill him. That would be going too far. Brooks finally decided to use a gold-headed, hollow-cored gutta-percha walking stick he owned, tapered from one inch at the top to three quarters of an inch at the bottom. Gutta-percha—hard rubber—was hard, but it would not cut and scar like a horsewhip.[6]

On May 22, Brooks—a combat veteran of the Mexican War—waited until all the ladies had left the Senate chamber. Then he walked over to Sumner's desk.

The Senator was bent over his pen. Brooks said, "Mr. Sumner." The man from Massachusetts raised his head and peered near-sightedly at him. "I have read your speech twice over carefully," Brooks said in a rapid Southern murmur. "It is a libel on South Carolina and Mr. Butler who is a relative of mine." Then he hit him.

Sumner threw up his arms and Brooks began to rain blows. The Senator's chair was on rollers, but he forgot that and tried to rise. His desk was bolted to the floor by heavy screws imbedded in an iron plate, but he made an awesome effort and actually tore the desk loose as he rose to his immense height, arms outstretched, and groped toward his assailant. Brooks retreated, whipping furiously. The gutta-percha cane broke and he continued to pummel away with the slivers until the Senator fell and men came running.[7]

Chapter 14

John Brown, Jr. later said he was planting corn when news reached him at his claim that Lawrence was being attacked. The same information trickled through the region and reached the settlers at Osawatomie the next day. By Wednesday evening, May 21, 1856, about thirty-four men —including the Browns—were together at the junction of the California and Westport roads, and late that afternoon they passed by the general store operated by Theodore Wiener and his brother-in-law, Jacob Benjamin, near Mosquito Creek.[1]

The area had been rife with rumors for days; it was known that Colonel Buford and his men had passed through and camped overnight. Free-Staters speculated that Lawrence would be attacked in force; most expected the pitched and bitter battle the newspapers on both sides had predicted for months. Wiener and Benjamin, fearful for their goods, loaded two wagons and Benjamin and his wife took them into the woods near the Marais des Cygnes to hide them from marauders, while Wiener—a large and reputedly fearless man—joined the Pottawatomie Rifle Company under John Brown, Jr.[2]

The men first stopped at Mount Vernon, across Middle Creek, and then—after a night's rest—began to move before daybreak on Thursday, May 22—the day that Sumner was caned. They reached the crossing of the Marais des Cygnes when a messenger from Lawrence appeared, saying the town had been taken without resistance. The Rifle Company digested this news with breakfast, and a vote was taken on whether to continue or turn back. Brown was eager to proceed: everyone recalled that later. The messenger had said, however, that Robinson was arrested, that the town was short of food, and no more men were wanted.[3]

This information was at startling variance with the great pitched battles predicted. It confused the men, and they continued doggedly in the direction of Lawrence. They were joined by men from Osawatomie, headed by "Captain" Shore, and also by a group calling itself the Pomeroy Guards. These reported that the Free State Hotel had been razed—and implied that much of the town was gone as well. The combined groups straggled on till they reached Shore's claim, near Prairie City, where they decided to spend the night.

The next morning Old Brown cooked breakfast; a chore he always liked. He also, apparently, had several arguments with John Brown, Jr., who was considered the leader and captain of the assembled men. The nature of these disputes will never be known precisely, any more than the number of men with whom the old man held brief, whispered conferences. Apparently his standing was not too high, for outside of his four younger sons—Owen, Frederick, Salmon and Oliver—only two men paid any real attention. They were James Townsley, who had a team of greys and a wagon, and Theodore Wiener the storekeeper, who had a pony.

The rest of the men, including Brown's two eldest sons—John junior and the oddly thin-faced Jason—watched in silence as Old Brown supervised the sharpening of a number of his sabers. A boy, Bain Fuller, obediently turned the grindstone.

"That looks like business," said nineteen-year-old George Grant.

"Yes," said Frederick shortly, "it does."

Then Grant, who had learned that Townsley was going to carry some of the Browns back to the settlement, wondered if he could ride with them. Frederick consulted with the old man and then said, "Father says you had better not come."

James Hanway, one of the settlers, hearing rumors of what Brown planned, went over and urged him to be cautious. At that the bitter, frustrated old man straightened up.

"Caution, caution, sir," he said. "I am eternally tired of hearing that word caution. It is nothing but the word of cowardice." He shook with passion.

Hanway recoiled. The vehemence was unexpected, and he wondered what was afoot. He talked to some of the others. They told him, and he was shocked. But—together with the rest—he watched in silence as the seven departed in Townsley's wagon, with the burly Wiener riding his incongruous pony alongside.[4]

While Brown and his handful rested in the ravine waiting for nightfall, the larger group of men under John junior decided to go to Palmyra, a hamlet about twelve miles from Lawrence situated on the Santa Fe Trail. Their new plan, formed after learning of Robinson's arrest in Missouri, was to wait there for the arresting party that was bringing the Free-State leader back to Kansas. When that party reached Palmyra they would waylay it, and release Robinson, by force if necessary.

That was a bold plan, and John Brown, Jr. may have had dreams of becoming famous by it; certainly he would have attracted national attention. But after they arrived at Palmyra they learned that the escort —perhaps fearing some such interruption—had changed its route. That left them tired and beginning to feel foolish. Thirsting for some sort of redeeming action, John junior went to Lawrence with two other men to assess the actual situation. He returned to report the damage, but also the fact that most of the stronghold was intact.[5]

By then the men were openly arguing about their purpose in remaining together, and John junior led the last independent effort of his brief career as a leader. He had learned that a Southerner, William Jones, who had a claim and a cabin near Palmyra, also had two slaves. He insisted that his own men release those slaves, and would hear of no disagreement. In this he began to resemble his father, and the men —or at least some of them—followed him to the Jones cabin, where Jones was ejected and the slaves carried back to camp, to be told they were free.

That information meant little to the slaves: they stood, bewildered and bereft, in a circle of roughly dressed men who told them, in effect, that they could wander out in the prairie to starve to death. Some of the men saw that, and an argument erupted. John Brown, Jr.'s wisdom in leading the venture was openly questioned and the matter was put to a vote. The captain was overruled, and a man named Clayton of Osawatomie returned the slaves to the Jones cabin. Jones' wife was so overjoyed that she gave Clayton her sidesaddle, obviously a prized possession, as a reward.[6]

It was now Sunday morning and John Brown, Jr.'s control over the men was slipping. A number had already left quietly, and the captain was further upset when—about two miles down the Santa Fe Trail— he and his remaining force ran into federal troops under Second Lieutenant John R. Church. The officer told him that orders had been issued for all armed bands to disperse to their homes.[7]

Most of the Osawatomie contingent obeyed, and John Brown, Jr. led his Pottawatomie Rifles toward Ottawa Jones' place near that region. Ottawa Jones was a half-breed trader whose hospitality was often abused. They were nearly there when, Jason said years later, a rider came by, his horse panting and lathered with foam. He shouted, "Five men have been killed on Pottawatomie Creek, butchered and most brutally mangled, and old John Brown has done it!"[8]

"This caused great excitement and fear among the men of our company," wrote Jason, "and a feeling arose against John and myself . . ."

They continued in the dark, with John Brown, Jr. and Jason the objects of sidelong looks, until they reached Ottawa Jones' claim, where they made camp near the fresh water of the river.

In the morning they discovered that old Brown, his younger sons, and son-in-law were back among them. Several of the men recognized Dutch Henry's grey stallion. There is no record of any open comment, but the men took a vote that Monday morning and dismissed John Brown, Jr. as their captain and elected H. H. Williams, his second-in-command, to his post. Then they headed toward Pottawatomie, and the Osawatomie men who had stuck with them traveled along. Paths parted for the two groups at Middle Creek, where John Brown and his handful turned toward the Brown claim. John Brown, Jr. and Jason continued on toward the home of their uncle, the Reverend Samuel Adair.[9]

Old Brown's crime—and those of his sons, son-in-law, Theodore Wiener and James Townsley—horrified the region. The news, communicated swiftly to Governor Shannon and other officials at Lecompton, was among the items that appeared in dispatches, though in jumbled form, within the next few days and weeks. Word of mouth, however, carried it farther and faster than even the telegraph could. Fear spread like a fog across the blue hazy climate of eastern Kansas, south to Missouri, west across the undulating plains.

The newspapers of the nation, however, were dense with accounts of what was called the "Sack of Lawrence," which was described in terms suitable to the fall of Troy or the collapse of Rome under the barbarians. Some dispatches depicted the town as ashes, with only a stray chimney left standing. The Southerners in Kansas were once again lumped under the term "Border Ruffians"—a synonym for everything low, loathsome, and mean in human nature.

These accounts sent premonitory shivers through moderates, and filled extremists with wild excitement—but they also had to compete for attention with the attack upon that idol of New England abolitionists, the tall, fair, and eloquent Senator Charles Sumner of Massachusetts.

Those who saw the attack did not consider Sumner seriously hurt, and in a physical sense his physicians caused him more pain and distress with their treatments than had Representative Brooks in his ten-minute onslaught. But Sumner had been gravely injured psychically, and would not recover entirely for years. Meanwhile, Boston newspapers screamed that he might be crippled for life.

Yet the name of John Brown, though not connected in the East with the Pottawatomie murders, floated through the Kansas Territory with uncanny speed. It was as if the significance of what Brown introduced into the disputes of the region struck some atavistic chord. He became immediately, immensely, important, though the men around him—and the men with him—could not quite define the essence of his new significance.

It is only after several generations that it can be seen, with terrible clarity, that Old Brown—by linking murder to his distorted version of religion, and by selecting victims who were innocent of any crime—had reintroduced the old, evil and pagan principle of human sacrifice.

Part II
ANGELS, DIRECTORS, AND STAGE MANAGERS

Chapter 15

Mrs. Mary Channing Higginson, semicrippled from a mysterious disease, had to be carried up and down stairs. Her husband, the Reverend Thomas Wentworth Higginson—tall, athletic, and bursting with innumerable enthusiasms and indignations—would take her to the beach in a wheelbarrow. He was also subject to some strange lapses in sensitivity. "I throw things down for her to pick up & show her off generally, like some wonderful quadruped, wholly gratis."[1]

William Channing Gannett observed that the Higginsons' relationship was fairly close to a standoff. "Mrs. Higginson is very queer," he wrote, "a great invalid from rheumatism, a perfect mistress in the art of abuse, in which she indulges frequently with peculiar zest & enthusiasm, she has a very dry & cutting wit and is very amusing."[2]

Mrs. Higginson had a talent for chilling the enthusiasms to which her husband was addicted; she disliked children—which he adored; she had to have her meals brought to her bedroom, which she seldom left. In the fall of 1855, Higginson tore himself away from his growing obsession with politics and antislavery, and took his wife on an ocean voyage in the hope that the change of climate would restore her health. It must have been a wrench to leave, for his part in the attempted rescue of Anthony Burns had brought him to the attention of the nation, as had his abortive indictment and his subsequent defensive statements.

He had also emerged as a contributor to magazines, and proved to have a popular touch in his articles. His most recent had been issued just before he and Mary sailed. Entitled "African Proverbial Philosophy," it appeared in *Putnam's Monthly,* and was little short of astonishing. Based largely on the travel accounts of another wide-eyed, enthusiastic cleric who had visited Africa, the article described an African village that existed only in Higginson's imagination: the natives were "active, commercial geniuses," with "a remarkable language and an even more remarkable collection of proverbs."[3] Higginson described them as being, in effect, black New Englanders, dedicated to commerce and mechanical marvels. Some have since searched for that village, or its remains, but without success.

The Higginsons sailed for the Azores. At the port of Horta, a port on the Portuguese island of Fayal, Higginson at first found himself enchanted by the towers left behind by the Moors centuries before, the

white houses, and the luminous sun. He was particularly impressed—
as was natural in his situation—by the island's "barelegged, uncor-
seted and vigorous women," especially as they contrasted with such
"diseased, tottering" American females as his wife.

As weeks and months passed, however, the cathedrals, bells and
priests, the monks, nuns, penitents, processions, incense, vestments,
and the entire climate of Catholicism aroused his New England prejudices. He decided that "natural religion" was better; it did not occur
to him that he was confronted with the religion of his remote ancestors: such a recollection is denied in the Protestant world. He chafed
and grew discontented; tardy dispatches from the United States told
of stirring events while he was chained to an atmosphere of what he
termed "nudity and dirt."

On June 7, 1856, the ship aboard which Higginson and his wife were
returning home was off the Massachusetts coast at Cape Ann. A dispatch boat arrived and Higginson read with indignation of the caning
of his close friend Senator Sumner—and of the sack of Lawrence. He
disembarked, rejoicing at the sight of well-dressed Boston, as compared to the "robust baseness" of the Azores.[4] Mrs. Higginson was not
improved, but he had done his best. His attention now turned to the
outrages of the "Border Ruffians" and the atrocities of Southerners in
general. He entrained for Worcester burning for the fray, and determined to make up for lost time.

The Reverend Theodore Parker loved books and bears. Twelve thousand volumes lined the walls of his study and even the stairways of
Green Hills, his home. His admirers sent him dozens of bear figurines,
statuettes, drawings. The famed Unitarian even called his wife, Lydia
Cabot Parker, "Bearsie." They had an odd exchange, often repeated.

"What are you?"

"A bear."

"And what must this bear do to be saved?"

"Have pups."[5]

They both grieved, however, over her failure to do so. Parker envied
the Howes their several healthy children; for a time he expected to
have their next. Meanwhile the tireless minister appeared in the Melodion every Sunday before a crowd of several thousand; in the winter
of 1855 he gave nearly one hundred lectures, and about eighty during
the spring of 1856.[6] But despite—or because of—his bewildering mix
of fanatic, scholar, religious dissenter, historian *manqué*, agitator, en-
tertainer, politician, writer, and reformer, Parker was burning his energies with a prodigality that was unnatural, excessive, and harmful to
his health. "I fear you would hardly know me," he wrote a friend in
1856, "I am grown so old in look. My head is bald and my beard is gray
. . . I have grown very old within the last three years; too much work
and too many cares have done this to me."[7] He was forty-six.

The caning of Sumner set Parker on fire; he was sure the United
States was in "a state of incipient civil war." In his lecture at the

Melodion, he pictured Sumner as the North and Brooks as the South, with Brooks stealing behind the seated Sumner when his arms were pinioned "in his heavy chair and his other limbs are beneath the desk, and on his naked head strikes him with a club loaded with lead."[8]

It was called the Bird Club but it had neither officers, rules, nor a structure of any sort. It charged no admission, had no initiation, oath, or membership roster. It was simply a table in Young's Hotel in Boston, where Frank Bird, a tall, thin, wiry, and wealthy paper manufacturer, sat every Saturday afternoon, chatting with his friends. That coterie, whose connections were amorphous, social, invisible, and impenetrable to outsiders, was important beyond measure in the city and beyond.

The "Kansas excitement" brought the club some newcomers, including George L. Stearns and Franklin B. Sanborn, but Dr. Samuel Gridley Howe had always been a member, and so had his closest friend, Charles Sumner. In 1856, Dr. Howe was the only universally acknowledged hero in the club—as well as its most famous member. He had won fame during the Greek war of independence in the 1820's. He was widely known for his treatment of the blind, deaf, and mute. Above all, he was married to the beautiful Julia Ward. That alliance had been made at a time when the difference in their possessions was so great that Julia's family thought Howe was a fortune hunter, and made him sign a contract to keep his hands off her money. Nevertheless, she gave him every cent she received from her income, and meekly accepted whatever allowance he granted her in return.

Howe shared an attribute with Frank Bird, who, says Stearns, "had this peculiarity, that the more kindly he felt to those who were unfortunate in life, the more antagonistic he seemed to be to those who were exceptionally prosperous. He appeared to have a sort of spite against handsome men and women, as if nature had been over-partial to them in comparison with others . . ."[9]

Although this "peculiarity" was not as well-known in Howe, he was nevertheless partial to the unfortunate. He used high-grade morons as maids, and was very proud of their efforts. He spent hours with the blind, or the deaf. Laura Bridgeman, who was blind, deaf, and mute, was both his prize pupil and someone with whom he liked to communicate. He was drawn to the insane, the imprisoned, the deficient, the crippled, and the handicapped. He shunned the society of brilliant people, and hated social gatherings—at which Julia Ward Howe both shone and sang. He avoided her "readings," which were famous in Boston, and forbade her to raise any money at these popular soirees, even for the causes in which he believed.

One of her achievements that aroused his deepest anger was publication, in 1854, of a book of her poems, entitled *Passion Flowers.* When the book went into several editions, Julia Ward Howe began to grow famous. To her dismay her husband, who himself had been famous for a long time, flew into a passion, refusing to speak to her for days on end. "Chev took it very hard," she wrote. His feelings were not improved when someone took the trouble to point out that one humorous effort in the collection, "Mind versus Millstream," satirized his efforts to make his wife obey him."[10]

For the next year, and the year after that, and into 1856, Dr. Howe found it difficult to approve of anything Julia did, said, or thought. He made this disapproval clear by cold withdrawal, which became even more frigid when she brought him her quarterly checks from New York, where, as she herself once said, she was "the daughter of the Bank of Commerce."

Then he asked for a divorce. She was stricken, and pleaded with him to change his mind. He dropped the subject, but switched to a legal separation. Though Julia hated their quarters in the Institute for the Blind, where she was always aware of the odor "of water closets and disinfectant," she protested, and wept, and tried to please in every possible way. But she could not, however, reduce her brilliance; which offended most.

No doubt she would have reacted differently had she known Dr. Howe's eccentricity better, but she was a superior woman, and although he told her he needed someone younger and more worshipful, it never occurred to her that there was already someone; someone younger and "worshipful" enough to come to his office for passionate trysts. That was something Julia learned many years later.[11]

At the time Julia thought her husband was difficult, often aloof and cold—but always a hero, always above petty intrigues and mundane motives. In the wake of the Sumner caning when he, the Reverend Parker, the Rev. Higginson, Stearns, Sanborn, and many others became active in the Kansas Aid Committee—a new, radical branch of the Emigrant Aid Society—she was so sure of the doctor's high-mindedness that she prayed this new interest would cure his mysterious malaise and bring them closer together. She had a marriage to save and children to raise, and it was a period when divorce was considered a failure, not an answer.

George Luther Stearns, a lead-pipe manufacturer, had to struggle for success, and he attained it. By the 1850's he controlled over half the sale of lead in New England. His wife was a niece of Lydia Maria Child and he moved in abolitionist and even transcendentalist circles, though his contributions were more in money than in ideas.

Like most upper-class Bostonians, Stearns found his life changed by the repeal of the Missouri Compromise and the Kansas-Nebraska Act. He was one of Charles Sumner's backers for the Senate, and also prided himself on Emerson's friendship. in particular. A member of Theodore Parker's Vigilance Committee, he bought a revolver to use against slave hunters. He was, in other words, a convert as were his wife and his children.

Beneath his respectable facade, Stearns had the instincts of a gambler. Early in the 1850's he went to New York City, borrowed heavily and sought to corner the market in lead. When his funds were exhausted the price began to drop and he was wiped out in three days.

He returned to Boston in despair, and called a friend, Peter Butler who was astonished to discover the erstwhile immaculate manufacturer "lying on his bed half-dressed and unshaven . . . His first words were, 'Butler, I wanted to blow my brains out in New York, but I thought of my wife and I could not do it.' "[12]

Butler raised some money for him; other friends assisted and Stearns worked out a repayment agreement. Fortunately for him gold from California and other factors created a boom, during which he recovered his position. In early 1856, having narrowly escaped the consequences of overreaching, George Luther Stearns plunged into the Kansas situation—and a new gamble that involved many more lives.

His parents reversed a famous name and called him Franklin Benjamin Sanborn, and he grew up in a liberal, literary, and politically radical New Hampshire family. He was immensely tall—six feet three inches. Steeped in books, addicted to poetry, he was also a lifelong hero-worshiper, growing up to adore Emerson, Theodore Parker, Lydia Maria Child, Margaret Fuller, the Channings, and also the entire transcendentalist circle. By his nature he was irresistibly drawn to the well born—and the well-meaning.

From the time he was eighteen, Sanborn had a high-minded attraction to Ariana Smith Walker, a young lady from Peterborough, a town near his own original home at Hampton Falls, New Hampshire. The daguerreotype of "Anna," as she was called, shows a beautiful face and her letters, as cited by Sanborn later, considerable intelligence. But Ariana was lamed by illness, subject to nervous spells, and had tuberculosis.[13] Nevertheless a love affair—hopeless from the start and nearly grotesque—was launched.

In the beginning, this liaison—limited throughout its life to sonnets, to long letters about Sanborn's potential and his gifts and possibilities—may have been rewarding to both these young people, and it continued despite objections from Ariana's brother. The objections were understandable; Ariana's chances of leading a normal life were slight—and she was an heiress.

Sanborn attended Phillips Exeter Academy and then entered Harvard's sophomore class in 1852, when he was twenty. He listened to Parker and was, predictably, thrilled. He had already read Sir Walter Scott, had kept abreast of contemporary authors like Hawthorne, and was capable of a good literary conversation as it was then judged. At Harvard he continued his flow of poems and letters to Ariana, to whom he became engaged, though it had been agreed the actual marriage would wait until he graduated and established himself. His ambition—and Ariana's for him—was to become a writer. But her health continued to worsen, her nervous spells became more frequent, and the likelihood of marriage seemed more remote as time passed.

At Harvard young Sanborn disagreed with those professors who held Emerson and all the transcendentalists in contempt. In order to hear Parker Sanborn had to have special permission to be absent from the school chapel on Sundays, and walk to the Melodion. That he underwent that ordeal was evidence of his admiration. More evidence was provided when he walked to Concord to see Emerson. Apparently he lost his nerve the first time, but in July 1853, he had become secretary of the Hasty Pudding Club and was brave enough to visit the great man. He was aware that ten minutes was the limit for such a first, uninvited call. Emerson was polite, and said he "hoped to see a good crop of mystics at Harvard College."[14]

After that, Sanborn called more often, interspersing these cautious efforts with visits to Parker and other Boston abolitionists until he became a familiar and accepted presence. In 1854, he also went through some fairly public agonies over Ariana's decline. They were married, to general wonder, with the bride pale and sinking, and the giant groom standing beside her bed, holding her hand. She died eight days later, in August 1854, and he inherited her estate. To that curiously mixed circumstance, Franklin B. Sanborn, or Frank—as he was known—became a gentleman with an income—much as had his idol Emerson years before.

The following year was his last at Harvard and Emerson suggested that he move to Concord and open a school. He did, bringing his elder sister with him as assistant. He rented the home of William Ellery Channing, a failed poet, and grew close to Emerson, Thoreau, and Bronson Alcott in particular. He also delved into the two-hundred-year-old records of Concord and made himself the town antiquarian, genealogist, and Boswell for his better-known associates and their visitors, friends, and audiences.

In January, 1853, Gerrit Smith went to Washington, D.C. as a Representative from upstate New York. His election was a surprise and a triumph for reformers everywhere, but in some quarters it was regarded with reserve.

The magnate bought a Washington home, had his horses shipped from Peterboro, traveled about the capitol in a new coach, and entertained often. Although no liquor was served, most congressmen accepted Smith's invitations. They discovered that his personal manners were more agreeable than his public positions. In the House, however, he soon showed cranky opinions—and an addiction to making long speeches.

Smith was a member of Congress when the Kansas-Nebraska Bill was carpentered by Douglas and he wrote a tract against it. His efforts did much to build sentiment against the compromise. By April 1854, when the debate was raging over Kansas-Nebraska, Smith made a long speech in Congress attacking the bill, the federal government, and the churches.

He became looked on as an unpleasant nuisance. He longed for applause, longed to shine in Congress, but more often than not was ruled out of order when he rose to speak. His disappointment was deep. Gerrit Smith was a man who could never understand that attacking other people does not win their admiration; in that respect he was like Sumner. Insensitive to the feelings of other men, he expected others to be highly sensitive and respectful of his own. But it was impossible for him to avoid the knowledge that despite his dinners, his hospitality, his fine house and rich furnishings, his glistening coach, and handsome horses, he was held in contempt by other Congressmen.

Unlike Sumner, Gerrit Smith could not be satisfied with praise from Northern newspapers and the encouragement of his own circle back home. His position galled him and in August 1854, he resigned.

In his public explanation of his resignation, Smith took very high ground. He complained that some congressmen would "use profane language, or defile themselves with tobacco, or poison themselves with rum." He hoped the time would come when "such coarse and insulting wickedness, of such sheer nastiness, and of such low and mad sensuality would not be allowed."[15]

After leaving Congress, Smith became relatively silent for a time, but was finally drawn irresistibly into the Kansas situation. The new Republican party, itself a response to that situation, seemed too tame for him—he was fiery in the abstract—and he joined the "radical abolitionists," as they called themselves, in 1855. It was at one of their conventions that he read John Brown's letters from his sons, and contributed toward Brown's tiny fund. By that winter Smith was with more radical abolitionists in Boston and helped create the American Abolition Society.

Through that season Smith and his associates listened to the agents of the Free-State government in Topeka, who came east to raise funds, and to urge more people to emigrate to Kansas. But he wavered to a great extent over these new developments. A noted pacifist, he was still a vice president of the American Peace Society.

These antiwar attitudes were so ingrained that he recoiled at an appeal to donate funds to a boy's military company, "The Union Infantry" in Washington, D.C. "I am sorry to disappoint the dear boys," he wrote," but I must. I am so afraid of war and patriotism, that I dare not help buy one musket—not even a boy's little musket."[16]

Then came the attack on Sumner and the sack of Lawrence. "Poor Brooks," Smith said, "I became acquainted with him in Congress and found him to be a frank, pleasant man. He allowed me to speak freely to him of his habit of drinking liquor . . . But for liquor he would never have committed his enormous crime."[17]

Violence, it would appear, was still the unforgivable sin. But Smith's position was now becoming inconsistent with the principles he had claimed for so many years: before the attack on Sumner he had sent $250 to A. A. Lawrence and the Kansas Emigrant Aid Company. Lawrence himself had weakened under propaganda, and his own principles of cautious restraint and obedience to laws had grown distinctly

uncertain, for he said, "I have thought that the money spent in rifles
has done the most good thus far, and may appropriate yours in that
way, unless you object."[18] Smith had replied, "Much as I abhor war,
I nevertheless believe, that there are instances in which the shedding
of blood is inevitable."[19]

Immediately after the news of Sumner's humiliation in the Senate,
the Syracuse *Journal* published a letter by Smith, calling for "real war
upon the Missourians," the raising of a fund of $1 million and 1,000
men—to which the onetime pacifist said he himself would contribute
$10,000.[20]

By June 1856 meetings and speakers urging similar efforts took
place in Boston at the Tabernacle, and raised three thousand dollars.
Reeder, Kansas' former territorial governor, suggested sending five
thousand armed settlers, with all their expenses paid for a year, to the
territory at once. In Buffalo, New York, in July, a meeting was held to
create a National Kansas Aid Committee with auxiliaries in every state,
county, and town in the North and West. Fifty-six delegates from
twelve states attended, including Gerrit Smith from New York, Dr.
Samuel Gridley Howe from Massachusetts, and even the famed evangelist Charles Finney from Oberlin College in Ohio.

A national committee of thirteen, including Smith, was voted into
office to supervise these efforts. Plans were made to raise two million
dollars and Smith helped draft a program to send "armed men into
Kansas" to defeat the forces of slavery "at whatever cost."

"Through the failure of government," said Smith, "we obey the
necessity of the case, and recognize ourselves to be the Government."
That was startling, but Smith's conversion was full-scale. "If our brethren in Kansas can be protected only by the shedding of blood," he
trumpeted "then blood must be shed."[21]

The movement that had started with a desire to save individual
sinners, to spread freedom and Christianity, to create a nation that
would be both a paradise and an example on earth to all others had
traveled a long way—and arrived at a strange crossroad.

Chapter 16

By the 1850's radical abolitionists were calling for blood; for sacrifices
in the name of liberty and, very often, in the name of God.

Their arguments rang oddly in the world at a time when slaves
abounded in the Orient, in Russia, in many parts of Latin America and,

for that matter, in Africa. The radicals could argue—and did—that slavery in other regions was beyond their power to end, and that slavery in the South was at hand, and an American responsibility.

If the antislavery argument, however, had remained within the bounds of politics, it would not have exacerbated as much passion as it did. The British, after all, had shown the way to eliminate slavery without either bloodshed or arguments among whites. In the British program to emancipate the blacks of their West Indian colonies, they compensated the slaveholders, and mandated a program of apprenticeship and graduated freedoms, so the completely freed blacks could earn their own livelihoods. That program, phased over a period of years, did not disrupt either the West Indies nor England itself.

The radical abolitionists, however, scorned the British example. Despite the knowledge that slaves constituted financial assets to the South, the radicals refused to consider their purchase. They refused to accept the legalities of laws passed when the nation was formed, and repeatedly countenanced afterward. They argued that slavery was a *sin.*

That brought religion into the issue, for the definition of sin is a theological matter. Once the radicals took that line of argument, their movement assumed a a religious rhetoric which evoked many hallowed echoes.

Some of these echoes were buried very deep in the American psyche, especially among the descendants of the Presbyterians and Puritans. Their movements had, after all, begun against the reigns of Mary Stuart and Charles I, when John Knox and his successors under Cromwell, had argued that resistance to "ungodly" authority was a Christian duty.

New England was populated with the descendants of Puritans; some of whom had emigrated before Cromwell, in the reign of James I, and others from those who fled during the Restoration. Their family traditions were that they should not obey a Parliament—or a Congress—that violated God's law.

The radical abolitionists, therefore, were stirring an old and powerful mixture. But although they used the old words and waved the ancient banners, there were some elements missing in their movement. The Knox Presbyterians and the Puritans had, after all, more than an argument with their governments to sustain them: they had a doctrine, a form of worship, a creed, and churches. The radical abolitionists had only one theme: antislavery.

The Southerners, being more theologically conservative, considered themselves good Christians, and were insulted almost beyond remedy by the radical abolitionist stand. Their ministers assured them they were not sinners in the eyes of the Lord. And what began as a political dispute took on many of the aspects of a religious one, with some curious and rarely-noted novelties attached. Among the more glaring of these was the call to apply the rules of Heaven on earth,

under pain of death. That demand was not, of course, ever openly
stated, but once the arguments against slavery were shifted from legal
and political grounds to the metaphysical, they ceased to be political
and became religious. Theologians have long recognized that slavery
is ineradicable in essence, so long as people are bound to vices, to
goods, to necessities and to circumstances of a worldly nature. To
confuse physical slavery, as it existed in the United States in the 1850's,
with slavery of the soul, as did the radical abolitionists, was to mount
an unanswerable challenge and to revive heresies dormant in the
Western world since the French revolution.

It was then, after all, that liberty, equality and fraternity were linked
—and death threatened to all who opposed that linkage. For this and
similar reasons, therefore, the eyes of European revolutionaries were
irresistibly drawn to the United States and the abolitionist movement.
Its combination of religious rhetoric—used even by persons unconnected with any church or creed—its calls for violence and its denial
of the laws of the majority constituted a movement of great and novel
potential. It marched under the banner of antislavery, but as it grew
it became clear that many causes could be furthered by the tactics it
developed.

Obviously so large and powerful a movement did not spring to life all
at once. It began, as all movements begin, in solitary efforts by individuals—some of whom are lost to history and others of whom are
barely remembered. Yet some left echoes of their efforts that still ring
—to some, mysteriously—through the years.

One of these was Dr. William Ellery Channing, who gradually drifted
from being an orthodox Congregational, that is to say, Presbyterian,
minister into the leading voice of the Boston Unitarians. Dr. Channing
lived in a mansion but slept in "a cold and cheerless attic." He was
wealthy but austere, and appeared everywhere: "on the streets, at
public meetings, ubiquitous, alert, robed in his blue camlet cloak, a
shawl about his neck, with his drawn, ethereal face almost lost under
an enormous hat . . . Every day, for years, it was known in Boston, he
fed with his own hands two poor old women who fancied that people
wished to poison them and would accept their food from him alone."[1]

Nobody on earth could have seemed less dangerous than Dr. Channing, but in reality he was like a prominent physician convinced of the
value of new drugs whose prescriptions created convulsions in the
community. The dons at Andover, who had created that seminary as
an antidote to the growing Unitarianism of Channing and others, were
among the few who were not deceived. Meanwhile the congregation
at his Federal Street Church swelled.

He had been deeply impressed by the English Unitarian Richard
Price, whose book, he said, "probably molded my philosophy into the
form it has always retained, and opened my mind into the *transcendental
depths*. And I have always found in the accounts I have read of German
philosophy in Madame de Staël . . . that it was cognate to my own."[2]

It was precisely this influence of Unitarianism from England—with its denial of the divinity of Jesus and of the literal truth of the Bible, its open scorn and dislike of whatever remained of Calvinism and Puritanism, and Presbyterianism—that made Dr. Channing anathema to the older, more orthodox clergymen of Boston. It was precisely his approval of the higher criticisms of German scholars who were shredding traditional Christianity into mountains of footnotes, denials and arguments, and icy drops of water that made Channing so popular with the young.

He "seemed to prove that one could be nominally a minister and yet almost free of creeds."[3] Two young Harvard professors—George Ticknor and Edward Everett—who had returned from their German studies to spread the new system of scholarly skepticism found Channing an enormous help to their efforts. And in 1824, when young Ralph Waldo Emerson, under the urgings of his aunt Mary, thought of studying for ministry, he went to Dr. Channing for advice.

Mary Emerson regarded her nephew's mentor with mixed feelings; she had no great opinion of Dr. Channing or his set, being an old-school Calvinist. When young Emerson echoed the younger professors and repeated old canards she cut him off tartly by saying he knew nothing of the creed except "a few bugbear words."[4] It was her hope that—Channing notwithstanding—the Harvard Divinity School would educate him into the ministry despite himself.

Slim and dapper, young Waldo, as he called himself, would walk to Dr. Channing's elegant home every Sunday afternoon to receive a list of readings. He found these brief visits surprisingly uncomfortable: Channing was a saint to the poor, a marvel in the pulpit, but distant, cold, and aloof in person. The experience was chilling enough to shake even Waldo's complacency, and he wrote some unusual self-criticisms in his journal.

His elder brother William, also aiming for the ministry, studied in Germany and was exposed to the higher criticism at its source rather than at second hand. In September 1824, he visited Goethe, who received him graciously. William asked the great poet-politician a question that had been nagging at him: "Could a minister hold different ideas than his congregation? And, if so, for how long?"

Goethe took an urbane view, and urged the young man "not to disappoint his family. Preach to the people what they want," he concluded, "your personal belief is no business of theirs."[5]

That reply shocked William Emerson; he received it at about the same time that young Waldo was discovering that Dr. Channing's position—impressive as a sunlit cloud bank at a distance—was equally misty, amorphous, and opaque at close hand. The reaction of the brothers to their better-known mentors was disparate: William returned home to announce he had abandoned the effort to be a minister and would become a lawyer instead. Aunt Mary was very disappointed and pushed even harder at young Waldo: she did not want to see a line of ministers that had lasted through seven generations come to an end.

In that she was helped, unknowingly, by Channing, whose disinterest in theology, fashionable ideas, and literature was taken by Waldo as a sign that being a minister did not necessarily imply accepting certain ideas. There was also, of course, the fact that he had no means of earning a living except by schoolteaching; his mother could not support him forever with her boardinghouses. So Waldo picked up from William, and entered the Harvard School of Divinity in 1825.

That was the same year Theodore Weld, as different from Waldo Emerson as an oak from a weeping willow, decided to enter Hamilton College, near Clinton in upstate New York. Like Emerson, he was descended from an old New England family and his father was a minister—but the resemblance ended there. Weld had earned his own way from his teens, was indifferent to whether he shaved or had his hair cut or not, slouched, and went his own way. He struck everyone he met as being some sort of natural phenomenon: puzzling and yet impressive. In repose at the age of twenty-two—Emerson's age—he looked like a pirate with a strange, dark, deeply seamed face. But when he spoke or smiled it was, as Whittier's sister Elizabeth said later, "as though an archangel had visited."

Weld had been at Hamilton only a few weeks when someone said that Charles Finney, the evangelist, was scheduled to speak. Weld was not interested. He had heard, as had everyone in the region, that Finney was something miraculous; capable of converting the most hardened skeptics, even whole villages. But evangelism was nothing new to the American landscape: its waves had appeared and receded since the time of Jonathan Edwards and the Great Awakening in the 1730's.

Weld, raised in a quietly devout family, scorned such excesses. "My father is a real minister of the Gospel," he said, "grave and courteous and an honor to his profession. This man is not a minister and I'll not acknowledge him as such."[6] He warned his younger schoolmates not to attend.

But Weld was not destined to avoid Finney very long. On a visit to an aunt in Utica he was asked to escort her to church, and was not told that the evangelist was scheduled to appear. By the time he realized he had been tricked he was trapped in a crowded pew with his aunt and her friends beaming beside him, and had to listen for an hour while Finney preached from the text, "One sinner destroyeth much good."[7]

Anger closes the mind, and Finney's eloquence on that first occasion did not convert Weld, who left, "burning with indignation." The next day he got into a discussion in a store—a usual gathering place for loquacious loungers. Towns were small in those days, and someone slipped away to tell Finney that Weld was being attacked before a group. The evangelist appeared but Weld shouted him down—a rare experience for Finney.

Later, thinking about that scene, Weld grew ashamed. The evangelist was doing what he believed was right; that did not entitle Weld to attack and humiliate him in public. He went to the house where Finney was staying, was admitted, and met Finney in the hall. Finney drew back. "Is it not enough?" he asked. "Have you followed a minister of the Lord to his own door to abuse him?" Then he saw Weld's face.

Both men sank to their knees and Finney thanked God. He had a new convert.[8]

To become a convert of Charles Grandison Finney was to embark upon a great and exciting adventure, for Finney was a tall, eloquent spokesman against virtually all the tenets of Calvinism that still bound most Americans together. A lawyer before his conversion, he scorned both theology and the educated ministry; and in that respect he was similar to Channing—although the two differed in almost every surface way. Channing's readings had been from the works of ministers alienated from their faith, such as Francis Hutcheson, who was refused by the Church of England, Joseph Butler, and Richard Price, a dissenter who found refuge in Glasgow. All of these were occupied in justifying the ways of God to men. And that effort was one of which John Calvin had said,

> . . . how exceedingly presumptuous it is only to inquire into the causes of the Divine Will: which is in fact and is justly entitled to be, the cause of everything that exists. For if it has any cause, then there must be something antecedent, on which it depends; which it is impious to suppose. For the Will of God is the highest rule of justice; so that what he wills must be considered just, for this very reason, because he wills it. When it is inquired, therefore, why the Lord did so, the answer must be, because he would. But if you go further and ask why he so determined, you are in search of something greater and higher than the will of God, which can never be found.[9]

Against this great acceptance—which the Puritans had taken so literally they did not expect all their followers to even become church members—worked the great leaven of evangelism, which argued that a sinner could attain salvation through his own will; one need only turn toward God. That was far more palatable to a greater number in the new country—as it had been far more palatable to the Church of England in the time of the early Stuarts. The Scots Presbyterians and the Puritans argued against that doctrine of Arminius, but where the warnings of Knox and Calvin alarmed, the promise of evangelism soothed.

By the time Finney appeared in Utica a religious revolution was well along, based on the evangelical idea that all society could be changed by converting all sinners. "Benevolent societies" had mushroomed. The Bible was replaced by "tracts," in which writers wove little inspirational stories based on single Biblical passages or on personal experiences. The days of great learned preachers, whose congregations listened in awe to descriptions of the mysterious workings of an inexplicable Providence, were drawing to a close. People wanted to hear that God was a reasonable being with whom it was possible to bargain and cajole. The evangelist was His agent, and could explain the rules.

Finney, with his legal background, was able to fill that role with marvelous skill. Six feet two inches tall, dressed in a grey courtroom suit, with "great staring eyes . . . never was a man whose soul looked out through his face as his did." Finney's musical voice and gift for spontaneous eloquence could reduce an audience to tears or lift it to ecstacy. His scorn for the language of classical Calvinism was intense, searing, and effective. He charged that the orthodox ministers confused the people "with you can and you can't, you shall and you shan't; you'll be damned if you do and you'll be damned if you don't."[10]

That hypnotic sort of chanting was linked to his own version of concepts whose depth and subtlety he denied, explaining them in ordinary language, and in simplicities that flattened their substance, reduced their meaning, and altered their influence. Original Sin, instead of being linked to defiance of God, was described as simple "deep-seated but voluntary selfishness . . . self-interest. . . . All sin consists," said Finney to his unlearned and feverish crowds, "in selfishness; and all holiness or virtue, in disinterested benevolence."[11]

In similar fashion he denied that there was any mystery to conversion: the sinner could make his own heart new, if he but chose. Putting these ideas together—and Finney thought he was explaining, not destroying—a sinner could first convert himself and then become holy through "disinterested benevolence." The evangelist made no secret of the fact that those who heard him were expected to change their own lives, and to dedicate themselves to "God's Kingdom." That meant they should "aim *at being useful in the highest degree possible.*"[12]

That message went through Theodore Weld like a bolt from Sinai, and he became, in Utica, one of the "Holy Band" who helped direct the crowds to their seats in the halls and the sinners to "the anxious seat"—a pew in front where they prayed, while the congregation prayed, too, that they might be saved.

As part of the "Band" the young Weld saw remarkable, seemingly miraculous, changes in people; watched as Finney would suddenly turn with pointed forefinger to one side of the hall and see the people flinch as though struck by a whip; hear weeping when Hell was described and shouts of joy at the assurance of Heaven. It was heady, exciting, and dramatic, new and raw and real—and addictive. Weld forgot Hamilton College and his own need to complete his education, forgot whatever plans he once held—forgot everything but to follow Finney and his message.

Weld was not alone in this fascination; Finney's "Holy Band" consisted of men from all walks, drawn into his wake. One was a retired British army lieutenant in his early forties named Charles Stuart—a bizarre figure even in that highly eccentric period—who wore a kilt and a tartan cape all year round. Stuart had retired, after thirteen years' service, with a pension of $800 a year, and settled in upper Canada.

In 1820, he published a guide to that region, came to the United States, and, somehow, to Utica, where he became principal of a boys' academy. Intensely though indefinably religious, he distributed Bibles at his own expense and was notably fond of children, with whom he would often stop and play—to general astonishment. Stuart heard Finney and was converted. He also developed a remarkable fondness for Theodore Weld.

In that same summer of 1825, John Brown moved his wife Dianthe and three small sons from Hudson, Ohio, to Richmond, a hamlet in Pennsylvania's Crawford County, near Meadville. A tall, sinewy, and stern young man, twenty-five years old, he had learned the tanner's trade from his father, who was a remarkable pioneer.[13] After a few years of schooling, Young John started his work life as a foreman for his father. That was a high beginning, and he developed a commanding presence that he never quite lost. When he was in his late teens he started his own tannery—no doubt helped by his father—with a foster-brother, Levi Blakeslee, as his assistant. Once the vats were built business was good. John Brown cooked for himself and Blakeslee until he prospered enough to hire a housekeeper, one Mrs. Lusk, whose baked bread he knew and bought.

Mrs. Lusk had a "remarkably plain" daughter named Dianthe who caught the young tanner's eye. They were married in June 1820; the bride was nineteen. Children came quickly and by 1824, the Browns had three healthy young sons. And business was excellent. Young John Brown, however, was a hard man to work under—or to live with. His apprentices and journeymen had to attend church and were forbidden to use profane language. Brown was quick to whip his children and to silence his wife, and he kept a Sabbath that even Puritans would have found excessive.

James Foreman, who worked for him in 1824, recalled that Brown once punished a journeyman who had been caught stealing, by forbidding anyone, in either the house or the tannery, to speak to the culprit for two months. To enforce such an edict, which was endured only to avoid legal prosecution, required—even in that time—a man of very unusual control over his establishment. It was remarkable that so young a man as John Brown, at twenty-five, had such control, but he had an oddly intimidating personality that not even ministers—who were widely respected—could face down.

With his father a leader in the Hudson, Ohio, community and his own business flourishing, one would not have expected John Brown to go through the expense of moving, but he did, though it must have been a difficult decision. In Richmond, a new town, he cleared twenty-five acres of woods and then built a fine new tannery. By early October 1825, he was again in business, and Dianthe, a plump, short, silent young woman, had the pleasure of knowing that relatives—a family named Delamater—were nearby.

The outlook appeared good for the Browns: the new tannery was

needed in the community. But a tragic problem soon emerged: Dianthe Lusk Brown was slowly growing insane.

The rising tide evoked by Charles Finney in upstate New York—in-
cluding the unprecedented novelty of allowing women to join in his
meetings—alarmed such Presbyterian stalwarts as the Reverend
Lyman Beecher, who began to mutter about dangerous innovations.
But this was light-years away from the concerns of Reverend William
Ellery Channing.

Channing's eyes were fixed on London, then the literary center of
the English-speaking world, and on his correspondence with various
luminaries who shone and orbited in that realm. In 1826, Channing
also produced a long review of a remarkable literary discovery: a book
by John Milton, lost and unknown for neary two hundred years. No two
men could, even discounting the vast period of time that separated
them, have been more dissimilar in their attitudes than the Puritan
Milton, secretary to Cromwell and dedicated Calvinist, and the cold
little Boston saint of the Unitarians—to whom the universe was their
own circle.

Channing devoted only a portion of his review to the long-lost
Milton work; the larger share went to his own opinion of Milton's
poetry and beliefs. He found much in Milton of which he disapproved,
and some opinions—on polgygamy and divorce—that he considered
too shocking to discuss. The lengthy effort appeared in *The Christian
Examiner,* a New England periodical that imitated, to some extent, the
approach and tone of the *Edinburgh Review,* then the most famous
high-level periodical in Britain. It created a sensation.[14]

It was unlikely that Dr. Channing's admirers included many who
read Milton, and it is doubtful that his own judgment of that writer
altered many opinions. It was Channing's temerity that was admired:
his tacit assumption that he and his contemporaries stood at a higher
level than Milton and the Puritans of Cromwell—this was what delighted many Bostonians.

Against these intellectual excitements, the scandal that broke around
William Morgan, a disillusioned member of the Free Masons, seemed
in another world. Morgan had moved to Batavia, New York, and made
arrangements to publish lurid descriptions of an allegedly secret and
criminal Masonic conspiracy; the articles were due to appear in the
Batavia *Advocates.* Mysterious disasters then began to engulf Morgan.
His house was attacked and he was threatened, and then imprisoned
on a debt claim. While he was in jail his house was ransacked and
strangers appeared to make inquiries about him.

These efforts to silence Morgan failed. Rumors began to circulate
and—after a long period of inattention—the Masons began to be whispered about as a shadowy and possibly sinister organization.[15] In
Europe, where the outlawed Grand Orient lodges had created a sensation a generation earlier, and where the activities of the Asiatic lodges

in collaborating with French authorities under the Napoleonic Occupation had given Masonry in Germany a bad and lingering name, such alarms were nearly endemic.

But in England and Scotland, the Masons—especially the Scottish Rite lodges—had long enjoyed not only respectability but considerable influence. A similar sort of influence had risen in the United States by the 1820's when Masons had achieved a quiet but tangible presence and considerable political power.

Calvinists linked Masonry to the French Revolution, but the Methodists and Jeffersonians in general poured into its lodges, as did Baptists. Politicians sought Masonic support; Jackson was a Mason, though John Quincy Adams, and other Federalist-Whigs were not. But "about a fourth of all Protestant ministers were Masons" though their congregations were not, "and like any group of private individuals interlocked against competition on economic, political, or social levels, they subverted the democratic process."[16]

Until the Morgan case focused attention upon the organization, however, the Masons in the United States had grown almost without notice. Many newspaper editors were Masons and sponsored a "free" press; Charles Finney, himself a Mason, estimated there were 2,000 lodges and 45,000 members. The treatment of William Morgan, however, shocked the country.

While he was in jail (on a trumped-up charge) in Batavia, strangers from Buffalo, Lockport, and other towns appeared. The printing shop which was to print his revelations was set on fire and Morgan himself was kidnapped from the authorities, driven in a closed carriage through Rochester, and taken along the Ridge Road to Lewiston, near the Fort Niagara Powder Magazine. Here, he vanished.

News of the kidnapping and murder swept across the nation like a hot flame and cast all Masons into odium overnight. John Brown, himself a Mason, told his children that on a visit to Meadville he had denounced Morgan's harassment and was threatened with lynching. That seems farfetched, but Masons everywhere were denying that a kidnapping or murder had taken place; they asserted the organization had nothing to hide. At any rate Brown broke with his prejudice against guns (according to John Brown, Jr. years later) and obtained a "sort of pistol that was half-rifle, and became very adept in its use."[17] Thanks to the Masonic scandal, John Brown was now being drawn toward the ideas of conspiracy and secret organization.

Chapter 17

Finney's crusade consisted of protracted meetings that ran all day and sometimes all night, ending in sunrise prayers; it expanded into invasions of houses to pray for "erring" husbands in tones that could be heard in the street; and it created paroxysms in which men and women, mingled emotionally together, sometimes made startling decisions about their future lives. But in general, prayer for "personal purposes" was discouraged; the idea was to pray for others—to pray for a better world.

The New England Calvinists, hearing of Finney's "new measures," grew alarmed. A meeting was held at New Lebanon, New York, where Lyman Beecher—flanked by the president of Amherst College, Justin Edwards of Andover, and Asahel Nettleton, a famous orthodox evangelist—debated with Finney. Having spurned seminary training, Finney was not inclined to take any directions from seminarians and rejected the suggestion that he should stop women from praying aloud at his revivals. He and his followers also successfully defended "audible groaning," and argued that "workers in one part of the vineyard" should not impose their judgments on others. In the end, Lyman Beecher lost his temper and a clear break appeared between the West and the Northeast. Finney returned to upstate New York to lead his followers into even newer trials, experiments, and victories, and a great schism yawned in Presbyterian ranks.

Reverend George Washington Gale sought to close the gap by creating the Oneida Institute, at Whitesboro, New York. Although none of the organizers seemed to know it, the institute resembled a monastery, in which manual labor was intermingled with theological studies. The end purpose was to produce trained ministers, but the manual work allowed students to pay at least part of their own way and, presumably, kept them from developing ivory-tower attitudes toward other men.[1] Weld enrolled, as did most of the younger members of the "Holy Band," but his attendance was intermittent because he was in such demand as a speaker. His tuition was paid by Charles Stuart—whose attention was also being drawn to the antislavery movement in Britain.

The strenuous, even earthy nature of these activities provided a great contrast to the atmosphere that surrounded Waldo Emerson in Boston, who had drifted through the Harvard Divinity School after being forgiven recitations on account of his eyes, and who occupied himself by reading. In October 1826, he was licensed to preach but remained irresolute. A friend of his—Sampson Reed, also a Harvard graduate—had produced a mirror-reflection of Swedenborg entitled *Observations on the Growth of the Mind*. Waldo's aunt Mary immediately attacked this "Swedenish" effort, and said the ideas came from Wordsworth.² That was astute: Wordsworth was a Swedenborgian.

Waldo worked up his only sermon, on "ceaseless prayer" and after delivering it several times around Boston without being invited to serve a congregation, he decided to take a sea voyage for his health. That led him to St. Augustine, Florida, the oldest town in the United States, where iron cages in which Spanish governors had once allowed prisoners to starve to death publicly were still to be seen hanging. In that antique, humid atmosphere, the no longer quite so young Waldo met Achille Murat, son of the former King of Naples and a nephew of Napoleon. Murat was married to a relative of George Washington and owned an estate near Tallahassee. He and Emerson were fellow passengers aboard a vessel to Charleston, and Waldo was shaken to meet a superior social personage who smoothly defended a worldly and assured atheism.

Proceeding on to Baltimore, Philadelphia, and New York, Waldo was welcomed by various Unitarian ministers and delivered his prayer sermon, and also laboriously contrived another on his theory of "compensation"—a subject he would repeat to the end of his working days —before returning to Harvard. It took him until 1829 to prepare himself fully for the ministry, and by that time he had met an heiress named Ellen Tucker, whose father, brother, and two sisters had died of tuberculosis, and who herself had already developed its signs.

In March 1829, Waldo was offered the pulpit of Boston's Second Church, an impressive edifice with windows three tiers high and a pulpit that towered over the congregation in the style introduced by John Knox. His salary was $1,800 a year, a handsome sum. But his fiancee was ill.³

The new minister said his purpose was to teach "right living rather than religious dogmas," and made it clear he did not intend to be "an ecclesiastical policeman." His pews began to fill with young people; Bronson Alcott was attracted, but Reverend Henry Ware, Emerson's superior, was privately, though silently, uneasy. Waldo found a minister's routine far from easy or idle. There was an endless cycle of duties and responsibilities, with prayers, readings, hymns, prayers, hymns, sermons, prayers, hymns, benedictions at services, and an eternal round of visits and community efforts. The new minister was against stereotyped prayers as a matter of principle, but was not skilled at extemporaneous praying, and this put him in an awkward position. He was unmusical and a poor singer, and with questionable tact, deprecated the efforts of his congregation.⁴

Once he made a visit "to the deathbed of Captain Green, a rough-and-ready old Revolutionary officer who lived next door to the church. Waldo was diffident and embarrassed; he fumbled among the clutter of things on the dying man's table, and began to talk about glassmaking. The captain became angry and told him if he had nothing better to do at a deathbed but lecture about glass bottles, he had better go."⁵

Yet he remained in the ministry, and married Ellen in 1829. He also launched a program of indiscriminate reading that included Mon-

taigne, Rousseau, Scott, Aristotle, Plutarch, Lamb, Swift, and Goethe
—works oddly lacking in theology. He subscribed to the *Edinburgh Review,* the *North American Review,* and the Boston *Daily Advertiser.* It was clear that Channing's example loomed large before him.

In February 1831, Ellen died. She was nineteen and they had been married a year and a half. He took the loss with apparent calm, and by June had obtained a legal opinion against her estate, which included a claim on her portion had she lived to be twenty-one. Rumors floated that the family protested but that the young minister was adamant. Meanwhile his eclectic reading continued and his sermons began to refer to Moses, Confucius, Socrates, and the ideas of the French philosopher Cousin.

These intellectual wanderings puzzled his congregation and worried Reverend Ware. He might, perhaps, have wondered even more had he known that a year after Emerson's young wife died, the youthful minister visited her tomb, opened the coffin, and stared.[6]

Charles Finney perfected his revival techniques and then encouraged his converts to accost people in the streets and visit them in their homes. Private prayers were discouraged in favor of loud and fervent public recantations and rejoicings. This rupture of the traditional lines between private and public attracted the admiring attention of the wealthy New York merchant-philanthropists, Arthur and Lewis Tappan.

The Tappans began to organize their approaches toward eradicating sin, and created a benevolent holding company, the New York Association of Gentlemen, which spun off several branches. One was a Female Retrenchment Society which sought to persuade women away from "coffee, tea, rich cakes, pastry, preserves, snuff and tobacco, as well as wines and cordials."[7] The New York Temperance Society, however, caused the deepest troubles. Although its name implies moderation, the society was actually in favor only of total abstinence. Its leaders led campaigns against taverns and bars, and even against truckers who transported liquor and farmers who sold grain to distilleries. The Puritans of old New England who had so enjoyed their beer and rum and even Calvin, who had liked his wine, would have been appalled.

The Tappans also funded a campaign to halt the mails and the passage of trains on Sunday, and backed a "Cold Water Society" that promoted "coarse" food and the avoidance of coffee and tea.

Theodore Weld was a convert to the "Cold-Water" theory, and began a lifelong custom of an icy-cold bath every morning. A comment from Finney that neglect of one's personal appearance betrayed an arrogance toward others deeply affected him; the implication of conceit had a lasting effect. For the rest of his life Weld was to believe that anything that furthered his own interest was forbidden to him. He began a habit of denying himself any opportunity to be conspicuous, to leave a record of achievement, or to place himself in the forefront of any cause or group. In the Middle Ages he might have been a saint and the old Church, which was familiar with such zealots through the centuries, might well have encouraged him to form his own order and to leave the larger establishments of society alone. But in the United States in 1830, it was all society itself that the new crusaders wanted to change.

Chapter 18

The British antislavery movement had several characteristics. The most obvious was a noble recoil against an ignoble trade. That sentiment was of old and admirable lineage; as early as 1772, a slave landing in Britain was automatically freed. In the late 1770's, various movements to emancipate the slaves of the West Indies and end the British slave trade were launched—although interrupted by the French Revolution.

After Napoleon fell—an event that altered the United States as much as any country in Europe—antislavery agitation was renewed in Britain. The British government was in a curious position. Had it not been in the hands of Christians there seems little reason to have expected it to mount its massive, expensive, and voluntary campaign against slavery. Slavery was essential to the West Indies sugar exports, and to their tax revenues. Yet the movement to be rid of the noxious traffic in human beings was inarguable, inexorable, and inevitable. By 1807, Britain forbade landing any more slaves in its colonies, though the edict was broken by privateers. Holland, Sweden, and Denmark withdrew from the trade. Britain actually paid Portugal £300,000 and Spain £400,000 to end their slave trades. But a labor shortage then arose, and smuggling slaves became a lucrative criminal practice. Being outside the law, it was conducted without conscience, and many of the horror stories of slave ships stem from this period.

Inside Parliament the situation grew tense. West Indian sugar and coffee had created some of the largest fortunes in England and the planters' lobby worked very effectively along the usual lines of argument-cum-bribes. The reformers, led by William Wilberforce, used methods even more effective: large mass demonstrations, lectures, protest meetings, and a river of tracts, books, and general literature.

Finney's disciple Charles Stuart, a Jamaica-born child of a British army officer and a stern, Scot-Presbyterian mother, was irresistibly drawn to this situation. He left Theodore Weld enough money to enter the Oneida Institution, said goodbye to the other members of the "Holy Band," and sailed for London. There he began to argue against the American Colonization Society—the movement to ship free blacks back to Africa—which until then had been supported by virtually all reformers in the United States, North and South. (Among the society's most influential backers were Smith, Channing, Weld, and Finney.)

Stuart moved at once into the front ranks of British abolitionists: those who demanded the complete and immediate emancipation, not the colonization, of all slaves. He was a welcome figure to the British reformers, being one of them in every sense, and he traveled and published his views at his own expense. One of his products was titled: *The West India Question: Immediate Emancipation Safe and Practical,* which appeared in 1832. Immensely popular, the work went through many editions, but it was only one of a stream that issued from his pen. He deplored the "malignant jesuitry" of the colonization societies, and there is no doubt that he was a catalytic and commanding figure in the abrupt switch of opinion on colonization that took place on both sides of the Atlantic.[1]

Stuart had left for England in the late 1820's and made himself famous by the end of the decade. In the same period Weld became celebrated for his lectures on temperance, and the Tappans moved into their crusades. Until Finney and Weld and the "Band" appeared, the two merchants had been content to donate their money—and to establish the *New York Journal of Commerce,* which refused advertisements for liquor, tobacco, circuses, theaters, and other sinful pleasures. But both Finney and Weld excited the two New York Tappans, who sought to bring the evangelist pair to the sinful city itself, to work their miracles.

The Tappans were not alone in their zeal: the American Bible Society had, by that year, distributed 65 million tracts on hundreds of "moralistic topics." The Sunday School movement, originated to overcome the secularization of public schools in New England and elsewhere, had enlisted 60,000 teachers and 400,000 pupils. The movement was just starting.[2]

The Tappans deplored the church practice of selling pews and reserving only a few hard benches for the poor, so they imported the Reverend Joel Parker, an evangelist from upstate New York, opened a hall, and established the first "free church." The Presbyterians, after a struggle, recognized it and the Tappans persuaded Charles Finney to become a pastor of the city's second free church. They also had great plans for Theodore Weld, but he was not interested in the city. He finally decided to become the Tappans' agent to tour schools and colleges, collecting data on conditions in the West with a view to locating and helping to create a single huge establishment along the lines of Oneida.

This carried Weld into the South as well as the West, where he began to see slavery for himself, and to make some notable converts—including James G. Birney. Meanwhile, impassioned letters kept flowing to him from Charles Stuart, who continued to fuel abolition arguments in Britain. Weld began to study the slavery question seriously.

Yet Weld did not change at once. He found Southerners were willing to talk about slavery, and who were also in favor of the Colonization Society. Not being commercially minded, he may not have appreciated that the South was burgeoning with new cotton millionaires, or that this prosperity, which benefited commerce in the North and West as well, was inextricably linked to slavery.

In Steubenville, Ohio, Ben Tappan, a brother of the two New York merchants, was of a different turn of mind. "Why can't you keep your religion to yourselves?" he wrote his brothers in exasperated tones. He received an illuminating answer. Lewis explained that he considered Ben's soul in danger, and that if he did not work to help save him that "your blood would be found on my skirts on Judgement Day."[3]

How that belief floated into existence is impossible to determine, but there is no question that it gradually permeated the crusade— which itself began to reach stupendous proportions by 1830. Evangelists of every description began to increase in numbers. They were once described as "men who fitted themselves more or less consistently into this mode of life—multitudinous little men, whose insignificance, poverty, roving habits and shifting careers practically defy analysis." They all argued that God demanded converts not only so that they would end their own sinning, but would denounce and, if possible, stop the sinning of others.

One flame lit by these embers was William Lloyd Garrison, who read the minutes of British parliamentary debates on slavery when they arrived in the United States. They were sent to Benjamin Lundy, an abolitionist with British contacts, who sought to keep Garrison abreast of their struggles. Lundy was respected; Lyman Beecher approved of him and also approved 6f colonization. Garrison, however, was a fanatic in search of a cause. A bitter son of an alcoholic seaman raised in icy poverty in Newburyport he had learned printing from the bottom, and leaned toward vituperation. Working for Lundy in Baltimore on a struggling little paper called *Genius of Universal Emancipation,* he read the acid, viperish accusations of British abolitionists against West Indian nabobs, found his style, and never thereafter lost it.

His first chance to use it came in commenting, in Lundy's paper, on a shipowner whose captain had agreed to carry a cargo of blacks to a Louisiana plantation. "Francis Todd," he wrote, "and his like should be sentenced to solitary confinement for life! They are enemies of their own species—highway robbers and murderers; and their final doom will be, unless they speedily repent, to occupy the lowest depths of perdition."[4] That brought a charge of libel and seven weeks in a Baltimore prison until one of Lundy's friends sent enough money for Garrison's release. He emerged flaming, convinced of martyrdom, quarreled bitterly one last time with Lundy, and left for Boston.

A year later, as the British campaign gathered momentum, the Tappans and Weld, together with George Bourne, Joshua Leavitt, and Simeon Joceylen, discussed the creation of a new society—this time in the name of antislavery. Weld was asked to head it, but he shunned such a public honor—and lost his place in history, though not his role. (He was, however, on the founding committee.) Support began to appear in reformist ranks. News of the society led a mob to attack Arthur Tappan's summer home; that gave the zealots grounds for pause. It was clear the time was not propitious; they decided to wait.

In Boston the balding young Garrison had no such qualms. Supported only by a local handful he launched *The Liberator*. Its first issue was unbelievably inflammatory. "I am accused of harsh words, and I admit the charge. I have not been able to find a soft word that describes villainy."[5] Despite its initial tiny circulation, Garrison's words landed like dynamite charges, and set off detonations all through the South, as editors in various newspapers picked them up and repeated them. Within eight months a slave named Nat Turner led a revolt in which blacks butchered entire white families, and burned plantations. For eight weeks of rage, fright, and excitement, fifty-five whites and approximately one hundred blacks were killed.[6] Finally captured, Turner was hanged with twenty of his followers. Many throughout the South credited *The Liberator* with having inspired the uprising.

The charge lacked proof, but a clear intellectual parallel could hardly be denied. What shocked white Southerners was the realization that men of their own race, in their own country, would consign them to death at the hands of another race. The Georgia Senate tried Garrison in absentia, found him guilty of inciting insurrection, fined him $500, and set a price of $5,000 on his delivery. That was a higher sum than Garrison and his circle combined could raise, and his continued liberty remained as much of a marvel as the speed with which he had entered the consciousness of the nation through words alone.

Chapter 19

William Ellery Channing followed his long review of Milton in *The Christian Examiner* with another even longer examination of Sir Walter Scott's *Life of Napoleon Bonaparte*. As much historian as storyteller, Scott held the view that the French Revolution had been an outburst of the worst elements for the worst reasons, and that Napoleon was to be credited with restoring the ideas of merit, patriotism, and rank to France.

That was a view disputed by Channing, who had been influenced early by the writings of Rousseau, Voltaire, and other "bearers of light." Channing criticized Scott's biography as too long—and said so in two long articles, separately published. Only two pages of the review, however, were devoted to Scott's work; the balance consisted of Channing's opinions of Napoleon, whom he considered "a mere soldier of fortune," a "low and vulgar" man; in effect a sinner.[1]

In 1829 that effort drew the attention of William Hazlitt, the editor of the *Edinburgh Review*. Hazlitt—who admired Napoleon's career—focused on Channing with the candor for which he was celebrated. Channing's writings, he said, "cannot be called mere commonplace, but they may be fairly termed ambitious commonplace. That is, he takes up the newest and most plausible opinion at the turn of the tide, or just as it is getting into vogue, and would fain arrogate both the singularity and the popularity of it to himself. He hits the public between what they are tired of hearing, and what they have never heard before."[2]

To be publicly whipped by Hazlitt was, however, an honor in New England, where few writers had ever before earned such international recognition. Channing's reputation took a sudden upward leap—especially among circles where open admiration of the French Revolution was becoming fashionable. Hazlitt had hit the target but Channing was riding real waves, and the young literati of Boston were dazzled by his rising eminence.

The Calvinists, who had no comparably fashionable figure to raise against Channing, were especially exasperated, for Channing had proceeded, in carefully spaced sermons at notable occasions, to attack the doctrines and beliefs of the orthodox. These attacks had begun obliquely, but gradually grew more pointed as his position—or the position he adopted—became more fashionable. He started by saying he desired "to escape the walls of a particular church . . . to live in the open sky, in the broad light, hearing with my own ears, and following truth meekly, but resolutely . . ."[3] Tom Paine had put it more candidly: "My own mind is my own church."

Channing was no Paine; he tunneled more often than he openly attacked. In the middle 1820's he was saying that much in the Bible was "poetical rather than scientific; much of it marked by the age in which it was written," and "it is necessary to look beyond the letter to the spirit." Reverend Moses Stuart observed that Channing was moving toward an editorial position, rather than an interpretive one, but Channing was merely beginning. In time he argued that belief in the Trinity was a form of polytheism, which gave rise to idolatry, and finally, that Calvinism was "immoral."[4]

In 1826 he compared the crucifixion to "a gallows, erected by the Father of Mankind, who then executed his own Son, as an example of His justice," and then quickly issued a stream of withdrawals. Two years later Channing declared the purpose of Christianity was to "exalt and perfect human nature"—a statement that placed God as the servant of humanity.[5]

When a storm of criticism broke around these intermittent probes toward some new theology, Channing was quick to respond that he meant no offense. In 1830 the most offensive of his sermons were collected and published and in a preface he voiced chagrin over some of his opinions being considered "crimes"; he said it was "one of the gross immoralities of our times, the practice of aspersing the characters of exemplary men," and complained of "assaults on freedom of religion and thought." The Reverend Stuart, however, observed that others had the right to dissent with Dr. Channing.[6]

But it was not Channing's attacks on doctrines alone that carried him aloft so much as his panegyrics on Nature and his praises of an amorphous God suffused through the universe, and whose existence, he said, was proved "by the structure of a leaf" and other evident, surrounding marvels.

These lyrical writings were part of a fashion—which took many forms—then coursing through England, Europe, and the eastern United States. In New York the Hudson River School of painting—in which landscapes portrayed majestic, edenic forests, waterfalls, and sweeping skies—soared into popularity, partnered by poems and articles about rivers, canyons, and trees. It was all part of a new Rousseau-like chorus that arose, hailing noble savages and keening over civilization. And it was echoed by Wordsworth in England, Longfellow in Boston, and the eclectic movement of Cousin in France.

Fashion was far from the concerns of Theodore Weld and the Tappans. Touring by stage coach, horseback, riverboat, and railroad, Weld preached the gospel of manual labor and education. He also began to shift against the idea of sending free blacks back to Africa— a shift that reflected Stuart's letters and activities in England.

After heroic travels, interviews, surveys, and sermons, Weld sent his report to the Tappans in New York. In it he traced the testimony of physicians and educators through the centuries, on the need to combine exercise with education. He contrasted various vigorous great men with indolent moderns, and in a subsequent brochure he made a series of recommendations that changed American education and led, eventually, to the land grant colleges.[7]

Meanwhile the Reverend Lyman Beecher—who believed it was still possible to reach a compromise between the all-out abolitionists like Garrison and those who favored the African colonization of freed blacks—agreed to become head of a new seminary in Cincinnati. Supported by the Tappans (who assured Beecher a high salary), the seminary would be called Lane. It attracted a great deal of attention in theological circles.

Most of the Lane founding class members came from western New York, where Charles Finney had caught them and their parents in his first great tour; others came from the Oneida Institute. Many of Weld's converts arrived from Utica and Auburn; some floated down the Ohio from Pittsburgh on a raft. A sprinkling came from Kentucky, Tennessee, and Alabama—they also were converts Weld made on his travels.

While these ardent spirits dedicated themselves to the betterment of humanity, John Brown was busy in his tannery at Richmond, Pennsylvania. He showed himself a good citizen by supervising the construction of a tax-supported common school and serving as the town's postmaster. But there was something excessive about almost everything that John Brown did. His wife was overworked, and her periods of "confusion," were well-known. Apparently, however, that condition did not stop her eternal round of pregnancies, for children arrived, one after the other, as soon as possible, even after the family settled in Pennsylvania.

There was also an excessiveness in the tannery that Brown built. It was two stories high and had eighteen vats. And Brown's two-story log home was large for the area and the time. Since the region was scarcely settled, there was no need for such an elaborate establishment. Consequently it was necessary for Brown to form a working relationship with a relative—Seth B. Thompson—in Hartford, thirty miles away. The arrangement called for Thompson to supply cattle that Brown would sell in the town of Randolph, while Thompson would sell Brown's hides in Hartford. Thompson sometimes sent hides of his own to be tanned; Brown sometimes bought cattle from Thompson.[8]

Thompson appears to have handled his business more efficiently. Brown often had to borrow from Thompson or have Thompson co-sign his notes to the banks, for Brown was often late and in trouble over debts. His laxity in that respect made a sharp contrast to his severity with his employees.

In 1831 the Browns lost a four-year-old son to illness. Dianthe grew noticeably weaker, had trouble with her heart, and continued to experience periods of confusion. In 1832 these problems overwhelmed her, and she died—shortly after giving birth to a seventh child, a son, who also died. She was lucid at the time of her death; this adds poignancy to a life that was neither happy nor particularly pleasant. She left five children ranging in age from three to twelve.

In 1833 the House of Commons ruled a state of apprenticeship leading to emancipation, in 1838, for slaves in the West Indies. Slaveholders would feed and clothe their slaves, and treat them as part-time workers, gradually shifting from a slave economy to an economy of free men in the sugar islands.

The news was as eagerly awaited by American reformers as by the British; they believed an example was set that they could repeat. In that humor the New York Committee established a central bureau under Elizur Wright, Jr., who had consulted often and earnestly with Weld. A newspaper funded by the Tappans, called *The Emancipator*, was launched; British and American tracts were printed and distributed; letters flew in all directions.

The overall plan was to demolish the American Colonization Society and to bring about the end of slavery. Weld, invited to the organization meeting in New York, said he was unable to attend; he was too busy at the Lane seminary in Cincinnati.

The new seminary was two miles outside the city in a secluded region; the campus was still covered with tree stumps. Lyman Beecher, its president, also served as pastor of the Second Presbyterian Church. The opening class of forty—most of whom, including Weld, were over twenty-six years old—consisted of college graduates or the equivalent.

Beecher, son and grandson of blacksmiths, was, in his middle fifties, still so energetic that he kept a large sandpile in the cellar to shovel when nothing better was available, exercised with barbells, and perpetually rushed to keep up with a crowded schedule. Cheerful, optimistic, and good-natured, he would soon discover he would need all these qualities, as well as some not yet conceived.

Lane was the first educational institution in the country to waive the color line: James Bradley, a black from Guinea who had bought his own freedom, was part of the first class. Beecher had made that a condition of his acceptance of the presidency.

But the most unusual feature of Lane was Theodore Weld. Tall, "very manly" and "noble-looking," he impressed even Beecher as someone extraordinary, "as logic on fire . . . As eloquent as an angel and powerful as thunder!"[9] That estimate was remarkably generous, for Beecher said later that Weld was "the president. He took the lead of the whole institution. The young men had, many of them, been under his care, and they thought he was a god.' "[10]

At first both Lane and the moves to organize an antislavery society went well. Weld taught one class; Beriah Green became president of Western Reserve College and the trustees there agreed not to interfere with the new crusade. In December 1833, the Tappans and Elizur Wright organized a mass meeting of delegates of the new society in Philadelphia. Again Weld said he could not attend; he shied away from the publicity of the event. It would have been "self-interest" on his part to have appeared.

The man who did appear, and who reaped the lion's share of the publicity, was William Lloyd Garrison. He accomplished that by virtue of having gone to England, where he was feted as the voice of the American antislavery movement, and where he shared in the glory of the British success in decreeing emancipation in the West Indies. By the time he returned to the United States, Garrison was generally considered a prime mover and shaker.[11] The Americans at Philadelphia listened while he described his meetings with Wilberforce, Brougham, and other famous English leaders, almost as though he had shared their labors as he shared their triumph.

The result was that although Lewis Tappan was president of the American antislavery meeting, Garrison composed its declaration of sentiments. It breathed the spirit of the original declaration, calling for agents to pour through the land to create a new social revolution, to "remonstrate, entreat and rebuke," to "purify the churches of their guilt of complicity with slavery . . . and to bring the entire nation to speedy repentance."[12] These words, which reflected Garrison's uncanny genius to offend, insult, and lacerate in the name of a noble cause, gave the new society a birth defect it would never be able to remove.

Chapter 20

It was during these years that Waldo Emerson found his distaste for the ministry increasing. In February 1832 he wrote a letter to his church (now missing from its records) and the church committee reported "a change in his opinions concerning the ordinance of the Lord's Supper, and recommending some changes in the mode of administering it."[1] He wanted to be relieved from the duty of serving at that sacrament.

In this he was reflecting growing Unitarian doubts; some of the young ministers said the practice was "superstitious." A group had studied the matter and decided, though softly, against change. Meanwhile Emerson's Second Church closed for repairs. When it reopened he was ill. Later in the year, when he was able to preach again, he spoke about the Lord's Supper as merely a Passover, with no new significance, and credited Paul with error in believing Jesus would return.[2]

By October the young minister was convinced that the soul does not need form and method. In this he was echoing Coleridge, Wordsworth —and Channing. He was encouraged in these conclusions by the visit of an English Unitarian, who told Emerson and others at dinner that Coleridge "ate opium," that the writer whose anonymous articles in a strange new style that were creating such a sensation was named Thomas Carlyle.[3] Obviously a whole new world of ideas was orbiting of which one could obtain only fleeting glimpses from Boston. Waldo yearned to explore it for himself.

Having won his legal right to inherit his wife's estate, Emerson had no financial reason to remain in a pulpit he found increasingly uncomfortable. When he resigned from the Second Church, however, the rumor was that he did so rather than perform communion. His decision created a sensation even in Unitarian ranks and his courage was hailed even by some who disagreed with that stand. One of these was

Channing, who approved of high standards, and whose approval shed a nimbus of saintly light around Waldo's head.

On Christmas Day, 1832, he sailed for Naples, leaving his grandfather Ripley in Concord convinced that he was insane, and his Aunt Mary deeply troubled. "I do believe he has no fixed faith in a personal God! His letters have been confused & dark—a mixture of heathen greatness—of worse than ancient good heathenism—a Swedenborgianism—Pantheism—hypothesis of nature & german rationalism . . ."[4] Which was, and would remain, as good a description as would ever be made.

Emerson's first stop was at Malta where he was impressed by the Cathedral of San Giovanni, but lodgings at Syracuse in Sicily later did not please him; he thought Sicily "a grey, ruined, shabby place." It was not until he reached Naples that the "true beauty of the churches stunned him."[5] He began to fill his journal with notes.

Rome almost overwhelmed him. He was there during Holy Week and saw Pope Gregory XVI wash the feet of pilgrims. The staggering collections of art from the centuries were more than he could describe. Yet, as with other Boston travelers, the presence of Americans helped cushion these shocks to his native pride. He also had the good fortune to meet a Jewish banker who gave him a letter to John Stuart Mill in England.

Even in its early stages, the trip was enough to shatter his Boston insularity. He met sculptors, wealthy travelers, dined with Walter Savage Landor. He toured Bologna, Ferrara, Padua, then Venice, Milan, and Geneva. In Paris he met his cousin Ralph Emerson—in whose honor he dropped the social use of his own first name—and Oliver Wendell Holmes, who was studying medicine. Paris, more than all Italy, made the deepest impression—especially a visit to the Eglise Catholique Française—an "independent" church founded by Ferdinand Châtel, where priests wore newly designed vestments and performed rituals to martial music played by a large orchestra accompanied by singers. Châtel's ideas sailed past even the Unitarians; Waldo decided he himself would go even farther and prove that Christianity was misunderstood "by all such as take it for a system of doctrines," when it was really "moral truths," that did not rely "on a book," but was "a rule of life." His mind became filled with images of a new church that he himself would lead.[6]

He attended lectures by Guizot, Cousin, Jouffroy, and Thénard and thought the French scholars lacked proper gravity. A visit to Jardin des Plante's exhibit of "an ascending order of shells, birds, beasts, insects, snakes and fish," arranged to prove that each was "its own, unique link in the chain of life" sent his mind to the opposite conclusion.[7] Lamarck's theory was in the air, and Emerson—like Channing—took his conclusions more from the air than from study.

But it was London that definitely altered his course. Here, Waldo also attended another private church, this time led by the Reverend Edward Irving, who had been ousted from the Church of Scotland for denying the divinity of Jesus—among other heresies. However, the literati attracted Emerson more than the clergy. He met "a short thick old man with bright blue eyes and a torrent of talk" named Samuel Taylor Coleridge and heard Dr. Channing praised. He also met Mill, who gave him a letter to Thomas Carlyle. Touring Scotland, he eventually found Carlyle on a farm sixteen miles from Dumphries. He was welcomed; the "tall, gaunt" Carlyle was lonely. He drenched Emerson with conversation and the New Englander responded; their roles were acolyte calling on master. They parted on very friendly terms, though Carlyle decided the American was "visionary and impractical" and Waldo decided the Scottish writer was lacking in "religious insight."[8] They were both right.

At Mount Rydal the traveler visited Wordsworth (who was wearing green goggles). Wordsworth told Emerson that Carlyle was clever "but probably insane" and declaimed his own poems as proof of greater genius.[9]

At the Lane seminary the first class struggled against cholera. It is to the credit of the students that none fled, and though many were stricken, all recovered. Weld was not infected but labored almost without rest, and by the time the siege ended his stature was enormous.

He launched a discussion on slavery. Beecher was swept into allowing this, but he soon developed doubts that were only too well founded, because the "discussion" turned into a revival, along the lines Weld had learned so well from Charles Finney. Meetings were held for eighteen nights, and their intensity mounted as students from the South voiced their guilt and told tales of cruelty they had heard or seen. Halfway through the session it was unanimously agreed that slavery was an abomination that had to be ended. Beecher's daughter Catherine presented her father's hope that antislavers and colonizers could work together; that was debated, and rejected. The outcome was the creation of an abolition society and a call for "immediate abolition"—to be brought about gradually.[10]

That was the Tappan-Weld conception of the British achievement and it was based not only on a misconception, but on a series of misconceptions.

These misconceptions were extensive. The American situation regarding slavery bore very little resemblance to Britain's. To compare their abolition campaigns was to confuse foxes with lions. Weld's New England forbears knew very well that England had exchanged the "divine right of kings" for the "divine right of Commons."[11] That was one of the reasons why they left that realm, and why the colonists later fought for independence to establish a limited government.

The American abolitionists did not seem to notice that the British colonies in the West Indies were—with new British colonies on the horizon—no longer as important as before. British control of the world oceans made the Orient and India far more alluring. It was true that West Indian wealth was still represented in London, and that the phrase "rich as a creole" could still be heard. But much of that wealth had been transferred to British investments. Their owners left the management of West Indian plantations to hired hands; the incomes from these properties were declining and therefore their maintenance less crucial.

There were some other realities of which the English were aware, and which the Americans did not seem to consider. The population of the British West Indies was ninety percent Black and only ten percent white. That meant that slaves in the West Indies performed all the functions necessary for a total economy, and had developed—and been educated—into all the necessary skills. That situation, extended over two centuries or more, had created a Black society integrated into the world marketplace.[12]

The Creoles in London were able, through bribes and political maneuver to delay the advent of abolition for a time, and were successful through the Napoleonic wars. But once those wars ended they were forced to retreat, step-by-step, by the rising power of the press and a mass movement created by some of the most eloquent and highly placed people in the realm. By the early 1830's it was obvious to the politicians in Parliament that they had much to gain and less to lose by joining that movement.

The result was a political change, and a majority was reached in Commons. Orders went out from London, backed by the full force of the government. No court in England can overrule Parliament, and English judges are limited to seeing that the laws are obeyed. The number of white Britons involved was very small compared to the mass of Great Britain, and those were largely persons of wealth able to maintain their fortunes.

Nothing very revolutionary was involved. The reformers turned their attention to working conditions, and to a lesser extent, to colonial problems in other parts of the empire.

In the United States, however, slavery was part of the economy of the North as well as the South. Most blacks lived in the South, and numbered over three million out of the nearly thirteen million people in the country in 1830.[13] Their condition was, generally speaking, deplorable. Most were employed on cotton plantations, which made millionaires of many once-poor families in that region—and of Northern bankers and merchants who provided loans, machinery, and goods, acted as factors in the international cotton trade, and were intermediaries with the rising textile manufacturers of New England.

This natural mixture of economic interest was not new: New Englanders had provided the ships and the captains for the slave traffic, as well as the rum and other articles by which the trade was conducted, and New York and Pennsylvania bankers and merchants prospered as slavery extended.

The American government was not, like the English, a seamless web of tradition and customs. It represented a sharp break with this tradition; a break far sharper than the American people realized.

For England maintained an ecclesiastical center of authority; officially, Britain was a Christian nation whose legal principles were founded on the Christian religion.[14] The United States was a government whose constitution claimed no higher authority than its own laws. That was essentially a lawyer's concept of civilization, and could be traced not to the church, but to Roman tradition.[15]

The novelty of a nation without an official religion was not fully appreciated in 1830—for no land was as crowded with churches and no people more prone to use religious terminology and Christian references in everyday speech, in their writings, and in their thinking, than the Americans.[16] There was no question of the piety of millions. There was equally little doubt that they did not fully realize that a land with no religious center is a land where religion is what anyone chooses to claim.

By the 1830's, says one commentator, "The church had fallen into a thousand pieces . . . It was not that religion itself was challenged—quite the contrary—but as a source of both organized social power and internal discipline the church had undergone a relentless process of fragmentation."[17]

What had risen as a social force was a rising number of "associations" and "societies." The new antislavery society was simply the latest of a long line of such groups that stretched back to the days of Cotton Mather.[18] They had fissioned into mass movements that included diets and rules of health, such as those promoted by Sylvester Graham, efforts to uplift fallen women, temperance, and an almost endless series of single causes.

Many such movements had taken on the aura of religion to their adherents, though few were even loosely connected, if connected at all, with any specific theology. Even antislavery, which Theodore Weld and his associates at Lane considered the essence of Christianity, had little or no connection with that religion, or with the Judaism from which it had emerged.

In the Old Testament "slavery was a voluntary servitude, where, except for the captives of war and criminals making restitution, a slave was free to leave at any time. Such slaves were men seeking refuge from the world of freedom and responsibility; they preferred security to liberty, because liberty meant troubles and possible losses, whereas servitude meant cradle-to-grave care."[19] In the Caucasus the slaves protested their release when the territory was conquered by the Tsar, because their tasks were restricted by hereditary rights and many of their "owners" were impoverished by the need to support them.[20]

John Randolph of Virginia was in a similar position. What Randolph and many Southerners (as well as some Northerners) perceived was that the condition of the blacks in the land could not be altered by abolition alone. Far more was needed to elevate this huge minority, which was uneducated, untrained, and dependent. The American Colonization Society wanted to ship them back to the Dark Continent; the abolitionists argued that freedom alone would work all the miracles necessary.

Even greater confusion and differences existed regarding the American government and society. Far from being the ideal document hailed and heralded in a sea of campaign oratory, the Constitution was a lawyer's contract that claimed no higher moral law than its managers, who represented themselves as reflecting the will of the people.[21] Since such a will was undefined and indefinable, lawyers made up the rules and procedures of government as they went along, within limits that were often ignored, slyly subverted, or poorly guarded.[22] In effect, the Founders had recklessly placed the government in the position of what ancient Greeks called a "tyrant"—which, in its original sense, meant a rule without divine authority.[23]

One result of this evasion of great issues was that the fabric of the new government was strained in every crisis. The first of these perils appeared at the Hartford Convention at the end of 1814, when New Englanders plotted secession. Controversy over the right of the federal government to interfere with overseas trade continued, and the South also threatened to secede.[24] The Missouri Compromise, which evaded the issue of slavery by accepting two new states, one from each section, limiting slavery below a certain line but giving Congress power over slavery in territories, was hailed as high statesmanship in 1820. But in fact it was an arrangement outside the boundaries of the Constitution, and more closely resembled lawyers making a deal outside a court—and outside the law.

What Weld and his associates did not realize was that the government of the United States had no official moral standard and was, therefore, fragile. They did not realize that Britain had weathered centuries of such crises and had developed a complex, subtle network of accommodations between the ideals of the people and the limits of their imperfections. They did not even realize that Christianity itself was not based on the eradication of sin, but on individual struggle against its myriad and eternal forms, including excessive pride in virtue. They completely overlooked, if they knew, that Christianity "did not demand that men remove others from sin, but themselves."[25]

These misconceptions were far from minor or unimportant. At the Lane seminary the large-souled Weld was fashioning a potent force of idealistic young men convinced that righteousness alone authorized whatever actions they chose to take. That in itself was a deviation from their goal of becoming ministers. And there was more to come.

Chapter 21

Early in 1833 John Brown recovered from a prolonged depression after the death of his wife and resumed his tannery operations. He hired a daughter of one John Day to cook, clean, and take care of his children and, after a few weeks, took on the girl's younger sister Mary to help her. The establishment was fairly large, for Brown had between twelve and fifteen journeymen and apprentices and when they all assembled for meals there were almost twenty to be fed. Cooking, washing the linen, keeping the place clean, and other duties kept both young women busy, and it was expected that Brown might marry the elder.

His eye, however, fixed on sixteen-year-old Mary. She was large, silent, and hardworking. His courtship was like a scene out of Dickens, who had a sharp eye for those whom others often overlooked. Brown wrote the girl a letter proposing marriage, and handed it to her one evening.

"She was so overcome," one of her daughters later said, "that she dared not open it but took it to bed that night and slept with it under her pillow. Next morning she found the courage to read it."[1]

The following day, when she went to the spring to get water for the house, Brown followed her eagerly and got his answer. It was yes.

It was not unusual for sixteen-year-old girls to get married, but the difference between the thirty-three-year-old John Brown and Mary Day was more than age alone: they were so disparate that their marriage appeared grotesque. He was the universal expert, who paraded his knowledge of the world from such books as Plutarch's *Lives, Josephus, The Pilgrim's Progress,* and the Bible, who disputed with itinerant preachers as though he was their dean, and who was the stern master of the tannery and lord of his little domain. She was simply a large, silent, ignorant young girl—only four years older than John Brown, Jr.

Her sister, who was mature, was astonished, and no doubt the journeyman and the apprentices looked at Brown with a new eye. He seemed more to be adding to his five children than choosing a new mother for them. Some sense of that might have seeped into even his self-assured crust, because Brown sent young Mary Day to school, apparently so she would be better equipped. Since he was not the sort of man to be troubled by the deficiencies of others in that respect, she must have been woefully behind. She later said the schooling "didn't amount to much," but that was when she was mature.[2] At the time the unusual gesture did not interfere with the arrangements; they were married in July, 1834 when she was just past seventeen. Fortunately, she could not read the future.

99

At Lane the students created an abolition society and gave all the posts to their Southern classmates. Then they organized a lyceum to lecture to free blacks in Cincinnati, and opened several Sunday Schools and Bible classes. Augustus Wattles was so enthused he that left the seminary and opened a school for blacks, where he was joined by Marius Robinson while others taught part-time for him. Four young ladies arrived from New York City to assist in these efforts. They were sent by the Tappans, who also sent $1,000.

News of these activities rushed through the town like a flame. Cincinnati had a population of about thirty thousand, an active waterfront, and heavy river traffic. Kentucky was on the other side and the city teemed with commerce. Yankee pilots and river crews, herdsmen and artisans were numerous, but in the main Cincinnati was Southern: in mood, temperament, location, and people. Southern planters and their families often arrived to stay at the city's leading hotels; servants were often slaves hired from their Kentucky masters.

A section called Green Town was inhabited by free blacks whose numbers kept slowly increasing; it was suspected they harbored runaway slaves, which was probably true. The black population of the city kept mounting. Five years before the Lane antislavery revival the authorities and people of Cincinnati had decided to expel all the blacks, but found that impossible. In 1830 antiblack feeling rose again and a series of bloody riots occurred.

News of the Lane movement—and of the arrival of young white women from New York—let loose a flood of scurrilous rumors. The entry of students like Weld and others into complete and fully equal social relations with the blacks became widely known. Feelings rose high.

Lane's discussions and resolutions, which were published and distributed nationally, led to new laws and resolutions all through the South forbidding the formation of abolition societies, and to other measures that were nearly astonishing. Laws were passed against *The Liberator;* the mails were stopped and searched. The South moved toward a state of siege: it would not relax for a generation.

In New England, where Garrison's newspaper was also causing great ill will and anger, Prudence Crandall, a Quaker schoolmistress, opened her doors to a black girl in her school at Canterbury. The whites then withdrew their children, and Miss Crandall opened a school for blacks. That provoked a storm. The town clerk said it made Canterbury "the Liberia of America." Merchants boycotted Miss Crandall, and her students were arrested on vagrancy charges. Garbage was thrown in her well, and her school was closed down.[3]

The Reverend Lyman Beecher thought Cincinnati might be more lenient, but the rising storm alarmed him. Returning from a visit to New England he called Weld into conference. "I can fill your pockets with gold," he said, "if you want to teach colored schools," but he warned that social equality would lead to dreadful reactions from the general community.

Weld took very high ground, and said "to make any distinctions in social intercourse because of color was an odious and sinful prejudice."[4] The men debated the subject till three o'clock in the morning on one occasion, but neither could budge the other. The *Western Messenger* appeared with an article attacking the seminarians; Weld replied in the Cincinnati *Journal.* Rumors were heard that the citizens might march on the school, and Beecher called a meeting to tell his charges that they were right, "but too far in advance of public sentiment."

Elizur Wright's reply was caustic. "In other words, we are not guilty of wrongdoing, but of doing right Too Soon."[5]

Others argued they were only doing at home what missionaries were applauded for doing abroad, but in that, they were on fairly weak ground—unless they proposed to help all the poor, and not just those of one race.

The crisis was postponed by summer vacation. The students scattered, though Weld remained in Cincinnati. Beecher went east to raise money, but the quiet was misleading.[6]

Garrison's diatribes were creating anger in more places than the South, and the New England clergy grew alarmed. At Andover the professors warned their students not to imitate the seminarians at Lane—or to follow the lead of Garrison. At Amherst the president ordered the college antislavery society disbanded on the grounds that it was "alienating Christian brethren, retarding and otherwise injuring the cause of Religion in the College and threatening in many ways the prosperity of the institution . . ."[7] Townspeople in Worcester mobbed a Methodist minister and in New Canaan a biracial school was hitched to a hundred yoke of oxen and dragged to a nearby swamp.

The attitude of most men—and men then ruled the land—was that other issues were of more immediate and pressing concern than slavery. The largest of these issues revolved around the Bank of the United States, whose charter was being threatened by President Andrew Jackson, the idol of the average man and anathema to virtually everyone else.

"Old Hickory" was not a profound thinker, but he was brave, loyal to his friends—and quick-tempered. He had had an awesome series of confrontations with Calhoun and the South Carolinians over the tariff; the outcome was a retreat on both sides. Then Jackson became angry with various members of the Cabinet because their wives snubbed Peggy Eaton, wife of the secretary of war. That tempest in several teapots opened the path for Roger Brooke Taney, the attorney general. Taney was tall, gaunt, and stooping, with bad teeth; his clothes appeared tailored for someone else. His voice was hollow and he seemed "consumptive." But when he spoke he had "an air of so much sincerity in all he said that it was next to impossible to believe that he could be wrong."[8]

That gift made him a very successful lawyer. William Pinckney said, "I can answer his arguments, I am not afraid of his logic, but that infernal apostolic manner of his, there is no replying to."

Taney was, in other words, a formidable personage who operated very subtly. He was also a lawyer with a connection to the Union Bank of Baltimore, which had several grievances against the Bank of the United States. On that dispute hinged one of the great convulsions in the American government: as attorney general, Taney prepared a series of papers that convinced Jackson that the Bank of the United States, with its many branches—and headed by the proud and socially prominent Alexander Biddle—was a national menace.[9]

The General, whose Cabinet voted unanimously to have the bank charter renewed, followed Taney's advice instead, and his entire reelection campaign raged around the issue. After being reelected, he was told by Taney that he could effectively destroy the Bank by withdrawing its governmental deposits. Cabinet members who disagreed were shifted; the secretary of the treasury, William J. Duane, was removed from office when he refused to carry out the order. Taney, nominated to the Treasury by the President, not only carried out orders he had himself inspired, but included the Bank of Maryland as one of the new depositees.[10] All this enraged Senate Whigs, who had fought Jackson and the Democratic party on the bank issue, and Taney's nomination was rejected. It was the first time in the history of the Government that a Presidential choice had been spurned.[11] That was in June 1834. Taney—though not generally credited with Machiavellian powers— had by then caused Jackson (through the destruction of the Bank of the United States) to create an immense financial crisis that depressed the national economy for years.

Both Andrew Jackson and Roger Taney escaped the odium of their efforts, as far as the general populace was concerned. Democrats hailed Jackson's destructiveness as a great triumph for the "people," and Taney shared in that curiously misplaced glory. When the rejected Taney returned to Maryland he was cheered, escorted, and banqueted, though he himself feared his public career was over.[12]

Fate intervened in a complex minuet that started when Supreme Court Justice Gabriel Duvall retired because of age. Jackson nominated Taney as Duvall's successor, but the Senate delayed its approval. During the delay Chief Justice John Marshall died and Jackson's second term ended. Elections were held, and the Democrats won, bringing Martin Van Buren into the presidency. Taney's nomination was passed by a narrow fourteen votes, and in early 1836 the new President —a true sycophant of his predecessor—swore Roger Brooke Taney into office as the fifth Chief Justice of the United States.

That turn of events contained multiple ironies. The campaign to destroy the Bank of the United States led Jackson and Taney to demolish, almost in passing and as part of the argument, a brake carefully contrived by Alexander Hamilton: it required that the secretary of the treasury report not to the White House but to Congress. By switching control of the Treasury to the Presidency, Jackson and Taney had removed one of the most important safeguards against possible one-man rule in the American Government. After their "triumph," interference with the nation's economy from the White House was to become an increasingly familiar feature of American life—though it is doubtful that either Jackson or Taney ever fully realized the far-reaching significance of what they had accomplished.

At the same time, other men were removing other safeguards against the sort of "enthusiasms" that the Puritans had so distrusted. Prior to the rise of the abolition movement the American Colonization Society was a national Christian undertaking. The society had a large liberal following in both South and North. It also had agents and a publication, it was generally accepted. Churches set aside one day's collection every year for its support.

But the abolitionists went into motion by making the colonization society their first target. This was essentially a revolutionary tactic, because liberals—not reactionaries—are always the first target of revolutionaries. To zealots, moderation is insupportable; it is held to be merely a moat behind which reactionaries remain secure in their castles. By draining the moat of moderation, the castle stands naked to attack.

That was the direction in which Garrison moved, guided by the instincts of a fanatic. He inserted his attack into the declaration he wrote for the American Antislavery Society at the convention he commandeered in New York, and he left no room whatever for moderation. "All laws," he said in part, "which are now in force, admitting the right of slavery, are therefore before God utterly null and void . . ."[13]

A few weeks later Garrison went back to Boston to his own New England Antislavery Society, which he controlled in dictatorial fashion. From there he pressed his campaign, added women's rights and several other features to his effort, and continued the castigations that enraged the South and moderates everywhere. The American Antislavery Society was left to argue for "immediate emancipation . . . gradually accomplished," in the British pattern. Garrison wanted immediacy, no matter what. Two abolitionist groups—still small—grappled for the field.

Weld, although he would never admit it, was virtually a third force in his own right. Working through converts, using the revival methods of Charles Finney, he pleaded that slavery was a sin, and that all that was needed for it to vanish would be the agreement of all good Christians on its sinfulness.

Weld's movement really started as a student movement. When New England college presidents banded together to outlaw such campus activities, the Lane trustees passed similar resolutions. Students who resisted were threatened with dismissal. The edict did not take effect at once; it had to be ratified and arguments extended through the fall of 1834. The Reverend Asa Mahan, a member of the board of trustees and a Finney convert, argued against ratification. The trustees were firm, however, and Weld led a group of fifty-three students out of the seminary. That created a sensation throughout the North. Other seminary boards discovered that their students thought Weld and his associates were martyrs. The Tappans did not break their word to continue Lyman Beecher's salary, but they cut off all further support. The famous evangelist, who had hoped to contain the "he-goat men, who think they do God a service by butting everything in their line of march which does not fall or get out of the way," surveyed the wreck of his hopes, and of the seminary, with bitter eyes.[14]

Even the Beecher family was split by the argument. Only Catherine Beecher, his eldest daughter, remained loyal to her father; Harriet Beecher—who would marry a Lane faculty member, Reverend Calvin Stowe—went over to Weld. And Beecher—who had first feared the awakening methods of Charles Finney, and then reconciled himself to them in the hope they would increase the Christian, and especially Presbyterian fold—now decided he had been fatuously optimistic. Virtually alone in the nation, he concluded that he confronted a new heretical movement, of the sort that had risen in the heady days of the Reformation, that he was marching down a strange, new, and dangerous road inspired by "the Oneida *denunciatory revivalry.*"[15] (Italics added.)

Ralph Waldo Emerson returned from Europe still a minister and still willing to ascend a pulpit and deliver a sermon. He even went so far, in the autumn of 1833, as to appear as a prospective candidate at a New Bedford, church, but did not sufficiently impress the congregation. That rejection did not trouble him: early in the year he had received the first installment of his inheritance from his wife's estate. It consisted of shares of bank stocks and shares of the Roxbury Mill Dam worth over $11,000. By the time he received the second installment he would be assured an annual income of $1,200—then enough for a handsome style of living.[16] It was true he would need to help his mother and his retarded brother Bulkeley, but he was now, essentially, financially secure. That is a situation that brings with it its own personal quality of assurance, unknown to those whose future is insecure. Thus bolstered, Waldo radiated a calm poise that would become famous.

His lectures began shortly before the inheritance arrived. In the first, entitled "The Uses of Natural History," Emerson paired the world and mind of humans, saying, "the whole of Nature is a metaphor or image of the human mind,"—as though a man could conceive of a parasitic liver fluke. Moses Curtis, a future botanist, attended, and said the lecture was somewhat "intangible."[17] Other titles included "Water," (not too well received), and "Lectures on Italy" (he both praised and patronized that country). He also dealt with great personages of the past: Michaelangelo, Luther, John Fox, Edmund Burke. These were all large subjects; the audiences were flattered to be invited to sit in judgment on them.

Meanwhile, the young minister made plans to move to Concord.

That was natural; Concord was the home of his forebears, and his mother's retreat in times of distress. All their joint belongings fit into one cart, and made a load for only one horse. Ellen's estate had lifted him far. They moved into the Manse, still occupied by Emerson's grandfather, Mr. Ripley. Waldo wrote in his journal, "Hail to the quiet field of my fathers."[18]

The Lane rebels at first continued their program of teaching free blacks from a large Cincinnati house placed at their disposal by a brother-in-law of a young lawyer named Salmon P. Chase. But several soon left for other seminaries; Weld was put on the payroll of the American Antislavery Society, and a new agent of change appeared with a new proposition.

John J. Shippherd was cofounder of a colony at Oberlin, Ohio—the land teemed with colonies—and was anxious to launch a seminary. The site he and his associates occupied was close to Western Reserve College, but that institution, although biracial and Presbyterian to the core, was not "severe" enough for Shippherd. His colonists were devoted to austerity in clothes, furniture, and fashion, opposed travel on the Sabbath, and favored unrestricted virtue. The Oberliners had built an elementary and secondary school, and needed seminary students; the Lane rebellion was Shippherd's opportunity.

Shippherd contacted Reverend Asa Mahan as possible president, and even dreamed of getting Weld as professor of theology. But Weld wanted no more of schools: he was now wedded to antislavery. Nonetheless he contributed an idea that made Oberlin a concrete rather than abstract project: Why not get Finney? It was an inspiration. Finney was growing weary of New York City and its eternal demands. Shippherd and Mahan went to New York and called on the Tappans, who were delighted to see a possible replacement seminary for Lane.

By the end of the year, only months after the Lane rebellion, Oberlin had a president, Charles Finney; it enjoyed the Tappans' support; and it was arguing over its rules of admissions. The college also decided to accept women—a radical innovation. But to general surprise the women objected to the admission of blacks.[19] That snarl took a little time to unravel but it was overcome with another innovation: the faculty, and not the trustees, would govern the school. The sequence was significant, because Oberlin, with its elimination of both racial and sex barriers, became the pattern for more "manual labor colleges" within a very short time. It made the highly respected Western Reserve College appear abruptly old-fashioned. Moderates, who could formerly relax in support of the older college, were given an alternative that moved directly into the abolitionist movement. The Lane rebellion, therefore, was not squelched so much as dispersed, and Oberlin itself soon became another seedbed.

After Oberlin was established Weld appeared there to speak against slavery. He lectured in the college's crude chapel, which had no plaster nor heat, and seats made "of rough boards placed on blocks." Weld spoke for twenty-one consecutive nights, and was heard by "five to six hundred males and females . . . every night"; they sat shivering, and with nothing to lean back against, until nine o'clock. One, James H. Fairchild, years later President of Oberlin, never forgot the experience —nor was he alone.[20]

When Weld left he took six recruits with him, to work in his campaign to carry the abolition gospel through Ohio. The group first went to Cleveland, to what one later called "a school of abolition," where Weld had already trained and sent out thirteen agents from New York.

Then the recruits fanned out. One went to western Pennsylvania, and one to western New York; the others remained in Ohio. Weld's tactics were Finney's. He preached against slavery as a moral wrong and spoke night after night, until he would finally call for repentance, conversion, and acceptance. His eloquence, according to all reports, was nearly supernal; at Steubenville he converted a youthful lawyer named Edwin M. Stanton; at Jefferson he won over two more lawyers: Joshua R. Giddings and his partner Ben Wade; at North Bend he was heard by still another young man: William Henry Harrison.

The Reverend Lyman Beecher, awakened to the danger, went east and tried, once again, to stem the tides that Weld was summoning, that the Tappans were funding, and that Garrison was turning stormy. He organized clergymen into The American Union for the Relief and Improvement of the Colored Race, and in January 1835 these held a meeting in Boston's Tremont Hall. The purpose was to rally moderates.

The meeting was invaded by Garrison and his followers, including a leather-lunged agitator named George Thompson, a British abolitionist whose cause had won in his native land, and who sought new fields to conquer. Thompson, Garrison, and their followers marched into Beecher's meeting, interrupted the proceedings with questions, and when asked to leave, launched a filibuster instead.[21] The ministers were caught off guard, and the publicity muffled their agreement that slavery was not a sin. Beecher had been pushed aside rudely; the Garrisons would brook no tactics, spokesmen, or activities but their own.

Their leader, meanwhile, carried his denunciations into new avenues. The theological position of Beecher and the orthodox Presbyterians that slavery was no "sin" led Garrison into denunciations of Christianity in the United States. The "drift of his thoughts toward anticlericalism was unmistakable as his obsession with conscience scattered before it questions of doctrine and policy."[22] He began, in other words, to attack the churches.

By turning in that direction, Garrison was merely expanding his targets; it could not be said that his positions were rational, for they left no room for other men to think. He was determined that everyone become perfect, instantly—even if everyone had to die to attain such a goal. His suspicions of anyone who disagreed with him were quick, violent, and unbounded. To those who criticized his abusive language, he replied that "language was, after all, a matter of taste," and "where is the standard of taste?"[23] A man who could ask such a question was unlikely to respect an answer.

He insisted that he was a pacifist, against all violence, but continued to make violent accusations. He did not stop at accusing individuals of bad faith, sinfulness, depravity, greed, lack of conscience, and honor; he attacked entire groups. One of the Garrison tenets was that Southern slaveholders and Northern businessmen "had a vested interest in corruption" and were "conniving to plunge the country into barbarism."[24]

Nobody was safe from Garrison's vitriol; not even the Reverend William Ellery Channing. Elizabeth Peabody told Channing that Garrison had accused him of "living on blood money derived from his father-in-law's ownership of a distillery engaged in the famous triangular trade."[25] Channing professed to believe that Garrison would never say anything so dreadful. The charge was heavy, for it contained an element of truth. Perhaps that was why, when Reverend Samuel May, an ardent abolitionist, spent an evening at Dr. Channing's home, he heard the frail Unitarian leader complain that abolition leaders were "too precipitate, and that they lacked tact, and that they were, in short, too violent."[26]

In October 1835 a Garrison branch organization, the Boston Female Anti-Slavery Society, scheduled a meeting but couldn't find a hall. The group settled for the offices of *The Liberator,* and the city was flooded with handbills offering $100 reward for anyone who "shall first lay violent hands on Thompson"—who was scheduled to speak—"so that he may be brought to the tar-kettle before dark."[27]

The ladies appeared, led by Mary Parker, a sister of Theodore Parker, but George Thompson, the doughty English abolitionist, did not show. Garrison was present, but retreated to a smaller office when the mayor of Boston arrived with the police to cancel the meeting. A mob had collected and after the women left began to call out for Garrison. He went out a window, across the back lane into a carpenter shop, and climbed into the loft where he hid behind a pile of lumber; but he was seen stealing into this refuge and great shouts went up. Some men seized him and prepared to throw him from the window. Then they changed their minds, coiled a rope around his middle, and led him into the street.

Their intention was to give him the tar and feathers prepared for Thompson, but the police intervened and Garrison was rescued at the cost of torn clothes. He was then whisked off to the Leverett Street jail for safekeeping. His behavior in this incident is disputed. Harriet Martineau, the English writer-abolitionist, who was in Boston at the time, said he showed "a want of manliness" and "excessive agitation." Others said he begged for mercy on his knees.[28] But his followers hailed him as a hero-martyr, and that version has outlasted all others.

Garrison's ordeal sent his name rocketing about the land, shamed moderates who deplored violence—though they had nothing to do with it—and brought him a new recruit: Wendell Phillips.

Phillips, a tall, blond Boston aristrocrat with a coolly eloquent gift for public speaking, was to prove as effective and almost as insolent as Garrison toward those who disagreed with him. He was the first of the city's upper crust to join the outcast movement; and after his appearance at Garrison's side a slow but significant trickle would begin to flow from the top. That trickle, however, was not entirely the work of young Phillips; it was due no less to the emergence of William Ellery Channing.

At this time, the eminent Doctor wrote a pamphlet called *Thoughts on Slavery*. It appeared in Boston only a few weeks after Garrison achieved new fame by being roughed up. The pamphlet also altered the climate amazingly. "Garrison could be dismissed as a fanatic, Maria Chapman as a flighty woman, Rev. Samuel J. May as a backwoods parson—but the Rev. Dr. William Ellery Channing, minister of the Federal Street church and acknowledged leader of the American Unitarian movement, was unassailable."[29]

Channing, in fact, made it official: antislavery had arrived in Boston.

Chapter 22

The entire North heard about the Lane rebels, the founding of Oberlin, and the activities of Weld and his new recruits. Among those drawn to these new activities was Owen Brown, John Brown's father, a trustee of Western Reserve College. Brown switched his support to Oberlin and became a trustee there. Family letters from Hudson, Ohio to John Brown in Randolph kept him abreast of developments. (One individual deeply involved—Elizur Wright, Jr.—was a former classmate of John's early youth.)

These events naturally affected John Brown. In November 1834, he wrote a long letter to a younger brother, Frederick, expressing his first recorded interest in black people: "Since you left me, I have been trying to devise some means whereby I might do something for my poor fellowmen who are in bondage, and having fully consulted the feelings of my wife and my three boys, we have agreed to get at least one negro boy, or youth, and bring him up as we do our own . . ."[1]

He went on to say that such a boy might be obtained from a slaveholder who would simply release him, or that he and his family might deprive themselves, save their money, and buy a slave. He added that "for years I have been trying to devise some way to get a school a-going here for blacks . . ." This seems somewhat unlikely, but Brown pursued the thought for several paragraphs, suggesting that "some first-rate abolitionist families" from Hudson might join them in such a venture. He then launched on a discussion of how education of the blacks would "operate on slavery like firing-powder confined in rock," and ended by asking Frederick to join him in the effort. The letter seems to have been more an echo of discussions floating in the air on a great national topic than a serious intention.

Meanwhile there were larger winds blowing than abolition. Andrew Jackson had destroyed the Bank of the United States and with it the stability of American currency. All that was left were state banks, which were printing money on credit with ignorant profligacy. The Erie Canal had ushered in a land boom, and lesser canal projects were being discussed as a result. Goods and commerce were flowing along the banks of the new waterway, and towns were springing up. Land sharks and developers proliferated, especially in northern Ohio. John Brown caught the fever, which was carried on the breeze like pollen, and heard, with shining eyes, how a new, smaller canal, built from Cleveland to Lake Erie, had jumped land prices from $11 to between $200 to $700 an acre, and was selling in ten-acre lots. Black boys and schools faded, and dreams of wealth took their place.

For a decade there had been rumors of a new canal, to be called the Pennsylvania-Ohio, that would run from the Ohio-Lake Erie Canal at Akron and carry traffic east to Beaver, Pennsylvania. That would expand American waterways immeasurably, creating access not only to New York through Akron and Lake Erie, but to the Mississippi—and thus the South. One town—Franklin—considered to be located along the banks of that project, was only six miles from Hudson, Ohio, where John Brown's father, Owen, lived, and where he had been raised for most of his life. It was John's thought that if he moved there he could share in the great prosperity to come. He decided to sell his holdings in Randolph and join the rush.

Brown therefore contacted Zenas B. Kent, an elderly, prosperous citizen of Franklin, and made an agreement to build a tannery there in partnership with Kent. Kent would put up the money, and Brown would be a junior partner. No doubt it started as an equal partnership; but Brown, unable to raise money from his Randolph property, suffered the humiliation of having to borrow from Kent to move with his family.[2]

At first Brown did not seem to realize that he had reduced himself, but he soon found that he was no longer master-to-be of a tannery. His position was more nearly that of an employee, and Kent, who attempted to give some orders, met with an astonishingly indignant response. The partners were soon psychologically parted and Brown's efforts were further delayed by Kent's reluctance to provide the money necessary for construction. No doubt he wanted explanations as work proceeded and materials were needed; Brown had never provided anyone an explanation in his life. His father had been indulgent and he had never before had to accommodate himself to another man. Work stalled while the difficult, stiff-necked Brown and the proud Kent each waited for the other to come to his senses.

Meanwhile the town teemed with Irish canal workers, who earned eighty cents a day. Carriages bearing top-hatted speculators ploughed through the muddy streets, hotel lobbies were crowded with men explaining plans, and the great boom shimmered in the air around them. That boom was what had drawn John Brown in the first place, and it had spread through the entire region. In Akron, where surveyors for the canal company had appeared, land prices leaped 400 percent. The Franklin Land Company was formed by twenty leading townsmen —including Kent—to sell water power and factory sites between the town and the Cuyahoga River; and men gathered in knots to estimate jealously the fortunes the company's organizers would make. That was galling for Brown, who was finding life on an allowance from his senior partner far from easy. The final blow came when he learned that Marvin Kent, his partner's son, who knew nothing of the tannery business, had already rented his father's share of the enterprise and would be the ultimate beneficiary of John Brown's efforts. Brown stalked in to see Kent and the older man, by now as sick of Brown as possible, was willing enough to lend him money for a yoke of oxen and a plow.[3]

Reduced to his small loan capital, John Brown then went to work like dozens of other poor men—mostly farmers in the region—digging mud and earth, in the heavy, exhausting, and antique labor needed to create the narrow and shallow ditch. He was engaged in that task in 1835 when he learned that the Franklin Land Company had bought some sites from Zenas Kent for $75,000 in Lower Franklin, and some other sites in Upper Franklin as well. The overall plan was to combine the water power of the two villages and connect it by means "of dams and spillways" at a settlement called Franklin Mills. That project would, it was widely believed, persuade the Pennsylvania Canal Company managers to select Franklin as a site for increased investments, and thereby outstrip other towns along the new waterway.

In late 1835 Brown went to Franklin Mills and walked around, burning to be a part of the boom. If Franklin was booming, why would not Franklin Mills? The thought was equal to the wish. He borrowed enough for a down payment from his younger brother Frederick, and bought Frederick Haymaker's farm in Franklin Mills. That was a gamble in itself, though it was his brother's money that he used as a stake, for he himself was not earning enough in canal work to pay the full price—estimated at nearly seventy-four dollars an acre—for the property. Brown was betting on the rise: on the hope that others, anxious to obtain land parcels for quick resale, would come running.

The Kents learned of John Brown's new venture without too much surprise. Both Zenas and Marvin Kent had formed their own opinions of his qualities. "Brown saw everything large," Marvin Kent said years later, "and felt himself the equal of anything. He had such fast, stubborn and strenuous convictions that nothing short of a mental rebirth could have altered him."[4]

At the time of the Haymarket farm purchase, however, Brown *was* undergoing a "mental rebirth." The man who angrily preferred to get into the canal ditch with a yoke of oxen rather than take orders as a junior partner had transformed himself into a real estate speculator— and done so by boldly taking possession of a house large enough for himself and his family, plus enough land to survey and divide into lots for sale, in one surprising jump.

Gerrit Smith had been caught first by the Temperance Society, and then by the peace movement. Both kept him busy, although his ordinary business day started before 5:00 A.M. At 6:30 he prayed with his family, and then opened his land office from 7:00 A.M. to 9:00 P.M. Between business correspondence he wrote his tracts, answered his groaning mail, and exchanged letters with zealots of every sort. His health remained, in his opinion, terrible. At the age of thirty-two, he wrote that he was an old man in constitution."[5] Yet his activities would have exhausted several average men.

His income ran between $80,000 and $100,000 a year, huge sums at that time, but Smith's accounts were kept in so many ledgers that the figures were hard to trace. That was, of course, his own business: it was a period when men kept whatever they owned, and when the government was pledged not to inspect their property but help them protect it. Not even Smith knew how much money he was worth; it was enough, however, to make him the target of appeals from all sides— which he fended with considerable skill.

Early in the 1830's Smith was visited by Benjamin Lundy, and was asked to help Lundy's newspaper. (Garrison was then working on the publication.) Smith refused; abolition seemed a small cause; temperance was the great cause. But by the middle of the decade, as the Tappans created the American Antislavery Society and Weld's activities became famous at Lane, Smith's interest was awakened. When a great word battle against the American Colonization Society began, Smith wavered, especially after being pressed by Charles Stuart, Theodore Weld's eccentric supporter. Smith had a high regard for Stuart: he called him "that precious child of God." Jubilant, Stuart wrote Weld, who also knew Smith from his days in the "Holy Band," that the magnate was "all but with us."

It was not that the magnate did not oppose slavery: he called it "robbery, that plunders its victim not of money or goods but of his mind, his soul."[6] The fact was that Smith did not merely like to join crusades; he wanted to be placed at their head.

In May 1835, however, he was persuaded, with many flatteries, to attend the New York State Antislavery Society convention in Utica. He arrived to discover that the Utica *Observer* had headlined the event, and

that a hostile mob had collected to break up the convention, consisting
of six hundred delegates in the Second Presbyterian Church. Led by
Congressman Samuel Beardsley—who termed the delegates "traitors"
—the mob attacked. The delegates fled, reassembled, and were invited
to hold their convention at Peterboro, where no mobs appeared.

Smith, the savior of the convention, now addressed it on the topic
that Garrison was raising in Boston: free speech. The abolitionists
were ecstatic; they had enlisted the mighty magnate.

Fired at last, Smith sent an open letter—published, as was his custom when denouncing a person, a group, or a cause—to Ralph Randolph Gurley, saying the colonization society was more interested "in
demolishing the Antislavery Society than in promoting the welfare of
Blacks . . ." Then he resigned.[7] That was a great blow; the colonization
society reeled.

The Tappans had tried, many times, to bring Weld to New York City,
saying that everyone, sooner or later, came to the metropolis. He
disagreed; he knew many who would never visit the city, and insisted
that the countryside was where converts could be made, and where the
nation could be changed. The Utica experience—which drove the New
York State society out of town to Peterboro, where the delegates not
only found refuge but saw farmers and their wives arriving in buggies
and wagons to hear the deliberations—changed minds at headquarters.

The antislavery society decided to expand the number of paid agents
to seventy—the number that Jesus had appointed—and to launch a
great drive. That push paralleled Weld's determination, and followed
his plan. Meanwhile, the leader—and despite the official posts of Elizur
Wright and others, there was little doubt that Weld was the intellectual
author of the movement, as well as its most outstanding speaker—went
to Utica. There he faced down the mobs that had chased off the six
hundred delegates, and began a great tour of upstate New York.

He met defeat only at Troy, where he was buffeted, stoned, egged,
and finally driven away. The experience took a great toll; no man can
become the "most mobbed man in the country" without paying a
price; Weld paid a price that Garrison never, and possibly could not
have, met.

In New England, however, reaction against abolitionist zeal was
stirring among the clergy. Like the Reverend Lyman Beecher, many
ministers began to fear that a surrogate religious movement was being
formed—a movement that imperiled not only civility, order, and the
nation, but religion itself. Beecher mounted his counterattack with an
eloquent sermon recalling the need to remain rooted in biblical principles, and in particular to honor the Sabbath. Other ministers, who
shared his anxieties, launched a move to censure or expel extremists;
in this effort they had the help of conservative members of their congregations. Pulpits once open to abolitionist clergymen began to bar
them.

The major Protestant denominations found themselves caught up in a great dispute. In 1836 the Methodists voted to bar further discussions on slavery as "too unsettling" and Garrison rose like some spirit of wrath to begin a series of denunciations of organized Christianity and its churches. His accusations shocked the country. He called the Methodist church "a cage of unclean birds and a synagogue of Satan." The Presbyterian church was anathema, the Congregational ministers were "at the head of the most implacable foes of God and man" toward whom "the most intense abhorrence should fill the breast of every disciple of Christ." Then, completely carried away, he "renounced all allegiance to his country and nominated Jesus Christ to the Presidency of the United States and the World . . ."[8]

That did more than verify fears: it brought anarchic principles into American political life for the first time in a serious sense. Lyman Beecher, still struggling to launch a liberal movement and to float his American Union, appeared at the Presbyterian general assembly to discover that Weld had lobbied the younger clergy at the previous year's meeting so effectively that the Presbyterians were polarized. It was impossible to reconcile the delegates: the Southerners were sure abolition was a child of heresy; Northern converts of Finney linked slavery to sin.

Beecher left defeated and convinced that all these troubles came from revivalism. He appeared before the Congregational Session of Connecticut to admit that his error had started early. "I wish to confess my sin," he said, "I was wrong . . . the system of evangelism . . . is as if a man should sit down and attempt to eat enough to last a whole year."[9]

By the time he had finished the Congregationalists of Connecticut closed their pulpits to "itinerant agents and lecturers," and Beecher was off to the general association of Massachusetts. Here he spoke again, and even the Boston abolitionists, who were ashamed of Garrison, agreed to follow Connecticut's example.

The speed and the force of Beecher's moves caught the abolitionists of New York off guard. Weld and others came running north, but they succeeded in saving only New Hampshire for their agents. It was a time when Massachusetts was tall in New England, and Beecher had captured the intellectual headquarters of the North.

Garrison was not distressed. Clergymen, he wrote, "are blind leaders of the blind, dumb dogs that cannot bark, spiritual popes—that they love the fleece better than the flock—that they are mighty hindrances in the cause of freedom."[10] He ignored the fact that even in his own Antislavery Society two-thirds of his delegates were clergymen, and that clergymen comprised the heart of Weld's gathering. Nor did he seem to notice that the entire abolition movement was, essentially, a revolt of young clergymen and seminarians, and he would have exulted had he known that he would reap the credit in history, long after the names of most of the clergymen were forgotten.

At Oberlin, however, the Reverend Charles Finney was deeply disturbed. He knew that Weld and many others had originally been his converts, but he had not intended any injury to Christianity: quite the contrary. In some agitation, he wrote Weld that ". . . we are in our present course going fast into a civil war.

"Will our present movement in abolition result in that? . . . Nothing is more manifest to me that the present movement will result in this, unless your mode of abolitionizing the country be greatly modified." Finney went on to say the danger could only be averted if "abolition was made an appendage of a general revival of religion." He added that many of the abolitionists were good men, "but few of them *wise* . . ."[11]

But the flood had begun.

These disputes could have been taking place on another planet as far as John Brown was concerned. Like most of the men not actually caught at the bottom in Franklin and other towns along the pathway of canals or proposed canals he was intent on riding the boom to its crest. His lots were laid out, and he accepted promissory notes in payment—as he himself had given promissory notes to farmer Haymaker for the land. These notes were in plentiful supply, as were bank notes, drawn on the myriad small state banks and their branches. In January 1836 Brown wrote his cousin, Seth Thompson, with whom he had a working partnership when he lived at Randolph as a tanner, offering to sell Thompson half the Haymaker land for seven thousand dollars. He urged Thompson to act swiftly.

Caught by the same lure, Thompson wrote back that he would buy, offering $1,134 in cash and $1,866 in a five-day note; he also offered four more promissory notes for $1,000 each, payable annually every January until 1840.[12] Brown used these notes—as was the custom—to pay his own debts, to repay his younger brother, Frederick, and to buy, via down payment, another farm and house near the village of Hudson. His mood may be surmised: he had made a giant leap and had landed in clover.

He was soon seen in a new buggy, drawn by a handsome horse, surveying other possible land sites; half the Haymaker property was sold but Brown had 150 lots left: he was on his way to wealth. People spoke of him as one of the smart operators; he was elected to an office in the Cuyahoga Falls Real Estate Association and became a director of the bank in that town.

His desire to pyramid was predictable as a sunrise. The more land he could get, via down payments, the more he could sell, and the more he could profit. He appeared at the Western Reserve Bank in Warren, Ohio, for a loan, learned the terms and rounded up six cosignors. They were his younger brother Frederick, who was pulled back into town, Joshua Stow, Henry Ogden, William Setmore, and Heman Oviatt.[13] With six thousand dollars in hand he put down the first payment for the farm near Hudson, and launched construction of a building on his lots at Franklin Mills. His thought was that the town, sure to grow, would need a hotel and a warehouse. Both structures, like his building at Randolph, were fairly large, and loomed stark on the landscape. Brown also laid out streets with resounding names, in classic developer style. He bought more land, too—or at least, made down payments. Then calamity struck.

It came from the White House—from President Jackson, who had been appalled to see the results of his victory over the Bank of the United States. Not that the General ever regretted that victory; it was just that the nation was engaged in an orgy of speculation and even Jackson knew there was only one conclusion to such a surge.

He was not alone. Missouri's Senator Thomas Hart Benton also voiced alarm. "I did not join in putting down the Bank of the United States," he shouted, "to put up a wilderness of local banks. I did not join in putting down the paper currency of a national bank, to put up a national currency of a thousand local banks. I did not strike Caesar to make Anthony master . . ." But he had.[14] The Bank of the United States as a stabilizing factor was gone. Now the currency of the nation ran riot, with promissory notes, bank notes, and company notes all mingling in a great cloud of paper that carried prices into the stratosphere, to fuel a boom in a thousand towns that mirrored Franklin Mills.

The White House announced that in future, federal land sales would be conducted only for hard coin. That created a howl of pain in Congress, which was stacked with speculators, and the order was delayed. Bitter arguments soared; Benton, whose fiscal ideas were limited to a conviction that people should use only gold and silver, received an ironical sobriquet, "Old Bullion," which he was to never lose. Meanwhile the entire financial structure of the nation trembled, and remained standing only because 1836 was an election year—no other event can compete with that exercise for the attention of American politicians. The deluge was delayed, but land prices fell like stricken birds while real estate speculators watched, frozen in terror.

Chapter 23

Shortly after he moved to Concord Ralph Waldo Emerson married Lydia Jackson of Plymouth. Also a descendant of an old New England family, she was well educated, bookish, spoke French and Italian, was considered a Unitarian with leanings toward Swedenborg, and had an income of six hundred dollars a year. The pair seemed suited in every respect. With Waldo's mother, they moved into a handsome house built for them by John Coolidge for three thousand dollars; it sat on two L-shaped acres of land that sloped down to Mill Brook, and had servants' quarters.

Emerson accepted several town posts; he was head of the library committee and a member of the school committee. He also gave an occasional lecture in the Concord lyceum and, from time to time, ascended the pulpit of his grandfather Reverend Ripley's church. But he dropped the posts after discovering the demands they made on his time; his aunt Mary, who kept a shrewd eye on him, decided he was lost "to the chaos of modern speculation."

She could not precisely date his departure, but she knew that the "humanitarians"—a term that then defined those who denied the divinity of Jesus and whose ranks included the Reverend William Ellery Channing—were responsible.

"What has his high-strained thought accomplished?" she asked of Dr. Channing. "It had chilled faith." She believed that if its supernatural character was strained away Christianity would be only "a straw in the tempest."[1] She believed in Calvinism, which did not make sin respectable: she scorned humanitarians because they denied a final judgment—and she began to identify the new transcendentalism with the worst in humanitarianism. She also identified Waldo with both, as did everyone else.

Like Aunt Mary, nobody can quite pinpoint the moment when Unitarianism spawned the transcendentalist movement. Hints of transcendentalist arguments appeared early in Channing's ideas, but the members of the new movement were so dazzled by so many trends—German scholarship, the philosophy of Swedenborg, the drift toward social reforms and against slavery, worship of dimly perceived paganism, the religions of the Orient—that defining the principles of transcendentalism is like packaging smoke. Yet transcendentalism was real enough to fuel a flight from the church by many of its most articulate and idealistic young ministers. The rebellion was spearheaded by Emerson.

In 1836 he and Lydia—whom he called "Lydian" for its antique Roman ring—had their first child: a son. Emerson was enraptured. "Now," he exulted in his journal, "I have joined the cult of childhood. I am Pygmalion."[2] That burst was inspired by Amos Bronson Alcott, a former clockmaker, farmer, itinerant peddler, and radical schoolmaster who had opened a school on Temple Street in Boston that was conducted, among the moppets, along Socratic lines, with dialogues on such lofty topics as sex.

Alcott believed children possessed intuitive wisdom, and could serve as "litmus paper sources of revealed truths for tasting the true meaning of the New Testament" in order to "bring that meaning within the comprehension of adults."[3] Alcott thought he was making a contribution to theology but was captured by a paradox, in which he considered children both intuitively wise and yet so pliant that their teachers could mold them into ideal forms. It did not seem to occur to him that using helpless children as research subjects was immoral or injurious. Although his experiments were grotesque he inspired many later imitators. At the time, when news of his undertaking and its nature became known, it created widespread indignation, anger, and horror: people came running to rescue their children and the Temple School collapsed. His self-assurance unruffled, Alcott moved to Concord to enjoy interminable conversations with Emerson, and to live off his bounty.

Another of the circle who appeared in 1836 was twenty-six-year-old Margaret Fuller, educated by her father into something of a prodigy. "Homely, long-necked and near-sighted," she read Ovid and Cervantes, Molière and Shakespeare as a child;[4] and also kept a voluminous journal—as did all the literati of Boston. (They sometimes exchanged them.) She went to Concord, recommended by Elizabeth Peabody, to spend three weeks with the Emersons by way of introduction.

The visit was in part practical; the Reverend Frederick Hedge, a product of Göttingen and one of the high priests of the new Germanic cult of Christianity-shredders, wanted to launch a transcendentalist publication, with Carlyle as editor and Emerson as a contributor. These meetings, moves, and plans were intertwined; serpentine, incestuous.

Emerson was meanwhile moving upward. His first ten Lectures, on "Correct Taste in English Literature," were a series of judgments in which authors were graded by transcendentalist standards, in which Coleridge was placed above Locke—and which earned Emerson two hundred dollars. Meanwhile, at Concord, he was putting together the observations of his life's readings, conversations, and reflections into a small book to be called *Nature*, only ninety-five pages long, and written epigrammatically. It appeared in September 1836 to the rolling of drums by all his friends, and their friends, on both sides of the Atlantic.

Essentially, the book was a long essay urging a "return" to nature, à la Rousseau, in which poetic descriptions of scenery were mixed with philosophic themes in bewildering fashion. "Standing on the bare ground—my head bathed by the blithe air and uplifted into infinite space, all mean egotism vanishes. I become a transparent eyeball; I am nothing; I see all; the currents of the Universal Being circulate through me; I am part and parcel of God."[5] That was, of course, pantheism—without the terror of the ancients.

The first five hundred copies of *Nature* sold out in a month. Reviews in the Unitarian *Christian Register* and the *Western Messenger* were flattering, even if the reviewers seemed puzzled. The *Christian Examiner* reviewer, Francis Bowen, observed that it was an attempt to revive the "Old Platonic School," and credited its inspiration to the Germans, whose language, he noted, had "a genius for novelty and vagueness." He took note that Emerson revealed "arrogance and self-sufficiency . . . no less absurd in philosophy than criminal in morals."[6]

Nevertheless the book's success gave Emerson's coterie such a lift that its members began to meet at the Reverend George Ripley's home in Bedford Place whenever Hedge came to Boston from his pastorate in Bangor, Maine. The group was called, on the inside, the "Symposium," in honor of Plato, but outsiders called it the "Transcendentalist Club." Members included Hedge, the ineffable Alcott, the Reverend Convers Francis, the Reverend James Freeman Clarke, the Reverend Orestes Brownson, Margaret Fuller, Elizabeth Peabody, and Emerson himself. William Ellery Channing was invited, but he preferred to be an inspiration.

However, Channing was not indolent. His tract against slavery had alienated many of his parishioners at the Federal Street Church: some crossed the street when they saw his diminutive figure and enormous hat approaching. But he gained followers throughout Unitarian circles. In 1836 he published an open letter addressed to James G. Birney, Weld's convert, entitled *The Abolitionists,* 7 which ranged him, definitely and forever, on the side of that movement—thereby irritating Garrison, who resented competition in leadership—especially from clergymen.

But Channing's open letter and the cerebral discussions of the transcendentalists seemed far removed from the activities of the American Antislavery Society in New York. That group had collected its seventy agents, brought them to New York, and there indoctrinated them at prolonged sessions that Weld headed—with the assistance of Garrison, who came down from Boston, Charles Stuart, Reverend Beriah Green, and others. Each session ran twelve hours, with a break for food only; Weld held forth for four days on "The Bible Argument Against Slavery" and sometimes spoke for as long as eight hours without stopping. His voice had already broken once, on his New England tour, and this additional punishment was more than his body could endure. By the time the sessions ended, he was reduced to a whisper, and his days of public speaking were over indefinitely.

The seventy left to spread the new gospel; Finney's great revival had been diverted into the great antislavery movement, and Weld, living in headquarters at New York, turned toward a new level of effort. He had sent the seventy into the country because that was where the bulk of the people lived. In his view, cities were only trading centers for a rural population. The statistics of the time proved the accuracy of his observation: propaganda is most effective when it reaches the largest numbers.

Breakthroughs, however, are not always a matter of mass movements alone. Significant individuals who break patterns are sometimes equally important. In early 1837 the aged Dr. Ezra Ripley, Emerson's grandfather, received an assistant who was ordained in Concord in February: the Reverend Barzillai Frost. Emerson was among the ministers seated on the dais during Frost's ordination. The charge was delivered by the Rev. Henry Ware, Jr., a Harvard professor—also a Unitarian—and very eminent.

The Reverend Caleb Stetson delivered an address as well. But Stetson was also a member of Hedge's "Transcendentalist Club," and he kept whispering jokes to Emerson, who found them delicious.[8]

Frost was hardly as eminent as these dignitaries. Emerson referred to him in his journal as the "young" minister, although he was only one year younger than Waldo. He came from poverty, managed to get to Harvard after a considerable struggle, and graduated late, at thirty-one. He was elected, as Emerson had been, to the Concord school committee, he had a list of three hundred parish families to call on, and was obliged to do nearly all the preaching. (Dr. Ripley was nearly blind —and nearly ninety.)

Emerson himself was preaching in East Lexington, on mornings, afternoons, and Sundays; and it was not until well into 1837 that he had a chance to attend the Concord church. At that time Reverend Frost baptized the infant Waldo, and also preached. Emerson was not pleased. "I cannot hear young men whose theological instruction is exclusively owed to Cambridge & to public institution," he wrote, "without feeling how much happier was my star . . ."[9] His aunt Mary would have enjoyed that; she had once been his star.

Emerson's journal contained many critical comments, but those on Frost were unique. He found Frost's sermons intensely annoying, and came back to that point repeatedly. He termed Frost's voice "a ragged half-screaming bass," and bemoaned his lack of originality. But if Frost was not a good preacher, he was a good pastor. "He was known as willing to talk anywhere . . . really outstanding in pastoral visits, as a presence to the sick . . . always cheerful, always healthy in mind." Frost was also active in the temperance and antislavery movements.

But Emerson disliked Frost. He once visited Frost's home and later wrote, "I looked over the few books . . . Priestly, Noyes, Rosenmuller, Joseph Allen & other Sunday School books . . . the dirty comfort of the farmer could easily seem preferable to the elegant poverty of the young clergyman . . ."[10]

Frost also offended Emerson by his faith: he believed in the Bible and in the miracles of Jesus. Emerson had disposed of such beliefs years before; had lectured in Boston that "If every man possesses . . . Transcendental Reason, the intuition of the absolute is possible for all, then the historical arguments for a particular revelation attested by miracles shrivels into triviality . . ."

As the heavy, somber New England winter enveloped them, Emerson's dislike of Frost blended into his dislike of their church. In February 1838 he gave up his agreement to serve as "stated supply" in East Lexington, and obtained the Reverend John Sullivan Dwight—another Unitarian—as his successor. In his journal he recorded the step, and added, significantly, that it cut "the last thread that bound him to that prized gown & band the symbols black & white of old & distant Judah."[11]

"Henceforth," he vowed, "perhaps I shall live by lecturing which promises to be good bread." *But he continued to preach,* while his journal castigated churches in general and Frost in particular. And it was while he was in this dark mood, of which the world was unaware, that he received an invitation to address the senior class of the Harvard Divinity School, "on the occasion of their entering the active Christian ministry."

He accepted, and filled in the time preceding the event by writing bitter comments on Frost in his journal—which even included insults to his grandfather, the Reverend Ezra Ripley. "Go hush, old man," he wrote, "whom years have taught no truth . . . Such Moabitish darkness, well typified in the perplexity about his glasses, reminded one of the squash-bugs who stupidly stare at you when you lift the rotten leaf of vines."[12] So much for glories of nature.

By summer Emerson finished his careful, painstaking efforts for the Divinity School address. It was composed, as always, of some new phrases but also of scraps and pieces used before: he was not a man to throw away a well-turned phrase when it did not fit the immediate need. When he needed a metaphor to describe "the poverty of our churches" he turned to his journal and his private remarks on Frost (who was never to know the extent of Emerson's antipathy).

The address itself was given on the second floor of Divinity Hall, with the pulpit at the north end facing a tiny class of six seniors and about one hundred Unitarian clergymen and guests. The room was packed. Waldo began with a long panegyric on Nature, "all reflecting One Mind or One Will," with new phrases but on a theme at least nine years old for him. Then he moved toward his definition of Jesus, whom he paraphrased as saying, "I am divine; through me God acts; through me, speaks" and went from there to say that this message had been misunderstood, distorted and into the "myth" of Christianity. Beneath the polished phrases lurked Emerson's own conception of the role of the preacher, and beneath that, his contempt for the Barzillai Frosts of the clergy.

He deplored a Christianity that "dwells, with noxious exaggeration about the *person* of Jesus." By then he had frozen the clergymen; the students, at first inclined to snicker, had grown still. Elizabeth Peabody was entranced; a newly ordained minister named Theodore Parker listened, wide-eyed, hanging on every word. Waldo went on to compare Jesus with Osiris and Apollo; Christianity was disdainfully placed amid a forest of pagan beliefs, and the audience was told to "dare to love God directly."[13]

He created a sensation, and a storm of reproach arose. Three hundred copies of the address were printed and distributed, as was customary. Emerson's grandfather, Reverend Ripley, was deeply disturbed; people began to link Emerson's name with atheism. *The Christian Examiner* rejected Emerson's doctrine, Princeton's *Biblical Repository* and also its *Review* traced the ideas to the Germans and the French Cousins, called the address an imitation of Carlyle, termed it "nonsense and impiety," and concluded that Emerson was an atheist. Pamphlets were issued, pro and con. To all outward indications the storm was brief, but that was deceptive. The spear had been aimed against the Unitarian clergy and its lingering vestiges of Christianity, and it had landed deep. Aunt Mary mourned that her favorite nephew had spoken "as though under the influence of a malign demon."[14] New England's intellectual life was shaken by a new schism.

Part III
THE CAST
ASSEMBLES

Chapter 24

By 1837 a depression had fastened its tentacles on the economy. President Martin Van Buren, told the people the government "was not established to give security . . . not intended to confer special favors on individuals or classes, or to create systems of agriculture, manufacture or trade."[1] Meanwhile trade shriveled, businesses went bankrupt, and banks fell like leaves before the winds of winter.

Banknotes, abruptly seen as worthless, were no longer accepted; loans were called, mortgages foreclosed; men began to barter. Lot prices that had soared to the sky fell below the surface of the earth; land was available everywhere for back taxes; construction on the Pennsylvania-Ohio Canal stopped. It was discovered that silkworms could not mature in the cold Ohio climate and the Franklin Silk Company, with its own elaborate money, vanished into chill air together with an army of other ambitious ventures.

John Brown moved his wife and children—there were now nine—to Hudson, Ohio and opened a small tannery on a farm in the town he knew so well. He had relatives there: his father, Owen Brown, brothers Oliver and Frederick, and numberless cousins. The tannery was a good center from which to barter; Brown's circumstances were still better than those of many others. But lawsuits flew after him, and settled, like so many crows of misfortune, right outside his doorstep.

The first of these suits was for the recovery of six thousand dollars Brown had obtained on a loan from the Western Reserve Bank of Warren. Brown couldn't pay, and judgments were obtained against his cosigners. Most of these men were as distressed as Brown, but one, Captain Heman Oviatt of Richfield, proved vulnerable to the extent of $5,260. Brown assured Oviatt he would turn over one of the other farms he had purchased—but he had not paid for the farm, did not own it, and Oviatt had to be satisfied with a "penal bond" of conveyance in which Brown promised to buy the property and turn it over. Oviatt, in other words, was given elaborate promises, while he was out more than five thousand dollars.[2]

Meanwhile seven more individuals and another bank entered suits against Brown. Haymaker, who had not been paid for his farm, not even when Brown obtained money from Seth Thompson, was threatening to sue—and so were those to whom Brown had sold Thompson's promissory notes.

In November 1838 Brown went east, to sell a herd of cattle that belonged to his father, friends, and neighbors. The cattle were taken to the firm of Wadsworth & Wells, buyers and sellers of livestock, in West Hartford, Connecticut. Brown apparently impressed Wadsworth & Wells as such a sagacious businessman that they made him a "partner"—a somewhat overblown term. Probably he told them that he could buy cattle for them in Ohio and drive them east; he would obtain a commission for his trouble. That would have been a good arrangement, and might have provided a fair livelihood in such terrible times.

But Brown had passed beyond the point where he could settle for a livelihood. He was loaded with debts and lawsuits, and it was a time when a debtor could be held in jail as long as a creditor was willing to pay one dollar a day for the expense. There were some men willing to pay that price for revenge.

Brown's most immediate concern, in terms of his obligations, was a farm property called Westlands. He still owed five thousand dollars on it. But he had already promised Captain Oviatt that he would make that final payment and turn Westlands over to him. That would have been a handsome settlement, but Brown did not want to lose the property. He did not want to lose any of the land he had pyramided. He had seen the lure of the big strike; it was to never leave his mind again.

He was so firm in that vision that he went to New York City and sought a large loan in several quarters, using his properties in Ohio as security. That was skirting the edge of legality—none of these properties was yet fully purchased—but the times were grim and men of all levels were seeking money. No doubt Brown was courteously received and just as courteously refused; each bank or financier would express deep regrets very softly, and suggest that some other quarters might be more receptive. Such conversations can almost give a desperate man the impression that he is actually conducting business.

Finding the doors of New York locked and bolted, Brown returned to Connecticut where he paused at Torrington, his birthplace and scene of his early childhood. Years later his visit was recalled by Henry B. Carrington, a Union general, who remembered that Brown spoke on abolition.[3] That fit, also. There are few devices that soothe a wounded ego better than allegiance to a noble cause—especially an allegiance that costs nothing to express.

Then he scurried to Boston, and searched out a financier he had known in Ohio; that individual had invested and apparently withdrawn in time. This visit, too, was later remembered for Brown inundated several businessmen of the city with letters. Finally he went back to West Hartford and actually bought some sheep—both ewes and rams —of "pure Saxony blood."

During all these activities he sent a deluge of pious letters to his family—now increased, by a new baby, to ten children—telling them of the possibility of a large loan from a Boston magnate. Similar letters went to Seth Thompson and, no doubt, to others. Where Brown got the money to buy the sheep remains a mystery, but he had negotiated the sale of his father's and his neighbor's cattle. Perhaps his commission was enough; perhaps he kept his father's share of the sale. In any event, he returned to Ohio with twenty-two ewes and ten rams, and talked about large sums of money that he expected very soon.

In March 1839 Brown again headed east and drove one hundred herd of cattle to Wadsworth & Wells in West Hartford. This time his status had improved with these men. His letters to his family breathed optimism and piety; toward the end of May he wrote Seth Thompson that he had been busy but would soon go to Boston to obtain the fabled loan.

Apparently he went to some other places as well, however, for he stopped at the New England Woollen Company in Rockville, Connecticut, and obtained $2,800 to buy wool for the firm.[4] That was not enough to solve his problems; the commission from such a purchase, even if shrewdly made, would not appreciably change his situation. But at that point he somehow contrived to steal $5,500 from Wadsworth & Wells.[5]

When the partners discovered the theft two days later, they threatened arrest, and Brown gave them the $2,800 he had obtained from the New England Woollen Company.[6] How he managed to convince them that he would return the rest remains a mystery; but the scene must have been painful for all involved.

Then John Brown returned to Ohio, where he had already mailed in the last five thousand dollar payment for the Westlands property. When he arrived home he went to the county recorder's office and registered the land in his own name,[7] breaking his pledged word to Oviatt, who had befriended him.

In early 1836 a book appeared under the auspices of the American Antislavery Society, entitled *Emancipation in the West Indies*. Based on data mostly by James A. Thome, one of Weld's holy abolition band, and rigorously rewritten by the leader, it argued that gradual emancipation and apprenticeship had been frustrated by the white planters, but that immediate emancipation, as in Antigua, had produced remarkable and peaceful results.

The success of the book was instantaneous; abolitionists purchased and circulated huge numbers. And the book presaged new tactics by the society. These were essential, for the Tappans' business was melting in the depression like snow in summer, and it was no longer possible to keep the seventy agents on the payroll. After a reorganization, the society was headed by James G. Birney, while H. B. Stanton from Lane, Elizur Wright, Joshua Leavitt, and Theodore Weld served as a permanent nucleus.

The above mentioned campaign tactic that emerged, rather than developed, was the use of petitions. The British Parliament, when confronted with a similar effort, had disposed of these with cool efficiency by categorizing them as either public or private. Private petitions were presented to individual members of Parliament. Public petitions went to a committee that kept records of their purpose and the number of their signatures, and presented periodic reports to the full body. That separated propaganda from grievance without violating the rights of citizens.

But the Congress of the United States no longer looked beyond the borders of the nation for guidance, inspiration, or even food for thought. The abolitionists' petitions were, of course, mainly public petitions, agitating for social change. The Southerners viewed them as conspiratorial; all or nearly all, Congressmen regarded them as threats to the parliamentary process, because if each were received, read, and discussed, no other business could be transacted. The gag rule seemed the only way to stop the flood. But as the petitions mounted and pressures against the gag increased, Southerners were accused of violating constitutional rights.

One who insisted on this point was seventy-year-old Congressman John Quincy Adams, who was nearly irrepressible in debate, and who insisted on discussing petitions. Calhoun hated him, and called him "a mischievous bad old man,"[8] and that opinion was shared by many. Adams also hated Calhoun—as well as most of the other senators and representatives. And yet, amazingly, the contest between the obdurate old man and all the others seemed nearly equal.

Adams was further determined that the subject of slavery would be neither smothered nor ignored. He devised strategems to insert this subject into debate, but he kept his distance from the abolitionist movement, fearing that the odium it aroused would destroy his political position. Abolition was not, in the late 1830's, a popular position.

Although gagged, the petition campaign—as it spread among the chapters and communities planted by Weld and the seventy, and in New England by Garrison and his followers—was accomplishing a silent revolution in an unexpected and unprecedented source of support: women.

The Antislavery Society had over a thousand chapters and over one hundred thousand members. These were dotted through upstate New York, New England, northern Ohio, Pennsylvania, and west across Michigan and Illinois.[9] Its volunteers made paid agents unnecessary, and women joined the chapters to assist in gathering petition names in increasing numbers. A decade before, only Quakers allowed women to speak at mixed meetings; the great revival had opened its religious gatherings to women, and Antislavery was now breaking down the sex barrier in politics.

Two women who became famous in these efforts were the Grimké sisters of Charleston, South Carolina. They came from a family that was not only prominent for its slaveholdings but known for its eccentricity. Sarah Grimké, the older sister, became a Quaker in Philadelphia, and Angelina followed in Sarah's path. When they issued a tract against slavery that outraged their family, city, state, and region, the sisters went north to attend Weld's training course.

Weld was, as usual, at the center of the wheel. He slept in a garret in the black district of New York and wore the cheap clothes of a workingman. He had neither a title nor salary, and drew only minimal expenses.[10] Yet he was the leader of the society; he knew it—and so did the others.

Daguerreotypes show the Grimkés grim and unattractive, but all who knew them were convinced of their beauty and charm. Angelina soon fell in love with Weld, whose dedication did not permit him to realize this—nor to realize, for some time, that he too was in love.

The Grimkés left for Massachusetts where Garrison arranged a lecture tour for them. It shocked the clergy and created a sensation. Newspapers reported the sisters' progress; arguments raged about the proper role of women and Weld frowned as Angelina and Sarah parroted Garrison's anarchic doctrines, which declared that only he and his followers properly served God.

Weld's letters to Angelina were highly critical; hers to him were gentle. Eventually he confessed his love, and the sisters returned to New York. Weld found a house in Fort Lee, New Jersey, on the South side of the Hudson across from New York City; Sarah would live with them. Angelina and Weld were married in May 1838. Many notables of the movement and its branches attended the wedding. Garrison was there—tall, bald, his glasses glittering, urbane as ever on a social occasion. Also present was Gerrit Smith—a massive figure with hair hanging over a "Byronic" collar, with large eyes and a mellow voice. Blacks attended as well; two were former slaves of the Grimké family. The ceremony was Quaker with no set words or form; the bride and groom spoke for themselves; each renounced "rights" in each other and the clergymen—both black and white—led everyone in hopeful prayers.[11]

It was, for those untroubled by the depression, a high-minded time. And it was Emerson's good fortune at the end of 1837, to receive the balance of his inheritance from his first wife's estate. This placed him in an independent position—and added a gloss to the growing popularity of his lectures, which began to lift his reputation to the point where Horace Mann, usually an acid critic, said Emerson was "to human life what Newton's Principia was to mathematics."[12]

Other individuals were far less amiable as general conditions worsened. The acerbic Garrison attacked Channing and other New England notables for what he perceived as their derelictions, and launched a raid against the American Peace Society. That succeeded in driving the society's clergymen from their own rented hall, and to the creation of a Non Resistance-Society, bound to "the laws of a kingdom which is not of this world."[13]

Even the enormously wealthy Gerrit Smith felt the pinch of the times: his creditors owed him six hundred thousand dollars but he could not collect enough to pay his own enormous debt to John Jacob Astor, his father's old partner. Troubled, as always, by a variety of minor ailments, the magnate vented his discontent in a series of public attacks on several public figures, including even the Reverend Jonathan Blanchard, a cold-water fanatic who was also zealous in every possible Goodness cause.

Amid rent riots and other depression upheavals, some surprising figures fell from financial heights. The Tappan brothers lost their fortune and the societies they funded fell on hard times. The Reverend Charles Finney and his family almost starved in 1837, and Oberlin College had to be sold to Baptists.

As usual during economic collapses, a great many turned toward utopian ventures; the Reverend John Humphrey Noyes, a Dartmouth graduate, began to organize toward a perfect society and was to have a lasting, though largely unacknowledged, influence on American thought. Another such figure was the Reverend William Miller, originally a Baptist, who began to convince some people that the end of the world was at hand.

That event, prophesied in Revelation, had long been considered by Christian theologians to be due only after a thousand Edenic years, the Second Coming, the Final Judgement, the ascent of saints and the descent of sinners. Miller, after years of labor, somehow reversed the sequence, and came to believe there would be a Second Coming first, then a Day of Judgement, the ascent and descent, and a thousand years of Eden. It did not occur to him to wonder who would be left after the Judgement to enjoy that Eden. His confusion, however, left a jangling argument between the traditional post-millennialists, who retained the biblical version, and the pre-millennialists. The dispute continues to this day.

At first Reverend Miller's calculations were of interest to a mere handful. Then the Reverend Joshua Himes, of the Chardon Street Chapel in Boston—a Unitarian, evangelist, temperance zealot and Garrisonian—was attracted to the new theory.[14] Reverend Himes began to call attention to Reverend Miller's prophecy about the end of the world. By November 1839 Himes and some other evangelists somehow obtained "the world's largest tent" and launched a revival, using Miller's dire prediction as a rallying cry.

The response, in troubled times, was phenomenal—perhaps because many longed to leave such a difficult world. The end-of-the-world movement began, to general amazement, and some individuals even began to dispose of their possessions in anticipation. One, Mary Cragin, wrote John Noyes, saying, "My dear husband one week since entered the kingdom . . . Bless the Lord, in the first week of December he will be without money and without business . . . How this rejoices me. We shall stand still and see the Lord provide . . ."[16]

That was in the last week of November 1839. It sounded an appropriate note amid tremors that shook the institutions of religion, law, and finance, as the nation slid into the 1840's.

Chapter 25

After recording Westlands in his own name, John Brown mortgaged the property, and raised some immediate cash—again without telling Heman Oviatt. He also fended off an executive of the New England Woolen Company, who had learned his $2,800 had not gone to buy wool, but to buy off a threat of arrest by Wadsworth & Wells. Brown's letters to this man pleaded expectations of a large loan, the temporary nature of the misuse of the money, and many promises to repay the sum, in time. The response drew attention to Brown's vaunted antislavery opinions, and the disparity between such noble sentiments and Brown's behavior. That drew indignation, and more promises.

Owen Brown, his father, sought to save him from complete disaster. The elder Brown was a trustee of Oberlin College—itself strapped for funds—and knew that the college owned a tract of land in Virginia from a donation by Gerrit Smith. In early April 1840, therefore, John Brown appeared before the Oberlin board of trustees and offered to survey and buy some of that land. What he planned to use for money remains unknown, but perhaps he had acquired land so easily during the boom that he thought boom conditions still prevailed, or would soon return.

In any event he emerged from Oberlin with a contract to survey the Virginia property for one dollar a day and his expenses. The college even provided some of the equipment he would need for the survey. Brown also saw the contract as a step toward a new home of his own. He wrote from Ripley, Virginia, to his wife and children that "I have seen the spot where, if it be the will of Providence, I hope one day to live with my family."[1] The college had agreed to let John Brown buy whatever thousand-acre lot he chose, at a nominal sum.

Brown, however, could not abandon the idea of the big strike. He continued to dream that work on the canal would resume, that he would sell his development, that he would keep his farms in Hudson and Westlands. Instead of surveying in Virginia and locating a new home, he let the assignment slide after a few preliminary trips, and returned to Hudson. There he resumed tanning, which provided a livelihood, and waited for the boom.

In July, 1840 a creditor—Daniel C. Gaylord—who had obtained a judgment of a little over two thousand dollars against him, obtained a court order to have Westlands sold to meet the payment. Brown was outraged, but on October 12, 1840, an auction was held, at which the only bidder obtained the property for approximately $1,600. That sum went to Gaylord, of course: the land went to Amos Chamberlain, a neighbor of Brown's, whom he had known since his youth.

131

Brown believed this was illegal, that he had been cheated, and swore he would launch a "tedious, distressing, wasting and long protracted war." He seems to have thought of himself as similar to a sovereign state, from which property could not be taken without force. His three older sons—John, Jr., nineteen, Jason, seventeen, and Owen, sixteen —were pressed into immediate service as an army, and dispatched to an old log cabin on the property, to repel invaders. When Amos Chamberlain and *his* sons appeared, Brown called out that Chamberlain would be shot if he put his head inside the cabin.

In due course this delirium brought a constable and his posse, to whom the Browns showed their guns. The constable retreated, but the sheriff of Portage County and his posse arrived later. Brown was at work in his tannery, and Jason had sense enough to run. But John, Jr. and Owen were arrested, and their father rounded up a little later. All three spent the night in the Akron jail. That ended Brown's first "war," but fueled his sense of the burning injustice of government.[2]

Meanwhile Levi Burnell of Oberlin wrote John Brown about the Virginia land and, receiving no reply, wrote John's father, Owen The New England Woolen Company also asked about the $2,800; Brown later said he hadn't the money to pay for postage to reply. The winter of 1840 wore on, and early in 1841 Brown finally wrote Burnell that he would accept "a thousand acres of land in a body that will include a living spring of water discharging itself at a heighth sufficient to accommodate a tannery."

By that time the Oberlin trustees were tired of John Brown, and wrote him a letter saying they had changed their minds. His response was, predictably, aggrieved: if "Providence intends to defeat my plans there is no doubt the best of reasons for it." In other words, he blamed God. A little later he wrote demanding thirty dollars, in payment of which he would "consider the institution discharged of any further obligation."[3]

Meanwhile he tanned on his Hudson property, his family swelled, and his creditors fumed. But Brown was in a plight shared by many men in those years; it was recognized that nobody could raise money in jail, and the courts were slow. Suits and judgments were discussed in legal chambers, and Brown had a facility for argument; there is no doubt he delayed many settlements by arguing their grounds. Nevertheless the mills operated by the lawyers ground away; eventually twenty-one lawsuits against Brown were filed. The wearisome details of these occupied him—on and off—until 1845, and their disposition, as is usual in such cases, was almost always far from the expectations of the creditors.

How John Brown persuaded Heman Oviatt to trust him again remains a puzzle; perhaps he had convinced him that all their troubles flowed from the failed promises of the mysterious Boston financier who had promised to lend Brown enough money to tide them all over. In any event, Oviatt had a large herd of sheep, and Brown talked himself into a working partnership in the sheep business. Captain

Oviatt, it was agreed, would buy the sheep; Brown would tend them at Richfield, Ohio.

The arrangement was reached some time in 1841, but Brown still lived in Hudson, worked the tannery and struggled over his lawsuits. He was saved from what would once have been a lifelong pit by the new federal bankruptcy laws, which enabled him to get rid of his pursuers by letting go of his remaining possessions. No objections being raised, the Brown family farm, furniture, and livestock was sold at public auction. The court allowed the Browns to retain some of their belongings, including eleven Bibles, two horses, two hogs, ten hens, two cows, some furniture, tools, and clothing. Then, an official bankrupt, but legally free of debt in 1842, he, his silent wife, and their twelve children moved to Richfield, where John Brown would launch a new, equally astonishing career in sheep.

In their establishment at Fort Lee, New Jersey, Theodore Weld, his wife Angelina, and her sister Sarah followed the famous Graham Diet, based on whole wheat flour, which the health leader, Sylvester Graham surrounded with many less sensible doctrines.[4] It was Angelina's custom to cook a week's supply of food in one day, which they ate cold through the week.

All three worked on a huge project Weld had conceived after a troubling conversation with his friend James A. Thome about slavery. Weld wanted to know what terrible scenes of cruelty Thome had personally seen, but Thome, who was from Kentucky, said he had heard of atrocities, but did not know of any personally. They were, he added, rare to his personal experience—though he was sure they were numerous.

That sent Weld to the New York Commercial Reading Room, which subscribed to many Southern newspapers, selling them for waste at the end of every month. Weld arranged to buy these, and he, his wife, and Sarah began to cull them, cutting out advertisements for runaway slaves and details of "whippings & shootings & brandings."[5] For six months the sisters searched through the papers gathering raw material, and the results were *Slavery As It Is.*

Culled from over twenty thousand papers, the indictment—for it was just that—presented one atrocity after another with all the force of fact. It was, of course, a one-sided and an incomplete picture of the condition of millions, as misleading as a compilation of arrest records and court cases would be in depicting the entire life of a nation. Had Weld and his two devoted helpers collected these dreadful tragedies for commercial purposes they would have earned a fortune, but such a thought would have appalled them. Publication was delayed because the American Antislavery Society was in bad financial and organizational straits.[6] In part this was due to the depression, but even more to the recoil of the Presbyterian Church from the excesses of the Philanthropic societies: that once mighty conglomerate of Goodness that the church had supported.

Nevertheless there was still an organization in New York, and *Slavery As It Is,* priced at 37½ cents sold over 22,000 copies in its first four months. At the end of a year over 100,000 copies were in circulation, and it sold in England as well. Reviewers in the North were ecstatic. Charles Dickens' chapter on slavery in *American Notes* in 1842 was based on *Slavery As It Is.* Until *Uncle Tom's Cabin* it was the most influential popular book on slavery in the land—and *Uncle Tom's Cabin* was also based on it.[7]

It led, also, to another and very important project. When Charles Stuart, Weld's mentor, discussed the book in England, some questions about the impact of slavery in the North arose. The society, apprised of this, authorized Weld to hire some assistants who gathered material that would later be useful as background in lobbying.

For the leaders had finally realized that their organizing, their propaganda, and their mass meetings were largely exercises in futility. The South barred their propaganda, the North reacted with violence, and they had not, despite millions of words, conceived of any coherent or practical way to end slavery in the United States. John Quincy Adams was right in terming the antislavery movement a large but misdirected effort.

One New York leader, James Birney, went so far as to appeal to William Ellery Channing in Boston for advice, but the famous Unitarian leader was, himself, surrounded by quarrels. The youthful Reverend Theodore Parker, who had a nearly incredible gift for learning to read and write different languages, had attended the Harvard Divinity School during the controversies of the 1830's and emerged to join the fray toward the end of the decade. Parker had entered the school as a devout Christian and emerged an ardent follower of the new German scholars and their skeptical theories.[8]

Obtaining a pastorate in West Roxbury, in the very heart of the Transcendentalists, with the Reverend Convers Francis as his first mentor and Waldo Emerson as one of his tallest idols, Parker also admired Dr. Channing and his theories. Two groups attracted him: one was called the "Friends of Dr. Channing," the other "Hedge's Transcendentalist Club." Both involved the same overlapping personalities; both were devoted to lofty discussions, and both were against the old-school Unitarians, those once-daring clergymen whose break with Calvinism had alarmed the orthodox, and who were now considered too traditional for the "ultras."

A prodigious worker, Parker published a weighty and unreadable tome on de Wette, a German scholar, and a series of labored reviews on other foreign theologians. He drew special attention in a favorable review of David Friederich Strauss' *Life of Jesus,* a book in which the author saw "nothing but myths" in the heart of the Christian doctrine.[9]

Orthodox protests reverberated from Princeton. At their forefront was the Reverend Andrews Norton, a Unitarian who had once led a revolt against Calvinism but had no intention of leading one against all Christianity. Many New England clergymen began to grow alarmed. They had good reason. By stages the Unitarian vanguard was headed toward the dissolution of the faith.

A Berry Street conference of ministers was held to decide whether clergymen who broke with all the tenets of Christianity should be "excluded," but this came to nothing, because the New England churches had no formal doctrine, no bishops—and lacking both fixed standards and higher authorities—neither basis nor authority to discipline or eject heretics. Parker—who was well aware that his own declarations were in part responsible for the conference—attended but was, unwontedly, silent. Later he raged in his journal: "This is the 19th century! This is Boston!" He seemed to think both those facts somehow released all the Unitarians from historic precedents.

The transcendentalists were also busy. The Reverend George Ripley, who had engaged Reverend Norton in voluminous polemics, Margaret Fuller, Bronson Alcott, the Rev. William Henry Channing (related to William Ellery), the Reverend Orestes Brownson, and Ralph Waldo Emerson, who had dropped his "Reverend" and also stopped going to church, launched *The Dial.*

When it finally appeared, Emerson disclaimed responsibility for it. The first issue carried some of his poems; with a few outstanding exceptions, they were efforts to rhyme prose, scraps from his dead brothers, Charles and Edward, some poems by Thoreau and some effusions by Alcott entitled "Orphic Sayings." These gave delight to skeptics: "Men shall become Gods . . . the voice of the private, not popular heart, is alone authentic . . ." Carlyle, who received a copy, wrote Emerson that it was "too ethereal" for his taste, and Emerson's apologies were almost abject.[10]

Meanwhile Brownson, the most original and independent mind among the Unitarians, issued—in his *Boston Quarterly Review*— a discussion of the "masses versus property, the Democratic Party" and "the laboring classes." The national depression, it was true, had by no means ended, but overall the United States was still remarkably prosperous compared to other countries. Brownson, however, saw decay on all sides and blamed these ills on "inequality of wealth." This was a new note and a highly significant one; he went on to attack priests and religions; they were meaningless, he said, unless they affected conditions. He concluded that the only way to "get rid of . . . evils is to change the system." From there he proceeded to declare that "banks and privilege" should be destroyed by "the use of physical force."[11]

That was startling enough to create a storm. The Whigs pounced on the article and circulated it as an exposé of the real designs of Democratic party supporters. Theodore Parker, hearing a new trumpet call, was elated and enthusiastic; Channing, who rose to every wind of change, gave two lectures "On the Elevation of the Laboring Classes."

In New York the American Antislavery Society met early in 1840 and virtually dissolved after issuing an appeal for its once far-flung chapters to pay its debts. The chapters rallied, and plans were made for a final convention in May. Garrison, who had long considered himself the nation's only real antislavery leader, attended with a boatload of followers, seized control of the name, and made himself master of the relic—though it was hardly worth the effort.

The fact was that the tides had moved beyond the society; reformers were turning toward the political arena and away from the churches. At Warsaw in upstate New York, Gerrit Smith and other abolitionists met and organized a Liberty party, with Weld's convert James G. Birney—who had married a sister of Mrs. Gerrit Smith—as nominee for the presidency of the United States. The new organization created instant disagreements among reformer cadres, with some believing it would siphon votes from Whigs or Democrat friends, others insisting that only a "pure" party could field the right candidates.

Most people paid no attention to any of these maneuvers, arguments, and schisms; the presidential campaign of 1840 was, in the words of historian Herbert Agar, "absurd."[12] The Whig leadership selected William Henry Harrison, an elderly Virginian of distinguished ancestry who had risen to the rank of major general in the War of 1812, had been a representative and a senator, minister to Colombia, and then faded to diminuendo as a farmer and court clerk. In 1836, at the age of sixty-three he had seemed fit only for the pasture when he was nominated. And he had lost to Van Buren. After four years of depression, however, Harrison seemed good enough to run again in 1840—even at sixty-seven. His running-mate in both years was another Virginian, John Tyler, who had fought Jackson on the bank, on nullification, and the tariff, and was therefore considered "an honorary Whig."[13]

Van Buren, of course, ran again, though to all observers he appeared doomed. American presidents always run again—or always want to run again, no matter how miserable their tenure in office. But the Whig campaign managers transformed Harrison into a military hero of the Jackson type, linking him to log cabins and hard cider. They also portrayed Van Buren—the son of a tavern keeper—who had struggled to the top through sheer wit and nerve, as a perfumed fop, aloof and aristocratic. This "lying, diverting and irrelevant" campaign carried the day in a carnival atmosphere whipped into spurious life for the occasion. "Tippecanoe and Tyler, Too" entered the top posts in early 1841. Unfortunately the canoe tipped quickly; Harrison died within a month of his inauguration, and the nation had President John Tyler, an unknown quantity, to assess.

With the great majority belonging to either the Democratic or Whig parties, it seemed absurd that the tiny Liberty party, which received only seven thousand votes—.03% of the total—could make any difference. It was, however, a party of ideas, and some of the ideas were being expressed by that spiritual but sensitive weathervane, William

Ellery Channing, in May 1841, only a month after Harrison's death.

Speaking at the Mercantile Library Company, Channing wondered aloud how the French Revolution had originated, and then answered that question himself. ". . . it came," he said, "from the intolerable weight of misgovernment and tyranny, from the utter want of culture among the mass of the people, and from a corruption of the great too deep to be purged away except by destruction . . ."[14]

Chapter 26

The Five of Clubs was an informal group of upper-class Boston gentlemen—all bachelors—who enjoyed one another's company and conversation. Two members of the club, Henry Wadsworth Longfellow and Cornelius C. Felton, were Harvard professors; all were Harvard graduates. Another member was Charles Sumner, who had served as a protégé of Supreme Court Justice Joseph Story for several years, and who had also been, for a season, a social lion in London by virtue of some good introductions and consummately tactful behavior.

A diligent legal scholar but a poor courtroom lawyer, Sumner returned to Boston in 1840 to resume practice with George S. Hillard, another member of the club. For a time he echoed his European success by regaling Bostonians with anecdotes of high society abroad. Even Waldo Emerson, hearing of these marvelous tales, invited him to Concord and waited, expectantly. He was disappointed, however, and later said "his talkative countryman" had "brought nothing home but names, dates and prefaces."[1]

Sumner, who had been virtually ignored before his European success, was equally tart. He pretended, as was fashionable, not to understand what transcendentalism meant, and said "the great mystagogue" did not produce "his winged griffins to take us into the Empyrean."[2]

Others were not as critical as Emerson, and Sumner found himself accepted on Beacon Hill, invited to various mansions to meet the historian William Prescott, Daniel Webster, and other luminaries. He also became a sort of unofficial social greeter for eminent foreigners. George Ticknor, who had launched Boston intellectuals on their discoveries of German scholarship, and who was the grandest of all social figures, liked Sumner—and so did Dr. Samuel Gridley Howe—who at that time may have been not just the most famous physician in New England but in the world.

Howe was ten years older than Sumner—who was a little over thirty

—but he too was a bachelor with time to spare. He was also a heroic Boston figure; for his exploits during the Greek War of Independence in the 1820's, when he was fresh from Harvard Medical School, the King of Greece had made him a Chevalier of the Order of St. Savior. His book describing the war and the Greeks had added to his stature. Howe also knew Lafayette, and he had been in Paris during the revolution of July 1830, when Louis Philippe was made "citizen king." In that same year, Howe had been imprisoned in Berlin by the Prussians for his work among Polish refugees in their uprising.

All this was astonishing enough, but Dr. Howe's greater worldwide fame came from his work with the blind, the deaf, and the mute at the Perkins Institution—an establishment he had made famous. Dr. Howe had found ways to teach the blind to read, write, to play musical instruments, and make themselves self-supporting. His greatest exploit was in reaching a blind, deaf, mute girl named Laura Bridgeman —and after her, others so terribly handicapped that until he proved otherwise, the legal opinion was that such unfortunates were barely human.[3] Ordinarily his accomplishment would have earned Dr. Howe fame in medical and legal circles, but not in the greater world, which is notoriously indifferent to the handicapped. But Howe's breakthrough came at a time when intellectuals were turning from the theories of Locke that man's senses were his means to comprehend God, and toward the ideas of Germans, who regarded intuition as superior to reason. To this rising school, Howe seemed to have physically disproven Locke and verified Kant. Therefore Howe moved in a nimbus of liberal and avant-garde approval, by virtue both of his experience as a successful revolutionary and as a medical innovator whose successes were not only along reformist lines, but were held to have deep societal and even philosophic implications. All this was enhanced by the doctor's tall, athletic presence, which made him seem younger than his forty years.

Sumner clung to Howe, and Howe—whose pride and thin-skinned lack of humor was well-known—developed a great fondness for the young lawyer. When Sumner stayed over, "they left the door between their rooms open, so that they could continue their conversation into the drowsy hours."[4]

It was during these days, when the Five of Clubs began to look more like a deuce, that Julia Ward and her sisters Louisa and Annie arrived from New York to spend a summer in the Boston environs. Very well known in New York society, where they were called "the Three Graces of Bond Street," the sisters were wealthy, beautiful, young, and unmarried. They came to spend a quiet summer, because their father and their brother Henry had both recently died. But that did not preclude visitors. Henry Wadsworth Longfellow (who was in fact short) appeared at once; Sam Ward, the eldest of the Ward children, was not only Longfellow's New York agent but a close friend.

Longfellow—nicknamed Longo—brought Charles Sumner along.

Sumner was dazzled. Although he found all the sisters remarkable, the red-haired, creamy-complexioned Julia outshone the rest. Sumner, who shied from women and was usually tongue-tied in their presence, unbent remarkably.

On one visit, Julia Ward expressed curiosity about Dr. Howe's famous Perkins Institution and Laura Bridgeman, so Sumner hired a horse and carriage. They arrived at the establishment—formerly a hotel, with a huge lobby from which corridors radiated out to various wings—to find that Howe was not in, but was expected. They waited, and Julia watched blind children running rapidly up and down the long steps, their fingers barely touching the railings. Some were deformed as well as blind, and she turned her head away. A little later she, Longo, and Sumner met Laura Bridgeman; who was thirteen and wore a green ribbon around her eyes. Laura touched them lightly with her fingers, and while they marveled at her questions—communicated through her teacher—Sumner looked out the window. He had seen Laura Bridgeman before, and she had complained of him. "He is not gentle," she told her teacher, ". . . I do not love or like Sumner . . ."[5]

Sumner called Julia's attention to the window: Dr. Howe was galloping a horse across the open field toward them. She looked out: the sight was impressive. Howe was equally impressive when he walked in a little later: almost six feet tall, dark haired, walking with a spring in his step; clearly, he was the master of the Institution. Julia Ward later said she fell in love at once.[6]

Their courtship was leisurely, as was customary, and not without its storms. Her family was not pleased: he was famous but older, and had only his salary, while Julia was an heiress. But they married—after he signed a contract to leave her money untouched. That proved relatively meaningless, however, for Julia Ward Howe gave him all her money, as soon as she received it, throughout their married life. In doing that, she made him financially independent—a circumstance he took as his due.

It was assumed that Sumner would be similarly attracted—if not to Julia, then to one or the other of her beautiful sisters. For a time he told his friends that he had some thoughts in that direction. He paid court to both Louisa and Annie, but when matters threatened to grow serious he said, "I have no desire in that quarter."[7]

The activities of the socially elite, however, were of little interest to more strenuous seekers of Utopia. Theodore Parker, an anxious striver, puzzled over the secrets of success—and especially of the success of William Ellery Channing. If he "could be ground over again, and come out a young man of twenty-five," he wrote in his journal, "give all the results of his reading, experience, life, all the insight, power, eloquence, Christianity he now possesses, but let him hold the same opinions as now, and preach them as he does . . . and be unknown to fame . . . he could not find a place for the sole of his foot in Boston. . . ."[8] That sounded a note of envy and wonder: Parker was unknown and struggling; Channing, therefore, was a mystery to be closely watched.

Others felt similarly puzzled about the reverend doctor, whose manners were somewhat intimidating. Hedge said that Channing's "uncompromising honesty" made conversations with him difficult, and "to a young man especially, somewhat embarrassing. You missed those smooth insincerities . . . You made your statement; if he accepted it, it was well . . . if he rejected it, it was equally well . . . but the chances were that he would turn upon you that calm, clear eye, and annoy you with an awkward sense of frustration, as when one offers to shake hands, and no hand is given him in return."[9]

That sort of honesty spread far, with some startling results. Emerson was called to the door one day by a delegation of young men, one of whom greeted him with an amiable "Good morning, damn you, sir," while another added, "We are hell-fired glad to be here." Puzzled, Emerson asked about their language, and was told, "Well, damn you sir, we are of the "Newness" and we wish to demonstrate that profanity is not the use of vile language spoken calmly, but spoken to relieve harsh feelings, so we put an oath in each sentence."[10]

The "Newness," as even Emerson called it, had many facets. One was a movement to force the churches toward abolition, and failing that, to urge congregations to "come out." Several abolition churches were created, and Gerrit Smith, who announced he had principled objections to communion, à la Emerson, planned to launch one such church near Peterboro. Another was epitomized by Theodore Parker's article in *The Dial* in midsummer 1840, claiming that "God will create a soul yet larger and nobler than Jesus," to lead the way "to a more perfect religion . . ."[11] That and similar effusions created such an uproar that other ministers refused to exchange pulpits with Parker; by the end of the year, Parker was defiant but self-pitying.

Meanwhile the Garrisonian reformers held a convention which was attended, said Emerson, by "Madmen, madwomen, men with beards, Dunkers, Muggletonians, come-outers, Groaners, Agrarians, Seventh-Day Adventists, Quakers, Abolitionists, Calvinists, Unitarians and Philosophers . . . to hide, or pray, or preach, or protest."[12] That gathering was called by the "Friends of Universal Reform": persons who disagreed on some of the specific errors of the world, but agreed that it was askew.

It was almost inevitable that these movements to improve society at large would also develop clusters to create perfect societies in miniature; oases of perfection; examples of how goodness could work away from an evil world. George Ripley, pastor of the Purchase Street Church in Boston, sold his fine library (to Theodore Parker) and, with some others, bought land at West Roxbury to launch Brook Farm in 1841. Reverend Ripley's intention was to show the world how to "escape the tyranny of the machine." There, artists and intellectuals would combine to farm, discuss, and create—and avoid the tides of industrialization that ordinary men worked to build.

The effort was praised by the transcendentalists in *The Dial;* (Ripley was a founder of that publication), but they were disappointed when Emerson, whose support was sought, wrote, "It seems to me a circuitous and operose [laborious] way of relieving myself of irksome circumstances, to put on your community the task of my emancipation which I ought to take on myself." He was less oblique in his journal, where he wrote that the scheme was "a room in the Astor House hired for the Transcendentalists."[13]

The fact was that Brook Farm, for all its idealism, was also an effort to escape the economic depression and its attendant worries, and offered more to some—like Nathaniel Hawthorne, who was poor—than it did to the financially secure lecturer at Concord. There was also the fact that Emerson had already tried his own society in miniature at Coolidge Castle, where the cook, maid, the penniless Alcotts, and the Emersons all tried "Liberty, Equality and common table."[14] That effort collapsed in general confusion. The Sage of Concord was, therefore, one up on the Brook Farmers, having discovered limits to communal living on his own—and having settled for a conventional household, with young Henry Thoreau as a working boarder.

Although Brook Farm received an inordinate amount of attention, thanks to the literary efforts of its founders, friends, and visitors, other Utopian settlements also began to appear. Typical was Hopedale, in Worcester County, Massachusetts, headed by the Reverend Adin Balou, who sought to create "a miniature Christian republic."

With these splinters breaking away from the churches in the direction of inner and cloistered reforms, the Liberty party fiasco drained away the remaining funds of the political abolitionists. Only Joshua Leavitt persevered. In Washington in early 1841, where he saw mounds of forgotten petitions piled in the corridors of Congress, Leavitt began to talk to Congressmen Joshua Giddings, William Slade, Seth M. Gates, and other antislavery politicians.

Forming what they called a "select committee on slavery," the congressmen plotted, through the winter of 1841, to introduce the subject of slavery whenever larger issues, such as the admission of Texas or the annexation of Florida were discussed. On such occasions a special speech would be prepared, delivered, printed, and circulated through the North by the abolitionists. But the congressmen lacked the time and the resources to research such material; a lobby was needed. The abolition leaders in New York issued an appeal for funds, to no avail, and the congressmen themselves put up some cash, rented rooms near the Capitol, and hired Theodore Weld.[15]

The practicality of the project thrilled Weld; and so did the anonymity of his task. He went to Washington and assessed the antislavery congressmen. Giddings of Ohio, one of his own converts, was the most outstanding. But all of the group were "professors of religion,"—openly religious, in the old sense—and five were elders in the Presbyterian church. Several were "revival men." All were products of Finney's "Great Revival" and/or Weld's abolition crusade.

Weld moved into Mrs. Spriggs' boardinghouse (it came to be known as "Abolition House") and the congressmen soon followed. Joshua Leavitt then took Weld to meet John Quincy Adams—a second cousin of Weld's father. A great polymath whose career was a marvel in itself, the former President not only joined the "select committee" but made himself its spokesman. He was a New Englander who considered Boston the proper center of the nation, and who, far better than his young associates, could appreciate how antislavery could become the lever to destroy Southern political power.

An American coastal vessel *Creole,* gave Adams and his followers an ideal opportunity to launch their campaign. *Creole* had been seized by black slave mutineers and taken to the Bahamas, where British authorities held them and the ship until they could clarify the legal aspect of the seizure. Did the high seas lift the laws of the United States regarding slavery? Or did the laws of Louisiana, where *Creole* was bound, prevail?

While that case was being prepared, Adams discovered a petition to remove him from the House Foreign Relations Committee and asked permission to defend himself. Permission having been granted, he launched into a tirade against slavery, and set the House into an uproar. Southerners were furious, the Whig leadership enraged. A caucus of leaders decided Adams should be censured at the first opportunity—which was not delayed.[16] Weld called on Adams to offer his help, and it was accepted.

The debate occupied days, created newspaper headlines, and provided Adams a platform he used with consummate skill and—despite his seventy-five years—inexhaustible energy. The spectacle of the diminutive lion holding the pack at bay was far too much for the party leaders; the motion to censure was tabled, as Adams had correctly foreseen, and antislavery had penetrated deeply into Congress. A few days later Giddings presented a petition for the *dissolution of the Union* (italics added) and used Adams' words, but without the same deep reaction. Giddings then presented a petition to open the *Creole* case and was censured. He immediately resigned, went home, and stood for reelection. The Whig leadership seemed to have won, but Giddings' district was in the Western Reserve—territory that Weld and others had thoroughly evangelized. He was reelected with a huge majority and returned, free to flout the leadership whenever and however he chose.

More to the point, all abolitionists in the House could now speak freely against slavery. The long compromise between Northern and Southern politicians was ended. Abolitionists inside the castle of government had opened a door for others to enter.

While touring upper New England in 1842, William Ellery Channing fell to one of the scourges of the time: typhoid fever, which stemmed from lack of proper sewers and sanitation. He died in a country inn at Bennington, Vermont.

He was buried in Mount Auburn Cemetery, while "the bells of the Catholic cathedral toiled, as for the passing of a saint," and eulogies welled from dozens of pulpits and appeared, black-bordered, in newspapers.[17] At least fourteen sermons on the meaning of his life were printed in the United States, thirteen in the United Kingdom. James Russell Lowell and John Greenleaf Whittier wrote poetical tributes and publishers began to collect Channing's works. His passing was internationally noted; he had corresponded with persons in many countries; Queen Victoria liked his writings and he was well known in Germany, France, Hungary, and Spain. His reputation was that of a devout Christian. But he had not believed in the Trinity, or that "omnipotence consisted of a power to alter the nature of things";[18] in the course of his life he had steadily discarded the entire Christian doctrine. In a most peculiar way, his life was a triumph of fashion over substance, but Emerson, years later, said, "He was our Bishop."

John Brown began life over again in Richfield, Ohio, a hamlet in Summit County not far from Akron. In October 1842 he was so humbled that he appeared before a justice of the peace, admitted his theft of $2,800 from the New England Woolen Company, and vowed to repay it. Twelve days later, his conscience still unappeased, he appeared again, pledging by affidavit to repay $5,667.96 to Captain Oviatt.[19]

Both these actions indicated a resolution to lead a new life, and John Brown now began applying himself to the sort of tasks for which he was competent. He opened a small tannery which thrived in a small way, and made an intensive study of sheep. He gradually came to be known for his expertise on these animals.

Tending sheep had a biblical significance for some; John Brown seemed to relish a job that most men found distasteful.[20] Perhaps it fed his image of himself as a patriarch; after all, he had twelve children ranging in age from twenty-two years to less than one year.

He ruled this brood, and his wife, with an iron hand. Sundays were days of silence; whippings were frequent. John Brown would note misconduct and issue demerits, to be paid in strokes. He was, in that respect, not unusual: many men of the time were severe and controlled their children by the rod, as the Bible recommended. None of the Brown children ran away, and the family appears—like many large families—to have been closely and affectionately knit.

In September 1843, calamity struck. Four of the Brown children died: Sarah, nine, Charles, five, Peter, two, and Austin, nearly one. This was a heavy blow to the parents. Nevertheless, death was a familiar visitor in every home in those days—and the Browns had eight children remaining. Brown continued to work hard. He began to win prizes at the Summit County fairs for his sheep, and to build once again, little by little, a reputation as a hard-working and honest man of unusual ability.

Chapter 27

In Mrs. Spriggs' Washington boardinghouse, Theodore Weld ate his usual bowl of milk, into which he crumbled some Graham bread. He also ate "mush, apples, vegetables, almonds, figs and raisins." He exercised every day, as of old, in a nearby park, running and jumping. His voice had returned—though not enough for public speaking—and his abolitionist congressmen began to increase in numbers, and to attract a steady flow of visitors and supporters.

Weld hated Washington. "The World's splendor which blazes around me, the pride and fashion, prodigality, ostentatious display and vanity, and desperate strugglings and vaultings of ambition, the envyings and fierce encounters of rivals for office and popular sway" disgusted him.[1] He wrote long letters to Angelina and Sarah; he missed his young sons (the elder had been named after Weld's old friend Charles Stuart). He missed the fifty-acre farm and the rambling, fifteen-room house they had bought in Belleville, New Jersey, with the sisters' inheritance.

As usual, he attended black churches, and described the pastors as "full of noise and shouting"; but their sincerity impressed him more favorably than the congressional chaplains'. The fact was that his once-flaming religious ardor had been greatly dampened. "That a vast amount of what passes for truth in the religious world," he wrote Birney, "is not taught in the Bible and is utterly contradicted by reason is clear to me . . ."[2]

He was, in other words, changed and tired. He had worked for years with Finney in the "Great Revival," and for many years in the antislavery crusade, but even his remarkable health began to falter. By early 1843 the number of antislavery Northern congressmen had increased; abolition was a subject that lit fires all over the Capitol. The Whig party, no longer able to maintain strict discipline, was sagging. The antislavers did not have quite enough strength to prevail, but they had rolled up as many as eighty votes on some sensitive issues—and were clearly a rising force.

At that point, in March 1843, Weld went home. Angelina was expecting another child and his presence was needed. He left behind an organization that had been shown how to operate; the American and Foreign Antislavery Society would establish a new abolitionist newspaper, *The National Era*. Weld also left behind a Congress that was filling with his Northern converts, including Thaddeus Stevens, and Illinois' Owen Lovejoy.

Weld's great force of seventy, however, was wearied with toils of battle. The editor of the *Oberlin Evangelist* was discovered to be a "thief and an adulterer," and the college itself was in arrears. Many of Weld's

144

longtime associates were also in dire financial straits. James Thome and George Whipple had not been paid; Elizur Wright barely eked a living selling his own books door to door. Marius Robinson was in poor health. Angelina Weld had joined the Millerites, and was expecting her baby, the imminent return of Jesus, and the end of the world.

So Weld turned his back on politics. His efforts had been remarkable for years, and his final project had provided a vehicle by which a host of later—and in most respects, lesser—men would rise to fame. But his private opinion of politicians was scathing. With the exception of the abolitionists, he considered most of them little better than dogs, "crouching on their marrow bones before public opinion fawning at their masters' feet, wriggling for the privilege of licking their spittle as it falls."[3]

That was a far cry from the wide-eyed young man who had once followed in the train of the Reverend Charles Finney. Lewis Tappan suggested a New York pulpit, but Weld wanted none of that, either. His antislavery beliefs remained strong, but he was never again to lead the movement. He had done a giant's work in anonymity, and he was now content to work his farm.

In Boston, Channing's passing left the field open for the rising voice of Theodore Parker. Brook Farm was near Parker's pulpit in West Roxbury, and he often dropped by for a visit.

So did Margaret Fuller, who attracted Hawthorne's caustic eye. Hawthorne later put her into a novel, *The Blithedale Romance:* "She was made for a stump oratress. Her mind was full of weeds. She made no scruple of oversetting all human institutions, and scattering them as with a breeze from her fan. A female reformer, in her attacks upon society, has an instinctive sense of where the life lies, and is inclined to aim directly at that spot. Especially the relations between the sexes . . ."[4]

But Hawthorne was unhappy amid the Brook Farm talkers; he was a writer out of step. Emerson's opinion was strangely similar. After attending a birthday picnic at the community, where the workers appeared in their own costumes, he marked it down in his journal later as "a perpetual picnic, a French Revolution in small, an Age of Reason in a patty-pan."[5]

(Emerson did not particularly notice, nor did the Brook Farmers, that when a road was built through Concord that year, it was built by Irish laborers—a sign that his own world, all New England, and the country at large, were undergoing far larger and greater changes than any they would devise.)

Parker, however, was content to survey Brook Farm from the practical view of an experienced farmer; he decided its methods were trivial. Already isolated from his fellow clergymen in the Unitarian movement who found his views distasteful, he toiled to expand, sharpen, and expound his theories and force their acceptance. The result was a printed effort entitled *A Discourse on Religion;* it was grandiose, complicated, and dissonant. Parker compared religion to the stars, and theology to human thoughts about them. He rummaged through his thousands of books and built mounds of footnoted comments about the climb of humanity from the worship of fetishes, through polytheism, and finally to monotheism, and he compared these to evolutionary stages—more than a dozen years before Darwin's name was tacked to this belief. Parker was echoing the German idea that God and life are a process. Had he stopped there, he might have raised some barks from Princeton and still have been fairly safe. Instead he went on to deny that Jesus taught Christianity, and to insist that He was not divine, saying He taught only piety and morality. Parker also rejected miracles, denied the Bible had a divine source, comparing it to the works of Newton, Descartes, the Veda, and the Koran. He denied Protestantism, dismissed concepts of sin, denied atonement, summarized God as goodness, and "each man as his own Christ."[6]

All this was a distillation from a series of lectures Parker had delivered, and which had created shocks. Brownson's *Quarterly Review* covered their essence and by early 1843 Parker had created enough of a stir to be called to a council of Unitarian ministers to explain himself. The only version of the conference that emerged was Parker's: he said he was attacked as not being a Christian, and that (instead of denying or admitting the charge) he had begun to expound his beliefs. The ministers found the discussion straying into odd directions. The Reverend Cyrus Bartol finally rose to call attention to Parker's sincerity. Some others seconded Bartol, and Parker fled in tears.

The upshot was that he refused to leave the association, though he was clearly at odds with most of the other clergymen. His position was that of a rebel against even the remnants of the orthodox doctrines. The transcendentalists considered him a hero, both for his rebellion and for his refusal to admit that he was rebelling. His own view was that he was bringing the world's most modern and advanced methods of scholarship to an ecclesiastical backwater, and deserved to be praised, not censured. He felt he was a martyr. His friends agreed.

Parker's difficulties might have attracted more attention had they not occurred at a time when the North was experiencing several other religious upheavals.

The most spectacular new movement in the early 1840's was that of the Adventists. From the time when the Reverend Joshua Himes launched a Boston revival around the predictions of the Reverend William Miller in 1839, this movement grew steadily into a large-scale phenomenon, embracing upper New England, upstate New York, northern Pennsylvania, Ohio, Michigan, and Illinois—with pockets in New Jersey and other regions.

The Adventist movement was given impetus when the most brilliant comet of the nineteenth century appeared in early 1843. Thousands listened to evangelists stressing Reverend William Miller's predictions as proof that conversion was now essential to avoid imminent doom.

Some eminent citizens joined the bandwagon; one was the Reverend Elon Galusha, son of a Vermont governor, a trustee of Columbia College in Washington, and a renowned Baptist leader.

The elderly Miller, whose calculations had set this mass into motion, was pressed to be more specific about the date of the Second Coming. He finally announced that 1844 was the fateful year, and that the event would occur between October and December. Under further pressure from zealots he named October 22. Some persons sold their property; thousands kept all-night vigils as the date passed without incident. Traditional Christians, like Angelina Grimké Weld, were not disturbed; the date might have been wrong but the prophecy remained. Nonbelievers, however, were indignant; mobs attacked, sacked, and burned Adventist meeting halls in Ithaca, Rochester, and other cities and towns.

If such demonstrations of anger because the end of the world had not arrived seemed irrational, they were at least no more irrational than the steady growth of "phalanxes." These communities attempted to bring to life the theories of Charles Fourier—with predictably sad results.

Fourier, who died in 1837, had lost his possessions in the French Revolution, a period that left a lasting impression of horror on his mind. He lived in obscurity as a bookkeeper and clerk, but created immense, highly structured fantasies. Believing that inhibited emotions led to discord, Fourier categorized "passions" into a group of twelve, with bewildering subcategories. He also dreamed of perfect villages—"phalanxes"—each limited to a precise number of people living in vast communal buildings. There, work and leisure was compartmentalized. Fourier was, of course, mad—but no madder than those who took him seriously. Among his more interesting fancies were his "courts of love," where everyone would move, like epicures, from one delightful experience to another as inclinations directed. In all of Fourier's dreams, private property and profits would be abolished—a familiar demand of the propertyless.[7]

Albert Brisbane, an American socialist who had helped save Dr. Samuel Gridley Howe from a Berlin prison in 1830, was an early, enthusiastic follower of Fourier, because as a youth he had experienced a "spontaneous intuition" that he would someday belong to a vast regimented army of selfless humans. After meeting the master, Brisbane preached his new message and ran a column, in Horace Greeley's New York *Tribune,* that launched the "phalanxes" in the United States. By 1844 one had been established in Michigan, by almost five hundred people;[8] others popped up in different places. Unlike the Adventists, the Fourierites did not attract marauding mobs.

Early in 1844, John Brown's situation finally improved; his efforts to learn everything about sheep brought handsome dividends. Colonel Simon Perkins, son of General Simon Perkins, a founder of Akron, engaged Brown to tend his sheep, and to prepare the animals and their wool for market. The arrangement was actually a partnership, allowing Brown to use a cottage—owned by Colonel Perkins—situated on a hill not far from Akron, at a nominal rent of $30 a year. The colonel's imposing mansion was not far away.[9]

In theory, Brown was to share in the losses as well as the profits of these efforts. Colonel Perkins was well aware that John Brown had no money; but he did not anticipate any losses. As for Brown, his prizes at fairs and his usual invincible confidence had brought him to the conclusion that he knew more about sheep than anyone on earth. "I had no controversy with John Brown," Perkins said later, "for it would have done no good."[10]

The Brown boys knew better. The agonies of their twenty-four hour Sabbaths continued at Akron, but whippings were beginning to abate as the boys grew taller and stronger, and became able to resist. At eleven Salmon fought so fiercely that his father laid the whip aside. And his older sons were now men—too burly for corporal punishment.

Mrs. Perkins did not care for any of the Browns. She thought John Brown was hard and violent, his sons overly mischievous. The boys bothered the Perkins' hired girls, and played crude, even painful, pranks. But there were not many men who wanted to raise the Perkins sheep in hope of a share in the profits, and Colonel Perkins had reason to believe that he had made a reasonably good bargain in 1844—especially in view of the intricacies that flourished as general prosperity returned.

Emerson's admiration for Bronson Alcott spread the philosopher's fame, but Alcott's books on his Temple Street experiments also enlarged the coterie of Alcott admirers. Some of these combined Alcott's methods with those of Pestalozzi and opened a school in England called Alcott House. When they invited Alcott to visit in 1842, Emerson was sufficiently pleased to give him passage to London.

The visit was such a success that Alcott returned with four Englishmen and a collection of books that was to serve as a library in a new, utopian venture. One of the Englishmen donated his life savings to pay for an abandoned farm and an experiment in communal life under Alcott—called Fruitlands—was launched.

Fruitlands (later described by Louisa May Alcott, Bronson's daughter, in one of the most hilarious books ever written[11]) could lay claim to a special niche in lunacy. The Englishman Lane, whose life savings vanished in the venture, believed that men at Fruitlands were enslaved by domestic animals, since they spent far too much energy caring for them. But the colony refused to use beef, milk or eggs, sugar, molasses, butter, and fish, for "nothing could be eaten that caused wrong or death to man or beast." Even the canker-worms that infested the apple trees were not to be molested: "They had as much right to the apples as man . . ."[12] Coffee and tea were held in as much horror as liquor; even salt was considered dubious.

Other special features included loose trousers and tunics for the men and linen bloomers for women.

After a butterfly summer the project trembled in the chills of autumn, and finally froze to death in winter after all but the Alcotts had fled. Bronson Alcott then took to his bed, turned his face to the wall, and refused to eat or speak for days. Mrs. Alcott finally took him a platter of hot food, telling him that she had sold much of their furniture, rented rooms with a neighbor and hired a wagon. They could move; the neighbor would pay Alcott laborer's wages and some of the women in the region would send Mrs. Alcott sewing. At that the philosopher revived; the couple embraced and later left through the snow with their possessions piled atop an ox-sled, leaving behind a failure later—and most improbably—redeemed by fame.

Chapter 28

The political abolitionists had put together the Liberty party. It held its second quadrennial convention in Buffalo in 1843 and again nominated James G. Birney for president. Its efforts were sullied by events in Boston the previous year—spearheaded, as usual, by Garrison and Wendell Phillips. This pair and their fervent followers had rallied around a fugitive slave arrested in Boston for theft. When it was discovered that he was a fugitive he was held for return to Virginia.

The Garrisonians whipped up a rally at Faneuil Hall—complete with placards, fiery speeches, and arguments on human rights. A large and predominantly hostile crowd was present. It shouted down Joshua Leavitt, Edmund Quincy, and others. Then Wendell Phillips rose. Tall, cool, and eloquent, Phillips called the crowd "white slaves of the north," and charged that the Bible outweighed the Constitution. "I say," he shouted, "my CURSE be on the Constitution of these United States!"[1] That tore the meeting apart; order vanished as fights broke out. The fugitive slave was finally released when someone bought his freedom, but the abolitionist movement was from that moment pointed toward new shores.

Garrison did not improve matters by issuing a series of charges against the Liberty party, which he considered an effort to deny his leadership of the abolitionist movement. The party was, he said, "conceived in sin"; it was unprincipled, and dominated by frauds. In the pages of *The Liberator* he ran down a list of names, and cried out that

all had betrayed the movement. The "traitors" included the impoverished Elizur Wright, Birney, and many others who had long toiled for
abolition.[2]

These onslaughts were damaging enough. But in the same year
other fanatics (including one Stephen Foster, not the song writer but
a man noted for disturbing congregations at worship by rising to
denounce them as thralls of slavemasters) issued a bulky pamphlet
titled *The Brotherhood of Thieves; or, a True Picture of the American Church
and Clergy.*[3]

Nevertheless the Liberty Party—whose members worked in the
Weld pattern of appeals to better instincts and to reason—had grown
respectable and its second convention was far better attended than its
first. It did not attract large followings; the masses were dominated by
the Whigs and Democrats, whose leaders had huge issues with which
to contend; issues the great majority of Americans considered far more
pressing than the plight of the Blacks.

The fact was that war loomed: in the Southwest and the Northwest.
American settlers on Mexican land had first occupied, then rebelled,
and finally, in 1836, established the independent Republic of Texas.
That creation was recognized by the United States and England. Mexico, torn by internal dissension and united only in hatred of the United
States, had not yet fully accepted the new situation, but in 1843 Britain
offered to mediate the Texas-Mexico boundary dispute—adding the
hope that emancipation of slaves would be part of any treaty.

That sent American suspicions soaring into the stratosphere, for
Britain and the United States were embroiled in a boundary crisis of
their own: over the immense Oregon territory in the Northwest—
embracing the present states of Washington, Oregon, and Idaho, as
well as parts of Montana and Wyoming. That region was jointly occupied, though it was generally agreed that a firm line separating Canadian and American sovereignty would have to be drawn. The American
newspapers wanted it drawn at latitude 54° 40' north. The British
would not consider that, and the dispute festered.

Therefore, the British offer to mediate between Texas and Mexico
could easily be seen as a perfidious plan to create a vast zone of British
influence in the Northwest and the Southwest. And, by adding the
Mexican territory of California and the region called New Mexico, the
British Empire might even lay claim to an area of the North American
continent extending from Canada, and down the Pacific coast, to
Texas.

The situation was compounded by arguments over Texas, in which
some Northerners claimed United States annexation of Texas would
expand Southern "slavocracy." Texas wanted to be annexed, and John
Calhoun negotiated a treaty to that effect; it was rejected by Northern
Senators. The abolitionist argument, in other words, had grown strong
enough to stop the expansion of the United States.

In 1843, Calhoun's chances to become president were no longer
tangible. But the abolitionist argument also worked, to some extent,

against Henry Clay, the nominee of the Whig Party. Clay was known as a balancing man; coming from a border state, he could thread his way through complex issues and emerge walking a tightrope to the satisfaction of moderates in general. That did not please the "ultras" —North or South.

In Van Buren, the Democratic Party had a possible nominee who was equally well-known and equally able. But when queried on the annexation of Texas, Van Buren took an antislavery position. That angered the South and although Van Buren entered the convention a favorite, backstage maneuvers resulted in a change of the rules, making a two-thirds majority necessary for nomination. The result was the selection of the first dark horse candidate in the nation's history: James K. Polk, of Tennessee.

The Whigs set up a derisive howl. "Who is James K. Polk?" they asked in bars and meeting halls throughout the land. The campaign, of course, made him better known. Polk campaigned on a platform to acquire Texas and to push the British out of Oregon. Both positions were popular, although Clay's moderation seemed more palatable to those who feared such bold measures.

When the votes were finally counted it was the widely scorned political abolitionists and their swing vote that decided the issue. Henry Clay went down to defeat by only 1.5 percent. The Liberty party collected 2.3 percent of the vote. That was only 62,197 votes out of the 4,-600,000 cast, but it was enough to turn a close election. It was also enough to establish the abolitionists as a national political force for the first time. But their success was bittersweet, for they had also—unintentionally—assisted into office one of the strongest men to ever reach the White House, a man whose platform and positions they bitterly opposed.

The election results were seen as national approval of the admission of Texas, though protest meetings were held in Faneuil Hall by the Garrisonians. Those zealots had moved, under the lashing of their leader and Wendell Phillips, against the idea that a majority should determine the direction of the nation, though they did not put it that way. Phillips had, belatedly, studied the Constitution and realized that the Founders had incorporated slavery. The discovery amazed and angered him, and he declared it was "a covenant with death and an agreement with hell."[4] He swung Garrison—already embittered against all institutions for not behaving according to his opinions— into quick agreement. As a result, the masthead of *The Liberator* soon blossomed with a new legend: A REPEAL OF THE UNION BE-TWEEN NORTHERN LIBERTY AND SOUTHERN SLAVERY IS ESSENTIAL TO THE ABOLITION OF THE ONE AND THE PRES-ERVATION OF THE OTHER.[5]

That slogan was far ahead of the tide, but it was not long before some others began to turn in the same direction. In the House of Representatives old John Quincy Adams and some fellow abolitionists circulated a statement warning that the annexation of Texas would "dissolve" the Union. In Boston Garrisonians thundered along similar lines; one listener was a young student from the Harvard Divinity School named Thomas Wentworth Higginson. The abolitionists, who had unwittingly engineered a Whig defeat in the elections, were now undermining the unity of that party, and the Union.

Their efforts, however, were puny when contrasted with the overwhelming majority of Americans, who regarded the Union as sacred and the Constitution as holy writ. And far beyond the abolitionist minority in Boston—which could fill a hall but would be lost in the city —loomed possible war with Mexico.

Mexico had repeatedly denied that Texas was independent, and repeatedly warned that its annexation by the United States would mean war. In that situation both Britain and France, as hostile to American growth as the American abolitionists, saw a chance to cage the eagle. Through their foreign ministries, both governments offered to mediate the Texas-Mexico dispute, and to guarantee Mexican borders thereafter against the Americans.[6]

That was a golden opportunity for Mexico City, and probably the only real chance it ever had to retain its vast territories of California and Arizona—which included present-day California, Nevada, Utah, Arizona, and New Mexico, and parts of Wyoming and Colorado. But the Mexican government was precariously engaged in internecine struggles and arguments broke out over the offer. Meanwhile the White House, suddenly apprised that time was pressing, moved the annexation of Texas out of the Senate and into the full Congress. Only a few days before Polk was sworn into office in March 1845, lame-duck President Tyler and Secretary of State Calhoun were able to present the nation, and Mexico, with a *fait accompli*. This was made even more impressive by the Mexicans themselves, who in an angry display of pride before intelligence rejected the offer of British-French mediation and guarantees.

Although some technicalities dangled, and legalists grumbled that the annexation was unconstitutional, the majority of Americans—long convinced that Texas was part of the United States anyway—were pleased. The Constitution, although hallowed in countless speeches, was tacitly assumed to be such an elastic miracle that it could be stretched or contracted to achieve any goal the nation chose.

Abolitionists, however, had injected the issue of slavery into the annexation of Texas, and that issue seethed even in the face of possible war with Mexico. Pamphlets against "slavocracy," and accusations of conspiracies in high places sowed seeds of doubt and dissension even in the midst of a great national surge toward the West.

Theodore Parker went to Europe, for the first time, in 1844, and found much to deplore. His journal notes read like compositions for future delivery. Hardly any sight shook his Boston confidence, though he was taken aback to discover that the German theological radicals sharply divided their scholarly biblical treatises from the sermons they delivered in their pulpits. He returned to West Roxbury in September 1844 and at once became the center of new storms. He had not been thrown out of the ministerial association, but he was nearly completely ostracized. Fulfilling a former agreement, Parker preached the Thursday lecture at the First Church in Boston and nearly brought that venerable custom to an end. Until he appeared the Thursday lectures had been subdued affairs attended only by "a score or two of venerable women [who] glided silently in at the hour of eleven and took their seats, well provided with bottles of *sal-volatile* against the probable effects of the discourse."[7] When Parker appeared the church was crowded with newcomers who heard him deny the divinity of Jesus, and praise Him as a man.

These resumptions of his attacks on Christianity brought the ministerial association together in another meeting to discuss his expulsion, but the talks ended, as before, in disagreement. That, coupled with his inability to find other ministers with whom to exchange pulpits, created a sense of burning injustice in Rev. Theodore Parker. He was unable to understand why he was not welcome to insult Christians in their own churches. Many of his friends shared that wonder, and in January 1845 a group formed, resolved that "the Rev. Parker should be regularly heard in the City," and hired the Melodeon theater for him every Sunday.

At first the idea of preaching in a theater seemed a contradiction, and even Parker was slightly appalled at the idea—especially in view of the entertainments that regularly appeared: "Dancing monkeys and Ethiopian serenaders," he said, "making vulgar merriment out of the ignorance and wretchedness of the American slave . . ."[8]

But crowds began to appear, and as time passed Reverend Parker's "Free Church" collected a solid core of attendance—a steady five hundred—swollen by visitors to the city who were attracted by his growing fame. In time he collected a mailing list of seven thousand—although some names were of citizens who virtually crept in and out. Garrison attended, however, as did Dr. Samuel Gridley Howe and his bride Julia and Charles Sumner. In time the Melodeon held the largest Sunday congregation in Boston, and Parker became the city's most famous preacher. West Roxbury was abandoned; the ministerial association no longer mattered.

While Parker gathered his following at the Melodeon, the other members of the coterie pursued different destinies. Worried over continuing deficits at Brook Farm, the former Reverend George Ripley and his associates finally accepted the idea that many trades were not likely to be established, and, impressed by the arguments of Albert Brisbane, became a "phalanx." Emerson, who read Fourier more closely than some of the others, disapproved, considering that the Frenchman had issued "a charter for libertines."[9] But the Brook Farmers were not so much attracted to "courts of love" as to the more mundane problem of keeping the venture from collapse. Fourierism was still very popular: they hoped to attract more people.

The Alcotts, abject after the miserable failure of their project, were saved by the Reverend Samuel J. May. An ardent abolitionist leader married to Mrs. Alcott's sister, May joined Samuel Sewall, his wife's cousin, to buy a farm called Hillside in Concord for the philosopher. For safety's sake they kept the title in their own names, and Emerson promised to keep an eye on the Alcotts, though he was fairly busy. He was, in fact, being generally helpful to Margaret Fuller and the Reverend William Henry Channing, but he refused to read Hawthorne's "somber fiction." That decision was prompted, no doubt, by the fact that Hawthorne's parody of the avant-garde, *The Celestial Railroad*, had appeared, to huge waves of laughter. In it Hawthorne repaid Brook Farm for his hours feeding the pigs. Written in the style of *The Pilgrim's Progress*, it included a German giant named Transcendalism, who was described as "a heap of fog and duskiness." Matters did not end there; Hawthorne would spend several years evening scores.

But the times were slowly changing; politics—a national obsession that was to grow into something close to a mania—diverted attention from the esthetes. When Emerson gave a lecture at Middlebury College in Vermont in the summer of 1845, the local minister prayed publicly to God "to deliver us from ever hearing any more such Transcendental nonsense."[10] In that atmosphere, Emerson began to pay more attention to what interested so many others. He met Garrison in Boston and praised his idealism, urged the residents of Concord to invite Wendell Phillips to speak, and refused to lecture at New Bedford because blacks would not be admitted.

Henry Thoreau, his protégé, was even more removed from politics. Thoreau built a hut on Emerson's property at Walden Pond, into which he moved on July 4, 1845. The village of Concord was a short walk away; the new railroad that carried trains to Boston was half a mile away, its trains within earshot. He strolled into town daily; his retreat was only from the Emerson household. A born naturalist, he began to study the smaller forms of life as avidly as other men watched the soarings of eagles.

On the same day that Thoreau moved into his hut, Charles Sumner, dressed for the occasion in "a long-tailed blue coat with gilt buttons, white waistcoat and white trousers," stepped forward on the stage of the Tremont Temple in Boston to address a crowd of more than 2,000 persons.[11] His speech was to be the culmination of the city's celebration of Independence Day, whose paraders had ended in the hall. There, before the assembled elite, with military officers in full dress behind him, and rows of beribboned Army and Navy officers in the seats in front of him, Sumner proceeded to orate—for two hours—on the proposition that "no peace is dishonorable and no war honorable."

In the course of this address Sumner dwelled on the horrors of war, blamed Christian churches for promoting such horrors, sneered at "exaggerated love of country," and called West Point "a seminary of idleness and vice."[12] At one point he leaned forward toward the officers who sat, rigid with indignation, in the seats before him, derided their uniforms and shouted that they were so incompetent they could not even be trusted to quell a street riot.

He concluded that the "true grandeur of nations" was in moral elevation, in feeding the poor and clothing the naked, in creating schools and hospitals. After these remarks, the atmosphere of the banquet was strained, and the fact that Sumner was allowed to escape an ugly scene was a credit to the patience of his audience, and the city. The performance ended his chances of becoming a professor at Harvard Law School when Justice Story died, and closed many Beacon Hill homes to him.

But these were closing in any event, for Sumner had undergone a startling change of personality since the virtual collapse of the Five of Clubs. Dr. Samuel Gridley Howe had married; so had Longfellow, and Sumner was—for a time—a lonely man. He retained Howe's friendship, however, and the physician drew him into two of his Goodness campaigns. The first of these was headed by Horace Mann, who was ardent for educational reform. Mann spearheaded a campaign against Boston's famous common schools. His methods, like those of Garrison and other reformers, were vitriolic. He charged that the Boston School Principal's Association was a mere club "for eating, drinking and telling bawdy stories."[13] He also charged that whippings and teaching by rote—methods used for centuries—stunted proper development. Tests were conducted to prove that assertion but the results proved, embarrassingly to Mann, that pupils so taught achieved higher scores than pupils exposed to Mann's theories. The immediate result of the campaign was a bitterly contested school board election. Sumner, a new candidate, lost both the election and five thousand dollars he had invested on behalf of some supporters—which they failed to repay. That created some bitterness in Sumner, but it did not lessen his zeal, nor cool his friendship with Mann and Howe.

Another reform in which Sumner was active with Howe involved the improvement of prisons and an effort to shift the emphasis of penal administration from punishment to rehabilitation. That effort was under way when Sumner was asked to be the Boston Fourth of July orator.

The nature of his address, delivered at a time when the entire nation was engrossed in the Polk cat-and-mouse game with Mexico over Texas and the war of nerves with Britain over Oregon, was enough to send Sumner's name soaring through the land. His friends thought he was immensely brave; his critics said he was simply insensitive. But the speech was made at such a crucial moment that it later became clear that Sumner had deliberately used the platform provided him to enter politics. His move was bold, farsighted, and crafty. It resembled, in a far less subtle way, the turns being made by Emerson and others toward the issues that engrossed the country.

Emerson, of course, had his books, his poems, and his coterie. Therefore he could discuss current issues in a disguised, lofty, and even mystical manner. Sumner, however, was a lawyer unsuited for the courtroom who had also grown bored with the possibilities of academe. He knew—for he was well-acquainted with Representative Robert Winthrop and other Whig Leaders—that a split was developing in the Party. In part the split was due to the loss of the presidential race; a defeat that always leads to party reorganization. And in 1844, that defeat could be attributed largely to the rise of the Liberty Party—and even beyond that, to the injection of slavery as an issue of national political dissension.

By 1845 the issue had become divisive. Some in the North charged that the acquisition of Texas was made to placate the South and expand slavery. They argued the annexation should be resisted. The Whig Party split on the question and Charles Sumner, by making an arresting speech against war, was in effect siding with one faction of that split. He did this without mentioning partisan politics, but by claiming what he considered the highest moral grounds.

The results were all he could have hoped for, though he was capable of such supreme rationalization that there is some question whether he ever admitted, even to himself, what he was doing, or what he had done. A spate of criticism from conservative and traditional quarters greeted his diatribe against his country and countrymen. But the American Peace Society reprinted and distributed his speech everywhere. It was used in Congress against Polk's war of nerves with Britain. It was hawked in the streets of Britain, where it was hailed as high statesmanship, and Sumner's aristocratic British friends wrote him admiring letters. The abolitionists were thrilled. Gerrit Smith, Theodore Parker, and Garrison all approached the tall, strong, and imposing Sumner at once.[14] The transcendentalists were delighted; they knew Sumner as an old admirer of the late William Ellery Channing, and Sumner's polished and florid language, with its classical allusions, was Channing in a new, stronger form.

Old John Quincy Adams was delighted and even Charles Francis Adams grew as cordial as his icy nature permitted. Samuel Gridley Howe was proud of his friend, and Representative Robert Winthrop, formerly close to Sumner, realized he might become a political rival.

That rivalry, however, was not as important as the tide that Sumner represented. For the first time in its brief history the United States was poised on the edge of a policy of expansion through war, and a minority was rising that opposed such an expansion—even opposed the growth of industrialism. This minority insisted the nation should not adventure abroad but should improve itself at home; America was embarked on an evil path, and should retrench, reform, and repent.

The majority of the people, however, were far more interested in moving forward. The drive to the West was called, in one newspaper editorial, "Manifest Destiny." In time the decade would be known as the "roaring forties." One man, often overlooked and almost always underestimated both then and later—austere, firm, and nearly mysterious—was determined that the urge of most Americans be realized and not smothered. He was James K. Polk; he was in the White House, and he meant to make the most of that opportunity.

Polk sent federal troops—ostensibly to guard newly acquired Texas —but actually to occupy a disputed strip of land on the Rio Grande. It was his intention to lure Mexico into the first move. He also sent the timorous though ambitious James Buchanan, his secretary of state, to settle the Oregon boundary dispute with Britain at the 49th parallel. The British suspected weakness and refused; they hoped for further concessions. Polk immediately withdrew the offer, and said he would stick at fifty-four-forty.

The newspapers began to shriek crisis; the patterns of the President's moves were disputed, clouded, and suspected. In January 1846, Polk went to Congress, described the tortuous progress of negotiations with Britain, and asked for one year's notice of an end to the "joint occupancy" of the Oregon Territory. That sent Buchanan into a bad case of the trembles, the press into paroxysms and Congress into dispute. The President, meanwhile, ignored the British offer to accept the 49th parallel. He was tired of bluffs from John Bull, and was far more interested in the reaction of Mexico.

It took Congress until April 1846 to give Polk his British package, but his diary shows that he remained calm while the dispute raged. On April 30, 1846, Polk records that he was touched by a delegation from the Perkins Institution for the Blind, which arrived at the White House escorted by Dr. Samuel Gridley Howe, and including "a female named Bridgeman who had been taught by signs with the hands and fingers to understand and communicate ideas and to write.[15]

That was the same day that Mariano Arista, a red-haired Mexican major general, led his force of approximately five thousand men across the Rio Grande at Longoreno.[16] The Mexican War was under way.

Chapter 29

John Brown had a plan that he described to Colonel Perkins. Like many other sheep farmers in 1846, Perkins was firmly convinced that the price of wool was manipulated by the large mills, whose agents and brokers persistently paid less than fair prices. Thus he listened with great interest when Brown proposed to establish an office and warehouse in Springfield, Massachusetts, and to act as a broker for wool growers of the West.

Had Brown stopped there, his proposition would have been eminently sound. For in the relatively short time of his partnership with Colonel Perkins, he had made a name for himself in the sheep business. Apart from winning prizes at many fairs, he had written a number of sensible articles for various wool industry publications, and he had ranged through Ohio, New York, New England, and other regions, buying and selling sheep and wool, getting acquainted and becoming known. All that was a sound basis for becoming a broker and expanding the sale of his and his partner's wool by selling wool from other growers as well.

But Brown had strong ideas about the wool market. Prices, he believed, should be based on the grades of wool, from fine to inferior. Therefore he had worked out a system of his own, which separated wool by grade. And in this observation Brown fell into a pit common to many men who do not believe a free marketplace sets fair values. The world is full of these: engineers who cannot understand why an expensively improved machine does not attract more buyers than a cheap but adequate one; men who insist that their labor adds value to a product, though labor alone does not make anything useful, necessary, or desirable; in short men who cannot understand that larger forces and events influence the price and profit of every trade, industry, and product.

Brown's second idea was based on the belief that the large mill owners of New England, with their great fortunes and mysterious methods, operated together to hold the prices of wool below proper or reasonable levels. That conspiracy theory is as popular in economics as are the delusions about quality, and is even less supportable by reason. The idea that an entire industry could maintain such a control —which not even governments can accomplish though they repeatedly try through the centuries—betrayed a lack of understanding of how marketplaces operate.

Yet Brown, whose arguments appealed to both pride and prejudice, proposed, in effect, to create just such a large-scale combination to lift prices, by asking all the wool growers to abandon their regular channels and to send him their wool to be marketed. He would grade it, and he would set a proper price, and he would force the mills and brokers to pay that price. How the ethics of his proposition differed from those he accused on the buying end he did not explain—nor did his listeners think to ask, as he marched across the landscape all through 1845, speaking at various wool growers' meetings. Neither did Colonel Perkins ask, although he put up the money for this mad adventure.

When experienced wool dealers learned why growers were sending John Brown huge bales of wool in Springfield, they were at first incredulous, suspecting some sort of swindle. Many dropped in to

Brown's office, to talk to the tall, neatly dressed proprietor—and to assess the new situation for themselves.

Brown was now at an age and of a bearing that impelled men to call him "uncle." He explained his nine grades, and his nine prices, and the fact that he would deal only in cash. That policy served as notice to manufacturers that their usual practice of paying ninety days later would no longer be accepted[1], as part of his plan to reverse the traditional buyer-seller relationship. His prices were even more wondrous. He set his best grade of wool at levels fifty percent above the marketplace, his worst twenty-five percent below.[2] This meant that his lower grades, if purchased, made it possible for another dealer to realize an immediate profit, while ignoring his better grades. His system for paying the wool growers themselves was to keep track of their bales, their grades and quantities, and to pay them the average of what all their individual wool sold for, in all nine grades, instead of what each bale was actually worth.[3] In other words, he had created his own system inside an ancient and traditional industry—which was then being flooded with British wool because the tariff had just been lowered. Furthermore, Brown launched his novelties just after the Mexican War started, when the marketplace was disrupted and prices swinging wildly. Men tried to explain this to him, because no industry likes newcomers who may add their own disruptions to difficult periods.[4] They soon discovered that was a useless exercise. His eyes would grow cold and his face would turn stern; his figure would stiffen. John Brown did not believe in economic ships that rose and fell in economic seas; his craft would steer along a logical plane, without dips or rises, according to the logic of his personal imaginings. He steered, like some creature of legend, according to navigational rules of his own.

It was the argument of the abolitionists that Texas was acquired to add more slaves to the United States, and that Mexico was invaded to extend a slave empire both south and west. Both arguments were fallacious; both became enduring legends. The Mexicans started the war, as they had said they would, and they were cruel and merciless fighters.[5] They had lost Texas originally by abusing American settlers, and as soon as the war with the United States began, the Mexicans committed a number of atrocities, including the murder of men and women who had given themselves up. The American field commander, Brevet Brigadier General Zachary Taylor, a thickset backwoodsman who despised schoolmen and the schooled and knew how to fight like a bear, took orders but could not plan an organized campaign. The United States Army had no general staff, but it had Major General Winfield Scott, a military genius whom President Polk detested for harboring perennial political ambitions. Against combinations of guerrillas and parade-trained troops, Scott was to mastermind a campaign that was to be as underestimated as it was brilliant.

Meanwhile, the President steered the United States into a settlement with Britain over Oregon at the 49th Parallel. It was a victory criticized by war hawks, costing him the support of many influential politicians, and seriously weakening his chances for reelection—although it was never criticized after the emotions of 1846 cooled. But before abating, those emotions rose to fever pitch.

In August, 1846 the fever broke into near delirium. President Polk's administration had introduced a bill for a two-million-dollar loan, to cover a "secret fund" with which Polk expected to pay the Mexican General Santa Anna's army, in the hope that Santa Anna would then become leader of Mexico and reach a peace with the United States.[6] Pursuing that objective the President visited the Vice-President's office in the Capitol, and left later when Congress neared adjournment. That evening the House debated the President's request. Robert Winthrop of Massachusetts, under fire from Sumner and others at home because he had voted for the war, wondered aloud if the President planned to buy more slaveholding land. That thought impelled David Wilmot, a freshman Representative from Pennsylvania, to offer a proviso to the President's money bill, forbidding slavery in any new territory added to the United States. At the time Mr. Wilmot introduced his amendment the last House session was advanced, and many members were drunkenly celebrating adjournment. The Southerners were inattentive, and the bill, with Wilmot's proviso not generally understood, passed.

News of the proviso crept through the capital over the weekend, and its significance sobered many minds. On Monday the Senate concluded the last session of the Twenty-Ninth Congress, and proceedings were dominated by other business. The President's bill, with its proviso, did not come up for discussion, mainly because Senator Davis of Massachusetts refused to yield the floor. Evidently he did not want the proviso to be debated, knowing it would lose; he preferred to let it die in abeyance, which it did. This meant that the issue of slavery in new territories remained—to hover, wraithlike, over the nation, clouding discussions of the Mexican War for months to come.

Abolitionists, transcendentalists, and Theodore Parker had already drawn their conclusions on the war: it was a conspiracy of Southerners to expand slavery. Henry Thoreau—who was so closely associated with Ralph Waldo Emerson that people said he walked, talked, and even looked like the Sage—made his own opinions clear by refusing to pay his poll tax. That landed him in the Concord jail overnight and provided a symbol of passive resistance that was to endure for generations. Emerson was annoyed with him. "Why should he poorly pound on some one string of discord, when all is a jangle?" he asked Alcott. The philosopher, who had no great love for the young naturalist, agreed, and Emerson, in a rare outburst, allowed that Thoreau's conduct was "mean and skulking."[7]

The war distracted Parker, to some extent, from themes he was beginning to develop at the Melodeon—themes which echoed the socialists of Europe, and which were to be echoed in turn in such newspapers as the New York *Tribune*. Parker, who seemed born to agitate the common mind and exacerbate the uncommon, argued that the class structure of the United States—the most egalitarian nation in the world—was divided, like Gaul, into three parts: "those who live on their capital, those who live by mental or physical skills, and those who live on their muscles." His solution was a "more Christian" society, and when he was reminded of American riches and a widespread rise in standards, insisted that this was not enough, because inequities persisted. "Poverty can only be eliminated," he said, "when its causes are removed. The alternative is revolution."[8] How that would remove the causes of poverty he did not make clear, but he was releasing ideas that were filled with European gases, that floated like balloons across the landscape, while all around him poverty was being overcome by ideas and men he despised.

To a considerable extent, President Polk represented such men. "What connection slavery had with making peace with Mexico is difficult to conceive," he wrote in his diary, and other practical men agreed. The South especially favored the war: Pierce Butler, Jefferson Davis, and Robert E. Lee were among many who won laurels, as did Northern officers like U.S. Grant and George McClellan. Volunteers mostly came from the South; the state of Tennessee alone produced ten times the number asked of it. Yet the eagerness of the non-slaveholding Southerner was not for slaves, but for Western lands.

But New England disapproved, as did Joshua Giddings from the Western Reserve, and the rhetoric of such new spokesmen as Charles Sumner poured acid into the wounds of war. "Blood! Blood! is on the hands of the representative from Boston," he wrote in a diatribe against Robert Winthrop, "and not all great Neptune's ocean can wash them clean."[9]

With several other young Whigs, Sumner bought a Boston newspaper to agitate against the war, charging that its promoters were slaveholders linked to the New England mill owners. His law office, no longer interested in courtroom practices or clients, became filled with men calling themselves "conscience" Whigs, as opposed to "cotton" Whigs, and Sumner made contact with such antislavery leaders as Salmon P. Chase and Joshua Giddings.

A wave of propaganda, in which attacks on the war were intermingled with attacks on the large mill owners of New England, washed across New England and the North. John Brown, for the first time, was situated in an urban setting where meetings, speeches, and agitators were present. One of his daughters later wrote that he went to considerable effort to hear women's-rights leaders Lucretia Mott and Abby Kelley Foster. For the first time Brown also began to meet free blacks —including two militants: Reverend J.W. Loguen of Syracuse and Reverend Henry Highland Garnet of Troy. Brown probably listened to them preach violent rebellion.

With its propensity for creating paper heroes—men of words and writing and instant celebrities—propaganda was irresistible to Brown. Not a man to admire anyone's success without trying to emulate that person, Brown sat down and wrote a crude, semiliterate satire called "Sambo's Mistakes," and sent it to the *Ram's Horn,* a newspaper published by blacks in New York City.[10] It was poorly constructed and spelled, more caustic than comical: the work of a man without education. The overall thesis was that blacks were too easily satisfied with small luxuries, too admiring of whites, and too docile in their situation. Whether the editors ever knew it was contributed by a white man seems dubious. But it appeared in the *Ram's Horn,* and there is something about it that still disturbs. The hatred it exuded—natural enough, under the circumstances of the day, in a black—was twisted in a white man.

Brown also began to talk about a "plan" for freeing the slaves. He was a man of many plans, though perhaps it might be more accurate to say, a man of many opinions, whose opinions were often announced as plans. Word trickled through the black community, through letters and conversations, that a wool merchant in Springfield was saying things that white men seldom said—or thought. In due course these interesting rumors reached Frederick Douglass.

Only nine years freed from slavery, and fresh from a tour of Britain where he had been received by the antislavery aristocracy, entertained in mansions, Douglass had already had ample experience of the peculiarities of American Goodness. Some abolitionists criticized him for allowing his freedom to be purchased; they held he should not have recognized the legality of slavery.

But Douglass was a realist, more gifted than those who gathered to hear him thunder. He thrilled audiences with his six-feet-tall bulk, his shock of hair that gave him a leonine appearance, his deep voice, and his natural eloquence. Largely self-educated, he was, in 1847, still feeling his way. Impressed by Garrison, he launched a newspaper of his own, called *The North Star,* in Rochester, New York. Gerrit Smith, Reverend Samuel J. May, Joshua Giddings, Charles Sumner, and other antislavery leaders all helped Douglass, but none to the extent that he was able to become independent. His newspaper was a step toward that goal. But like all free blacks in the United States, Douglass could not enter lyceums except as a speaker, was barred from social gatherings except those of special nature, was condemned to continual snubs, insults, and rudeness.

He therefore led three simultaneous lives. In one, he was a lecturer and circuit lion, in another a newspaper editor struggling with bills and circulation, and in the third, a "stationmaster" on the "Underground Railroad"—the famous secret passage that carried fugitive slaves to freedom. The Underground Railroad had central depots in Baltimore, Philadelphia, New York, Syracuse, Rochester, and Buffalo. Rochester was a jumping-off-place to Canada, where network agents received the fugitives and helped them build new lives.[11] Both whites and blacks maintained the railroad; John Brown had no connection with it.

But Garnet and Loguen were both key figures in the network, and when they mentioned the Springfield wool merchant to Douglass, he noticed that "their voices would drop to a whisper." Douglass was sufficiently interested, to say he would like to meet the man, and in due course an invitation was passed along. Douglass appeared at the offices of Perkins & Brown and was impressed. He decided the proprietor must be "a man of considerable wealth."[12]

He was pleased when Brown—"clad in plain American woolen, shod in boots of cowhide leather and wearing a cravat of the same substantial material, under six feet high, less than 150 pounds in weight, aged about fifty"—invited him to his home. Douglass thought Brown's bearing was "singularly impressive." He noted that "his eyes were bluish-gray, and . . . full of light and fire. When on the street he moved with a long, springing, race-horse step, absorbed by his own reflections . . ." Douglass walked with him—a lion to Brown's fox—away from the "prominent, busy street" where Perkins & Brown had their offices and warehouse, into a "small wooden building on a back street, in a neighborhood occupied chiefly by laboring men and mechanics—respectable enough, but not quite the place . . . for the residence of a prosperous and flourishing merchant."

Douglass masked his surprise on being ushered into a home he described as "Spartan." Mary Brown and her brood were inside, and Douglass was served "tea." With his lively sense of humor, he described this—beef soup, cabbage and potatoes—as "a meal a man might enjoy after following the plow all day, or performing a forced march of a dozen miles over a rough road in frosty weather." It was served on a crude, unvarnished table. Douglass also noted that Mrs. Brown and the children waited on him and Brown without pretense—and also that Brown ruled his household absolutely.

After a long preamble in which he cursed slaveholders as bitterly as a black man Brown unfolded his plan cautiously. Douglass, schooled in patience by hard experience, waited, watched, and listened. In essence, Brown wanted to create an armed force in the heart of the South. He brought out a map. Pointing out the Allegheny mountain chain, which stretched south from New York, he described the range as the basis of his plan: "placed by God for the emancipation of the Negro race."

He discussed how small bands of men could hide in the Alleghenies. "I know these mountains well," he lied, "and could take a body of men into them and keep them there despite all the efforts of Virginia to dislodge them." He went on to say he needed, at first, "only about twenty-five picked men, and begin on a small scale—supply them with arms and ammunition, and post them in squads of five on a line of twenty-five miles." From time to time, the men would persuade slaves to join them. When they numbered a hundred, they would have a new band.

Douglass wondered how these men would subsist, and Brown said:

"upon the enemy. Slavery was a state of war, and a slave had a right to anything necessary to his freedom." That was an anticipation of the later sermons of Theodore Parker, who would argue that slaves had a right to kill for freedom.[13]

Douglass objected: if the plan moved well, the slaveholders would sell their slaves farther south. "Then," said Brown, "I would follow them up." Douglass said they would hunt him with bloodhounds. "The chances are, we should whip them . . . . But you might be surrounded and cut off." Brown thought they could fight their way out, "but if the worst came he could but be killed, and he had no better cause for his life than to lay it down in the cause of the slave."

Douglass looked around at the barren little house and the children, and Brown, as if reading his thoughts, said he had "adopted this simple manner . . . to save money to carry out his purposes." Douglass was impressed; Brown was a man of remarkably open manner; his Biblical phrases and cadences flowed so spontaneously and so appropriately than even Douglass—who had heard and would continue to hear a great deal of hypocritical piety—was impressed.

Douglass spent the night and was, apparently, able to sleep. But he was deeply shaken. He had been spouting the Garrison line of peaceful resistance: that was one of the reasons he was welcome on so many different platforms. Garrison, Wendell Phillips, and many ministers managed to make that line sound plausible, reasonable, and even hopeful. But Brown's brutal words had carried with them something real. Nobody knew better than Frederick Douglass that slavery was a harsh fact in a violent world. In Salem, Ohio, he said openly, for the first time, that slavery "could only be destroyed by bloodshed." So-journer Truth interrupted him, and asked, "Frederick, is God dead?"

"No," he answered, "and because God is not dead slavery can only end in blood."[14]

John Brown, a white man, had introduced a new note that encouraged violence by blacks against whites.

Chapter 30

New notes were being sounded all over New England. In September 1847 the church at Newburyport, a town forty miles from Boston, was packed with people attending the ordination of a new young pastor, the Reverend Thomas Wentworth Higginson. His cousin, the Rev. William Henry Channing, spoke of George Whitfield's revival over a century before, and how it had split the Newburyport Presbyterians; Channing said he was willing to see another such split, proposed "a redistribution of landed property, a new sliding scale of wages, and a new system of equitable commerce." He alluded to the "enigma" of Jesus, and concluded, "all forces must converge to create a perfect society."[1]

The Reverend James Freeman Clarke then rose and urged the young pastor to speak, "regardless of who is offended by that honesty." He was followed by the Reverend Thomas T. Stone, a contributor to the now defunct *The Dial,* and well known for his criticisms of American "love of material wealth."

The congregation that heard this series of avant-garde opinions was one of the most conservative in the region. Newburyport was Garrison's birthplace, and its newspaper was where he had learned his trade. One of its leading merchants was Francis Todd, whom Garrison had slandered in a Baltimore paper (and had been jailed for doing so). The attack on Todd can be said to have had at least part of its genesis in an old animosity.

Once a leading seaport, the town had declined and almost died after the War of 1812. Its merchants had then built large glass display windows for their stores and invested in textile steam mills; five of these were working day and night when Reverend Higginson arrived. Newburyport's population burgeoned with its new industry, which employed huge numbers of women. The First Religious Society connected the mills, the banks, the newspaper, and the old elite. But pulpits yawned empty all over New England, as the new doctrines of Harvard and the new movements lured young men away from the ministry, and Newburyport was willing to accept even Rev. Higginson —and his radical sponsors—to keep its church alive.[2]

For his part, Higginson had a legacy from his grandfather, but a pulpit was a podium; and it was the podium he wanted. His terms were freedom of speech, freedom of exchange, freedom of six months' notice, freedom to choose his own way. These had been accepted. However, hardly had Higginson been installed than the Newburyport *Herald* editor warned its readers that the new pastor "seems tinctured with those radical and imaginative notions . . . which would seek to govern society more wisely than God has seen fit to guide it ever since the dawn of creation."

Shortly afterward Higginson married Mary Channing, his second cousin, to whom he had been engaged for nearly four years. She was twenty-seven; he was twenty-four. They moved into a pleasant house a block from the Pleasant Street Church, and a maid was hired to spare the bride, whose health was uncertain. Mary Higginson was also offended by "the ugliness" of Newburyport, and found its people "unfascinating."

Her husband had other objections. The fumes from a rum refinery displeased a temperance preacher, as did the sight of numerous drunks. One of the town's steam mills was next door to the church. But

Higginson's preliminary talks with the elders seemed to go well; they were Whigs and not overly enthusiastic about the war. The town's leading Democrat, Caleb Cushing, was fighting in it—and paying for his own regiment. But Newburyport was Webster territory—which meant that it was, basically, for an expanded and expanding United States.

In early October, 1847, Higginson invited the Essex County Antislavery Society to hear Parker Pillsbury, a famous abolitionist notorious for his attacks on the churches, and Reverend Samuel J. May, the Garrisonian. The speakers went through their usual accusations and then added the Whigs to their demonology. The audience grew angry and shouts drowned the orators; the meeting broke apart in disarray.

It was not an auspicious start, and Higginson, delivering his hand-tooled sermons—from a pulpit that towered two stories high over the Pleasant Street congregation—did not noticeably improve on it. His topics were not religious so much as societal. He attacked conditions in the Newburyport mills, declared crime was a product of the town in which it appeared, and dwelled on the evils of rum. The congregation, which numbered about five hundred when he started, soon dwindled visibly. Offended by Mary Higginson's condescension, the ladies of the town withdrew their invitations and stopped calling. The Higginsons found themselves isolated. And Higginson began to feel sorry for himself. He went to Theodore Parker for advice, but found Parker "so strong and self-sufficing" that he left even more depressed. Even the poor with whom he worked seemed to lack gratitude and appreciation. By June 1848, at the Unitarian convention, he rose to complain that younger ministers were not sufficiently encouraged and wondered aloud if there should not be "a new social organization to include Christianity," rather than a strictly Christian Church.[3] The pulpit, in other words, was not enough.

Gerrit Smith found life physically and socially more comfortable, though his familiar demons of discontent continued to gnaw at him. His hypochondria kept him in daily expectation of painful death, he sifted through mounds of letters appealing for money every morning, and penned heated denunciations of sin between business details. Very few persons or events entirely pleased Gerrit Smith; he was accustomed to returning even his wife's letters, when he was traveling, with corrections of their grammar, spelling, and ideas.[4]

The economic distress of the early 40's, which had ruined John Brown and hundreds of thousands of others, had squeezed Gerrit Smith as well: at one point he had planned to sell his mansion, and his wife and daughter Elizabeth had gone to work in his office. But by 1845 he had recovered and moved back to the mansion, and a modest investment in land along the Oswego Canal turned out—unlike John Brown's speculations—to be a bonanza. Smith's business acumen was, in truth, phenomenal. In 1846, again surveying the world from financial heights, he set in motion vast land sales of 750,000 acres at public auction. Some of the fairly worthless land was to be given to free blacks.

In April 1848, Smith and John Brown met at Peterboro for the first time. As previously mentioned, Brown convinced Smith that he was intent on helping blacks and Smith agreed to sell him some land so he could settle his family among the black beneficiaries of Smith's bounty. Brown moved his family into that remote Northern location and after settling the family in, he took off to look after the wool business.

John Brown saw Frederick Douglass depart, and returned to his wool business—which had been in serious difficulties from the start, no matter how impressive the office and warehouse may have appeared to outsiders. Correspondence had piled up to such an extent that John Brown, Jr. (who had now obtained an education, married, and settled in Ohio), was persuaded to come to Springfield and function as the company clerk—a difficult task under a disorganized and obdurate proprietor.

Despite the anguished pleas of growers, who needed the money, Brown refused to sell wool at whatever he regarded as an unfair price —either high or low. In order to placate those who pressed too hard, however, he began to borrow money from the banks. The man who would not deal with others on credit used credit to keep himself afloat.

Around him the nation boiled. The Wilmot Proviso to prohibit slavery in new territories had inflamed the South into meetings and demonstrations to expand slavery. Hotheads in Alabama, South Carolina, and Virginia rose to make fevered speeches that matched, in vitriol and hatred, the diatribes of the abolitionists. New men appeared, fiery and one-eyed, "ultras" in every sense. Around this steaming cauldron tiptoed such men as James Buchanan, trying to find a safe spot. Buchanan favored extending the Missouri Compromise, with slavery allowed in the South and forbidden in the North, all across the country. But firebrands in both sections were loose—and running.

In that atmosphere the 30th Congress met late in 1847. Angry debate raged over the Wilmot Proviso. A representative from Illinois named Abraham Lincoln raised his voice against the war, while others argued over slavery and whether it should be allowed in Oregon, in California, and the lands expected to be wrenched from Mexico.

The debates were still under way when the Mexican government collapsed. Santa Anna and his staff fled from Mexico City, and General Winfield Scott, "mounted on a heavy bay horse, his powerful figure resplendent in full-dress uniform, gleaming epaulettes, and nodding plumes, his aides clustered about him" entered the Mexican capital as a conqueror at the head of his troops.

In early 1848, by the treaty of Guadalupe Hidalgo, the United States took, as spoils of war, a vast tract embracing the coast of California, the deserts of Arizona and New Mexico, the green fields of eastern Texas and its sandy western wastes—a total of 850,000 square miles, completing the nation's expansion from the Atlantic to the Pacific.

The treaty debate was under way when John Quincy Adams, eighty-two years old and still fighting all comers, fell in a convulsion in his chair. He was carried to a waiting room and spent hours dying. Joshua Giddings, his congressional heir, waited through the ordeal and reported his last words.[5]

That cooled the air. Adams had been the last prominent link with the Revolution; his life had been a marvel of energy, intelligence, and courage. His death restored some sense—even in Congress—of the larger qualities that sustained the nation. The lawyers in Congress halted their eternal, serpentine coilings long enough to pass the treaty —and then resumed their arguments.

Their bitter strife however, clouded, even for future generations, the immense accomplishments and amazing will of President Polk. He had expanded the boundaries of the United States farther than any president except Thomas Jefferson, who only had to pay some money. Polk had matched his wits against the fabled diplomats of Britain and emerged with both land and honor; he had led the nation in an inescapable war and won it quickly.[6] He had also met several other promises he made when campaigning; he never wavered from them. He had no intention of running for office again; had said so when elected —thus unintentionally opening the gate to unending struggles for succession. His last year in office was unpleasant; his accomplishments were derided, shouted down and scorned; and his entire difficult but successful term was cast into historical shadows by the arguments that raged between North and South over slavery.

In early 1848, Ralph Waldo Emerson—who had long ago dropped his reverence—was in England. His first visit was to Carlyle; the two men had helped one another professionally but their reunion, after fourteen years, was like a reacquaintance. Once again Emerson was surprised by Carlyle's vigor and lack of scholarly airs, and Carlyle was surprised by Emerson's "moonshine" and "intellectual sonatas." But they got along well, and Emerson proceeded to triumphs seldom—if ever—achieved by any but a British writer on that insular island.

Although Scotland was impressed, London proved to be Emerson's great stage, at a time when to be accepted in the cultural capital of the English-speaking world was to soar beyond other Americans. In one letter Emerson jubilantly wrote that he dined with Macaulay, Bunsen, Lord Morpeth, Milman, and Milnes on one occasion, with Carlyle, the Lyells, and the Butlers on another, and on a third with Lord Monteagle, Cobden, and Lady Baring. He was elected an honorary member of the Athenaeum, a recognition dealt only to the most eminent. He met Lord Palmerston, the prime minister. He went to Oxford and chatted with Palgrave, Froude and other Fellows of that university. He became better acquainted with Dickens and with Tennyson. He also saw Chartists street riots being suppressed.

It was the year of revolutions in Europe. In Paris, where Emerson had an apartment on the Rue des Beaux Arts, he saw the revolutionists Blanqui and Barbés. He heard Michelet lecture, and was offended by his sarcasms on Hindu philosophy. He was also received by de Tocqueville and his English wife. On his return to London he lectured with fair success. The Duke of Argyll, son-in-law of the Duchess of Sutherland, invited to meet Emerson, complained that he was "somewhat cloying, wanting bone and gristle."[7] Otherwise the duke was charmed by the American's reserve and his slightly aloof courtesy.

Before he left, however, Emerson ventured to criticize Cromwell to Carlyle, was alarmed by the latter's passion. Emerson decided that his friend was "no idealist in opinions, but a protectionist in political economy, aristocratic in politics and epicure in diet," that he favored "murder, punishment by death, slavery and all the pretty abominations, tempering them epigrams."[8] The two parted friends, but Emerson was shaken.

He arrived in the United States in July 1848 to find some more surprises, he had assured his shipboard friends his wife would be at the dock but she did not arrive. At home he discovered she had resumed going to church, and was—to his silent shock—turning toward the orthodox faith, that she had prepared "a protest against Transcendentalism, and a philosophy she found insufferable," and had been joined in this intellectual rebellion by their eldest daughter.

Dr. Samuel Gridley Howe became interested in morons, and examined hundreds before deciding they could be trained, to a limited extent. Despite this clear evidence of sympathy for their circumstances, the physician's theories regarding the causes of such congenital handicaps were severe. "There must have been sin," he would say firmly.[9]

Like his close associates, Howe felt surrounded by sin, including sins against society. Blending the religious with the medical, he traced the physical results of violations of moral laws. Intemperance, for example, "lymphotized" the body and "demolished the fibrous part." Idiots were the result of the principle of the sins of the fathers being visited on their children.[10] "They have been too tenderly treated," he said of these unfortunates, "they must be *taught.*" That seemed stern, but in his personal relations with such pupils, as Superintendent of the first Massachusetts School for Idiotic and Feeble-Minded Youths, Howe proved patient, helpful and kind. Like Frank Bird of the Bird Club, he tended to be partial toward the handicapped, neutral toward the average, and sharp with the exceptional. Such prejudices were harmless enough on a personal level, but Dr. Howe and his closest associates tended to project these judgments onto society as a whole. To ascribe all injustice to sins of heredity or of entire classes within society was to foster indignation and even anger.

That sort of anger smoldered all through the ranks of the extreme reformers to give their statements and efforts a profoundly disturbing effect. It was enhanced by their claims to be motivated by ideals beyond those of other men. Garrison spoke in the name of nonviolence and brotherhood, and scalded clergymen and churches as betrayers of the faith, but he never described the doctrine he considered true. Theodore Parker denied the divinity of Jesus, mocked the Trinity, scorned predestination, and held all society sinful in tone. He also made it clear that any deviations from his opinions would uphold, defend, or represent sin.

And where Parker and Garrison led, others followed, creating a chorus that lent weight and volume to the assumptions of the leaders. Charles Sumner spoke of peace as Christian and war as un-Christian: this would leave all Christians defenseless. Howe spoke of natural deficiencies as the result of sin. In the process, these voices were forging a creedless, churchless religion that did not call so much for individual reform as for converts to carry their new versions of Goodness into political changes.

Whig party leaders were aware that the reformers burned to improve society—and their own positions. When Webster—the fiery-eyed, eloquent Senator from Massachusetts—toured the South in early 1848 seeking support for the Whig presidential nomination, these party leaders suggested to the reformers that the senator was too much of a "compromiser" to deserve support.

Howe and Sumner took the bait, and helped undermine Webster's chances for the nomination. Then the Whig elders calmly steered the nomination toward General Zachary Taylor, a hero of the Mexican War—and a slaveholder. Unable to admit publicly how thoroughly they had been duped, the enraged reformers bolted the Whig party.

Their new creation, the Free Soil party, was, as its name implies, a collection of single-eyed zealots with little beyond their convictions against slavery to offer the average voter. The Democratic party, on the other hand, nominated Lewis Cass, a homely bear of a man, who had sidestepped both Southern and Northern extremists by suggesting that settlers in the new territories should decide for themselves whether or not they would allow the peculiar institution.

The free-soilers, the malcontents of the Whig party, attracted—far more than its leaders realized—malcontents from the Democratic party as well. Their platform was not generally popular, being centered on demands for radical change that hardly anyone considered practical beyond their inner circle, but they nevertheless managed to make a great deal of noise, applauded one another, and created a coalition for the future. In the process they created platforms denied by the leaders in major organizations. Led by Richard Henry Dana, Jr. and Sumner, joined by the political poet John Greenleaf Whittier, and backed by the wealthy manufacturer Frank Bird, they welded reform elements (and won the blessings of the transcendentalists). Higginson was invited to join and was tempted. He agreed to take the stump and speak for the new party, if it nominated Martin Van Buren and Charles Francis Adams. It did, and he plunged.

Higginson's congregation was appalled, especially by his articles attacking General Taylor as a slaveholder. Now their young pastor frequently disappeared to make stump speeches. Mary Higginson approved: she had initially steered her husband onto reform paths. Her approval did not extend, however, to opening her home to Higginson's political associates: they could stay at the Old Wolfe Tavern. She did not relent simply because some were well known. Charles Sumner drew her acidulous comments because "he has not very good manners . . . always sits in the rocking chair, gapes almost constantly without any attempt at concealment and picks his teeth."[11] (But she approved of Sumner's moral sentiments.) Others did not fare much better. Reverend Hedge, transcendentalist star, was "unbearably pompous and egotistical." Higginson, however, adored such visitors: to have them seated before his fireplace, chatting with him on great national and intellectual issues, made him feel a part of the great and important world of events. George Luther Stearns, who had attended the Worcester Convention, was among the men who crowded into Sumner's Boston law office, earlier in 1848, to discuss the exciting revolutionary happenings in Europe. There, he heard Sumner describe his meetings, years before, with Mazzini, Louis Blanc, and other revolutionaries. He also listened while Samuel Gridley Howe chimed in with his own revolutionary experiences and revolutionary opinions.

Stearns was a member of the Bird Club, and as was Rev. Higginson, and the mutterings of conservatives were as unimportant to both as the change of the seasons. Even Julia Ward Howe, who was not a political person, and found entertaining the humorless Sumner a sometimes difficult chore, began to see that her husband had found an obsession, and would not soon let it go. Watching him leaving the Institute, with rapid step, Sumner at his side, she began to sing to her babies:

Rero, rero, riddety rad;
This morning my baby caught sight of her Dad.
Quoth she, "Oh, Daddy, where have you been?
With Mann and Sumner, a putting down sin!"[12]

The course of the presidential campaign so greatly excited Reverend Higginson, that even the experience of exchanging pulpits with Reverend Theodore Parker—and the opportunity to orate before thousands in the Melodeon—did not assuage him when he saw a Newburyport torchlight Whig parade that was funded by his own parishioners. That led him, in fact, to deliver an anti-Whig pulpit jeremiad so vitriolic that Garrison praised it, and the Democrats circulated it as a campaign document. That recognition from larger circles led Higginson to console himself with the thought that Newburyport would, in time, awaken to recognition of his talents.

Unfortunately, even activities unconnected with the elections further widened the hostilities between the young minister and the town. The local *Herald* editor was not pleased when Emerson appeared at the Lyceum, and termed him "a professed Pantheist." That antipathy was not lightened when it was learned the Lyceum committee had actually voted against Emerson's appearance in the first place, and that Higginson and his remaining friends had taken advantage of an inadequately attended meeting to reverse the vote.

Other collisions of a similar nature arose: Higginson spoke against the mill operations and the local distillery, and argued fervently to improve the lot of the mill workers—although most observers agreed that New England mill conditions were then the best in the world.

By that time the 1848 presidential elections were over; the torchlight parades had ended, the platforms were empty, the speakers silent. "Old Zack," General Zachary Taylor—a shrewd but unschooled man with a heavy torso, short legs, and a seamed backwoodsman's face— was in the White House, slaves and all. The Free Soil party in Massachusetts, however, had reason for pride: it had garnered 40,000 votes in the state and nearly 300,000 in the nation, to account for 10 percent of all votes cast. It was clearly a new, influential force in the North. Higginson could console himself with the fact that he had not worked with illustrious literati and ardent reformers in vain—although that was cold comfort after the campaign, when he became unhappily aware that his situation in Newburyport had worsened.

Dr. Howe was in a secure position and Reverend Theodore Parker was prodigiously active in the pulpit. Only Charles Sumner, moving with unexpected dexterity, toiled for righteousness and his political prospects at the same time. In 1849 he hoisted a banner, "Equality Before Law," that neatly appealed to diverse groups.

Sumner also brought suit to break down the separation of the races in the common schools of Massachusetts. His argument in this case, however, was not based on law—the precedents were against him—but on "philosophical and psychological grounds." He argued that children of both races were injured by education in different facilities, and that such a system differed "in spirit and character" from what constituted a proper common school.[13]

As chairman of the Free Soil party's state executive committee, Sumner also helped steer his party toward a coalition with the Democrats, breaking with the Whigs forever—and also with Beacon Hill. At the age of thirty-nine, the former protégé of Justice Story, the law student who hated to leave college, a darling of London society, had completed a transformation. His remaining friends were so impressed that they considered him a near-saint, because he insisted that he moved only from conviction and not from any "selfish" purpose. He often rejected suggestions that he enter politics in earnest, saying he planned "a great historical work." That work was never started, however, and Sumner's political presence grew larger with every passing month.

By 1849 the firm of Perkins & Brown was rumored to be in trouble. The rumors were accurate. John Brown had proved to be so difficult an individual, so prickly in his opinions, so arbitrary in his prices, that buyers stopped calling on him. He scented conspiracy; it did not occur to him that even business is a human relationship and that men will not go out of their way to seek trouble. Instead, he wrote that manufacturers were "obstinately holding back not withstanding that our prices are decidedly below European prices. They are evidently trying to get rid of us permanently and get the wool again under their own absolute controll."[14] He clung to that thought, but the fact was that manufacturers saw no reason to deal with John Brown for cash when they could obtain wool on two months' credit. Brown could not grasp that his own terms put him at a competitive disadvantage, or that his grades were not needed in a marketplace that bought on lots, and in which growers would send in uncleaned wool, packed with dirt and other foreign matter for mill owners to clean, weigh, and grade.

With his business on the verge of collapse, he decided to ship his wool to England, then to follow it personally, and sell it in that country. During May, June, and July 1849, he sent ahead 200,000 pounds—690 bales—and left Boston on the steamer *Cambria* on August 15, bound for Liverpool. He was, of course, behaving eccentrically: wool can be shipped overseas and sold without the proprietor following it to conduct a personal auction—although some wool merchants with whom he had corresponded promised to attend his London sale, But Brown was obsessed with the idea that sinister forces and evil men dominated the trade; he trusted nobody but himself, though he expected everyone else to trust him.

His letters from England were those of a farmer: he wrote his son John, Jr. about the appearance of horses, hogs, breeding mares, and sheep. In London on August 27 he learned the sales would not begin for nearly a month, and crossed the Channel to Paris. Then—a restless, lost, and worrying soul—he took a train to Brussels and Hamburg. Nothing he saw impressed him much; he had the true bumpkin's inability to be impressed by anything new or different, having no standard other than familiarity to guide his judgment.

At Brussels he stopped, disembarked, and walked around the site of Waterloo, squinting to connect the contours of the land with the movements of the several armies that had contended there, and afterward boasted he had achieved, mentally, in a few hours what would take the most highly trained military staff officer a long time to approximate. After that private charade he proceeded to Hamburg, no doubt to see other merchants. Later he told Frank Sanborn that during this period —about ten days—he watched military reviews, looked at various battlefields, and examined German agriculture. This was somewhat vague, but as usual he had sharp, clear, and critical opinions on all these subjects. He completely misunderstood the German cooperative farms, whose owners shared their labor and lived in villages; Brown thought they deprived their land of "natural manures."

In mid-September he was back in London, where he endured a scalding humiliation. The British buyers ripped his bales open, and in some—despite his often-repeated boast that he examined, washed, and graded his wool—found "twigs, mud and other impurities, placed by growers hoping to add to he weight of their bales."[15]

That demolished Brown's credibility and he watched as bids dropped to levels lower than those he had fled in the United States. After seeing 150 bales go at these embarrassingly low prices, he stopped the sale. Even then, exposed before a group of openly scornful buyers, he could not admit that he had misrepresented his wool as being washed, cleaned, graded, and in perfect condition. Instead, he wrote John, Jr. "I have a great deal of stupid, obstinate prejudice to contend with as well as conflicting interests, both in this country and the United States . . ." His enemies, therefore, were still engaged in a conspiracy—this time a transatlantic one—and had added bigotry to their evil machinations.

Having decided that English sales agents were unreliable, Brown now undertook to make his own sales, and went on a tour of mill towns. Again, he misunderstood the trade. English mill owners had their agents, who operated in sales centers, and the agents were not interested in itinerant sellers from abroad who appeared without notice on their doorsteps. Brown sold his best grades at a loss, pegged his lower grades at prices the English would not meet, and then sailed for Boston in October, leaving one hundred thousand pounds of unsold wool behind. From Springfield he arranged for a ruinous sale of that wool.

John Brown had been warned against his trip abroad by Thomas Musgrave, a wool manufacturer who had offered him sixty cents a pound before he left. Shortly after Brown returned, Musgrave dropped in on E. C. Leonard, a wool merchant with offices near Perkins & Brown, and invited Leonard to share some fun. "Then he went to the stairs and called Uncle John and told him he wanted to go over to the Hartford depot and see a lot of wool he had bought. So Uncle John put on his coat, and we started. When we arrived at the depot, and just as we were going in to the freight-house, Musgrave says, 'Mr. Brune, I want you to tell me what you think of this lot of wull that stands me in just fifty-two cents a pund.' "[16]

John Brown saw his own London wool, baled, with the stamp of Perkins & Brown on it. He wheeled quickly and stalked back to his office with "his brown coat-tails floating behind him," leaving Musgrave and Leonard staggering about in helpless laughter.

Chapter 31

In the spring of 1849 the Reverend Thomas Wentworth Higginson attempted to avert the fate of George Hannewell, a black who had been sentenced to be hanged for burning down his own home and killing his parents. Higginson intervened because he was against capital punishment, and his argument, inside that larger one, was that Hannewell had committed arson only "to frighten," and without intent to kill. His campaign failed even to excite attention: Newburyport refused to honor him to the extent of being annoyed with him.

Disconsolate, he went on an extended vacation and in June finally went to Concord to call on Thoreau, whose book he had praised to Emerson. He found "a little bronzed square man" alongside his father, making pencils in the family business. Emerson had mentioned Higginson to Thoreau, whose welcome was warm. Higginson was struck by "the most unvarying facsimile of Mr. Emerson."[1] In a few years people would make the same observation about Higginson.

Later, Higginson told Emerson he was "lonely and unsupported" and Emerson invited him to join a "town and country club," which he and Alcott had created with twenty-nine other men earlier in the year, and which had no settled headquarters. The group was impressive in transcendentalist terms: the Reverend Frederick Hedge, and the Reverend John Dwight, the Reverend William Henry Channing, the Reverend Theodore Parker, Henry Wadsworth Longfellow, James Russell Lowell, and even Garrison were members. Lowell called it a collection of eccentric particles gathered to make their own planet. Higginson, strangely, was not even happy at this recognition. He observed that Lowell did not respect anyone else's opinion—and apparently Lowell was far from the only offender. Higginson also noted that no women were members, and decided that a Negro would not be acceptable either.[2] He dropped away.

He also dropped away from his pulpit. At first he tried to assume the attitude of one being driven away, but the fact was that he had driven his congregation away. In early autumn 1849, he gave six months' notice, to few and faint demurrals. The trustees accepted his decision with embarrassing alacrity, and muttered about differences of opinion.

Mary Higginson was pleased; she often spoke of the "littleness" of the people of Newburyport, and the couple moved to Artichoke Hills to live with a distant, aged relative, Mrs. Mary Curzon, whose income was large enough to allow them free lodging. Deciding to lecture, Higginson began to take notes on nature. In this he was following many footsteps: Emerson's, Channing's, and Theodore Parker's. Years before, when he was launching his ministerial career, Parker had written his fiancee that, despite his wisdom, "a single walk along the banks of the Connecticut . . . have taught me more than Mr. Emerson and all the Boston Association of Ministers." Robert C. Albrecht, the historian, later remarked on this: "That scholars should value most highly their non-literary experience may seem ironic, but in their view the reading was done to find support for opinions derived intuitively, and to learn what other men said, rather than to appreciate how they said it."[3] Higginson was entering a well-trodden path, and he would have to run to catch up. He was handicapped by a certain literal quality of mind as well: he could see neither order, design, nor morality but simply "a voluptuousness" in nature that bewildered him. Emerson sought to enlighten him, but Higginson grew angry, "and felt like stopping his ears."

Nevertheless he began to lecture, receiving fifteen dollars an appearance—as opposed to the twenty-five dollars usually paid to Emerson or Parker. He enjoyed the experience. It was well that he did; there was little else in his situation at that time that he could enjoy; life with wealthy and aged relatives bears its own irritations, and although he had an income of his own from his grandfather's estate, Higginson was drifting.

Abolitionist agitations, mounted by a relative handful, had proceeded now for a generation. In that time its rhetoric had gradually entered every public issue and every national debate, and had created irritations everywhere. Abolitionist lecturers, writers, and leaders had risen, inch by inch against violence and heavy odds, to convince overseas observers of their importance and to create sweeping though resentful changes in the South. Even the war with Mexico and its great victories was clouded by abolitionist protest. Arguments over whether the new territories should enter the Union as free or slave states distorted congressional debate even after the 1848 elections, and in the weeks before Old Zack Taylor was sworn into office in 1849.

Even the discovery of gold in California and the great land rush did not end the controversy. It penetrated every issue and darkened every debate. Would California be admitted as a free state? Would New Mexico be admitted as a slave state?

The Underground Railroad was transporting a small but steady trickle of fugitives out of the South; the possibility of new free-state senators would upset the balance of power between the regions. Abolitionist agitation in the North, although barred from the South, injured the reputation of the United States abroad, soured personal relationships in the Capitol, and stifled the dialogue between North and South.

The South smarted under a wave of denigration that issued from hundreds of Northern presses and hundreds more lecture platforms. The South's culture and religion were denied, its classes mocked, its heritage and accomplishments ignored. Millions of Northerners regarded the South as a region of nightmare and evil. The reality was far different. The South was a region not simply of Calvinism, but of the religious principles inherited from John Knox and Scotland. It was a region where the Bible was revered as the base of Western civilization, and where such ministers as the Reverend Theodore Parker were regarded as malignant in their influence. Lacking roads, with even its better known cities relatively small, with a population undisturbed by the streams of immigrants who poured through the North, the most important regions of the South—in South Carolina, Virginia, Tennessee, and other states—reflected the Scots Presbyterianism of an earlier age.

The ranks of upper-class Southern planters had been increased by the rise of King Cotton, and newcomers to these ranks imitated the manners and mores of their predecessors. In their close-knit families and customs, the planters resembled the "county families" of an older England more than they did the rising Victorians. The Southern poor white resembled the rural Scot, and believed, as did Bobby Burns two generations before, that "freedom and whiskey gang together." Even in poverty the Southern white was a landowner, proud of belonging to a superior race.

There were variant-pockets throughout the South, as throughout the North; towns and counties where Catholicism rather than Presbyterianism was dominant; cities like New Orleans with a different heritage and ethnic mix than in upcountry Louisiana. There were also pockets of abolitionism, and areas such as Virginia, where slaves were barbers, clerks, house servants, and housekeepers rather than field hands. But in general the South had remained unchanged since the Revolution. Its culture and social patterns were set and familiar. Duels were still fought. Men drank, gambled, and wenched as in the 18th century, while Victorianism, with all its pruderies and pretenses, its red light districts and its hypocrisies, altered the North. Southern anger rose steadily under a Northern barrage that insisted the South revolutionize itself, dislocate its economy, and change its pattern of relations between the races—all to please the consciences of men in another region who would suffer no pain, loss, or change of status from such changes.

At first the South was content to seal its mailbags against Northern propaganda and to issue denials and refutations. In time, abolitionist propaganda led to a worsening of the conditions of blacks; efforts to educate slaves were halted, and emancipations made more difficult. The conditions of free blacks declined remarkably. The South moved toward the condition of a garrison state in its own nation.

As immigrants filled the North, as its wealth and commerce increased, as Northern settlers moved west, Southern leaders began to see their political power decline in the government and the nation. If more free states were admitted, each with its senators and representatives, the precarious balance of power maintained since the Missouri Compromise of 1820 would tilt, and the South would inevitably become helpless against Northern votes.

At that juncture two Congressmen, Joshua Giddings—now white-haired but still ardent against slavery—and gangling young Abraham

Lincoln of Illinois, planned ambitious new moves. Giddings wanted to end slavery in Washington; Lincoln emerged with a plan to end slavery in the district through purchase, apprenticeship, and gradual emancipation over a period of years.[4] News of these plans traveled through Washington, and Whig leaders, alarmed at the reaction, warned both men to drop their projects. They did, but too late. John Caldwell Calhoun, political-intellectual master of South Carolina and the living voice of the defiant South, had heard the rumors, and rose like an angry hawk.

Calhoun's first response was an attempt to organize a "Southern Rights" party. In this he was opposed by all "standpatters," averse to change on principle. He was also opposed by senators Thomas Hart Benton of Missouri and Sam Houston of Texas, who opposed slavery and had voted for a free Oregon Territory. But Calhoun was supported by Jefferson Davis and James M. Mason of Virginia and, significantly, by other younger men. In the end the Southern caucus that Calhoun summoned decided only to issue a lukewarm statement of protest—though Calhoun's own fiery document was also printed and widely distributed through the South, where its argument slowly sank into many minds. A shift in power, said Calhoun, would be accompanied by a reinterpretation of the Constitution, the emancipation of slaves, and "the overthrow of Southern whites." He warned that "in the hours of abolitionist triumph the blacks would be raised to favor, office and power. The South would then become the abode of disorder, anarchy and wretchedness."[5] Calhoun argued that a unified South might avert this fate, and that its appearance alone might deflect the Northern drift and direction.

In New England these rumblings seemed faint and unimportant. Old Zack Taylor was sworn in as President, and as the year 1849 progressed the Free-Soilers were delighted to see that—slaveholder or no —Taylor favored the admission of both California and New Mexico as free states. Even more surprising, Free-Soilers dominated the cabinet and the administration. The most prominent influence over the President was that of New York's Senator William H. Seward—a thin, somewhat unprepossessing man whose persuasiveness appeared best in small groups. Behind him loomed Thurlow Weed and the Democrats of New York.

The Whigs, who had chosen a nonpolitical military hero to thrust into the White House, were now appalled to see their candidate pursue a policy that split the Whig party, both North and South, into angry factions. The Massachusetts Whigs were among those discomfited, and Charles Sumner, moving now "with muffled oars," steadily steered Free-Soilers into a coalition with Democrats.

The South grew thoroughly alarmed as the year went on. Calhoun's words, deprecated earlier, hung in the air like the predictions of Cassandra over Troy, and echoes began to be heard all through the region. This growing uneasiness was not improved by a bumper cotton crop and a corresponding drop in prices. Southern propaganda, long dormant, took a leap upward: a book called *Letters,* by the Reverend A. B. Longstreet, asserting that slavery had biblical sanction, began to run through successive editions, and the problem of runaway slaves suddenly surged to the fore.

In Boston, where a vigilance committee to help fugitive slaves had been formed—with such members as Theodore Parker, Dr. Samuel Gridley Howe, and George Luther Stearns—a series of meetings over the slavery issue continued to keep the subject alive. Early in 1849, at a meeting in Faneuil Hall, Wendell Phillips had thundered that Washington might pass "its little laws" but that "Faneuil Hall repeals them in the name of humanity . . ."[6]

Friday, August 3, 1849 was declared a day of fasting by President Taylor to lift the curse of a cholera plague. The New England Antislavery Society, disdaining that purpose, decided to use the day to celebrate West Indian emancipation, and called a mass meeting in Worcester, Massachusetts. Boston alone sent fourteen carloads of zealots. Speeches were made by Parker, Emerson, Adin Ballou—the Christian anarchist—and Wendell Phillips, before a crowd of five thousand.

The South then learned of various laws, in Massachusetts, Rhode Island, and other Northern states, that barred the arrest of fugitive slaves; Senator Butler of South Carolina estimated the cost of runaways to the South was now two hundred thousand a year. Some Southerners warned that the new federal law forbidding slave auctions in Washington would be followed by laws abolishing slavery in all federal installations, to create abolitionist pockets even in the South.

That possibility evoked hearty cheers from the New York *Tribune* which, thanks to high-speed presses and some remarkably gifted writers, was rapidly attaining an unprecedented circulation throughout the North. Its editor-proprietor, Horace Greeley, was more avid for power and influence than for money; among his assistants was the former Reverend George Ripley, whose Brook Farm had collapsed, and who was living in poverty in New York, ignored by his Boston transcendentalist friends.

Finally alarmed, Mississippi held a convention in October 1849; it was attended by both Whigs and Democrats who warned the federal government against antislavery moves and scheduled another convention—of all the Southern states—for June 1850. South Carolina followed suit, and though other Southern states did not go so far, all Southern governors instructed their senators and representatives to make a stand at the next session of Congress in December 1849.

When Congress assembled it was soon learned what all this meant: the contest for speaker of the House of Representatives was split between Whigs, Democrats, and Free Soilers. Day after day, week after week, vote after vote was taken with no candidate receiving a majority. Americans slowly grew aware that something new and ugly was underway; ballots were taken again and again, and as the fortieth, fiftieth, and sixtieth ballots were taken with no resolution, the nation began to realize that all the thunder and lightning had not been idle show. A hurricane had arrived; it threatened to blow the United States of America apart.

After a Southerner, Howell Cobb, was finally elected speaker a storm of argument broke forth over fugitive slaves, Northern abolitionists, Southern intransigence. Threats of secession rose, and carried with them—for the first time in a generation—an ominous sense of reality. Senator Thomas L. Clingman of North Carolina described how the Southern states could become independent, maintain ties with Britain, and survive on their own—and he threatened to hold up all Congressional business indefinitely. Northerners pounded their desks, and in the White House, Old Zack, confused but ready to lead an army anywhere he was pointed, proved unable to penetrate the issues, clarify them, or even confront them.

Such clear signs that the South was on the edge of a fight cooled some Northern leaders. But others, accustomed to the overblown rhetoric of the South and the exaggerated language of the times, were not impressed. As usual, men farthest from the argument were the most adamant.

In this crisis the seventy-three-year-old Henry Clay, balding and wrinkled but dapper and genial as ever, rose on January 29 to propose a series of compromises that admitted parts of the Northern and Southern demands. Most of these had already been suggested, piece by piece, by young Senator Stephen Douglas of Illinois. Clay's presentation was calm, measured, and persuasive. "Ultras" remained unmoved, but moderates were cheered—and their numbers were greater.

However, although Clay presented his compromise with great skill, Senator Seward convinced President Taylor to reject it. That left Clay at the mercy of the Northern abolitionists and Southern fire-eaters—and also led to the final appearance of the gravely ill Calhoun, who summoned his powers for one last convulsive effort. He had to be helped into the Senate chamber and seemed, when he arrived, the very image of death. He sat and surveyed the hall with burning eyes during the reading of his speech by Mason of Virginia.

The address spelled out the situation and its origins from the Southern viewpoint. Calhoun warned that even if emancipation was not accomplished, the Union would collapse "by the gradual snapping of the bonds that held it together." Some of those bonds, writes historian Allan Nevins, were religious. "The slavery issue had rent the Methodist, the Baptist and the Presbyerian churches asunder."[7] Political parties were divided, the people of the North and South were growing strange and foreign to one another. Calhoun's proposals to heal this situation were, in effect, a call to roll back Time: for the North to abandon its campaign and for both sections to unite in a new constitutional amendment that would, once again, make both North and South equal in political power. If this were not done, the South should resist and secede. The speech ended, Calhoun was helped toward the door. Stopped by some admirers, he was heard by Richard Henry Dana, Jr., to say, "At any rate, be men!" In his eerily accurate view the future was already present; the South was doomed.

Then the Senator from Massachusetts, Daniel Webster—for years the pride of his region but more recently a wounded champion, stabbed from behind by his old Whig supporters—entered the situation. While the debate was under way he had been pressed from many sides. The New York *Tribune* and other abolitionist voices reminded him of his words on freedom in the past; Webster had never liked slavery. Meanwhile he had toiled alone, sustaining himself with "oxide of arsenic and other drugs,"[8]—for he was no longer young. When he rose on March 7, 1850, nobody knew what to expect.

He spoke, he said, ". . . not as a Massachusetts man, not as a Northern man, but as an American . . . for the preservation of the Union . . ." He summed up both sides objectively, and then concentrated on the evils that would result from a rupture. He examined the economic and geographical realities restricting expansion of slavery, discussed the right of Southerners to have their property respected, and warned that peaceable secession was a chimera. The nation faced internal war —unless it agreed to peace. When Webster sat down, covered with perspiration, there was no question that he had spoken at the expense of his personal interests, and in favor of his nation—and that the terms of a settlement had been placed within reach. By all standards it was the greatest contribution Webster had ever made to his country, and it was to cost him more than anything he had ever done.

Letters of praise poured down on Webster from all parts of the Union; Whig leaders were delighted and the Boston *Advertiser*—the voice of Beacon Street—hailed his courage and his statesmanship. Invitations to speak arrived by the hundreds. Webster's address in the Senate was also a turning point for Congress. Members moved to draft the proposed compromise into law, and included in its provisions a strong fugitive slave clause, in which identified slaves were to be taken into custody immediately and returned to their owners.

Meanwhile a wounded roar went up from abolitionist ranks; it was so loud and piercing that it seemed to split the sky. Webster had hit them hard: in one passage he had said, "If the infernal Fanatics and Abolitionists ever get the power in their hands, they will override the Constitution, set the Supreme Court at defiance, change and make the laws to suit themselves. They will lay violent hands on those who differ with them politically in opinion, or dare question their infallibility; bankrupt the country and finally deluge it with blood."

He was answered in kind. Theodore Parker thundered that Webster "was making a bid for the Presidency; an act and a motive that can only be compared to those of Benedict Arnold."[9] Edmund Quincy spoke of "the ineffable meanness of the lion turned spaniel in his fawnings on the masters whose hands he was licking for the sake of the dirty puddings they might have to toss to him." John Greenleaf Whittier wailed poetically, "So fallen! So lost! The light withdrawn which once he wore!" Emerson deplored Webster's "profound selfishness."[10]

Webster's character and habits—his drinking, his lordly manorial style at Marshfield, where his favorite horses were buried upright and where he gloried in thousands of cattle and sheep—rose to choke the angels of austerity. But his style was a minor fault compared to the whiplike words with which he lashed out at his enemies.

"There are men," he said, "who are of the opinion that human duties may be ascertained with the exactness of mathematics. They deal with morals as with mathematics and they think that what is right may be distinguished from what is wrong with the precision of an algebraic formula . . . If their perspicacious vision enables them to detect a spot on the face of the sun, they think it good reason why the sun should be struck down from heaven."[11]

In the Senate, Seward rose to express the pure abolitionist doctrine. He opposed slavery in any new land and in the District of Columbia, and he favored its extinction by gradual but deliberate effort. A fugitive slave law would be immoral. Seward also cited a Higher Law than the Constitution. Henry Clay, shaking with anger, rose to ask, "Who are they who venture to tell us what is divine and what is natural law? Where are their credentials of prophecy?"[12]

During all these explosions, Senator Douglas was launching Webster's compromise—in committees, hearings, drafts, and private arguments—and earning the eternal hatred of the abolitionists. Senator Seward, meanwhile, held Old Zack in his spell. It was by no means easy to foresee how the compromise—even with Webster and the moderates, North and South, behind it—could become law as long as the President was against it. Taylor was, after all, a man of many fixed opinions, which he considered principles, and he held it a grave weakness in a man to change his mind.

At that point a greater force intervened, against which even the most highly placed were helpless: Calhoun died. Although his passing cost the South a heavy toll in terms of intellectual coherence, stature, and inspiration, his passing also removed the prime catalyst of secession. The South would have other leaders and hear other arguments, but none would ever make its argument as intelligent or as farsighted as Calhoun's.

Another—and far more unexpected—change was the death of President Taylor. As long as Taylor held the White House the Free-Soilers held, in effect, the balance of power. But in mid-July 1850, the sixty-five year old President endured a long open-air ceremony under the blistering Washington sun, and later drank large quantities of ice-water, milk, and cherries. Many believed that mixture to be responsible for the high fever that developed, but the doctors muttered about cholera. Recovering, Taylor was then stricken by typhoid fever, which took his life—and brought former Vice-President Millard Fillmore to the helm. Free-Soilers were aghast. Fillmore was conciliatory by nature —and Webster and other Whigs had his ear. That transfer of power, and not persuasion, gave Webster's compromise tangible form. Its various sections were sewn into law—including a strong Fugitive Slave Act—and the crisis seemed over.

During all these fateful events, John Brown was, as ever, intent on his own affairs. They were tangled, dismal, and depressing. The firm of Perkins & Brown had failed signally to do what it had promised: to sell wool for dozens of growers at a good price. Brown visited these growers, told them his version of the distressing influences that had overcome him, paid them what he had collected for their wool, and persuaded others to return overly generous advances he made to them. This effort took him through northwest Virginia, the Western Reserve, and Pennsylvania, in which places he wrote the usual lengthy and pious letters to his family. Meanwhile lawsuits followed him like so many carrion birds. But he was fortunate beyond compare in having Colonel Perkins as his partner.

Perkins listened to Brown's recital of troubles in early 1850, and instead of reproaching Brown, encouraged him to do his best. Brown wrote Perkins a letter brimming with gratitude—a rare sentiment in his life, but one that was fully justified. It would not, it seemed, be necessary for Brown to use his North Elba retreat; the colonel wanted the partnership to continue.

Later that year, however, Brown's presence in Springfield was disturbed by the need to talk to lawyers, to make depositions, and to respond to lawsuits. These took time to file and longer to come to court: they included a suit by Henry Warren of New York, charging he had not been paid enough for his wool; another by Burlington Mills of Vermont, for recovery of a sixty-thousand dollar loss (in part representing money advanced to Brown for his trip to England, part representing sales of Burlington wool that Brown had failed to pay the company); and by parties variously known as Pickersgills, McDonald, Jones, Patterson, and Ewing.[13]

In October 1850, the Free Soil party of Massachusetts held a convention to attack the new Fugitive Slave Act and select nominees for the state elections. Higginson, an eager participant, was named to run for Congress. In the background the Free-Soil leaders worked closely with the Democratic party against the Whigs, in a coalition created by antipathy to Webster, who had resigned his seat in the Senate to become secretary of state under Fillmore. The Democrats and Free-Soilers sought to control the state legislature—which would elect Webster's successor—and to fill the state offices. Higginson was not expected to win; he was a propaganda candidate, but he took the stump with pleasure, delivering speeches against slavery and Webster's compromise. He had a newspaper column in the Newburyport *Union,* a Democratic paper newly opened to him, and he printed, at his own expense, an "Address to the Voters."

Ordinarily the decision of the government to compromise great issues and to issue strong new laws would have been seen as an end to any argument. Most moderates, at any rate, so regarded the outcome of the situation in 1850. The South, satisfied that its rights were honored and would be respected, dispatched a number of slave hunters to the North to locate and return fugitives. Two such fugitives were Ellen and William Craft, who had reached Boston in 1848. Ellen Craft was nearly white, and had posed as a man to carry William with her as her slave. Both were well known in the city, largely through the dramatic nature of their escape. When warrants were issued for their arrest the Vigilance Committee headed by Theodore Parker—and whose members included Higginson, Stearns, and Howe—swung into action. Higginson urged the Crafts to test the law. "Disobey," he told them, "and take the consequences." He also advised physical resistance.[14]

Within hours the case got out of hand. The slave agents were arrested for slandering the Crafts by calling them slaves and for conspiring to kidnap them. Parker whipped up emotions, mass rallies were held. The Crafts were hidden by Howe and others. At this time also, Parker called the Crafts to his book-lined study—where a Bible and a sword lay on his desk—and married them. Arrangements were made to send the couple to England and freedom. Faneuil Hall became filled with indignant citizens who called for an end to lawless activities that flouted the government.

After the Crafts were shipped to safety and the slave agents sent back to Georgia empty-handed, Parker wrote a letter describing his illegal activities to President Fillmore, saying he had presented William Craft with the Bible and the sword, and had suggested their "appropriate use." Earlier, he had told critics: "There is no supreme law but that made by God; if our laws contradict that, the sooner they are broken why, the better."[15]

Coming in the middle of an election campaign, the Craft case marked a significant turn in the abolitionist road. For years these zealots had secretly broken laws and created the Underground Railroad to subvert the peculiar institution. But after the Webster compromise they rose in open defiance. For the first time the United States government was faced with a revolutionary movement that denied its authority and its power to exert that authority. The movement was a minority, but its leaders held high and respected positions. The number of clergymen in its ranks and their arguments—in Parker's words —that "antislavery is the Law of God," and "the constitution was not morally binding"[16] made them difficult and embarrassing opponents. There was no doubt they had won converts in high places; Senator Seward of New York expounded their arguments, and there was no law against their speaking themselves.

When the abolitionists of Boston began to argue, however, that a Higher Law entitled them to defy the government, the situation shifted into a new phase. The difference between covert resistance and an open clash with the authorities is more than physical. Underground efforts tacitly recognize the legality of the rules being broken. Open physical resistance is a deliberate denial of the authority of government. The abolitionists' new position was that the national laws could be broken in the name of national progress. Theodore Parker, Higginson, the manufacturer George Luther Stearns and the physician Samuel Gridley Howe and their associates, by accepting that argument, turned down a path untrodden in the United States by men of high position since before the Revolution.

With such stirring events and fighting words crowding the pages of the New York *Tribune* and other Northern publications, it was no wonder that John Brown's interest was awakened. He had spent most of the year traveling, and would resume after the holidays, but he had the period between Thanksgiving and New Year's Day to read about newly famous men and exciting rallies—and such statements as Parker's remarks about how he would react if anyone sought to enslave him. "I would kill," said the clergyman, "with as little conpunction as I would drive a mosquito from my face. It is high time this was said."[17]

Years earlier John Brown had sketched an ambitious plan of armed resistance to Frederick Douglass and other black leaders, and although nothing had come of that fantasy, Brown had maintained his contacts inside the black community. With several weeks in Springfield to temporarily forget his troubles, he drafted another plan, and in January 1851, he collected his black friends and told them about it.

What Brown had in mind was a new organization, to be called the United States League of Gileadites. Its statement of principles mentioned the struggles of the Greeks against the Turks, the Poles against Russia, the Hungarians against Austria, and compared these to the "sufferings of more than three millions of our submissive colored population." Then the statement offered some specific suggestions. "Should one of your number be arrested," it said, "you must collect together as quickly as possible, so as to outnumber your adversaries . . . Your plan must be known only to yourself, and with the understanding that all traitors must die . . ." Then Brown himself proceeded to give some instructions on creating "confusion and terror," saying: "after affecting a rescue, if you are assailed, go into the houses of your most prominent and influential white friends; and that will effectively fasten upon them the suspicion of being connected with you, and will compel them to make common cause with you, whether they would otherwise live up to their professions or not . . ."[18] Brown then listed nine resolutions that ended on a patriotic note.

Forty-four blacks signed this document, which was purported to represent only the Springfield branch of the league—although the League existed only in John Brown's mind. Whatever the forty-four signers thought as they left the meeting is unknown, and Brown himself seems to have turned his attention back to his lawsuits and personal problems.

A few months later he moved his family from North Elba back to the comfortable house that Colonel Perkins had provided near Akron, and no mention was ever again made of the League. Yet it was significant, for the tactics it recommended were clearly reflected by the surging crowds of Boston. And although the circumstances of the document indicate that it was the effort of a distracted man during a brief interlude of escapism, it is significant that some of its tactics, like Brown's earlier plan to invade Virginia, were later put into action.

Webster had moved on to become secretary of state and the Massachusetts state legislature had to elect his successor. Despite previous backstage deals, the actual election of Charles Sumner, the Free-Soil candidate, was so distasteful to so many that it teetered in the balance, first for weeks, then months. Ballots were taken all through January 1851, then through February and March. Many Whigs hoped to stall the outcome until the next regular elections. Meanwhile the abolitionist issue continued to provide a lurid backdrop. Shadrack was arrested, the vigilance committee swung into action, and he was rescued. In April another fugitive-slave case erupted and the authorities ringed the courthouse with so many guards that rescue was impossible. During the hearings, Higginson shocked one lawyer by suggesting that a crucial Southern document, lying on a table as evidence, be stolen.[19]

Sumner's election would be such a clear victory for abolition that even many Free-Soilers were reluctant to support him openly. Aware he was regarded with suspicion, Sumner wrote a letter to the legislators saying he would "wait and work patiently under and through the Constitution."[20] Meanwhile, he remained conspicuously absent from the mob scenes that marred Southern attempts to return fugitive slaves from Boston.

His backers finally ordered a secret ballot: the twenty-fifth. Taken April 24, 1851, it elected Charles Sumner to the United States Senate —by a margin of one vote.

A little over a week later, Waldo Emerson spoke at the Lyceum in Concord, and said the South was a separate nation, that "infamy was in the air, and Webster an archbetrayer." Stern and cold, he said "all the drops of his blood point downward." Then, carefully withdrawing from any suggestion of violence, he pronounced the British plan the best: "buy the slaves."[21]

He took the new lecture on tour and was interrupted at Harvard by "hisses and groans, interspersed with cheers for Webster, Clay, President Fillmore, Edward Everett and Old Harvard."[22] But there was no doubt that Emerson's emergence was significant; it would not have made the students at Harvard groan had it not been. Channing, the old bishop of the transcendentalists, was gone, but the new bishop of the Movement was in place, and its Savonarola, Theodore Parker, was in his pulpit at the Melodeon theatre. In the wings, new actors, as yet unseen, were preparing.

Part IV
THE PLAY RESUMES

Chapter 32

John Brown's murder party rejoined the Osawatomie men at their encampment on Ottawa Jones' claim sometime near midnight on Sunday, May 25, 1856. The men were drowsily aware of their return, but it was not until daybreak and breakfast that they noted Dutch Henry's prize grey and the other horses. All of them had heard of the grisly discoveries the previous morning along the banks of the Pottawatomie; they knew how those horses had been obtained. But the murderers were large men with guns and sabers; it would have taken far braver observers than these peaceful settlers to have forced an issue.

That hard task remained for Jason Brown, the tall, hatchet-faced tinkerer, so gentle he carried pieces of cheese in his pockets to feed stray dogs. He trembled, as he afterwards admitted, but he was the only man in the company with the moral courage to confront his father.

"Did you have anything to do with the killing of those men on the Pottawatomie?"

His father turned a face of stone toward him, but his eyes flickered. "I did not do it," he said shortly. Then he added, "but I approved of it."

"It was uncalled for, wicked act!"

"God is my judge," the old man said shortly. "It was absolutely necessary as a measure of self-defense, and for the defense of others."[1]

He turned away with an offended air, and Jason rushed toward Frederick—the wild one of many moods.

"Do you know who the murderers were?"

Frederick's face worked. "Yes, I do, but—I can't tell you."

"Did you kill any of them with your own hands?"

"No," Frederick said, and began to weep. "When I saw what manner of work it was, I *could not* do it."[2]

The Osawatomie men started back to their homes under their new captain, Henry H. Williams, with their heads averted from the Browns, Townsley, and Wiener. Those men lagged behind, and when they reached Middle Creek, turned south toward the Brown claims. John Brown, Jr., disgraced and distraught, and Jason—still deeply shocked—walked through the brush toward Osawatomie on their own, the roads being "lined with men," Jason said later, searching for the murderers.

They reached the cabin of Adair and their aunt after dark. The minister came to the door with a gun. When he learned who they were he said at once, "Can't keep you here. Our lives are threatened. Every moment we expect to have our house burned over our heads."[3]

Jason begged the Adairs to let him stay, and offered to sleep anywhere, even in the outhouse. His aunt came and asked, "Did you have anything to do with the murders on the Pottawatomie?"

Jason said he and John had nothing to do with it, and their aunt let them in, but she said grimly, "We risk our lives in keeping you."

The two men, emotionally and physically exhausted, were given a mattress; the Adairs went to bed, but all four talked until midnight in the tiny cabin—or at least the Adairs talked to Jason. He was the second eldest but peculiar-looking; his face seemed oddly pressed together. He also lacked the assurance of his brothers. But he could talk that night, while John, Jr., the onetime Free-State delegate and leader—his father's pride—could only groan.

Mr. Adair and Jason finally fell asleep but Florilla Brown Adair lay awake. Sometime during the remaining course of the night she heard John Brown, Jr.'s voice, speaking in the darkness.

"I feel that I am going insane."[4]

Ordinarily a mass murder, committed by known parties and hunted through the region, could have only one outcome. The Lykins County seat at Paola, a hamlet of thirteen houses and one hotel, where United States District Judge Cato had arrived, was only fourteen miles northeast of Dutch Henry's Crossing, and news reached the court very quickly. On Monday morning dispatches were sent to the governor by the commander of the militia and the Paola prosecuting attorney *pro tem.* That night Governor Shannon forwarded the information to Colonel Edwin V. Sumner at Fort Leavenworth, asking him to replace troops in Lawrence being transferred to the Pottawatomie region.[5]

For several days no official court business was recorded; which was less a sign that the massacre had created unusual tension—though that was present—than that the authorities were trying to define its origins and purpose. Witnesses were collected and investigations launched, and on Saturday, May 31, 1856, capias writs—calling for arrest on sight —were issued for John Brown, Sr., Oliver, Frederick, Salmon, and Owen Brown, Theodore Wiener, Henry Thompson, and James Townsley. Also issued were warrants for their arrest for murder.[6]

Other action soon followed. Dutch Henry charged that his grey horse and some of his cattle had been stolen by John Brown, Wiener, Townsley *et al.* An indictment was handed down against John Brown and associates for robbing the post office operated by Postmaster Allen Wilkinson. Still another indictment was returned against John Brown, Jr. for horse stealing.

Nor did the Lykins County grand jury stop there. In the week following the murders, and after hearing a stream of witnesses from the Osawatomie region, the grand jury handed down an indictment of conspiracy against ten men who had all been conspicuous in the Osawatomie meeting of April 16, 1856. These included the real Osawatomie Brown, John Brown, John Brown, Jr., and seven others. The basis for that indictment was the men had openly conspired to resist the laws of the territorial government, by force if necessary. The reasoning of the authorities at Paola was fairly straightforward. A meeting had been held by the accused and its leaders had vowed to resist the territorial government. Then a series of murders and robberies had taken place against men who had worked with that government. The expedition to Lawrence fit in that sequence, for Lawrence was being occupied by territorial and federal troops, and the same men active in organizing resistance, and associated with those who committed murder, had headed toward Lawrence, and on their return had illegally released some slaves. The pattern of rebellion appeared clear —and deadly.

With so many witnesses, with a logical chain of evidence, with cold murders, open robbery, and defiance loose—and with peaceful settlers at hand and willing to testify—Judge Cato appeared to have ample reason to issue, as he did on May 28, 1856, a warrant against John Brown, Jr. for treason.[7]

By the time the warrant was issued John Brown, Jr. was in custody, after being flushed out of the woods around Osawatomie by Southerners from Buford's Emigrant Aid Society. There is very little reason to doubt that he was mad;[8] he had fled into the woods the day before and one of the settlers found him hallucinating. But the Southerners had no way of knowing that he was not feigning, and the federal troops to whom he was turned over were certain he was a malingering, faking murderer.

They did not deliberately mistreat him. Captain Thomas J. Wood, the commander in the field, later became a Union general; throughout his entire career he was known as a man of character and judgment. John Brown, Jr.'s arms were tied behind his back and he was forced to march toward Paola, and he was chained at night. That treatment was customary at the time, and Brown's dementia alone would have justified it, especially if he was suspected of brutal murder.

Nor was Jason Brown mistreated after his capture by some Missourians when he emerged from the Adair cabin. According to Jason's story, he was taken on horseback to Paola, where indignant crowds—including many Osawatomie men waiting to testify—surged forward, determined to lynch him. "Then," said Jason, "came what changed my whole mind and life as to my feeling toward slaveholders. I can't see a Southerner or a Southern soldier, now, whatever he thinks of *me,* without wanting to grasp his two hands."[9]

What happened was that three respectably dressed men decided matters had gone far enough. One of these, the former Judge Jacobs of Lexington, Kentucky, calmed the crowd and took Jason into his home. There, although still a prisoner, he was treated like a boarder, and would have been very comfortable but for the brief presence of Mrs. Mahala Doyle, who had lost her husband and two sons to Jason's father.

In none of these proceedings had the territorial officials abused their authority. It was true that in the first week after the murders the only two Browns arrested were the brothers innocent of murder. Although the crowd that captured them and the soldiers who transported them thought they were murder suspects, the officials of Paola soon decided that they had not been involved at Pottawatomie. They were indicted and held for treason: for having participated in the April settlers' meeting that defied to the government, for having joined the expedition to Lawrence with the intention of carrying their defiance into practice, and for having assisted in the unlawful invasion of a settler's home and releasing his slaves.

After two weeks in Paola seven men, all from Osawatomie, including John Brown, Jr. and Jason, were taken back to the settlement for a preliminary examination on the treason charge. John Brown, Jr. was still demented and in poor condition, but he and all the prisoners were shackled in pairs and marched the eight miles back to the settlement in stages.[10] On one overnight stop John Brown, Jr. made so much noise and proved so difficult to quiet that a soldier beat him unconscious.

They arrived at Osawatomie to undergo examination regarding the Pottawatomie Rifle Company, its purpose, and various other aspects of their activities. As a result Jason and two others were released, and four, including John Brown, Jr., were held over for trial in the fall.

While his eldest sons were under arrest and threatened with various reprisals, John Brown led his four younger sons—together with Townsley and Wiener—into new lives: as outlaws.

After parting from the main body of Osawatomie men on Monday, May 26, 1856, John Brown led his group into a hidden clearing on Vine Branch, near Middle Creek. His party now included Augustus Bondi, Wiener's brother-in-law and partner in their general store. They were met, soon afterward, by Orellius Carpenter, who reported that John Brown, Jr.'s cabin on the Brown claims had been sacked and burned in reprisal for the murders, that a war of retaliation had started, and that Brown and his gang should move to another, secret location near Ottawa Creek. From there Brown and his men could operate against the Southerners.[11]

On May 28, two days later, Charles Kaiser, a veteran of the 1848 revolution, arrived as a recruit, as did Ben Cochrane of the Pottawatomie Rifles. They reported the arrest and departure of John Brown, Jr. and Jason. On May 29, "Captain" (a title the settlers bestowed upon anyone in temporary leadership) Samuel T. Shore of Prairie City appeared. Shore, no doubt, had learned the location of the gang from Carpenter; the elder Brown, through his leadership in murder was seen in a new and important light. Shore wanted John Brown and his gang to combine with a force being organized in Prairie City; Brown said he would consider it.[12] The next afternoon a Northern newspaperman appeared in John Brown's camp.

The wide-eyed behavior of the territorial and federal authorities in Kansas was entirely aboveboard, but the movements of the Free-State leaders remain mysterious and heavily veiled. "Captain" Shore did not leave any evidence of his talks with John Brown: these were reported by Bondi and other members of Brown's gang. But it was clear that the murders in the Pottawatomie area had coincided with a series of organizing moves to drive Southern settlers out of Kansas, to destroy Southern settlements, and in particular to strip Dutch Henry of his possessions and claims.

The appearance of such deliberate and coordinated violence, however, could not have been possible, nor could it have proceeded, without a covering legend by Northern newspapermen, who shrouded its significance from the nation. That legend was woven and spread by a small coterie of rabidly abolitionist journalists in the territory, and soared on the occasion of the "Sack of Lawrence." That greatly exaggerated event was first described to a startled nation in an extra edition of the Chicago *Tribune* on May 26, 1856. It described the Free-State "Athens" as "devastated and burned to ashes," by "Border Ruffians," with only "a few bare and tottering chimneys, a charred and blackened waste" remaining.[13] The dispatch—apparently written by Richard J. Hinton, an ardent abolitionist and correspondent for the Chicago *Tribune* and the Boston *Traveler*—went on to say that a "reign of terror" was underway in the territory, and left no doubt in the minds of readers that this was the result of federal and territorial troops working with "Border Ruffians" to destroy and drive away all Free-State settlers.

The dispatch was picked up by other Northern newspapers and created a great wave of anger and indignation. It succeeded in etching an ineradicable image into the mind of the nation—an image that later and more accurate accounts could not change. It was a remarkable instance of the power of journalism, fueled by the new high-speed presses—but it was even more than that. Beyond its imaginative mendacity, which remains to shame national journalism, it appeared just before the opposing forces launched a *real* reign of terror. Wrote Major John Sedgewick of the First Cavalry of Leavenworth, who was also on the scene:

> No one can defend the action of the marshal's posse at Lawrence, in burning the hotel, destroying the printing-press and other outrages, but no life was lost, no one was threatened or felt himself in danger. In retaliation for this act, inoffensive citizens have been plundered, their houses robbed and burned, and five men were taken out of their beds,

their throats cut, their ears cut off, their persons gnashed more horribly than our savages have ever done. I sincerely think that most of the atrocities have been committed by the free-soil party . . .[14]

The major was not a Southern sympathizer; he later lost his life as a Union general in the Civil War.

One of the magicians of confusion, expert at misdirecting attention, was the journalist James Redpath, who appeared at John Brown's camp on the afternoon of May 29, 1856. How he found the camp remains a mystery. What he and John Brown discussed remains essentially unknown, except for a fable that Redpath wrote three years later, in a mendacious book about the scene. Here, he described Brown as both a Cromwellian figure, all Biblical quotes and stern rules for clean living and high thinking, and as chief of noble outlaws sequestered in the forest.[15]

At the time that Redpath met Brown in his camp, however, there could well have been more than journalistic curiosity involved. Redpath was a friend of the unscrupulous Jim Lane—the Free-State leader who had escaped the treason dragnet cast out by the territorial government—and who had his eyes on Dutch Henry's Crossing. Brown, whom Redpath and everyone else in the territory by now knew to be responsible for the Pottawatomie murders, was a man who seemed worth contacting, and Lane—according to Charles Robinson later— was in favor of using terror as a means of gaining power and property. None of this was ever hinted at later by Brown gang member Bondi, or by the Brown sons, On the surface all that happened was that Redpath penetrated the outlaw camp, was impressed, and departed. And if some wondered that so well-placed a journalist would keep secret the location of a nest of murderers, the wonder seemed well answered later, in Redpath's smoothly romantic account of the meeting.[16]

While Brown was in his camp and "Captain" Shore was organizing a force at Prairie City, some Missourians made plans to invade the region, avenge the murders at Pottawatomie, and restore the flagging spirits of Southern settlers. The force included groups from the Missouri militia, and prominent among the militia officers was Henry Clay Pate, former student at the University of Virginia, a deputy U.S. marshal, and a correspondent for the St. Louis *Republican*.

It was Captain Pate who had rounded up Jason and John Brown, Jr. and turned them over to Kansas territorial authorities. Pate and a small force were camped along the Santa Fe Trail at Black Jack Springs. Before daybreak on June 2, 1856, Brown's party—augmented by Prairie City men—stole up on Pate's camp.

The pre-dawn hour was Brown's favorite time to attack. He succeeded in surprising Pate's company though the men were not asleep but preparing their breakfasts. There was no charge: the attackers opened fire on the camp from two sides—Brown's and "Captain"

Shore's. The fire was returned, and a disorderly series of exchanges ensued with some men from both sides fleeing the scene: no plan had been prepared and it was every man for himself. Pate later said he was running low on ammunition and sent a runner out with a white flag, but that Brown refused to parley with anyone but the leader. Then, said Pate, he saw reinforcements approaching to assist his attackers, and he came out himself with a white flag. That was an error.

When the old man loomed before him, Pate immediately said he was a deputy U.S. marshall, looking for indicted persons.

"I know exactly what you are, and do not wish to hear any more about it," Brown responded. His voice was as hard, cold, metallic, and dangerous as the pistol he pointed at Pate's head.

"You can't do that; it's against the rules of war," Pate protested, and Brown responded by telling him to surrender "immediately."

"Give me fifteen minutes," Pate pleaded, but Brown was adamant.[17]

There was nothing for Pate to do; he was ignominiously marched back to his men, who threw down their guns as fifty other men, wearing Free-State armbands, drew up to reinforce Brown. Similar groups had risen, as though by magic, across the region, but these were from Lawrence—that "charred and blackened waste."

Pate and his twenty-four fellow Missourians, prisoners of Brown and the now enlarged force of Free-Staters, were placed under guard and held for nearly a week. During that week Brown and others conducted a series of raids against pro-southern settlers. Two of these incursions were against the general store of Joab Bernard on the California Road near the county line, with booty worth an estimated four thousand dollars.[18] From such forays, John Brown and his men were soon well-mounted, well-dressed and heavily armed.

With these and other raids under way, Governor Shannon sent Deputy Sheriff William J. Preston into the region with federal troops, instructing Preston to use his best judgment. But it was Colonel Sumner, who also took the field, who located Brown's camp, ordered the prisoners released, and told all the men to go home. Legends remain to the effect that Deputy Sheriff Preston recognized Brown, but lacked the courage to arrest him. That was unlikely; the federal troops could have handled anyone the deputy pointed out. The fact was that Brown was not known by appearance to very many, and looked like an old and harmless farmer. Released with his men, however, free to ride and raid, with armed bands rising like dragons' teeth in the wake of his murders, he not only must have felt vindicated by events, but may have believed he was leading a charmed life—which he was. The spells, however, were cast by other men far away.

One such spellbinder was Richard Hinton, correspondent for the Chicago *Tribune*. A friend of Redpath and as ardent an abolitionist, Hinton filed an account of the Pottawatomie murders that was as helpful to the Free-State movement as had been his previous account of the "Sack" of Lawrence.[19]

Horrible stories are told in Missouri of the murder of five Pro-Slavery men at Osawatomie. It is said that their throats were cut, and their corpses mangled and chopped into inches. Of course the Free-State party, as a party—every Northern man and every Southern man with Northern principles—in the Territory is accused by the organs of the Ruffians with this imaginary and revolting atrocity.

It is stated that their houses were entered at Midnight and victims of this outrage murdered in their beds.

I remained a day at Prairie City, in order to find out the truth of this report. I sent a messenger to Osawatomie to investigate the circumstances.

The facts, of course, refute the Missouri version of the affair.

Five men were killed. There is no doubt of that fact.

Their names are William Sherman, better known as Dutch Henry; a father and two sons, named Doyle; and Mr. Wilkinson, a Member of the House of Representatives of the Bogus Kansas Legislature.

They were shot by a party of Free State boys—at least I infer so, from the cause of their summary execution.

These men have bullied and threatened the lives of the Northern Squatters in that section ever since the invasion of November last. Doyle and his sons have been particularly active in harassing and assaulting the Free State men.

On the day on which these men were killed, a flag inscribed "Head-Quarters of the Pro-Slavery Army," was hoisted over Sherman's store. A Free State man went in and inquired the price of powder. The man told him he charged ten cents a pound to pro-Slavery men, but as he was a d--d nigger thief he would have to pay twenty-five cents.

Some angry words passed between the parties. Wilkinson then seized on the squatter, and told that, as he refused to acknowledge the Territorial laws as valid enactments, they would give him a lesson to teach him what his principles would lead to. They said he ought to have been hanged long ago; and as now they had him in their power, by G-d they would give him his due.

They kept him confined an hour or two. After dark they took him out, went down with him to the woods, put a rope around his neck, and an end of it over the limb of a tree, and were preparing to hoist him up.

"Fire!"

The report of five rifles was heard simultaneously with this unexpected command. Five corpses—the bodies of the Doyles, Sherman and Wilkinson were seen stretched on the grass as soon as the smoke cleared away.

"Fly!" cried the same voice who had given the order to fire.

The man whose life was so mysteriously and unexpectedly saved, as soon as he removed the rope from his neck, went into the woods and shouted for his friends.

But they had disappeared as suddenly and mysteriously as they came.

This act will be made the excuse for arresting every man in that section of the State, who has made himself obnoxious, or is likely to be a leader in defending the lives and property of Northern men.[20]

That version, with modifications, spread through the Northern press together with various other accounts of Southern violence.

Chapter 33

"The blossoms were falling from a large cherry tree in the front yard," and some ladies were having a sociable afternoon chat in the Stearns' home in New Bedford when news arrived that Senator Sumner had been assaulted in the Capitol. The ladies were shocked, and several wept. Finally one said, "What a sermon Theodore Parker will preach about this next Sunday!"[1]

She was not disappointed. Parker thundered, and so did hundreds of other ministers throughout the North. A spontaneous mass rally of protest and indignation was held in Boston; Parker, Wendell Phillips, the Reverend James Freeman Clarke and others spoke. Even the conservatives were aroused and gathered at Faneuil Hall, with the governor present and the Reverend Edward Everett Hale as lead orator. The radical abolitionists were ignored in this collection of respectables, but Dr. Samuel Gridley Howe was prominent as was the wealthy manufacturer George Luther Stearns, frowning over his remarkable beard.

These rallies remarkably resembled the highly emotional gatherings once addressed by Theodore Weld. Biblical language poured from the rostrums. When William M. Evarts, addressing a throng of four thousand in the New York Tabernacle, read resolutions of condemnation against slavery and Southern aggression and mentioned, among the resolutions, the name of Sumner, the audience gave "Peal after peal, cheer after cheer . . . like the discharge of heavy artillery." Whenever Representative Brooks' name was mentioned, there was "a spontaneous outburst of groaning and hissing . . . ."[2] The effect was of a revival meeting, with its evangelical exhortations toward higher aspirations, its denunciation of sin and the Devil transferred to the political arena, its spokesmen against slavery hailed as angels of light and the South as a region of the damned.

The rallies were still under way, the editorials were still being composed, when the Chicago *Tribune* report of the "Sack" of Lawrence reached the nation. That launched more outcries, more sermons, more speeches, more rallies. The Republican party, composed of former Whigs like Abraham Lincoln, former Democrats, and inpouring Free-Soilers, combined the events into a twin slogan: "Bleeding Sumner" and "Bleeding Kansas."[3] The New York *Tribune* printed Sumner's "Crime Against Kansas" speech, with its vituperative language and loaded charges, and sold them at cost, to send an estimated one million copies rolling across the landscape like so many political grenades.

The symbolism of martyrdom, deeply imbedded in Christian theology, was used to elevate Sumner into living sainthood and to cast the Southerners into the role of demons, in both Washington and in the Kansas Territory. The theme evoked deep responses all through the

199

North and West, though it contained its own ironies. For in both instances—the beating of Sumner and the "Sack" of the Free-State stronghold—the Southern response had been in reply to repeated goads and insults. Southern attempts to point out that Senator Sumner was not greatly injured, that Lawrence was still standing, were of little avail. The Southern reaction was not always sophisticated. Many Southerners cheered Sumner's beating, and others said Lawrence had received what it invited.

In Worcester, where the recently returned Reverend Thomas Wentworth Higginson headed a "free church" in the Parker Melodeon style,[4] an intense recruiting effort sprang into life. Higginson cast off all restraints; he helped pay for newspaper advertisements seeking guns, and men, for Kansas. Within a few days after news of the twin outrages had reached the town, Higginson was able to shake hands and smile at forty-seven men led by Dr. Calvin Cutter, and including one Charles Tidd, who would later join John Brown, as they left for Kansas. Their departure was dramatic: heavily armed, they marched down the main street to the strains of martial music played by the Worcester Cornet Band, with the blessings not only of Reverend Higginson and other clergymen, but also of Town Hall.[5]

All through the first weeks of June 1856, Higginson preached and traveled. He went to Boston, Bedford, and other places, and back to Worcester. It was his opinion that the Emigrant Aid Society had been too peaceful in its methods. Eli Thayer heard that, and said he believed "men like Higginson feared a peaceful settlement in Kansas would quiet the Northern conscience." He went on to add that Higginson, *et al*, "yearned for violence, agitation and strife, to advance their cause." Thayer was right, but he misunderstood the energy, vigor, and determination of such dissatisfied men like Higginson, Howe, Parker, and their set. Action in Kansas and campaigns against slavery—a distant sin of which they were themselves free—provided much deep-seated gratification.

Howe was no less eager than Higginson for new scenes, new sights, new deeds. As Sumner's closest personal friend he was indignant over his friend's martyrdom; and as a spokesman for equality he was indignant over slavery. Howe was the moving spirit, in its early stages, of a new Massachusetts Kansas Aid Committee—a new and deliberately more virile arm of the Emigrant Aid Society. To Howe, as to Higginson, Parker, and Stearns, "aid" now meant guns.

In upstate New York the longtime pacifist Gerrit Smith was of the same mind. The news of Sumner's caning was still warm when a letter of Smith's appeared in the Syracuse *Journal* calling for "real war upon the Missourians," measures to raise "one million dollars and 1,000 men." Smith, added that he would contribute ten thousand dollars toward such an effort.[6]

That interesting proposition was relayed to John Brown in Kansas by his daughter Ruth Thompson, after the old man sent a letter to North

Elba from "near Brown's Station." In this message, the first since he led his murder party and entered upon an outlaw life, John Brown glided, with the ease of long practice, over the terrible events and grisly truths of his activities, hinting that he and Ruth's husband and her brothers were being unaccountably hounded for their opinions. But Brown added quickly, "We are not disheartened." He described John Brown, Jr.'s being brought before "a bogus court," injected some misleading descriptions of Black Jack Springs, and concluded: "if under God this letter reaches you so that it can be read, I wish it at once carefully copied in Ink & a copy of it sent to Gerrit Smith." Then he said, untruthfully, "I know of no other way to get these facts & our situation before the world."[7]

That was false, because Brown was already in touch with journalists and various Free-State forces in Kansas. But the touch about Gerrit Smith was interesting: John Brown had not forgotten how Smith raised funds, how and why he read his son's letters to the radical abolitionist meeting in Buffalo a year before.

News of the turbulent events in Kansas and the outrage in Washington created great indignation in peaceful Concord. Emerson, calling Sumner "the whitest soul I know," encouraged young Frank Sanborn, his children's tutor and his own general acolyte, to assume the chairmanship of the Essex County Kansas Aid Committee.

The Sage also took part in a fundraising effort in Concord, and observed that the one thousand dollars collected "in a few days" amounted to one percent of the valuation of the town. In a speech at Harvard, Emerson went on to say that "all the right is on one side." He charged the government of the United States with responsibility for Kansas atrocities. Emerson's support was both so well-known and so helpful to the cause that in November 1856 Garrison asked and received permission to include Emerson's portrait in a lithographic composite that included Theodore Parker, Wendell Phillips, Joshua Giddings, Gerrit Smith, Reverend Samuel J. May, and other antislavery heroes.[8]

As usual, however, Emerson did not neglect his career. His book, *English Traits,* appeared in August 1856; it consisted of fulsome praise of the English people, together with his own idiosyncratic mixture of doctrines, fantasies, and epigrams. He offered a personal version of history that included a description of the invading Normans as "20,000 thieves,"—Emerson was anti-French—and many statements lauding a "Teutonic heritage." Praise came across the Atlantic from Carlyle; the English were delighted to be so highly estimated and although most of the contents of the book were familiar to those who had heard Emerson lecture, sales were excellent.

Such calm sideline activity was beyond Dr. Howe, who left for Kansas personally. His first stop was Buffalo, where he appeared as a delegate from Massachusetts at the national convention that created and authorized the National Kansas Aid Committee. Twelve states and Kansas were represented. Headquartered in Chicago, the organization was dedicated to raising two million dollars to send, in Gerrit Smith's words, "armed men to Kansas to conquer armed men who came against her." Reverend Charles Finney was among the delegates who cheered and passed this warlike manifesto. A national committee of thirteen members, including Gerrit Smith, was elected. To resounding cheers, Smith pledged $1,500 a month—indefinitely—to the Kansas Aid movement. In Illinois Abraham Lincoln's law partner, a fervent admirer and correspondent of Theodore Parker, submitted Lincoln's name as a member of the Illinois central committee. Lincoln, less easily influenced, refused to serve.

In July 1856, Howe left the Buffalo convention to carry instructions to Kansas Free-State forces. He was accompanied by Thaddeus Hyatt of the New York Tabernacle Committee, an allied organization. The two rode horses across the plains from Chicago; the Missourians had closed river traffic to Northern interlopers. Howe saw parallels, everywhere he looked, with the English Civil War. He mentally considered the antislavery forces—a label he automatically attached to every Northerner or Westerner—the equivalent of the Puritans and Presbyterians of that earlier conflict. These were notions derived from reading Sir Walter Scott rather than history; Howe did not recall what the religious principles of the Puritans might have been: in his mind antislavery had assumed the force and coherence of a religion. He dashed off letters to Julia from almost every stop, picturing a landscape peopled with heroes, fair ladies, and Virtue on horseback riding to battle against demons, devils, and dragons.

At about the same time that Howe left for Kansas, John Brown left his hideout and went to Lawrence. That center of idealism was no longer concerned about the murders on the Pottawatomie; various Free-State groups had become involved in raids and fights, and matters had undergone a qualitative change. Brown had read an account, written by Henry Clay Pate, of how he had been tricked into surrender at Black Jack Springs. In rebuttal the old man wrote his own version of that mini-battle, which took on epic proportions as he pictured himself as a fearless military leader. He met William A. Phillips, correspondent for the New York *Tribune,* and that paper not only printed Brown's tale but began a fulsome press campaign to impress the nation with the idea that a new Cromwell had appeared in Kansas.

The North badly needed such an image: martyrdom can raise a flag, but victories are essential for recruits. The battle of Black Jack Springs entered the propaganda lists with two conflicting versions, and Pate—enraged at finding himself branded a coward—visited still another *Tribune* correspondent, Hanscomb, in his lodgings and assaulted him.[9] That did not help; the Brown story was given greater exposure and became lodged in the Northern mind as a triumph. Inevitably the various references to so many confusing Browns—John Brown, Jr., the murdered E.P. Brown of 1855, G.W. Brown, the editor of the *Herald of Freedom,* and O.C. Brown, the original Osawatomie Brown—began to converge into multiple images of one: "Captain" John Brown.

Phillips accompanied Brown to Topeka, where the Free-Staters were scheduled to hold their "legislative" sessions. Colonel Sumner had federal orders to forbid the gatherings, so he waited until those Free-Staters out of jail had assembled, and then saw to it that they dispersed. He deplored the necessity, which led Secretary of War Jefferson Davis to remove him from his command. The North screamed prejudice.

Brown played no role whatever in the legislative gathering or its dispersal. But Phillips, who was preparing material for a book, in classic war-correspondent fashion, found the old man's conversation excellent material. The book appeared late in 1856; it painted a picture of John Brown as a biblical believer, a sage of the prairie, "an inexorable old man" feared by Missourians.[10] That too, built the legend, but, as in the case of the Redpath visit, the combination of the known murderer and the journalist for the New York *Tribune* seems to have contained more than either man ever afterward admitted. Radical plans for Kansas were being promoted in the North by the abolitionists, who in many instances were unconscious stalking-horses for ambitious politicians. It was, after all, a campaign year—and Kansas was a campaign issue.

Jim Lane, who had been making a series of remarkable speeches through the East, was raising a "Northern Army"—the strange term used by the Brown murder party at Pottawatomie—to enter the territory through the overland route via Iowa and Nebraska. Wagon trains of actual emigrants, to be accompanied by armed recruits financed by the Kansas Aid organization, were slowly converging on Nebraska City at the time Phillips and Brown held their conversations.

When Phillips departed, Brown rode back to his camp near Ottawa Creek. His son Owen was ill and thin; the others wanted to leave Kansas. They had their fill of outlaw life. Presumably, their father calmed them saying he would leave Kansas himself. At least that is what he wrote John Brown, Jr., in prison at Lecompton. His eldest son was relieved to hear it. He had recovered his reason with the passing of danger, and replied "I am convinced you can be of more use where you contemplate going than here . . ."[11]

However, Brown was only going to Nebraska City, to meet Lane—who now termed himself a general.

Dr. Howe and Thaddeus Hyatt also met "General" Lane, at Tabor City, Iowa. Howe described Lane as "clean-shaven, narrow forehead, deepset, flickering eyes." Hyatt, phrenologically sophisticated, commented unfavorably on Lane's skull. Howe, who also believed that cranial contours predetermined character and intelligence, agreed that Lane did not have a good head.

This stiffened their conviction that Lane was too reckless. They proceeded to "demote" him from his "generalship"—at least so far as the Kansas Aid Committee was concerned. Lane's armed band, which numbered several hundred mounted men, was virtually in rags and nearly penniless. Howe and Hyatt knew not only that Governor Shannon wanted federal troops to intercept this "army," but that if Lane led an actual armed insurrection the North would lose its moral case. They left, leaving repeated warnings against rash behavior ringing in the air.

While this meeting was underway, John Brown packed his sons and son-in-law into a wagon drawn by an ox team, and headed for the mass rendezvous in Nebraska City. En route he joined some other travelers and was in turn joined by Samuel Walker. Walker had been assigned to guide the huge emigrant trains on the border, and he knew Brown. Later, he said he had decided that Brown was insane, as a result of the Pottawatomie murders and the effect they had on his conscience. That conclusion was enough to make Walker both wary and watchful.

Among other things, Walker noticed that Brown would always go off and camp by himself. One morning Walker saw him leaning against a tree, asleep, with a rifle across his knees. "I put my hand on his shoulder; at that moment he was on his feet, his rifle at my breast. I pushed the muzzle up and the ball grazed my shoulder. Thereafter, I never approached Brown when he was sleeping, as it seemed to be his most wakeful time."[12]

Walker's curiosity could not be contained entirely. Riding along with Brown, he turned the subject to the Pottawatomie murders and said he wouldn't have them on his conscience "for the world." Brown said he had not raised a hand against any of the victims, but admitted he had been in command of the murder party, and that he had ordered the "executions." He charged that Lane and Robinson were the instigators, but would not now sustain him. Nevertheless, he believed that what was done was in the "best interest of the country."[13] Walker did not press the matter.

Near Nemaha Falls, Nebraska, Samuel J. Reader was marching with some other Free-State men to join Lane's army, when "Someone in front shouted, 'There he is.' Sure enough it was Brown . . . as we passed the old man on either side of the road, we rent the air with cheers. If John Brown ever delighted in the praises of men, his pleasure must have been gratified, as he walked along enveloped in our shouting column. But I feared that he looked on such as vainglorious, for if he responded by word or act, I failed to hear or see it. In passing I looked at him closely. He was rather tall and lean, with a tanned, weather-beaten aspect in general. He looked like a rough, hard-working old farmer . . ."[14]

Such was the miraculous effect of newspaper stories. In his wagon the old man had his son Owen, ill, thin, and feverish; his son-in-law Henry Thompson, convalescing from a bullet in his side received at Black Jack Springs; Salmon, who had been kicked by a horse; and Frederick and Oliver, who longed to go home. Kansas—where they had sought freedom and independence—had proved to be another of their father's painful traps.

John Brown found Nebraska City and the encampment a fine opportunity. He again met *Chicago Tribune* correspondent Hinton, who was later to describe this meeting as their first. Brown also met a tall, dark-haired young man with a rich voice and commanding presence who called himself Captain Charles Whipple. Whipple was already known as a Free-State raider; it was less well known that he had deserted from the United States Army, after murdering an officer. He was twenty-five; his real name was Aaron D. Stevens.[15]

> In his later recollections Hinton described how Stevens drilled his raiders:
> "What are you doing here, men?"
> "Holding a town meeting," they would shout in unison.
> "Where are your ballot boxes?"
> "Here!" and each man would bring his hand down in a slap against his Sharp's rifle.

John Brown was in congenial company among men who could make such grim jokes about democratic proceedings. Within a day or so he seemed to have become transformed in a white suit, a broad-brimmed straw hat and a fine horse. Riding about the encampment he was an object of awe; many thought he was some prominent personage incognito.

Lane, who now called himself General Jo Cook, had a plan to rescue the Lecompton prisoners by force. Mad as it seemed, that plan was supported by Governors Salmon Chase of Ohio and Grimes of Iowa.[16] In Massachusetts, A. A. Lawrence, who had White House connections, worked for the prisoners' pardon.

The new Republican Party wanted to keep the Kansas pot bubbling because it was a campaign issue; its candidate was John C. Fremont— the son-in-law of Thomas Hart Benton. The Democrats nominated James Buchanan—unspotted because he had been out of the country in recent years—and the American—or Know-Nothing party—nominated former President Millard Fillmore.

None of these parties wanted to resolve the Kansas issue in any clearcut way; the South would be enraged if the territory became free, the North if it did not. All politicians wanted to capitalize on the situation but all were divided on how it should be resolved; Illinois' Senator Douglas was the most important leader who thought the answers should be left entirely to sincere settlers, and to time.

To the radicals the best possible situations was continued disorder. Higginson, a paradigm of unrest, longed for eternal excitement. Learning that the forty-seven men he had recruited and dispatched under Dr. Cutter had been ignominiously disarmed aboard a Missouri steamboat, he impulsively decided that Kansas needed his own inspiring presence.

By early September Higginson was in Chicago, sending long letters to his arthritic wife Mary and various friends, and—for the world—dispatches to the New York *Tribune,* the Chicago *Tribune,* and the St. Louis *Democrat,* under the transparent pseudonym "Worcester." Higginson did not like to hide his light. At first he wrote of having "spoken daily with men who sacrificed all their property and were ready to add their lives for revolution." But as he neared the territory his private letters said that "things look discouragingly safe."[17]

He found Nebraska City rustic and calm. From "a vile little tavern" he wrote an appeal to "Eastern Capitalists" to "invest in transforming this whole blighted area into an industrious North." In that demand, Higginson revealed that he simultaneously held capitalists responsible for evil and capable of producing good.

He was stirred by the appearance of Northern men who appeared "bearded and booted and spurred and red-shirted, sword and pistol by their side—only their sword is a Bowie knife—wild manly looking riders." He met General Lane-Cook who seemed unconcerned over his demotion by Howe and Hyatt; Lane was so sure of himself that he named Higginson a brigadier general immediately, and invited him to join "the fight." The eager minister was not as impressed as he might have been by the honor. Appointed brigadier by Lane at the same time was Sam Tappan, a reporter for the *New York Times* and the Boston *Journal.* Higginson reveled, however, in his role as a guardian of a wagon train rolling slowly across the prairie. He wrote his mother: "Imagine me also patrolling as one of the armed guard for an hour every night, in high boots amid the dewy grass, rifle in hand & revolver in belt."[18] No attackers ever appeared.

Despite these naive letters, some mystery does hover over Higginson's Kansas visit. He always later denied that he met John Brown there. But he did meet Lane—and Brown was with Lane. So was Samuel Walker. In fact the three left Nebraska City together at the head of a mounted party of about thirty men, galloping toward Lawrence—supposedly in response to a mysterious message.[19] The nature of that message and its source remain unknown. What *is* known is that shortly after Brown and Lane returned to Kansas a series of savage raids, robberies and violence against Southern settlers erupted in the Pottawatomie region.

August 1856 was a bad month for peaceful settlers in Kansas. The names of Lane, Brown, Whipple, Cline, Walker, Harvey, and James H. Holmes became infamous as settlements were raided, homes burned, cattle and horses stolen, and men killed. The fighting was sporadic, stealthy, and cowardly in nature; settlers were forced to declare for North or South—often before men whose purposes were hidden until after the declaration was made.

One of Lane's first acts, after returning to the territory, was to send word to the prisoners at Lecompton that he would bring his "Northern Army" to their rescue. The prospect alarmed them; Robinson and others knew that high-level efforts were being made on their behalf and they sent word to Lane to forget about rescuing them. An impression remains that John Brown, who sent a similar message to John Brown, Jr—and received a similar response—was acting as though he, and not Lane, was the Free-State leader to whom others should look. Certainly he did not accept any orders and was not a member of Lane's "Northern Army." He was a presence, of a peculiar sort, and one whose name cropped up regularly in the dispatches sent by correspondents Phillips, Hinton, and others to newspapers in the East. It was almost as though Lane, Walker, and other men were the instruments of actual action, while Brown served as a symbol of that action —because his personality and ability to utter Cromwellian phrases made him important in a special dimension and role of his own.

But Brown was on the periphery of events. A new settlement near the Marais des Cygnes—consisting of families financed by Colonel Buford's Southern Emigrant Aid Society—was raided. A raid was conducted against Franklin as part of a concerted plan to reduce all Southern settlements between Lawrence and the Missouri border. Entire families fled from the territory. Brown, however, had no position of leadership at this time.

Nor was he present when fifty men from Lawrence under Captain Samuel Walker attacked "Fort" Titus at daybreak, and conducted what amounted to a minor battle, complete with a cannon that fired slugs of melted type from the old *Herald of Freedom*. In the end the defenders surrendered and Walker appeared in Lawrence with "thirteen horses, four-hundred guns and thirty-four prisoners, six of whom were badly wounded." Colonel Titus was among the wounded; his home had been looted and burned after his surrender, and $15,000 was stolen from him by "a Free State man."[20]

Some indication of the climate at Lawrence was provided by the fact that Walker and his men (eighteen of whom were wounded) were met outside the town by a group demanding the summary execution of the prisoners. Walker refused, but inside Lawrence, while he was placing the wounded Titus inside a house, a "committee of safety" met and passed a sentence of death on the Southerner, for unstated reasons. Walker rejected that verdict also, and then, guided by some instinct, ran to the house where Titus had been taken. He arrived just in time to prevent a desperado from shooting the wounded man in his bed. That peril averted, he heard Brown and a Dr. Avery outside, haranguing the crowd, and calling Walker himself a "public enemy" for refusing to obey the mandate of the committee.

A few days later Titus was saved by Governor Shannon, who came to Lawrence, he said in his official report, "at the imminent peril" of his life. Shannon negotiated the release of Titus by exchanging him for five prisoners held at Lecompton for the Franklin raid; he left no doubt that the idealists at Lawrence had defied the law, and would not obey orders under any other arrangement. That situation shamed Shannon, who was relieved by President Pierce; the prisoner exchange and Shannon's admission it was necessary were two of the last acts of his administration.

Meanwhile news of an inevitable gathering of Missourians reached Lawrence, and John Brown made arrangements to go south to the region of Dutch Henry's Crossing: area of Pottawatomie and Osawatomie, where his interest remained concentrated. Reverend C. G. Allen wrote that it was around August 18, 1856, that he saw John Brown "purchasing mules from Eldridge at Lawrence." Although he had heard much of Brown he commented that on first sight, "I saw nothing remarkable in his appearance that impressed me." Allen did not realize how remarkable it was that Brown had money to buy mules. Eldridge was the leading horse-and mule-dealer in Lawrence.[21]

Brown was not alone in heading toward Dutch Henry's Crossing. Two other freebooters moved in that direction: "Captain" Holmes, with fourteen men, "Captain" Harvey, with his "forty thieves." It is possible that Jim Lane—who eyed the crossing as a hawk eyes a pullet —was also in the region.

Brown impressed Augustus Bondi when he did appear near Osawatomie "with a spic and span four-mule team, the wagon loaded with provisions; besides he was well supplied with money and all contributed by the Northern friends of Free State Kansas, men like Thaddeus Hyatt."[22] That was disingenuous, but Bondi was, after all, one of Brown's raiding companions. And there was also a splinter of truth in the explanation: Howe and Hyatt had been sent west to dole out money and orders for supplies and weapons; and for that matter, so had Higginson, who was touring the territory and holding many unrecorded conversations.

It is known that Higginson met Martin Stowell—his old companion in the May 24, 1854 assault on the Boston Court House, where a guard had been killed—now settled in Plymouth, Kansas. Higginson also visited Leavenworth, which he disgustedly described as a settlement of "50 saloons in a town of 2,000." He was contemptuous of the Southerners he saw; "a puny race with good manners and bloated faces," and came to some fierce conclusions about the future course of events.

"Kansas may be crushed," he wrote the New York *Tribune,* "but not without a final struggle more fearful than that of Hungary; a struggle which will convulse a continent before it is ended, and separate forever those two nations of North and South which neither Union nor Constitution has yet welded together."[23] Horace Greeley shook his head at this dire prediction. He printed it, but was sure it was too pessimistic; Greeley was positive all issues would be solved by the ballot box.

John Brown's handful was only one of a number of armed groups that converged on Linn County, south of Osawatomie. Samuel Anderson, Captain Cline, and others arrived with their bands; "Captain" Holmes, already working closely with Brown, led Frederick Brown and Bondi into a raid against the claim of Martin White, and left with

White's horses. That coup helped John Brown persuade Holmes and his men, as well as Cline and his followers, to join what the old man called the Kansas Regulars.

Brown had a fondness for drawing documents: for the combined force of about thirty men temporarily under his orders he drew a covenant swearing his recruits to obey him and the "Laws" of this association. These laws consisted of twenty three articles, most of which involved the division of "valuable property taken in honorable warfare," but which also included some old Brown injunctions against liquor, "uncivil, ungentlemanly, profane, vulgar talk," and the like. Some of the articles were more remarkable. Article Twenty, for instance, said: "No prisoner shall be put to death or subjected to corporal punishment, without first having had the benefit of an impartial trial."[24] In effect, John Brown had come to see himself as a sovereign power in his own right, able to conduct war, command armies, and hold the powers of life and death over American citizens—all in the name of "the Free State cause" and "the maintenance of the rights and liberties of the Free State citizens of Kansas." Persons other than Free-Staters were, apparently, enemies, and Brown considered his men to have enlisted for "the war."

That "war" consisted of raids south of Osawatomie—in the Sugar Creek district inhabited largely by Southern settlers. The raids were promiscuous and somewhat confusing: houses were burned and cattle driven off.

After these sweeps the Southern settlers in Linn County formed their own parties and retaliated, burning the homes of Ben Cochrane and Samuel Kilburn, both Brown followers, and actually capturing George Partridge, another Brown man. In the course of these events, conducted back and forth over several days and nights, news reached Lawrence that a large force of Missourians had gathered, complete with a small cannon, and was once again heading to exterminate Lawrence. Messengers were sent to Holmes, Cline, and other Free-State leaders in the southern region, telling them to come back to defend the stronghold.

The free-state freebooters turned back, but their progress was slow; they were burdened with wagonloads of booty and herds of cattle and horses. John Brown, however, appeared in Osawatomie, late in the afternoon of August 24, 1856, "looking very good-natured," and wondering if anyone wanted any "proslavery beef." He said he had got some that was "number one. That he had been out that day collecting taxes. I afterward learned that he had taken some fine cattle from the plantation of a Border Ruffian."[25] That statement of an eyewitness was proof of how terms had altered: a "Border Ruffian" was originally someone from Missouri pretending to be a settler; by late August 1856 it was any Southern settler.

Brown's appearance alarmed the settlers of Osawatomie: they feared Southern retaliation for being associated with Brown's plunder. But after enjoying his triumphant parade, the old man withdrew across the Marais des Cygnes with his herd of seventy-five stolen cattle, to camp on the Crane claim. He had, apparently, no intention of soon leaving the region. His son Frederick, who had turned back with him from Nebraska, had intended to go to Lawrence to assist in the defense of that town but felt ill, and decided to spend the night with his uncle, Reverend Adair. Everyone knew the Southerners were coming, but the raids by the Northerners had been so incessant and tiring that the "Northern Army" was somewhat disheveled.

The Southerners were closer than the free-staters realized. They had organized a large force under Major General David A. Atchison, with Brigadier general John W. Reid, a veteran of the Mexican War, and Colonel P. H. Rosser of Virginia. The entire force numbered more than one thousand men and had a cannon; its plan was to level Osawatomie, Hickory Point, Topeka, and Lawrence.

Osawatomie was a small settlement, more or less led by one Dr. Updegraff. Its remaining members had built a crude blockhouse. The Southerners circled the town on their way north, then sent a contingent to enter it from the west—an unexpected quarter—early on Saturday morning, August 30, 1856. The force was sighted and horsemen galloped ahead to give the alarm. Word was sent to Brown at his Marais des Cygnes camp.

Frederick Brown emerged from the Adair house just as the first Southerners entered; Martin White was with them. White had been erroneously branded a proslavery man, but his horses had been stolen, and his life threatened, by the free-staters. Having been rejected from one side, he was working with the one that accepted him. He later told the Kansas House of Representatives, where he was known and respected, what happened. "Frederick Brown, one of their guard, advanced toward us. We halted and I recognized him and ordered him to 'halt,' but he replied, 'I know you!' and continued to advance towards me. I ordered him a second time to 'halt.' By this time he was getting very close to me, and threw his hand to his revolver; to save my own life I shot him down."[26]

The bullet went through Frederick's heart and the "wild one" of the Brown clan fell dead.

The main body of the Southerners took some time to arrive; John Brown and his men were on their way, and Cline and his contingent headed toward the defense as well. The Southerners moved down the ridge road in two lines; when they met fire they dismounted and reformed, and brought their cannon forward. Dr. Updegraff and his Osawatomie force left the blockhouse but Southerners were detailed to circle behind them. Firing was general and disorganized on both sides; Brown, Cline and their men were on the scene, but joined the general retreat across the river. Holmes escaped by swimming and one man later recalled that John Brown "cut a queer figure, in a broad straw hat and a white linen duster, his old coattails floating outspread upon the water and a revolver held high in each hand over his head, while balls whistled around him."[27] Six of his men were wounded, but the old man escaped.

General Reid had used two-hundred-fifty of his men to take the settlement. Brown had made a mistake in crossing the river, and thus cutting himself off; he escaped death by sheer accident. The Southerners looted the houses and burned some. They took John Brown's seventy-five stolen cattle with them when they left to rejoin their main force at camp on Bull Creek. Reid's report stated that his force had killed a son of Old Brown and perhaps Old Brown himself. He thought his troops had killed a total of about thirty free-staters. Reid also deplored the burning of houses, saying he could not stop the men. But he did not consider the affair very important, saying it was like "driving out a flock of quail."[28]

But Reid was, in fact, upset over the incident at Osawatomie: his men had broken ranks and disobeyed orders, and had the resistance not been completely mindless, would have suffered greatly. He conferred with Atchison and Rosser, and they decided to return and reorganize their force, dismount the horsemen—who were the most unruly—and to return against Lawrence with infantry on September 13.[29]

The retirement of the Southern forces gave the free-staters a respite; the burning of Osawatomie was heralded as a dastardly deed and served to cloak the previous Linn County raids to some extent. Southerners under Hays had burned Ottawa Jones' house, but that was balanced, to some extent, by Dr. Calvin Cutter—the leader recruited by Higginson in Worcester—who attacked and looted a wagon train homeward bound for Missouri from New Mexico.[30]

On September 7, 1856, Brown created a sensation by riding into Lawrence. Henry Reisner of Topeka was awed by his impassive appearance, by his bent figure slumped on a grey horse, by his gun on the saddle before him. The cheering, he said, "was as great as if the President had come to town, but John Brown seemed not to hear it and paid not the slightest attention."[31] He had hidden at the Hauser farm, less than three miles from Osawatomie, with his son Jason and Luke Parsons, who was ill.

Brown now wrote a letter home, giving his version of the battle of Osawatomie—in which heroic defenders held off a force of four hundred, killing and wounding from seventy to eighty of these attackers, and losing "Four or Five Free State men." Jason, the gentle one, was described as fighting bravely; Frederick's death received one sentence. The letter ended on Brown's usual note: "May the God of our fathers bless & save you all."[32]

The Osawatomie action almost immediately underwent the eerie process of exaggeration that attended all Brown's activities. It filled columns of type in the press; it was later described by Senator John J. Ingalls as "the most brilliant and important episode of the Kansas war. It was the high divide of the contest. It was our Thermopylae. John

Brown was our Leonidas with his Spartan band."[33] That version took a little time to establish.

On the day he arrived in Lawrence, according to C. G. Allen, John Brown went to Harvey and asked for help.

> He came in front of my tent where I lay sick unable to sit up, and asked Col. Harvey for some of his men. Said he, "I want some of your men to go & assist me in repelling the outrages of the Border Ruffians. I have suffered from Free State men every indignity they could heap upon me, yet I am determined to serve through the war." Harvey talked rather discouragingly. "Well," said B., "if you can think about & give me an answer after a while." This was on Sunday. Gen. Lane was in town & several speeches were made. Brown was sent for to make a speech. He replied, "I would not come if Gen. Lane himself should send for me."[34]

Brown was, it seems, laboring under great excitement. Osawatomie was a defeat; the cattle he had stolen were taken by Reid's men; conferences to which he was not a party were under way; Charles Robinson, the "Governor" of the free-state forces was on the scene again; and Brown's own band was dispersed. E. A. Coleman said later that Brown came to his house near Lawrence and told him and his wife that God had used him as "an instrument for killing men," and would use him "to kill a great many more." Others heard Brown say that he had his mission just as Christ did—that God had appointed him "a special angel of death" to destroy slavery with the sword.[35]

No wonder that Allen said, "I heard several say that they thought Capt. Brown to be insane after the battle of Osawatomie."[36]

Higginson was also in Lawrence then, which makes his claim not to have met Brown at the time seem very odd. The minister had traveled widely through the Kansas Territory, from Plymouth to Leavenworth to Topeka to Lawrence, speaking to many men, and he was anxious to share—if not physically, at least vicariously—in all the excitement of the moment. For him to have failed to search out the increasingly famous Captain John Brown seems out of character in many ways, because Higginson was, of course, in the territory as an agent of the Kansas Aid Committee. He had funds and orders for supplies and weapons to disburse; most Free-State leaders were anxious to meet him and to obtain some of this largesse.

The same was true of Franklin B. Sanborn, the Concord schoolteacher whose entry into the Kansas Aid Committee campaign had got him into the Bird Club in Boston, and brought him into prominence generally. Sanborn set out for Kansas, as an agent of the committee, in August 1856, when the disorders in Linn County were at their height. The trip was his first outside New England and his letters reveal that he regarded it, in part, as a sightseeing tour. He mixed business with pleasure; in Chicago he stopped at the offices of the National Kansas Aid Committee and met, among others, Captain Webster, who later served as Grant's chief of artillery in the Tennessee Army. In Iowa, Sanborn discussed the loss of state muskets—loaned by Iowa to Kansas emigrants and never returned—with the adjutant general of the state visited Iowa's governor; and proceeded to Council Bluffs via "filthy coaches, with all sorts of companions, and lodging at all kinds of stage-taverns."[37]

Like most of the Kansas Aid Committee leaders, Sanborn considered himself a man dedicated to lofty principles, but his opinions of the people he met were apt to be low. He took time to visit a Mormon encampment and "held some conversation with these poor creatures, mostly of the lowest English classes and with their shrewd and selfish American leaders."[38] He also noted that some of Nebraska's "cities" had only two or three houses, being real estate developments. But he did not enter Kansas Territory, where sporadic fighting was under way.

What was Sanborn's mission? "Inspection and consultation."[39] "To inspect the emigrant route through Iowa, in order that it might be kept open for men, arms and ammunition during the autumn of 1856."[40] Years later, he wrote "I believe I met Colonel Higginson at Worcester . . . before he went out to Kansas." It was all very vague, years later, hidden amid luxuriant descriptions of scenic wonders.

Higginson had, of course, the benefit of his cloth. On September 8, 1856, the day after a distraught John Brown wandered around Lawrence telling men he was "an angel of death," Higginson delivered a sermon warlike enough to satisfy the most belligerent. He took his text from Nehemiah: "Be ye not afraid of them; remember the Lord, which is great and terrible, and fight for your brethren, your sons and daughters, your wives and your homes."[41]

The next day the new governor, John W. Geary, arrived. Geary was a veteran of the Mexican War and mayor of San Francisco in its most turbulent period; in Kansas, he spoke of conciliation but moved decisively. His arrival coincided with the release of the treason prisoners on bail. That reduced a great Northern complaint at once. But Geary was also empowered to create a new militia, and to swear that force into the service of the United States government. That made future resistance treason beyond argument.

The new governor was hardly settled in Lecompton when he sent for various troublemakers to tell them that Kansas had changed, and to convince them that a strong hand was at the helm. Higginson was one of those summoned. He did not enjoy the interview, and left no record of what was said. A six-footer, proud of being able to look down on most men, Higginson did not enjoy looking up at Geary, who stood six feet five and a half inches tall. He left the interview muttering that the new governor was "a little Napoleon"—but he left Kansas as well.

Chapter 34

The United States had three major political parties in 1856. One faced the future, one faced the past, and one sought to hold the center. The Republicans were futurists: they had chosen a young man, John C. Frémont, whose name conjured images of the adventurous West, idealism, and progress. Around him the Republicans, who ranged from former Whigs and Democrats to former Know-Nothings, unfurled an exciting banner: Free Speech, Free Press, Free Soil, Free Men—Frémont and Victory.

That sounded as open as air and as exciting as the dawn, but it also carried a heavy underload of animosity against the South, which had become associated in the minds of millions with the scenes depicted in *Uncle Tom's Cabin*. That novel was taken as literally true; Mrs. Harriet Beecher Stowe, who had drawn on Theodore Weld's *Slavery As It Is* for its specifics, believed God had dictated its pages to her.

Elderly Whigs, whose party was dead but not yet officially buried, were not dazzled. Wealthy manufacturers and merchants, the more worldly literati, they saw seeds of national agony in the fervor the Republicans radiated in the North—and the anger they created in the South. Rufus Choate, a leading lawyer in Massachusetts, warned that the new Republican Party had forgotten the unity of old, was incapable of rising above the moment, and was naively caught in the "glittering and sounding generalities of natural right which make up the Declaration of Independence."[1]

In an effort to check the rising tide of radicalism, the Whigs nominated former President Millard Fillmore and made a deal with the leaders of the American Party, the Know-Nothings, to combine in that nomination. Fillmore accepted, but he did not campaign on an anti-foreign platform: he championed a renewal of the spirit of the compromise of 1850.

Against both of these movements, future and past, the Democratic Party, with a following in North, South, and West, took the logical course and the middle ground. Its candidate, James Buchanan, genial, white-haired, and experienced, promised a safe and sensible administration, and deplored extremism.

With so many controversial and divergent issues, the 1856 campaign inevitably fell into the trough of virulent and unbridled propaganda. Frémont's illegitimate birth was hoisted as though he was responsible for it; his religion was misrepresented, and his military and business career traduced. Southern Democrats threatened to secede from the Union if Frémont were elected. The Republicans attacked slavery, the South, compromise, and the patterns of the past.

Amid all this excitement, which created more attention than previ-

214

ous elections—since the campaign convinced virtually everyone that truly momentous matters hung on the outcome—it was essential to the Democrats that the Territory of Kansas and its violence, which had so helped the radical Republicans, be removed as an issue.

Governor Geary appeared in Lawrence, flanked by two hundred federal troops, and held a conference with Robinson and other free-state leaders not associated with atrocities or crimes. He assured them that if they did not resist the Southern army moving toward the town from Missouri that it would be no threat. Whatever else he said is disputed, but there is no doubt he made it clear that continued organized resistance to the laws of the territory would no longer be possible. Then the giant governor made a speech to the crowd, assuring them their worries were over, and rode away with his escort.

Robinson sent a note to various free-state followers, and one went to John Brown. "Governor Geary has been here and *talks very well.* There will be no attempt to arrest any one for a few days, and I think no attempt to arrest you is contemplated by him. If convenient, can you come to town to see us? I will then tell you all what the Governor said and talk of some other matters."[2]

On the back of that note, however, was another from John Brown, Jr. to his father saying he, John Brown, Sr., would be arrested, voicing fear that Geary's plan was to implicate free-staters in the arrests, and adding: "Captain Walker thinks of going east *via* Nebraska soon. I do hope you can go with him, for I am sure you will be no more likely to be let alone than Lane. *Don't go in to that secret refugee plan as talked of by Robinson, I beg of you.* "[3]

Ignoring his son's advice, as usual, Brown went to Lawrence at once. He arrived during the last big scare. Southerners were headed toward the town in force from Missouri, and feverish defensive preparations, of a somewhat amateur nature, were under way. Brown's journalistic friends later made much of this activity, and placed the old man at its center as a military commander at least equal to Wellington.[4] Brown also met Robinson and, apparently, was told that the free-state movement inside the territory was, for the time being, ended. The cause of free Kansas was being transferred to the East and to the national political arena. The time of riding freely and attacking settlements at night, burning houses and running off horses and cattle was over—at least for a while.

Brown's response to whatever Robinson told him is unknown; but his lifelong attention to his own situation remained as bright as ever. He asked Robinson for a letter attesting to his own activities in the cause of human liberty, and the politician obliged.

Lawrence, Sept. 15, 1856

Capt. John Brown: My Dear Sir:—I take this opportunity to express my sincere gratification that the late report that you were among the killed at the battle of Osawatomie is incorrect.

Your course, so far as I have been informed, has been such as to merit the highest praise from every patriot, and I cheerfully accord to you my heartfelt thanks for your prompt, efficient and timely action against the invaders of our rights and the murderers of our citizens. History will give your name a proud place on her pages, and posterity will pay homage to your heroism in the cause of God and Humanity.

Trusting you will conclude to remain in Kansas and serve during the war the cause you have done so much to sustain, and with earnest prayers for your health and protection from the shafts of Death that so thickly beset your path, I subscribe myself,

Very respectfully,
Your Ob't Servant
C. Robinson.[5]

Robinson also wrote:

To the Settlers of Kansas:—If possible, please render Captain John Brown all the assistance he may require in defending Kansas from invaders and outlaws.

C. Robinson[6]

A day later the vanguard of the Southern forces appeared, but Governor Geary and federal troops appeared as well. Robinson watched the subsequent byplay bitterly, and described it to his wife Sarah, who was east on a tour to promote her book on Kansas. Robinson said, in part, "It was all a farce. The Gov & the Missourians wanted to pretend to do great things. So they pretended they were going to overwhelm us & the Gov pretended to come just in the nick of time & save us from an awful fight. The Missourians now think they have got rid of some of the disgrace of their defeats & the Gov thinks he has placed the Free State party under everlasting obligation . . ."[7]

This was, essentially, correct. General Reid later wrote that when he and his force were twenty miles from Lawrence he learned that Geary had disbanded the free-staters; and therefore decided not to enter the town against Geary's wishes.[8] Both men had combined, in other words, to achieve a peace for the Democratic party, and the threat of Kansas, which had clouded the country for months, began to diminish.

Back in Worcester, Higginson unpacked his valise and put his revolver in a trunk. His wife was now so crippled she was confined to her room. A wave of sadness swept over him. He felt as though "all the tonic life was ended . . . it seemed as if all the vigor had suddenly gone out of me, and a despicable effeminacy had set in . . ."[9]

Soon, however, he was in Vermont, talking to Governor Ryland Fletcher and appearing before the Vermont legislature, asking for funds to "repel federal interference" in the Kansas Territory. Higginson was not going to give up the fight without a fight.

Gerrit Smith was equally reluctant to drop the cause. A month after Geary had halted the Southern "invasions" and federal troops had rounded up nearly a hundred free-booters, turning them over to be sentenced to prison, the New York millionaire addressed a meeting of radical abolitionists in Buffalo. He not only repeated his call to arms, but also drafted a statement that called "all existing Governments, at home and abroad conspiracies against human rights." Smith also called all churches "spurious."[10] Thaddeus Hyatt of the New York Tabernacle Committee agreed: he wanted a meeting of what he termed "rebels" to be held in Boston to reconsider military intervention in Kansas. Higginson proclaimed that in Kansas he found "free soilers better prepared for revolution than they had been a few months previously." He was pleased to report "less of that spirit of blind, superstitious loyalty to the U.S. Government which I feared to find. On the contrary, the people of Kansas are just as ready to fight the U.S. Government as the Missourians, so far as feeling is concerned."[11]

The zealots watched Geary's "pacification" with dismay. George Luther Stearns had created among his customers and suppliers a network to raise funds for Kansas; he was reluctant to disband it. Mrs. Stearns had worked with her husband, and collected clothing and supplies; she found it difficult to suspend these activities. Her aunt, Mrs. Lydia Maria Childs, had produced a dramatic book on Kansas violence; peace in Kansas would hardly enhance her standing as a political expert. William A. Phillips, correspondent for the New York *Tribune,* had written a book called *The Conquest of Kansas by Missouri and Her Allies,* containing romantic descriptions of John Brown and other free-state leaders. The book appeared in Boston just as Geary's peace threatened to make his observations ridiculous.

Frank Sanborn, newly returned from his tour of the exciting West, and earning recognition for his efforts with the Kansas Aid Committee, saw his eminence in danger of being eclipsed. Dr. Samuel Gridley Howe was, of course, busy with his Institute, his schools, and the fortunes in the coming election of his close friend, the martyred Senator Charles Sumner. But he did not regard the Democratic moves in Kansas with any pleasure—and neither did Theodore Parker.

Parker, however, was not dissatisfied over Kansas alone. At forty-seven he had grown bald and his beard was white; he was astonished to discover that he looked distinguished—but old. His activities remained phenomenal; in 1856 he gave seventy-three lectures in addition to his weekly sermons and wrote over a thousand letters.[12] But his health was crumbling; he had had a breakdown in 1855 and was to have another shortly. This troubled him as he struggled against an avalanche of mail and invitations; people sent him monographs on bears as his fondness for those creatures became more widely known. Large puzzles troubled him most: he could not understand why the blacks did not rise en masse against their oppressors. This led him into a swamp of racial analysis in which he betrayed some extraordinary confusions. But his political opinion of the national situation was prescient. By October 1856 he had despaired of a Frémont victory and was predicting "civil war within four years." He had been spending $1500 a year on books, but stopped "to save money for his wife": he believed that when civil war struck, "his property would be confiscated and himself hanged."[13]

All of them—Higginson, Smith, Stearns, Sanborn, Howe, and Parker—were out-shouted and shoved aside by the tumult and noise of the political campaign. The Republicans were mounting their first presidential candidate but lacked in-depth organization in many regions—even in the North and West, to which their appeal was limited. The Whigs hoped to throw the issue into the House of Representatives, for the conservatives believed more wisdom resided there than in the populace. The Democrats had the best organization and were the only party organized in all sections. Their candidate, the sixty-four-year old bachelor Buchanan, had angled for the top office since his days under Andrew Jackson; and he now promised to keep the status quo. That promise included vows not to interfere with slavery in the South, and to allow territories to become proslavery or antislavery according to what Calhoun had acidly called the principle of Squatter Sovereignty. Geary's "pacification" made the promise seem still reasonable.

Geary created a new militia (which included both Southerner Titus and the Northern Walker, who had burned Titus's home and taken him prisoner), sent troops out scouring the territory for outlaws who refused reconciliation, and put others to patrolling the border. The latter move was made after he learned that the journalist-adventurer James Redpath had entered the territory with two hundred armed men.

The governor's first few weeks, therefore, were somewhat frantic. It was during that time that Brown—who had vanished from Lawrence as soon as he received his letters of endorsement from Robinson—would have been expected to leave Kansas. Brown retreated, as usual, to the Osawatomie region, and there collected John Brown, Jr., Jason, John, Junior and Jason's wives, and Owen, and prepared to leave the territory. John Brown, Jr., who had preceded his father to Kansas and gained brief eminence, was—as were his brothers—once again and forever chained to his father's activities.

Those activities had grown mysterious. With a new and vigorous governor in the territory and newly authorized militia—officered by some of the very men with whom John Brown had shared an outlaw life—scouring the landscape, it would have seemed natural that the old man would flee as quickly as possible. Lane had already fled: an emigrant in Nebraska City left a graphic picture of him as he clattered into that town at the head of forty men "all handsomely mounted with new saddles . . . Lane said they were going to rest . . . they had fought the battles of Kansas (but) would be around . . . until they were wanted again . . ."[14]

But Brown's departure was oddly delayed. He said later—or his sons said—that he was ill with "dysentery, chills and fever." Perhaps the long strain of his activities had weakened him. Or perhaps he had some messages to send, and receive, in Lawrence, where he returned. On the outskirts of that unlovely collection of "stone houses, log cabins, frame buildings, shake shanties and other nondescript erections,"[15] he found refuge, surprisingly enough, with Augustus Wattles.

That connection—one of many puzzling coincidences in Brown's bizarre career—was fairly remarkable. Wattles had once been a student with Theodore Weld in the Lane Seminary, years earlier. As one of the original Lane rebels, he had left the ministry to become an antislavery zealot. At the time John Brown, his sons, and their wives crowded into his home, Wattles was associate editor of the newly revived *Herald of Freedom*. He had to know whom he harbored, and why John Brown was sought. The fact that he saw no injury to his conscience in accepting such fugitives provides a fascinating glimpse of the distance he had traveled since he thrilled with indignation and pity at Weld's eloquent denunciations of man's brutality.

At this time, free-state forces in Lawrence were off balance. Geary's offer of amnesty, together with his acceptance of both Free-State and Southern outlaws as leaders in his new militia, disrupted and disorganized the Northern organization. Arms were still being distributed; and both S. W. Eldridge and William Hutchinson, agents of the Kansas Aid Committee, were besieged with applicants. On one occasion, an applicant was told no revolvers were available: these were reserved for John Brown's company.[16]

That company—the Kansas Regulars—included men whose names were being placed on affidavits by both Free-State and Southern settlers in the Osawatomie and Pottawatomie region as horse thieves, raiders, and arsonists. It was clear, however, that John Brown had managed to gain enough acceptance from the Free-State and Kansas Aid agents for his volunteers to be included in whatever plans were under way, and to be armed in order to carry them out.

Wealthy and Ellen, the wives of John Brown, Jr. and Jason, were sent east from Lawrence by riverboat, since that traffic was once again open to all travelers. But on October 1, 1856, after two weeks at the Wattles house—during which time he undoubtedly had conversations with the aid committee agents and others—John Brown was back in Osawatomie. On that night another coincidence occurred.

". . . in October (1), 1856, five or six men came to the door of our house with their faces blacked," said Mr. Thomas Totten. "Mr. Sherman was at our house at that time. They wanted him to leave the Territory by the next day at noon, or they would kill him. They had their guns, and looked like they were going to shoot him every minute. He was taken prisoner at the door and was a prisoner then. He told them that he wanted leave to stay and bury his brother (Peter). They gave him for that purpose till noon the next day. His brother Peter had died at our house, and his body was then lying in our house. They asked Sherman where his horse was, he said he had turned it loose. They left two or three men to guard Sherman, and the others went and found his horse. They asked for his saddle: he pointed to the side of the house where it lay, and they took it. I did not know any of the men, all but one of them had their faces blacked . . . After one of them had got on to the horse he told Sherman he was not to meddle with the cattle which they had driven up to Prairie City and were holding there. They said they had levied on his cattle for the benefit of the free-state party . . . When they ordered him to leave they said they would kill him if they ever caught him in the Territory again . . ."[17]

"Mr. Sherman" was, of course, Dutch Henry Sherman, whose claim at the crossing—and whose cattle and horses—had excited so much envy and animosity. It was Dutch Henry whom John Brown had been seeking along the Pottawatomie the previous May, and it was Sherman's brother Bill who was slain and left lying with his skull split, in the water. After the catalytic crime Dutch Henry's home had been burned, and he and his brother had lived with various other settlers, some of whom worked for him. He had, said Mrs. Totten, "no other business save that of buying cattle and farming."[18]

The manner in which the Totten home had been invaded, the inquiries about the horse and the saddle, and the cool statement that theft and murder were in the name of a higher purpose resembled the approach of the Pottawatomie slayings too closely to doubt the origin of their inspiration.

It was only after that final sweep that John Brown turned the command of the Kansas Regulars over to James H. Holmes, known as the "Little Hornet." "Captain" Holmes was bold and unscrupulous. He later said his orders from Brown were "to carry the war into Africa."[19] The phrase carried its own irony: few of the men associated with blacks, slave or free; all of them used antislavery as their claim to morality amid murder.

The old man and his sons moved across the plains in two wagons. The first, drawn by a four-mule team, was heavy with weapons and ammunition. The second was a small covered wagon, driven by a man the Browns hired; none would ever name or describe him later. Apparently the idea was that John Brown could slip past patrols more easily if a stranger did the driving, while the old man lay inside, covered with hay. Jason later said that John Brown had a fugitive slave as a companion under the hay inside that wagon,[20] but that seems to have been a retroactive touch, intended to lend a note of nobility to what was, in reality, an ignoble retreat.

The description of the Browns' flight is sketchy; the clan later provided various nuggets about narrow escapes. These were not all invented: Lt. Col. Cooke, an army officer patrolling the border, reported on October 7, 1856, that "I just missed the arrest of the notorious Osawatomie outlaw Brown. The night before (October 5) having ascertained that after dark he had stopped for the night at a house six miles from the camp I sent a party who found at 12 o'clock that he had gone."[21]

Cooke did not pursue Brown far: he had his hands full trying to check on incoming emigrants. Three days after Brown slipped through, on October 10, 1856, Cooke came upon one long wagon train of two hundred forty men walking and driving. Halted, they proved to have with them only five young women, no children, no furniture or farm implements, but crates of muskets, Sharp's rifles, sabers, revolvers, and ammunition.[22]

Tabor, Iowa was a village settled by religious families who followed the Oberlin pattern. Anxious to do their part in the great antislavery crusade, they opened their homes to long trains of emigrants and, in the wake of Geary's pacification, to retreating warriors. The Browns, with their four-mule team and their one-horse covered wagon, came straggling into Tabor in mid-October 1856, and were made welcome. John Brown rested for a week, stored his wagonload of weapons and ammunition, and headed for the national headquarters of the National Kansas Aid Committee in Chicago—*where his arrival was awaited with interest.*

The National Kansas Aid Committee, like Higginson, Stearns, Sanborn, *et al,* was reluctant to halt its activities merely because Governor Geary was bringing peace to Kansas. It had collected an expensive number of wagonloads of Sharp's rifles, boxes of ammunition, crates of sabers, cartons of clothing, and even a brass cannon, all stored at Tabor; and another wagon train of guns, ammunition and war equipment, led by Dr. J. P. Root, was en route to the town.[23]

The escort of Root's wagon train included Salmon and Watson Brown. That lifts—though only partially—a curtain on some of the ties between the Browns and the Kansas Aid Committee. The Brown boys had left the Territory to stay with their mother and sisters at North Elba, but had then learned with anger of the shooting of their brother Frederick in Kansas by Martin White. "Assisted by Gerrit Smith, Frederick Douglass and other friends"[24]—who remained unknown—they obtained funds to go from North Elba to Chicago, where they joined the Root train. Obviously, there was a working relationship between the Browns and the Kansas Aid Committee that was, in all likelihood, continuous ever since John Brown, Jr.'s letter had been read aloud at Buffalo, in June, 1855.

But John Brown was not an agent of the aid committee. He was an independent force, who operated outside all organizations and rules. Asked about the wisdom of letting the Root wagon train proceed with its weapons, and told that his sons were part of its escort, he said the arms might be confiscated if sent into Kansas. He also sent a message to Owen, telling him to stop his brothers. Watson heard and obeyed, but Salmon proceeded. Brown also agreed, however, to go back to

Tabor and take charge of the committee's arms shipment; Root was to be outranked.

Before he left Chicago, however, he received a note that accidentally escaped destruction. It was from Horace White, the assistant secretary of the National Kansas Aid Committee, telling Brown that Mr. Arny, their general agent in Kansas, was due in the city the following day. It also added an interesting sentence, never later explained: "Reverend Theodore Parker is at the Briggs House & wishes very much to see you."[25]

November was an interesting month in Kansas, especially in matters that could affect John Brown. As order was slowly restored—excepting for the activities of Holmes in southeastern Kansas—settlers began to appear to level charges against various raiders, arsonists, thieves, and killers. John Brown was among those accused, as were Holmes, Partridge, and others. Governor Geary made a tour of the southeastern region and there is little doubt that the Pottawatomie murders were mentioned, though Geary's reports to Washington continued to stress, inaccurately, that blissful peace reigned everywhere in the territory.

Dutch Henry was still being harassed and hunted and great arguments were underway over land. Geary decided that only land sales would end the disturbances, by halting claim-jumping and open thefts. Exhuming past offenses seemed to him an effort that would exacerbate rather than end difficulties.

There were, after all, few Pottawatomie witnesses left to testify. Mrs. Doyle and Mrs. Wilkinson, the two widows, had left the territory. Other witnesses were available but their testimony was largely circumstantial. Mr. and Mrs. Harris, whose home was the last invaded on the night of May 24, and who saw the men who took Dutch Bill out to slaughter at the water's edge, were aware of their danger. John Wightman had prudently vanished. That left only Jerome Glanville, a settler on Ottawa Creek, who had been in the Harris home that night, who spoke of John Brown's bloodstained hands—and who could identify the killers.

On October 30, 1856, Glanville was driving his wagon toward Missouri when he was first overtaken, passed, and then stopped by four horsemen a hundred yards west of Bull Creek. Two riders appeared on each side of his wagon, and told him to stop and hand over his money. His oxen could not stop right away. Glanville reached for his rifle, and was shot in the back.[26]

The following day Glanville gave an affidavit to Mr. A. Street, a justice of the peace, in Westport, Missouri and said, "I think these four men who attacked me belonged to Captain Brown's company, the notorious abolitionist of Osawatomie."[27]

As was its custom the Lawrence *Herald of Freedom* credited "proslavers" with the crime. *The Star of Empire,* a Southern paper, unwontedly accurate in this instance, wrote a scathing editorial against Free-State journalism. Evidence later found indicates Glanville died from his wound.[28] As far as John Brown's situation was concerned, that was unimportant. What mattered was that Glanville, an eyewitness, vanished from the territory. With the Browns gone, and with the storekeeper Wiener gone, and only Jim Townsley (the driver of the wagon that carried the clan to the scene of Pottawatomie) still in the territory, with the remaining witnesses terrified—it appeared that "Captain" Holmes was doing more than simply "carrying the war to Africa."

Chapter 35

Boston—the once proud and secure city on a hill—was split into warring factions. Its clergy was at odds and its congregations did not speak. Beacon Hill hated Senator Charles Sumner, and its windows remained shuttered as a sign of contempt when he returned after being caned by Brooks. He looked hale but walked like an old man.

Floods of illiterate Irish immigrants, bibulous, violent, and Catholic, crowded into loathsome slums, gave rise to unemployment and crime, and evoked open prejudice that stained the lofty pretensions of the city's intellectuals. The rise of Garrison, Theodore Parker, and the vigilance committee, which welded the revolutionary doctrines of Europe to abolition, disrupted Boston's upper class, divided families and separated the city's merchants from its intellectuals. A shift of transatlantic trade routes from Boston to New York narrowed Boston's ties to Britain and Europe and reduced its commercial importance. Its theater and arts declined in every sense as New York's rose, though its literary reputation continued to flourish. But even that remaining eminence was flawed by internecine disputes. Emerson and his coterie remained aloof from Cambridge and deplored the popularity of Hawthorne and Melville on one hand, and resented the international fame of Ticknor and Prescott on the other.

By a subtle, invisible, but inexorable process all subjects—religious, artistic, literary, social and commercial—had gradually been tainted by abolition. The radicals despised the merchants of the city—who struggled to maintain ties of friendship as well as commerce between North and South—as narrow and short-sighted, and proslavery. While Boston had increasing problems of its own, its radicals insisted that the energies of its citizens—and of all New England—should be concentrated on changing conditions in another region. What would happen after slavery was ended in the South they did not say, though the flavor of their rhetoric in favor of abolition at any cost implied that the nation would then enter a new Eden.

The rapid rise of first the Liberty party, then the Free Soil party and finally the Republican party, together with the flowering of an abolitionist Northern press, seemed to promise that these changes—so ardently desired by the radicals and so fiercely resisted by the South —would be peacefully accomplished through politics and elections. But the violence in Kansas disrupted that illusion, and the campaign of 1856 was remarkable for threats of secession from the South and "disunion" from the North. As election time drew near, and as the moderate majority swung toward the status quo, it became increasingly evident that Frémont might lose.

A. A. Lawrence attended a meeting on November 5, 1856, with U.S. Senator Henry Wilson of Massachusetts, Charles Robinson of Kansas, about twenty Kansas agents, Higginson, and others, to discuss their reaction to a Buchanan victory. Higginson outlined a plan to raise two million dollars from the state legislatures of the North, to outfit an army of ten thousand men and station these in Iowa, and also to send ten thousand Northern emigrants into Kansas. Lawrence was appalled, and protested; so did Senator Wilson. But Higginson, who said he wanted to "involve every state in the war that is to be," insisted that "the scheme is approved by all the best men," and then added, "nobody seems disposed to lead in it unless I do."[1]

That was the atmosphere on the eve of elections. Shortly afterward, when Frémont lost and Buchanan was assured of the White House (though with less votes than the Republicans and Whigs combined), shrieks of rage and hatred welled from radical ranks. Frank Sanborn, young enough to be a weathervane of the movement, summed up radical reaction when he said, "I am convinced we need something different—submission for the next four years seems to me out of the question."[2]

His attitude, and that of his associates, was as though he—together with the blacks—was held in slavery. Identification with a cause could hardly go deeper, or be further from what men had previously considered realistic. Rebellions had traditionally been mounted by those who suffered oppression. To launch a rebellion not against one's own circumstances, but over the circumstances of another race was unprecedented in history, and resembled the rise of a new religious movement more than a political one.

Buchanan's election made the prospects of raising money from state legislatures dwindle. Martin Conway, a former free-soil member of the Kansas Territorial Legislature and an agent of the Kansas Aid Committee, seeking state funds in Vermont, said disgustedly, "the election of Buchanan has played the devil with . . . these low-lived politicians. Their backbones have become entirely relaxed."[3]

But Higginson was spurred into new efforts. In a letter to Gerrit Smith on November 12, 1856, he spoke of "a *private* organization of picked men, who shall be ready to go to Kansas in case of need . . .

against any opponent, state or federal." In order to launch that clearly revolutionary movement, he told Smith that "Garrison, Phillips and others see that the time is come for resisting the U.S. Government in Kansas, and sustaining such resistance everywhere else."[4]

The organization for such a force would begin, Higginson continued, by calling a "Disunion convention" in Worcester, his own city, in early January. The participation of Garrison, notorious for his pacifism, was curious only on the surface. For many years, Garrison had been considered the most radical of the abolitionists. Now his radicalism had been exceeded, and his pacifism was to be a shield behind which an effort to expand by violent means would be mounted.

Gerrit Smith replied at length. He was enthusiastic about resistance to "state or federal" authorities in Kansas, but the millionaire had a businessman's caution about making commitments. He would prefer, he said, to "see the South take the lead" in the matter of disunion, and thought he would be unable to attend the Convention.[5]

In Tabor, Iowa, John Brown took charge of Dr. Root's wagon train and stored two hundred Sharp's rifles in the cellar of the Reverend John Todd's residence.[6] Then he returned to Chicago, taking his young son Watson with him. Brown had reached the stage where he disliked solitary traveling; from this period on he was nearly always accompanied.

The goal of his return to Chicago was money—his eternal need. He also picked up a letter at the headquarters of the Kansas Aid Society from George Luther Stearns, inviting him to come to Boston and offering to pay his expenses. That letter, and whatever he obtained from the aid society's Horace White in Chicago, made December 1856 a promising month for John Brown. John Brown, Jr. and Jason had already left to rejoin their wives and children in Ohio, and John junior was surprised at his father's speed in traveling east after them.

Brown next visited the abolitionist governor of Ohio, Salmon P. Chase, another supporter of the Lane rebels of years earlier, and asked for a letter of endorsement. Chase was cautious in his phrases: "Captain John Brown of Kansas Territory is commended to me by a highly respectable citizen of this state as a gentleman every way worthy of confidence. Upon these testimonials, I cordially recommend him to the confidence and regard of all who desire to see Kansas free."[7]

He *also gave Brown twenty-five dollars.* Since nobody hands anyone else money without some encouragement, it was clear that John Brown was fundraising as he traveled east. He would continue to do this for the rest of his life.

He raced through Hudson, Ohio, where he probably saw his father, some old friends, and other relatives, then took a train to upstate New York and headed toward Peterboro and Gerrit Smith. He had taken the precaution of sending his new credentials ahead, and in response received a letter from the millionaire that was Dickensian in its effusiveness. "Captain John Brown! You did not need to show me letters from Governor Chase and Governor Robinson to let me know who you are. I have known you for many years and have highly esteemed you as long as I have known you. I know your unshrinking bravery, your self-sacrificing benevolence, your devotion to the cause of freedom. May Heaven preserve your life and health, and prosper your noble purpose!"[8]

That was indicative of John Brown's new status: he was a Northern star. He had arrived at Peterboro at Christmas time, and although Gerrit Smith had turned against both clergy and churches and denied the significance of holy days, the season nevertheless cast its warming glow on the occasion.

Yet there was a sinister series of developments, far from Peterboro, that influenced the larger landscape. Rumors of slave uprisings on the borders of Arkansas and Louisiana, involving three hundred slaves, were reported to have taken place. When captured, the slave leaders had said their destination was "Kansas and freedom."

Still another slave rebellion—scheduled for the Christmas holidays but stopped before it started—was reported along the Kentucky-Tennessee region and the Cumberland Valley. Another uprising, also slated for Christmas, was uncovered in Virginia, and still more were disclosed in South Carolina, Alabama, Florida, and Mississippi.[9]

No doubt Gerrit Smith learned all this in the New York *Tribune,* which reported alarms from "seventeen Southern papers from eight different states."[10] If Smith and John Brown discussed these reports, they must have done so with satisfaction.

It is unlikely that Brown would have mentioned another development—this time in Kansas—that occurred on November 22. On that day Dutch Henry led a posse to the claim of John Townsley, the man who wagoned the Brown clan and Wiener to Pottawatomie, and pointed him out to the officers.[11] Townsley was arrested on warrants outstanding since the May indictments, which had also named John Brown, his sons and son-in-law, and Wiener.

On December 13, 1856—when John Brown was in the vicinity of Hudson, Ohio—Townsley was arraigned and pleaded not guilty. Subpoenas were issued for witnesses. The *Herald of Freedom,* noted for its vociferous nobility, was strangely quiet. Even the tender conscience of Augustus Wattles, touched by the plight of slaves and ardent for universal justice, did not appear aroused over the possibility of justice in the case of the murdered settlers. Because witnesses proved strangely difficult to locate, the trial was put over till the next term. Since the charges were first-degree murder in four instances, Townsley remained incarcerated in Tecumseh without bail.[12] To assume that the cool John Brown did not know this when he was entertained at Peterboro would be to assume a great deal.

After he left Gerrit Smith, Brown called on Frederick Douglass in Rochester. Douglass was not in a position to close his door to Brown —nor, for that matter, to any of the white zealots who looked him up.

Whatever Brown told him on the Christmas season of 1856 remains a secret.[13]

Douglass, however, was not a member of the Kansas Aid Committee —though he knew its leaders and many of its supporters. It is unlikely that he was aware of all its activities, which appear to have been so extensive that not even A. A. Lawrence was kept fully informed. It is, therefore, unlikely that Douglass knew what all the committee's Kansas agents probably knew: that John Brown and most of his sons were murderers. Certainly Charles Robinson knew about Pottawatomie.[14] Higginson later admitted he knew.[15] Martin Conway knew; Jim Lane knew; many other men knew. In accepting that knowledge—and by silence and protection accepting the principle that innocent lives could be destroyed in the name of Higher Law—all these men darkened their cause and altered its essence. Under the weight of what they knew, it is no wonder that none of them could—then or later—either disavow or deny John Brown and his career.

John Brown did not stop at North Elba to see his wife and daughters, though as usual he flooded them with letters and sent them money. He paused at Albany, and then left for Springfield, Massachusetts. He knew that town—the former site of Perkins & Brown—very well and had contacts in both the free black and the general community. He talked to George Walker, a lawyer with whom he once dealt, and obtained a letter of introduction to Frank Sanborn, the secretary of the Massachusetts Kansas Aid Committee. Brown placed great emphasis on these letters, though in this instance it was clearly redundant; he was going to Boston and was expected. Perhaps he also obtained a "contribution" from Walker; he apparently sought funds from everyone he met. But perhaps he also wanted such letters to assure himself as well as others of his respectability.

Finally Brown entrained for Boston. He sat busily jotting in his notebook with his huge son Watson silent beside him. Brown was well into the second notebook; most of the entries centered around raising money. He was going to set up his own competitive enterprise in the abolition business, as he had set up his own grandiose project in the wool business, and in the real estate business before that. One note gave a hint of its nature. It read: "Remington and Sons, Ilion stop Herkima (can make spears)."[16]

Finally, on January 4, 1857, he entered the School Street office of the Massachusetts Kansas Aid Committee. The tall, thin, eager figure of Frank Sanborn rose to greet him.

There are many curious things about the timing of John Brown's appearance in Boston in January 1857. For one thing, it was just before the "Disunion Convention," when Kansas would be held aloft as a burning issue. For another Brown was no stranger in Boston; he had been in and out of the city numerous times while in the wool business.

He called on A. A. Lawrence, who had had dealings with Perkins &
Brown in the past, and the financier noted in his diary that "he looks
a little thinner than when he went to Kansas with his sons."[17]

That was on January 6, 1857. The following day Lawrence and
Brown met again, and the financier recorded his visitor was "a calm,
temperate and pious man, but when aroused is a dreadful foe." Apparently Brown did some convincing bragging—an art in which he was
skilled.

Brown saw Lawrence to insinuate himself into the financier's good
graces. Lawrence's purposes were more complex. Working with his
stepmother in the White House, and with Mrs. Robinson, he had
pulled wires in the Pierce Administration to have Geary nominated
territorial governor of Kansas. At the time Brown called on him, however, Lawrence had proposed that an abusive press campaign be
launched against the governor—using James Redpath of the N.Y. *Tribune* and G.W. Brown of the *Herald of Freedom*—to force Geary into the
free-state camp.[18]

It was Lawrence's argument that if Geary remained neutral he
would, in effect, be proslavery.[19] But, while lighting fires under the
governor, Lawrence planned to help him stay in office—if he was
cooperative. Lawrence considered himself a skilled political operator.
Letters he wrote later made it clear that he received Brown mainly to
size him up for future possibilities.

But Lawrence represented only the conservative wing of the Kansas
Aid Committee. The radical faction saw matters in a different light. It
had no single leader in the Massachusetts branch of the aid committee:
it was a coterie including Higginson, Parker, Howe, and Stearns. All
were either famous or wealthy men who shared a common despair of
the wisdom of their countrymen; each seemed to believe that slavery
could only be ended by revolution.

John Brown appeared among these men with a reputation created
by James Redpath of the N.Y. *Tribune,* attested by Richard Hinton of
the Boston *Traveller* and the Chicago *Tribune,* enameled by Phillips of
the *New York Times* in his recent book on Kansas, by the *Times'* Sam
Tappan, and by Richard Henry Kagi of the New York *Post.* His story
was dramatic; the Brown clan claimed to have been martyred by the
"Border Ruffians" and the territorial legislature. One son had been
killed. The old man provided biblical justification for what radicals
now lusted to see: a bloody resolution of the slavery issue.

They clustered around Brown as soon as he arrived in Boston.
Conferences were held in Howe's domain—the Institute for the Blind
—where they could be neither seen nor interrupted. Frank Sanborn,
the volunteer secretary who had turned his Concord school over to a
Harvard student to manage, was delighted to be a member of such a
heady and significant group. Julia Ward Howe, excluded by her husband from any knowledge of the family finances or his activities—in
keeping with his theory regarding the proper place of women—may

have suspected her husband was deep in an abolitionist plot, but had no specific knowledge.[20]

Like all plots and committees, it had its own pattern. Higginson, according to Brown, had met him in Kansas, though the minister denied it. Parker had met Brown in Chicago and may, at that time, have heard his plan, although he never later alluded to any such knowledge. Gerrit Smith in Peterboro was probably aware of the plan, but later denied so much that whatever he knew at any time remains uncertain. Therefore the Boston committee of six—Howe, Higginson, Parker, Smith, Sanborn and Stearns—started out by keeping secrets from one another, and were never to be wholly honest with the world.

Brown's project was fairly simple. He wanted thirty thousand dollars to arm and provision a force of one hundred men under his leadership to "fight for freedom" in Kansas and "carry the war into Africa." Geary's "pacification" of Kansas would make such an effort useless, if not mischievous. But Brown assured the six that the Kansas "peace" was only a lull, and that the Missourians were preparing a new invasion for the spring. Men believe what they choose, and the six chose to believe that.

These discussions were interspersed with more public, social occasions in which Captain Brown was lionized in a manner later made familiar to many momentarily famous revolutionists when received by wealthy radicals. Theodore Parker threw open his home to a reception for the hero. Wendell Phillips, who lived next door, appeared—and so did Garrison. As always, the famous firebrand was courteous in person, but he engaged Brown in a debate on his use of violence. Both men quoted the Bible, with Parker "injecting a bit of Lexington into the controversy."[21] No minds were changed but Brown apparently refrained—in this polite and substantial gathering—from his usual sarcasms, and came off undamaged in the eyes of his admirers. Only Parker openly expressed the real attitude of the committee of six. "I doubt," he said, "whether things of this kind will succeed. But we shall have a great many failures before we discover the right way of getting at it. This may well be one of them."[22]

In other words, John Brown was an experiment.

On January 7, 1857 the Massachusetts Kansas Aid Committee met—with Stearns sitting as chairman and Sanborn as secretary—and voted to give the Hero the two hundred Sharp's rifles stored in the cellar of the minister, Mr. Todd, in Tabor, Iowa, plus four thousand ball cartridges and thirty-one thousand percussion caps. The only string tied to Brown was that he report how the rifles and ammunition were used "so far as it is proper to do so." Another string, which the Bostonians did not bother to mention, was that their title to this ordnance was somewhat uncertain.

There was also the fact that the weapons and ammunition were double the number Brown needed for his force of one hundred men.

That problem was solved, some months later, when he was authorized to sell half, and "apply the proceeds to relieve the suffering inhabitants of the Territory." No record of any such largesse exists; apparently the clan represented enough of these sufferers to satisfy John Brown.

On the same day that Brown received his military hardware, an item appeared in the N.Y. *Tribune*, with a Boston dateline:

> Old Brown of Osawatomie is in town. He is a hale and vigorous old man of fifty-seven, with a spare figure, with piercing dark-blue eyes, and face expressive of indomitable will. He is accompanied by one of his sons. It is proposed by the friends of Free Kansas here to present him with a purse, to enable him, if Kansas is again invaded, to continue his invaluable services for Freedom. Certainly there is no man more deserving of such a testimonial.
>
> J.R.

"J.R." was, of course, James Redpath, the newspaperman who had so opportunely appeared at Brown's hidden camp after the Pottawatomie murders, and whose initial article had started Brown's awesome newspaper legend rolling. No doubt the two men had many matters to discuss of which no record remains, but it is known that Redpath took the Hero to meet the Martyr: Senator Charles Sumner.

Senator Sumner's physicians were already locked in argument over the extent of his injuries and their nature. The press was divided, along partisan lines, on whether or not he was malingering. The Senator looked well: his voice was "strong and manly as usual, his intellect was bright and strong, but, when he tried to rise from his chair, he had to reach out for support, and he 'walked with a cane and quite feebly.' "

Brown asked to see Sumner's famous coat, the one he had been wearing when he was assaulted by Representative Brooks. The Senator struggled to his feet, made his way painfully to the closet, swung it open and handed the coat "still stiff with blood, to Brown." Brown examined it at length and "said nothing . . . but his lips compressed and his eyes shone like polished steel."[23]

The Sumner incident is often retold as an illustration of how the Senator burnished his role as victim, and is considered interesting because it brought together two figures then high in the martyrology of abolition. It is less often observed that Brown probably got the idea that he, too, could use some exhibits—for not long after he met Sumner he claimed to have the very chains that had once been used on his sons.

The act built, bit by bit. On January 11, 1857 Brown had dinner with the Stearns family in their mansion at Medford. He held them fascinated by his habit of rocking in silent laughter, and appalled them with his tales of the sufferings of free-state settlers in Kansas. Asked about various free-state leaders in the territory, he damned most of them with faint praise—excepting only the brutal and unscrupulous James Montgomery. But he also interjected bits of "grim humor" that impressed Mrs. Stearns with the thought that a warm spirit lived beside his "indomitable will."[24] The eldest Stearns boy wondered what the Captain had been like as a boy. Brown promised to write an account and send it to the boy later. (He did—and it would have done credit to Parson Weems.) The boy also offered his tiny savings to help the Kansas settlers; Brown pocketed that mite gravely—no contribution was too small. When he left he had enlisted the entire Stearns family forever.

The Disunion Convention, called on January 15, 1857, by Higginson and eighty-eight others, was little short of astonishing. Its appeal was reproduced in the Worcester *Daily Bay State* inside a black border. Other newspapers waxed equally sarcastic.

Frank Bird, the jealous, wealthy leader of the Bird Club, served as the convention president; Garrison was a vice president; Wendell Phillips and Higginson were conspicuously active on the program. Some famous names were absent, including Senator Henry Wilson and Representative Joshua Giddings. Theodore Parker sent his regrets to Higginson, saying "other business" kept him away. His other reasons ran an interesting gamut. He was against the Union because it was "a failure," but at the same time he didn't want to see it divided, because "it was wrong to leave four million poor whites and four million slaves under that government." An ordinary man might have blushed to utter such blatant contradictions, but Parker was serene in his ability to face in every direction at once, like some omnipotent being. He concluded, however, on a somber note: "I used to think this terrible question of Freedom and Slavery would be settled without bloodshed; I believe it now no longer."[25]

Others who did attend betrayed similar contradictions and came to less concrete conclusions. Garrison stressed his pacifism, and hoped the Union would, peacefully, dissolve. Wendell Phillips was bolder; he defended treason and shouted "We have a right to change and abolish governments!"[26] In the wake of an election defeat, that sounded hollow; it was obvious the majority of the people were not in favor of such radicalism. But Higginson sounded the loudest bugle. "Give me a convention of ten," he said, "who have drawn their swords *and thrown away the scabbard* and I will revolutionize the world."[27]

One man to whom such words sounded both familiar and realistic was Colonel Hugh Forbes, a former officer under Garibaldi in the Revolution of 1848. English-born, fluent in both French and Italian, Forbes was editor of a small Italian language newspaper in New York. He was also a fencing master and a translator at the New York *Tribune*—a paper that harbored many revolutionaries including Karl Marx—among its European correspondents. Interestingly enough Colonel Forbes had been brought to Higginson's attention by Senator Sumner, who had a wide acquaintance among European revolutionaries.[28]

Another man cheered by such proclamations was John Brown.

There is little doubt that he was introduced to Forbes at the convention, and that they agreed to work together on Brown's army.

A week later Brown was in New York and appeared, uninvited, before the National Kansas Aid Committee, which had convened to discuss ways to approach state legislatures. The officials found their meeting sidetracked into a debate over John Brown's plan for his own army. Sanborn was present, and added his enthusiastic echoes to the Captain's argument. The immediate issue was the two hundred rifles in Tabor. The national committee had a claim on these and some members were against giving them to Brown. They knew more about Brown than did Sanborn; especially Mr. William F. M. Arny, who had taken Abraham Lincoln's place in Illinois, and who had been to Kansas. Another Westerner, Henry H. Hurd of Chicago, was blunt. "If you get the arms and money you desire, will you invade Missouri or any other slave territory?"[29]

Brown took high ground, and would not answer. "I am no adventurer," he said, in an unconsciously revealing phrase. "You all know me. You are acquainted with my history. You know what I have done in Kansas. I do not expose my plans. No one knows them but myself . . . I will not be interrogated; if you wish to give me anything I want you to give it freely. I have no other purpose but to serve the cause of liberty."[30]

That did not satisfy the Westerners but the Eastern members were more radical; they had before them a list—suitable for a boy's expedition—that Brown had drawn up, of blankets, wagons, and provisions he thought would be necessary to outfit fifty men. In the end the national committee donated twelve boxes of clothing enough for sixty persons, turned the disposition of the rifles in Tabor over to the Boston committee, and ordered a draft of five thousand dollars "for any *defensive* measures that may become necessary."[31] That was not as generous as it sounded; the committee had to raise the money, and the opposition that arose was not a good omen.

Brown found another disappointing omen in the somewhat cool reception Gerrit Smith gave him when he made a quick trip to Peterboro to report on his progress. The millionaire said he had already committed one thousand dollars a month toward Kansas aid, and implied that the pledge was growing onerous.

Brown was, however, finally able to visit his wife and children in North Elba. There were complaints there also; Henry Thompson had never been paid for building the clan a house, and little Ellen, who was only two, shrank from her father, a stranger.

The Massachusetts Kansas Aid Committee had hopes of raising a large sum from the state legislature. Captain Brown was needed as a witness at a committee hearing to discuss an aid bill, which Sanborn, a busy young man, had drawn up. The other two witnesses were Martin Conway, an agent of the Kansas Aid Committee who knew all about Pottawatomie but had political ambitions, and E. B. Whitman. All

spoke, but Sanborn had the highest hopes for Brown, whom he introduced with appropriate flourishes.

"Ask this gray-haired man, gentlemen," said Sanborn, "—if you
have the heart to do it—where lies the body of his murdered son—
where are the homes of his four other sons, who a year ago were quiet
farmers in Kansas."[32]

Brown had a prepared speech ready, but soon threw it aside in the
manner of a man carried away. He described the losses of his clan,
which he placed at seventy-five hundred dollars, and said he had "in
his hotel room, the very trace-chain which his son wore under the
summer sun of Kansas." He also mentioned the insanity of John
Brown, Jr.: "a maniac—yes, a maniac," he said, "and wiped a tear from
his eye."[33]

That would have upset John Brown, Jr., at that moment comfortable
with his family on his Ohio farm, but it did not move the men of
Massachusetts. A new administration was due to take office the following month in Washington; the nation was beginning to calm down after
many months of fever, and the Massachusetts legislature was not responsible for deeds, or misdeeds, in the West. Sanborn, Brown, Conway, and Whitman left, disappointed.

Brown had assumed that he would make a lecture tour and raise his
own funds, at least in part, all along. His experience after the Buffalo
meeting in 1855 had shown the way; his experiences in Kansas had
provided the reputation. He had some circulars printed, which show
signs of his own inimitable hand, heavy with a mendicant's appeal.

——This will introduce a friend who visits in order to secure means to
sustain and secure the cause of Freedom in the U.S. and throughout the
world.

In behalf of this cause, he has exhausted his modest means as to place
his wife and three daughters in circumstances of privation and dependent on the generosity of friends who have cared for them.

He has contributed the entire services of two strong sons for two years
and his own services for three years.

During this time they have undergone great hardship, exposure of
health and other privations.

During much of the past three years he had with him in Kansas six sons
and a son-in-law who together with him were all sick.

Two were made prisoners and subjected to the most barbarous treatment.

Two were severely wounded.

One was murdered.

During this time he figured with some success under the title of "Old
Brown" often imperilling his life.

He himself is endorsed as an earnest and steady-minded man and a
True Descendant of Peter Brown of the *Mayflower* pilgrims.[34]

That was crude, but a more polished version soon appeared in the
New York *Tribune* and other newspapers, that ended on a more proper

note of martyrdom in a higher cause: "It is with *no little sacrifice of personal feeling* that I appear in this manner before the public." Brown even acquired a treasurer—W. H. D. Callender of Hartford. He also acquired the lecturer's polish; his talks were dramatic. He shook the chains at the audience—the chains which, he said, once shackled his sons; he drew a bowie knife from a sheath in his boot; he said the knife had been taken from Captain Pate in the famous battle of Black Jack Springs.

On March 1, 1857 he spoke at Collinsville, Connecticut. The next day he was in the village drugstore and showed the bowie knife again, then turned to Charles Blair, a blacksmith, and asked how much it would cost to fix such a blade to "poles about six feet long."[35] Blair thought he could make a thousand for a dollar each; Brown said he would order them. Later some correspondence was exchanged and Blair sent samples. Brown sent in an order for the thousand. He wanted spears, and not for settlers.

The day after Brown left Collinsville for his next lecture date—March 2, 1857—was the day that his "Little Hornet," James H. Holmes, finally caught up with Dutch Henry Sherman. Dutch Henry was on the prairie, at least a mile away from the house in which he had been staying. Archie Cansdell, who was with Holmes, shot him "against," said Holmes, "my orders or expectations."[36]

The wounded man staggered toward his home; the "Hornet" and Cansdell followed and cared for him briefly, while someone went for a doctor. Dutch Henry lingered two days and then died.

Augustus Bondi said, "Sherman's claim had been jumped during the winter and the jumper's cabin was the hangout of Holmes, Archie and other questionable characters and Archie killed Sherman for his money belt and probably divided with Holmes."[37] That was a quick explanation of some elements of fact, but it was too quick. Bondi, after all, was close to John Brown, and even closer to Wiener, the store-keeper who had murdered along the Pottawatomie with Brown. Bondi would not want to remind anyone of that prior crime.

Southerners who had watched the Kansas situation in growing frustration had no such reservations. They charged that Sherman was murdered by "a remnant of Old Captain Brown's desperados" so he could not testify against any of them."[38] That was possible: Holmes was under indictment and Dutch Henry was a witness against him and against Townsley—who was in custody at Tecumseh—for the murder of his brother Dutch Bill. The Harrises, who were also witnesses to murder, theft, and arson, had been threatened. Glanville, another witness, had been murdered.

The fear created around the crime and its criminal aftermaths in the region was so great that Governor Geary was informed that "on account of the murder of Henry Sherman no one would qualify as county officers." The governor's secretary, J.H. Gihon, denied that murders were being committed to cover up other murders. He said Dutch

Henry had been slain "simply for his money, of which he had collected a considerable amount."[39]

Meanwhile another sort of cover-up was under way. Dutch Henry's neighbors, former employees, his physician, his undertaker, his lawyers, his customers, and his suppliers began to present bills or claims against his estate. His remaining cattle were driven away on the pretext he had sold his herd and died before the sale was registered; the coffin-maker's bill was high, as was the doctor's; lawyers charged fees for handling the estate, and for representing claimants and/or heirs. The county and state demanded taxes, suits were filed and fought, and years passed while the estate gradually dwindled until, in the end, no final accounting was ever made.[40]

Before that, however, and coincident with the latest murder, a land company was formed, named Sewanoe, after a Pottawatomie chief buried under a mound, "located at Pottawatomie Creek, at the crossing of the old California Road, at an old established point, known as Dutch Henry's Crossing."[41]

A week after Dutch Henry died, John Brown arrived in Concord. He was the guest of Frank Sanborn the first night, at the home of William Ellery Channing, who was away editing the *Mercury* in New Bedford. At noon the next day Sanborn took Brown across to Mrs. Thoreau's boarding house for lunch. Thoreau was waiting, and after lunch the trio sat in Mrs. Thoreau's parlor while Brown launched into his well-polished description of the Battle of Black Jack Springs. He described his own force as a minuscule nine—pitted against Captain Pate's twenty-odd.[42] Sanborn, to whom the tale was ever green, left to look in on his school. After a while Emerson, "who had returned from his Western lecture-tour, came up, as he often did, to call on Thoreau, and was introduced by him to John Brown."

Emerson was charmed, and invited Brown to be his guest at Coolidge Castle. The invitation was accepted, but the Sage later learned he already had so many house guests that there was no room. This was not unusual: Emerson was so often crowded out of his own home that he rented a spare room at a nearby farmhouse. Brown could use that chamber, as a guest of the Emersons.

Emerson was famous, among other attributes, for his ability to disengage quickly from bores, or persons with whom he was not in sympathy. But Brown was a man with whom he agreed, and by whom he was charmed. He and Thoreau chatted with Brown through an afternoon and into the evening hours. It was during this long exchange, said Sanborn later, that Emerson and Thoreau acquired "that intimate knowledge of Brown's character and general purpose which qualified them . . . to make those addresses on his behalf which were the first response among American scholars to the heroism of the man . . ."[43]

The hero of Osawatomie convinced them both that he was "a transcendentalist above all, a man of ideas and principles—that was what distinguished him."[44] Thoreau was sensitive: he often chafed against the Emersonian coolness, but Brown's manners impressed him deeply. "I noticed," he wrote

> that he did not overstate anything, but spoke within bounds. I remember, particularly, how, in his speech here, he referred to what his family had suffered in Kansas, without ever giving the least vent to his pent-up fire. It was a volcano with an ordinary chimney-flue . . .
>
> When I expressed surprise that he could live in Kansas with a price set upon his head, and so large a number, including the authorities, exasperated against him, he accounted for it by saying, "It is perfectly well understood that I will not be taken . . ."
>
> Yet he did not attribute his success, foolishly, to "his star," or to any magic. He said, truly, that the reason why such greatly superior numbers quailed before him was, as one of his prisoners confessed, because they *lacked a cause* . . .

"He is so transparent," chimed Emerson, "that all men see him through. He is a man to make friends wherever on earth courage and integrity are esteemed, a pure idealist, with no by-ends of his own."[45]

Later, Emerson recalled that Brown said, that night, that he "believes in two articles—two instruments, shall I say?—the Golden Rule and the Declaration of Independence; and he used this expression in conversation here concerning them. Better that a whole generation of men, women and children should pass away by a violent death, than that one word of either should be violated in this country."[46]

The Sage repeated this non sequitur as though it made sense; perhaps because it resembled so much of his own amorphous rhetoric. Both he and Thoreau were delighted with Brown; they agreed that they had discovered "a transcendentalist saint."

They came to that conclusion together on the same night that—by eerie coincidence—James Townsley, under arrest in Tecumseh for the Pottawatomie murders, was provided a file by parties unknown, and sawed his way to freedom.[47] The escape was barely noted even in the press of the Territory; the *Herald of Freedom* had remained oddly silent about Pottawatomie and even the murder of Dutch Henry. The evening of March 13, 1857, therefore, marked the moment when John Brown was released from the weight of pursuit for five murders, and entered the literature of the nation—as a hero.

Chapter 36

The murders committed by the Brown party in Kansas had escaped attention because they occurred at the same time that Lawrence was "sacked" and Senator Sumner was caned. Brown's emergence in the lecture halls and parlors of New England similarly escaped national attention because by early March the Supreme Court was on the eve of announcing its decision on the Dred Scott case—and a new president was about to enter the White House.

Both events cast long shadows. The Dred Scott case was tangled in the free-state–slave-state issue in bewildering fashion, and rumors had already been spread through the press about it. Buchanan's career was shadowed by the case even before he took office, and there was material enough for interminable disputes and the darkest of suspicions to be creditably floated.

Scott was the slave of Dr. Emerson, an army surgeon who had taken him to Illinois and Minnesota: both free-state regions. In one of these Scott had married Harriet, another slave, and had a child. In 1838 all three were conveyed by Dr. Emerson to Missouri, where another slave child was born. Then Dr. Emerson died and left his slaves and other property in trust for his children, in the care of his wife. She remarried a politician named Chaffee, and Scott was turned over to the care—for he was retarded—of a friend named Taylor Blow.

Blow grew tired of the expense and sought the advice of lawyers regarding the best means of releasing Scott. Their solution was to sue Mrs. Emerson for fourteen years' back wages, on the argument Scott and his family were freed by virtue of residence in a free state. From there on the case went into the legal mills of Missouri. The first court ruled that Scott was free. An appeal court reversed that verdict. In the interim Scott's ownership had been transferred to Mrs. Chaffee's brother, John Stanford of New York—and a suit was filed to resolve the constitutional principles. The case was transferred to the federal courts and went on the Supreme Court docket in 1854. It was argued in December 1856.

By that time it was clear that issues fought over in Kansas were inherent in the case. Many prominent persons were drawn into the affair, including Reverdy Johnson, a leader of the Maryland bar, former Senator Thomas Hart Benton, Senator Henry S. Geyer, and others. The newspapers awakened to the importance of the issue. Observers in the court agreed that the presentation for both the owner and the slave were brilliant, according to partisan views. The justices retired to consider the matter, and rumors mounted while they deliberated.

The composition of the Supreme Court was critically examined from a sectional vantage. Five justices were from slave states, four from free. In chambers the justices at first thought a decision could be made on narrow grounds. But as discussion continued it also became clear that the Court, if it chose, could resolve an issue that had been dividing the nation for a generation. The prestige of the Court at the time was immense. Caleb Cushing had told the justices that the Court was "the incarnate mind of the nation."[1]

That incarnate mind, however, found itself grappling with itself in terms that resembled, in chambers, a microcosm of the arguments that exacerbated the nation. Justice Curtis of Pennsylvania wrote his uncle, George Curtis Ticknor, who had argued in the Court for Dred Scott's freedom and was in Europe: "The North is now quiet after a sectional excitement . . . but I am greatly mistaken if events do not arouse it again to overthrow what is called the 'slave power,' even greater than that recently made. . . ."[2]

That was indiscreet, but it was in a private letter to a relative out of the country, and a leader among lawyers. Ticknor could hold his tongue well. Far more injurious to the Court was a speculative article written by James Pike, Washington correspondent for the New York *Tribune,* who said there were "hints" that the Court would rule that Congress could not restrict slavery. Pike ventured the opinion that "the moral weight of such a decision would be at least equal to a political stump speech of a slaveholder or a doughface."[3] That was a poor prediction, but the article provoked a wave of other speculation, and the *Tribune* pressed its persistent argument that the entire United States government was weighted on the side of slavery.

Meanwhile the justices prepared to write their own decisions. Chief Justice Taney, in his eightieth year, had long encouraged this practice and little expected the mischief to which it would lead. He was the same Roger Taney who had, once before, pushed the nation into crisis when, as attorney general and, later, acting secretary of the treasury under Andrew Jackson, he had precipitated the Bank of the United States argument. On that occasion Taney had acted with such subtlety that few of his contemporaries could accurately assess his behavior. As Chief Justice he had been equally persuasive but his popularity and prestige were far more impressive.

President-elect Buchanan was, naturally, greatly concerned about the decision; like the rest of the nation he was aware the Court was going to rule on the constitutionality of whether states could mandate freedom for slaves legally held in other states. Unless he had a clearer picture, this terrible subject could become a most embarrassing point in his March 4 Inaugural Address. Justice Catron sent him a helpful message:

> The question involving the constitutionality of the Missouri Compromise line is presented to the appropriate tribunal, to wit, the officers of the Supreme Court of the United States. It will decide and settle a controversy which has so long and seriously agitated the country and

must ultimately be decided by the Supreme Court. And until the case now before it . . . is disposed of, I would deem it improper to express any opinion on the subject . . .[4]

Nothing could seem more neutral than that, but President Buchanan and the Court were working, at this point, against the power of the press to poison the air of the nation. In covering Buchanan's speech, James Pike of the New York *Tribune* called the President's remarks "on the side of an open, undisguised, entire devotion to slavery . . . gradually forcing its way, through fogs and murky darkness . . . until at last this policy bursts upon the nation in the inaugural . . . and the coming decision of the Supreme Court . . ."[5]

Pike's article, which spawned a rash of angry rumors that Buchanan was conspiring behind the scenes with the Court, appeared on March 5. The following day, March 6, 1857, Chief Justice Taney read his opinion. It was not the "majority" opinion, for there was no majority on the points of the argument—only on the decision.

Chief Justice Taney was a man who, in 1857, recalled happy fox-hunting days in Maryland in the 1790's, the death of General Washington and the tears of Revolutionary War veterans, and the climate in which the Constitution was drafted and accepted. His reasoning was based on that memory and period, and on the assumption that the nation could be frozen in that mold. In a way, his assumption was an unconscious tribute to the power of propaganda to make the Constitution seem unchangeable, even though he himself had played a large role in making many changes in it—both as a cabinet officer and as Chief Justice.

Taney was a pious Catholic who waited in line among Negroes for his turn in the confessional; his first criminal case as a young lawyer had been the defense of a black accused of raping a white child.[6] He was personally gentle and generous, whenever his own interests were not involved, and he had released his own slaves many years before, excepting in cases of their poverty and old age, in which he supported them.

But it was his opinion that the Constitution accepted slaves as property, and beyond that, that Negroes were an inferior, conquered race. He contrasted them with Indians, whose freedom, he said, "has constantly been acknowledged." He argued that Negroes had no rights "excepting those granted to them by those who had the power to grant." They could be reduced to slavery, and had "no rights that the white man was bound to respect."[7]

Therefore Dred Scott and his wife and children had no right even to sue in court. The Court had no jurisdiction over them. With only two dissents, the other justices produced tortured arguments sustaining the decision. One dissent was entered by a justice hopeful of the Republican presidential nomination in the future. The other—which sliced Taney's reasoning to shreds—was entered by Justice Curtis, who resigned in protest over the decision.

The Northern newspapers erupted. Radicals rejoiced, for Taney had, by the sweep of his statement, provided their cause with ammunition that they had never dreamed of receiving. The South also rejoiced, for it was the general view that the North could not now continue its argument. Moderates remained cool; Lincoln thought the decision was "erroneous," but noted that the Court "had changed its mind before and could change it again." He added, "we offer no resistance to it." The nation was—by the overly ambitious step of the Chief Justice and six of his associates—across an irreversible boundary and in a new and perilous position. For the North would not accept the ruling, and that meant that the rule of law would give way, or be broken.

The Dred Scott decision was issued at a time when violence in Kansas was on the wane, and when a great election victory by moderates had cooled the nation's temper. The decision of the Supreme Court, however, tore asunder the accomplishment of the Democratic party. From that cleavage a new spirit rose in the land, in which the savage doctrines of John Brown found new adherents.

Brown was carried upward by the Northern reaction against the Court. S. G. Hubbard of New Haven, Connecticut wrote, advising him to limit his lectures to what he had seen and experienced in Kansas and why he expected another invasion—but to keep his own plans unstated, pending "a private meeting of our friends for a consultation of plans ..."[8] Thaddeus Hyatt, who had accompanied Higginson to Kansas and was highly placed in the Kansas Aid Committee, wrote more boldly of the possible necessity of annihilating to a man the proslavery legislature in Kansas, and " 'Old Brown' is our hero when God's work of vengeance is to be executed upon our enemies when their cup shall be full."[9]

In New York, Brown conferred with Colonel Forbes. Based on his military experience with Garibaldi, Forbes had written *Compendio del Volontario Patriotico*, in two volumes, published in Naples. His rank of colonel under Garibaldi had been real, and the Italian leader recommended his books as a manual for volunteers.[10] The colonel explained this to Captain Brown, who had long dreamed of mountain warfare. Brown agreed to pay Forbes one hundred dollars a month to distill and summarize the lessons of Italy in English for Brown's own projected volunteer "army", and further authorized him to draw six hundred dollars advance pay from his treasurer, W. H. D. Callender. Once Forbes's *Manual of Patriotic Volunteers* was ready, the colonel was to join Brown in Tabor, Iowa to share in the task of military preparation.

There is little doubt that Forbes thought Brown's was a large and serious undertaking, backed by important personages in the United States. He did not realize that Brown's Boston coterie consisted of men who believed, for the most part, that words were all the realities the world needed. Instead, Brown appeared to Forbes as an angel of unexpected good luck, for the colonel was in dire poverty and worried almost out of his mind by letters from a nearly destitute wife and family in Paris.

Forbes sought to raise funds by appeals to sympathy, but Brown—who also needed money—had more originality. A letter was sent to the old man by his son Jason, saying that a federal marshal was enroute through Cleveland with a warrant for Brown's arrest. That marshal was never heard from again, but Brown used Jason's letter as a device to rush to Boston and seek refuge.

That refuge was provided by Judge Thomas B. Russell and Mrs. Russell in their home on a quiet Boston street. The Russells were ardent abolitionists unknown to all but a handful in the movement, since they chose to play a quiet background role.

Brown carried off his end of the charade with a skill that would have earned him a place on the stage. He chilled Mrs. Russell by producing "a long, evil-looking knife," and some shorter ones, as well as revolvers. He told her: "If you hear a noise at night, put the baby under the pillow. I should hate to spoil these carpets, too, but you know I cannot be taken." Then he barricaded himself in his room for hours.[11]

Mrs. Russell and the Judge were also regaled, at dinner, with tales of how Brown had "eaten joints and toes of crawling," and imaginary, creatures. He laughed without sound, would "in utter silence rock and quake with mirth."

Unfortunately his scare did not work; there was no rush to see him, or to press money into his hand. One day he came downstairs with a bitter document headed "Old Browns *Farewell:* to the Plymouth Rocks; Bunker Hill, Monuments; Charter Oaks; and Uncle Toms, Cabbins." Long lines followed that described his sufferings and needs, with many underlinings to stress significant passages, in his usual manner. The paper ended piteously, *"How Are the Mighty Fallen?"*[12]

Brown read this aloud in a suitably dramatic voice, to Mrs. Russell. Her reaction must have been satisfactory, for he asked her to send for Mrs. Stearns in Medford. When she arrived he read his lament to her. She was touched and said she would show it to her husband. Brown then made a number of copies that he mailed to various contacts—the complaint's effect on the ladies being sufficient proof that the effort might work. It worked so well on Mrs. Stearns that, awakening the next morning in "the splendor of the spring sunshine" in her luxurious home, she felt so guilty about the Captain's sufferings that she suggested to George Luther Stearns that they sell all their possessions and turn over the proceeds to Brown.

That brought Stearns to the Russell home. He handed Brown a letter of credit for seven thousand dollars, but added a significant string. Brown could draw on the letter only in Kansas, when his force was in the field, and "actually engaged."[13]

Brown was jubilant, and wrote John Brown, Jr. that his "collections I may safely put down at $13,000. I think I have got matters so much in train that it will soon reach $30,000."[14] Then he described his lament, and said, "The effect on a Boston merchant who saw the manuscript was that he immediately gave me a letter authorizing me to draw on him on sight $7,000 & others were also moved to be in earnest."[15]

The letter was intended to enlist John Brown, Jr. in his enterprise; the Captain had been upset to learn from his wife that all his sons except Owen had "decided not to fight any more, in Kansas or anywhere else." The old man was angry at this; his sons were his instruments and the thought of their independence was insufferable. He warned them, through Mrs. Brown, that "there may be *possibly* in their day that which is more to be demanded."[16]

He also demanded more from his supporters. He had spoken so often about his "sacrifices" that he had come to believe them himself. And he began to stress the dangers he would face, the possibility of his death, and his concern over his family. That led to an appeal to A. A. Lawrence for "One Thousand Dollars cash" with which he proposed to buy land in North Elba from Gerrit Smith "to procure a Subsistence should I never return . . . my Wife being a good economist and real old fashioned business woman."[17]

Lawrence replied he did not have that much cash to spare, and Brown then pressed to see if his supporters could not combine to raise it. Lawrence went along with that and so did Stearns; between them they put up $570. The rest would take a little longer while Wendell Phillips and others were solicited.

The Captain was working hard to put his enterprise on a sound financial basis, but as the weeks passed the situation in Kansas and the nation began to change. The discovery of gold and the opening of new lands, the construction of railroads and development of new towns and cities had led to rising prices, expanded credit, and feverish speculation for a number of years. The speculation was a natural part of a boom but it reached unprecedented heights by the end of 1856 and was then affected by a number of overseas events.

The most important of these was the collapse of Louis Napoleon's Crédit Mobilier—a huge government creation that franchised private companies to launch grandiose projects that gradually entangled financial centers in Spain, Austria, and Germany as well as France. Crédit Mobilier began to buckle in 1857. France, working through the Rothschilds, attempted to extricate itself by siphoning gold from the Bank of England and by presenting certificates for redemption. This led the English to drain money from American securities, which led to a wave of selling.[18]

On the surface all remained prosperous and substantial in the United States through the spring, even though the supports of the economy were slowly eroding. Prices remained high and speculation persisted. In such a climate almost all plans appear practical and appealing.

Higginson was, therefore, not alone in believing that Brown's plans were practical, and that they offered opportunities for an expanded future. Enlisted to gather funds for Brown in the Worcester area in early April 1857, he announced on April 10, that he would resign his pastorate of his free church. Higginson knew that Theodore Parker was failing, and believed Parker's condition to be the result of overwork, as it may well have been. Yet he wanted to "lecture, preach and write without being similarly drained. In the present condition of the country," he wrote his mother, "there will be an increasing demand on me from outside."[19]

It was a significant step. Higginson later produced an article in the *Atlantic Monthly* advocating, as usual, physical action, and said: "One of the most potent causes of the ill-concealed alienation between the clergy and the community, is the supposed deficiency, on the part of the former, of a vigorous, manly life."[20] He wanted to be seen as a man of action; not a clergyman. In May 1857, speaking at the American Antislavery Convention in New York, he made his hopes clear.

"The question of slavery is a stern and practical one," he said. "Give us the power and we can make a new Constitution . . . how is that power to be obtained? By politics? Never. By revolution, and that alone."[21]

Despite that faith in action—shared by Howe, who gave Brown his rifle and two revolvers, and the rest of the "Secret Six"—the situation in Kansas grew steadily more peaceful. A. A. Lawrence, who went west to survey the situation from the several levels of his interest, had never believed in revolution and was shrewd enough to see that conditions were changing. "There must be a collapse in land speculation all over the West," he wrote in May 1857. "Now is the time to sell . . . and lend money . . ." He advised the officers of the Kansas Aid Company to sell half their Kansas property and put the money out at interest, or they would lose everything.[22] The officers ignored his warning—and in time did lose everything. Seeing that his advice was spurned, Lawrence resigned, and sent a letter of warning to Charles Robinson in Kansas.

. . . avoid all disagreement, or controversy with the E.A. Company, you are not strong enough to stand against it in this part of the country a single day. Its financial power is trifling; the whole capital paid in & invested in Kansas is trifling. But its moral power *here*, if exerted against any individual, would destroy his influence & his standing. This arises from the character of most of the men who compose its Board of Directors. An opinion they might deliberately form . . . on almost any subject . . . would be final & would have more weight here than the ruling of the U.S. Court.[23]

That was true enough in New England, but even the Emigrant Aid Committee could not move against the inexorable economic tides that were beginning to run. In Kansas a new governor, Robert J. Walker of Missouri, arrived in May 1857, and the free-state groups began to shift their focus. Robinson, Lane, and others—even James H. Holmes, the "Little Hornet"—were deeply involved in land deals and town sites.

Settlers from the Ohio Valley, from Indiana and other Northern states, but not particularly from New England, were pouring into the territory. Matters were still tangled, with Southerners continuing to rant in the territorial legislature. But the new governor—with the forceful F.P. Stanton as his secretary, and with General William S. Harvey, another ally, in command of federal troops in the region— proceeded to restore rationality with outstanding speed. His main problem was to persuade free-staters to vote instead of maintaining their boycott and illegal organizations.

Walker arrived with Senator Henry Wilson of Massachusetts and Dr. Samuel Gridley Howe. All three gave speeches; Charles Robinson and Jim Lane were persuaded to cooperate and by July, A. A. Lawrence wrote, "We look on the great question as now settled and all political movements in Kansas as having chiefly a local interest . . . Now we must be magnanimous to the South. Slavery cannot be extended. Whether it can ever be got rid of in this country is doubtful. It is a curse imposed by the sins of our ancestors and we must bear it patiently . . ."[24]

Meanwhile over seven thousand immigrants arrived in Kansas City; the population of Leavenworth soared to nearly four thousand; land prices rose like rockets. By midsummer it was estimated Kansas would have one hundred thousand people by October. Nine-tenths of the settlers came from free states and that fact—more than all the plots, plans, and perils of the combatants—was making the final outcome inevitable. Efforts to raise money in the South to win Kansas were halted.[25]

Nevertheless Southern anger rose high: the admission of a free Kansas would tip the scales Northward in the Senate and end the balance so long maintained. Minnesota and Oregon were on the horizon and would soon enter the Union; antislavery forces were rising even inside Missouri. The "ultras" of the South began to rise, the directory of Southerners around President Buchanan warned that secession plots were underway—and were justified.

In the United States, Europe's economic troubles seemed distant and unimportant; few Americans outside export and banking circles paid much attention to them. Many factors, however, combined to create changes: the end of the Crimean War and the reentry of Russia into the grain markets hurt U.S. agriculture, sales began to drop and some New England mills, with bulging warehouses, began to suspend operations. Still business boomed through July 1857; it was not until the Ohio Insurance and Trust Company collapsed that the bankers became alarmed. The firm had failed, ironically enough, through internal embezzlements and not external conditions, but in two days seven small New York banks sank and panic ran through the city like a forest fire.[26]

Loans were called, creditors dunned, stocks plunged, demands for collateral sent out. Fear began to make its presence felt. As the banks sought to protect themselves by forcing their customers to suicide, old respected institutions began to cave in; bank runs began by the end of summer. The panic spread to Chicago; it affected railroads, factories, land developments, all commerce. When Boston caught the virus, the Emigrant Aid Committee lost its holdings, investments, and contributions—and sent word to John Brown that its five thousand dollar draft was no longer valid; the committee was virtually out of business in Kansas.

Until then, John Brown had been doing well. By July his friends had raised the one thousand dollars he said he needed to provide a home for his wife and five minor children, and he had spent the months of May and June contacting everyone he knew or to whom he was recommended, ceaselessly raising money and seeking further contributions. He was anxious about Colonel Forbes, who had drawn the six hundred dollar advance salary with impressive alacrity, and had his progress checked. On June 22, 1857, Brown had a conference with Gerrit Smith in Chicago. The millionaire gave his "old friend" $350 and when pressed, on the grounds that Brown had unpaid debts, another $110. Later, Smith had a conference with Forbes (whose participation in the project was, therefore, known to at least some people); and also wrote: "We must not shrink from fighting for Liberty—and if Federal troops fight against her, we must fight against them."[27]

George Luther Stearns, whose zeal was unquestionable, tried to raise one hundred thousand dollars for Brown from the New York State Legislature to "organize a secret force, well-armed and under the control of the famous John Brown, to repel Border Ruffian outrage . . ." He also sent Brown a draft for five hundred dollars and turned over one hundred of the Sharp's rifles in Tabor. By the end of July Sanborn went to North Elba with one thousand dollars cash for Brown's family home, and was somewhat taken aback to discover that Brown already owned 244 acres of land purchased from Gerrit Smith years before. The thousand dollars were meant, it appeared, to pay for another parcel, of which half was intended for his son-in-law Henry Thompson and his daughter Ruth. Even that did not cost one thousand dollars. Sanborn, whose faith would not have been shaken at any revelation, decided it was all for the best, and happily gave Mrs. Brown the remaining money.[28] The Captain was, meanwhile, enroute to Tabor, Iowa, and his great undertaking in Kansas.

Had Brown proceeded directly to Tabor he might well have organized at least some of the one hundred men for whom he had collected so much money, arms, and provisions. But it took him nearly three full months of apparently aimless wandering across the landscape to proceed from North Elba to Iowa.

Letters signed with various imaginative names, replete with mysterious hints and interspersed with demands for money, marked a trail that led from Hudson, Ohio to Cleveland, to Milwaukee, to Chicago, and back to Ohio. Brown wrote gratefully about the successful one thousand dollar subscription raised by A. A. Lawrence, George Luther Stearns, and Frank Sanborn which expanded his family's holdings in North Elba; but he followed it at once with complaints that he was not receiving the support he needed for his great venture.

While he meandered—from time to time sending explanations that he had been felled by "ague" or "fevers"—the situation in Kansas changed. The radicals were still hopeful of violent action, but floods of new free-staters far outnumbered Robinson's old League for Freedom, and a combination of federal troops and energetic territorial officials brought not only peace, but arguments that an outlaw free-state government was no longer reasonable.

As the summer passed and Brown delayed, an exchange of letters made it clear that his hopes were more obsolete with every passing week. He sent word to Augustus Wattles that he would be in Tabor, and enclosed a list of names of men whom he wanted to join him at his new headquarters. Wattles wrote back that if Brown planned to return to Kansas, to "Come quietly as possible, or not come at present, as you choose."[29]

Wattles' employer, G.W. Brown, was busy with his *Herald of Freedom* and less in favor of violence.[30] Charles Robinson had obtained a large parcel of land and was planning a town to be called Quindaro.[31] The free-state leaders had scheduled a convention for August 26, 1857, at which they planned to advise their followers to drop their boycott of the territorial government and vote in a general election in October. That would mean the end of the covert civil war and the troubles in Kansas.

Radicals were appalled. Violence had become their livelihood as well as their method. Funds contributed to the Kansas Aid committees in the East had provided an easy living for a clutch of adventurers, including a coterie of young newspapermen—Redpath, Kagi, Realf, Phillips, John E. Cook, Richard Hinton, and others.[32] Their dispatches had inflamed the nation and sowed deep seeds of North-South discord that not even the passage of generations would sooth. An end to the troubles in Kansas would mean an end to their meteoric careers. And they were not alone.

Captain Holmes, the "Little Hornet" whom Brown had left in charge of his minuscule Kansas Regulars, wrote Brown: "Several times we have needed you very much." He was eager to continue "the business for which I believe you have a stock of material with you"— meaning weapons—and added, significantly, "If you wish other employments, I presume you will find just as *profitable* ones."[33]

Brown did not arrive in Tabor, Iowa, until August 7, 1857.

Colonel Forbes, who had completed the English version of his manual, had also waited until the end of summer to make the trip; his delay was due to Brown's. Before leaving New York the colonel sent his daughter back to her mother in Paris, having forwarded a goodly part of his six hundred dollar wages to his family. He had a chat before leaving with Horace Greeley, and told the publisher he was going to fight for freedom in Kansas. Greeley gave him twenty dollars, and his friends in New York's Garibaldi-Mazzini colony—exiles, like himself, from a failed revolution—made up a modest purse. Forbes then went to Peterboro and saw Gerrit Smith. Explaining that he would work with Brown, he showed Smith the manuscript of the manual. Smith was delighted and impressed. He gave the colonel $150—most of which Forbes spent to have the manual printed.[34] Forbes then proceeded to Tabor, arriving two days after Brown. He was appalled to discover a serene religious community and—instead of a small army of eager young men—nobody waiting for him but commander-in-chief John Brown and Brown's son Owen, who had a crippled arm.

Two weeks later the Panic struck.

Between the last week in August and the early weeks of September there was a series of nationwide economic debacles. The banks of Philadelphia suspended specie payments. The banks of New York followed suit and ceased honoring rural notes; runs began on banks everywhere. Natural disasters added to the crisis; the steamer *Central America,* carrying two million dollars in needed gold, sank with all hands. The Panic spread to Chicago, to Boston, and south to New Orleans and Charleston.[35]

Speculators felt the impact first, then debtors, and finally ventures of every sort. But in Massachusetts young Frank Sanborn, comfortably situated, remained more intent upon the progress of Brown than on other matters. Pressed for money by Brown, he sought to persuade Higginson to part with three thousand dollars of Kansas Aid Committee reserves that had been collected in the Worcester area:

> He is as ready for a revolution as any other man, and is now on the border of Kansas, safe from arrest, but prepared for action, but he needs money for his present expenses, and active support. I believe he is the best disunion champion you can find and with his hundred men, when he is put where he can use them . . . will do more to split the Union than a list of 50,000 names for your convention—good as that is.
>
> What I am trying to hint at is that the friends of Kansas are looking with strange apathy on a movement that has all the elements of fitness and success—a good plan, a tried leader and a radical purpose. If you can do anything for it *now* in God's name do it—and this ill-result of the new policy in Kansas may be prevented.[36]

The new policy was, of course, peace in Kansas. That appeared a terrible possibility to Sanborn. And although he was not specifically informed on how much Brown had retained from his collections, he was accurate in assuming that more money was needed. Brown had arrived at Tabor with only twenty-five dollars.[37] The rest had been squandered in aimless and incessant traveling; on purchases that were never explained, and also on the clan.

Having pressed Sanborn to press Higginson, Brown turned the full force of his persuasions on George Luther Stearns:

> I am now waiting further advice from Free-state friends in Kansas, with whom I have speedy *private* communications lately started. But at this moment unable to move *very much* from an injury of my back, but getting better fast. I am in *immediate* want of from five hundred to one thousand dollars for *secret service* and *no questions asked.*
> *Will you* exert yourself to have that amount, or some part of it, placed in your hands subject to my order?[38]

Soon after that appeal, which did not work, Brown prepared his friends in the East for more delay: "I am still waiting here for additional teams & means of paying expenses or to know if I can make a diversion in favor of our friends in case they are involved in trouble."[39] He also told Sanborn to assure Stearns that he intended to keep the arms entrusted to him safe "so that he may be remunerated in the end."

He was, clearly, in a tight situation. If he entered Kansas with the murders hanging over him, he could not be sure he would not be arrested and tried. His reputation, after all, was terrible, and he had criticized Robinson and other leaders in the East to the point where he could no longer be certain of their support. That left Jim Lane. Lane wanted the Tabor guns, and wrote Brown: "We want you with *all the materials* you have. I see no objection to your coming to Kansas publicly."[40]

Brown wrote back that he needed "three good teams with well covered wagons & ten really ingenious, industrious men (not gassy) with about $110 in cash . . ."[41] Lane wrote back that he was sending all he had, fifty dollars, and "ten true men."

Brown kept the money, and grumbled to E. B. Whitman, the Kansas Aid agent in Lawrence, that it was "only about enough to pay up my board bill here with all I had in hand. I need not say my disappointment has been extreme."[42] The letter was handdelivered, via Charles P. Tidd, a recruit. Whitman sent Tidd back with $150 he had scraped together for Brown, and a message saying "General Lane will send teams from Fall City so that you may get your guns all in. Make the Tabor people wait for what you owe them. They must."[43]

While this cross-purposed correspondence was under way, Brown and Forbes held conferences about their phantom army. Brown had decided to "carry the war to Africa"—and invade Virginia.

Forbes was appalled. At Brown's request he had drafted a document entitled *The Duty of a Soldier; Presented with respectful and kind feelings to the Officers and Soldiers of the United States Army in Kansas.* It was followed by three printed pages of argument, designed to lure the federal troops from the American flag to Brown's command.[44]

Copies were sent to Wattles, Sanborn, Parker, and even to Governor Salmon P. Chase of Ohio, among others. Each man also received a handwritten note from Brown asking for an opinion of the argument, and for money. Gerrit Smith was the only one pleased; he replied to Forbes' accompanying letter with twenty-five dollars, saying he thought the document was "very well-written." Sanborn and Parker were less favorably impressed.

Meanwhile Forbes explored the potential of John Brown's army —with growing dismay. Brown thought he could raise troops by offering an officer's commission to army privates to lead a slave insurrection. He intended also, at the head of "25 to 50 well-armed men, colored and white mixed" to "beat up a slave quarter in Virginia."[45] Forbes wondered how agitators would circulate through slave regions to rally the blacks, but Brown assured him that the entire black population of the South was ready to rise at the first opportunity, and that "between 200 and 500 slaves would swarm to his standard the first night."[46] Brown would take part of this horde and move against an arsenal, seize more arms, destroy what he could not carry, and retreat to the mountains with an instant army. It was his old plan—the one he had outlined to Frederick Douglass, when he traced the Appalachian range southward on the map— though with some additions.

The most significant of these was that his supporters and financiers in New England would call a convention to "overthrow the pro-Slavery Administration" in Washington.

Forbes pointed out the fallacies inherent in every step of his plan. First, the slaves would not rebel. Second, the military forces available would soon pursue and destroy them if they did. Third, the New Englanders would not dare emerge until all danger was over. Forbes was, of course, accurate and realistic in all observations, but John Brown had an immediate scorn for any man who argued against him. The colonel discovered that, and concentrated on an attempt to blend Brown's purposes into a more reasonable effort. He had in mind the distant but impressive Eastern contacts whom Brown had, unaccountably, persuaded to support him.

While Brown and Forbes debated, the Panic spread. The fund-raising efforts of the Kansas Aid Committee were among its casualties. These funds were the real basis for the influence of the committee's agents, and had also paid to enlist newspaper writers whose talents provided the zealots with their propaganda.[47] The Panic, therefore, was helping to bring peace to Kansas, and cooling the sectional dispute between North and South—though only in the sense that a hurricane halts disputes among a ship's crew.

Trade unions and the unemployed held mass rallies in the great cities of the East; men marched on City Hall in New York bearing banners that read: "Hunger is a Sharp Thorn," and "We Want Work." *Hunt's Merchant's Magazine* reported: "The whole monetary system of the United States has fallen with a mighty crash,"[48] and its editorialists discussed the paradox of full granaries, operational machines and factories, and ships ready to sail, while willing workers were unemployed.

On October 19, 1857, Parker wrote: "There never was so much mental suffering in any two months as in the last five weeks. Think of the men who never thought of want, except as the proud angels think of suffering—as something fit only for the lower classes—now left without a dollar! All property is depreciated. My income will not be half this year what it was last. But 'I still live,' only I shall buy no books; and it makes a gap in my charities."[49]

But George Luther Stearns, secure in his lead-pipe business, wrote Martin Conway in Lawrence: "Our world is now engrossed with the impending financial crash. If it would snap the South as well as the North I would welcome it, so much do I hate the present state of affairs."[50]

Prejudice could hardly go farther.

Forbes finally persuaded Brown to agree to a "Well-Matured Plan" which involved a "Committee of Management," to which the colonel would belong. But that was a paper compromise; Forbes had perceived what the Easterners could not, or would not, admit: that Brown had "a bigoted mind and limited instruction" and was not "a truthful man."[51]

Meanwhile the weeks went on, and both men worried about money, though Forbes suffered more than Brown. North Elba had been prospering, according to its dismal level, ever since the head of the clan had entered the abolition business. But the colonel was not receiving his one hundred dollar a month salary. He noted that only one recruit arrived from Kansas, "an unscrupulous scoundrel who joined—only for loot and plundering," and his remonstrances with Brown against such a volunteer were ignored.[52] The days passed with Forbes in agony; his family in Paris was in need, and the wealthy men in the East remained oblivious to his cares. Bitterness began to well within him; he had been fooled by Brown, who had approached him with such glittering patrons. He decided to tell them the truth; he was sure that they would gladly transfer their trust once they became aware of what he had learned.

Brown overhauled and cleaned the Sharp's rifles in Reverend Todd's cellar. He also watched his son Owen and the colonel engage in target shooting and read about mountain military tactics. He had filled up his second notebook and had given it to Sanborn before he left the East; the young man treasured it as a holy relic. In his third notebook Brown made some notes on the activities of the Spanish guerrilla Minas, and added a list of place names. Each location noted harbored an arsenal, but all ranged across the South, and were jotted down in no particular geographical order.

Newspaper fame—which tends to be evanescent—was all his reputation relied upon. But John Brown had been described as a modern Puritan; a man of firm biblical faith, clean-living, and high-minded.

That attracted the Reverend H.D. King, a resident of Tabor, who sought him out.

> I tried to get at his theology. It was a subject naturally suggested by my daily work. But I could never force him down to dry sober talk on what he thought of the moral features of things in general. He would not express himself on little diversions from the common right for the accomplishment of a greater good. For him there was only one wrong, and that was slavery. He was rather skeptical, I think. Not an infidel, but not bound by creeds. He was somewhat cranky on the subject of the Bible, as he was on that of killing people. He believed in God and Humanity, but his attitude seemed to be "We don't know anything about some things. We do not know about the humanity matter. If any great obstacle stands in the way, you may properly break all the Decalogue to get rid of it."[53]

What King did not realize was that Brown's beliefs were widespread in the ranks of radical abolitionists, and bore very little resemblance to Christianity. They had evolved, over the years, from the time of Weld's crusades, and they had used the evangelical methods of Rev. Finney. But they had many fathers. Most of these denounced slavery "not as a wrong, a crime, a blunder, a folly—but as a sin against God, to be immediately repented of and abandoned. Thus they set themselves up not as expositors of mere human science, not as teachers of morals, and political economy, but as expositors of the will of God, and according to the usual course of things, from being expositors, they had proceeded to act as God's vice-regents, judges and executors . . .

"Hence it is easy to understand and explain the fierce spirit of indistinguishable hatred, never forgetting and never forgiving with which they pursue all with whom they differ . . ."[54]

Many were influential in areas beyond Garrison, Wendell Phillips, *et al.* Lysander Spooner, for example, believed slavery was against "Natural Law." He specifically denied Christianity and said a belief in miracles was "a product of a diseased imagination." He claimed to be a deist. Although he failed in journalism, his writings were influential in legal circles.[55] He was among those who approved of John Brown. Reverend King would have been astonished had someone of Spooner's ability described, as Brown could not, the new doctrines which Spooner and others believed, and to which the intellectually limited Brown was converted through the pages of *The Liberator* and other radical abolitionist publications.

Forbes would also have been astonished. The colonel was so steeped in the revolutionary doctrines of Europe that he did not realize he was associating with heretics of a new sort. The New England coterie's patience with Captain Brown stemmed from its members' knowledge that he shared their vision; the colonel was unaware of that. Still bemused, and hopeful of replacing Brown, he joined an eastbound wagontrain on November 2, 1857. John Brown saw him off at Nebraska City, and even mustered sixty dollars for him. No doubt he believed that would be the last he would see or hear of the colonel.

By the time he said goodbye to Colonel Forbes, Brown had already managed to disrupt the complex plans of Jim Lane in Kansas. The key to his disruption was not so much cunning as his single-minded devotion to his own plan to "carry the war to Africa"—and his iron insistence on keeping in his hands the Tabor rifles and ammunition.

Lane had sent a man named Jamison as an emissary to Tabor. On arriving, Jamison said he had ten men "thirty miles back."[56] Brown said that was not enough, and handed back Lane's fifty dollars. He also gave Jamison a note for Lane, saying his "poor state of health" made it impossible for him to turn over the rifles on such short notice. It is unfortunate that no record remains of Lane's response when he received that message; it must have been colorful.

Lane was, after all, leader of the radicals, and the radicals in Kansas had hoped to upset the peaceful process of electing a new territorial legislature—which would draft and submit a new constitution. From Massachusetts, young Frank Sanborn, still functioning as an officer in the Kansas Aid Committee, pleaded with Brown to assist in thwarting peaceful efforts. In September, he wrote protesting again the plans of free-staters to vote in the October elections, and said: "Should Kansas be admitted under such a constitution and a state government organized, the officers must be immediately seized and *hung*—nothing milder will serve the purpose . . ."[57]

On October 19, 1857, Sanborn followed up with a letter voicing the hope that Brown would cooperate with Lane, whom "Whitman [the Aid Committee agent in Lawrence] assures us is true and powerful in the Territory."[58]

Despite this, Brown refused to turn over the rifles to Lane, and delayed at Tabor. The October elections took place, and free-state settlers proved more numerous than the radicals had claimed. The new legislators gathered at Lecompton to draw a constitution, on the same day—October 19—that Sanborn's second letter was written. Two days before, the Leavenworth *Herald* reported: "Jim Lane said the Convention would never meet . . . that its members would all be hung on trees around Lecompton . . ."[59]

On the day it did meet, Lane gave a speech in Lawrence threatening to break it up, while six companies of federal troops ringed the territorial capital. The situation in September and October 1857, therefore, had been heavy with threats of violence—but Lane needed the rifles in Tabor to which the old man clung.

Later, G.W. Brown, editor of the *Herald of Freedom* in Lawrence, wrote:

> The business men of Lawrence will remember the *insane* movement of
> James H. Lane and these anti-peace men, who projected the idea of

murdering the delegates to the Lecompton Constitutional Convention, while on their way to resume their labors on October, and the *ordering* of the whole country to assemble at Lecompton with arms . . . to take that town and hang the members of the Convention . . .

Then [A.W. Brown continued], was organized the secret oath-bound league, the object of which was to *murder*, in cold blood, every officer elected under the Lecompton Constitution, be he a Free State man or otherwise. The pass-word to that secret organization was LANE. The whole plan of assassination, or relays of horses for the executioners, are in the possession of good men in Lawrence.[60]

None of these plans, or John Brown's role in them, were known to Colonel Forbes when he was at Tabor: he would have been astonished to have learned the old man was playing such a complicated hand in so complex a game. But enough coincidental material remains to make it clear that Frank Sanborn's "idealism" in Massachusetts was not of the sort the term usually implies.

But Brown was not to be moved by the plans of Jim Lane, nor by the "secret, oath-bound" organization,—even though he had received word from Whitman that his presence was requested "at a very important Council, Free State Central Com., Ter. Exec. Com., Vigilance Committee of 52, Generals and Capts of the entire organization."[61]

That message had arrived with the $150 entrusted to Tidd. "I trust," Whitman wrote, "the money will be used to get the guns to Kansas, or as near as possible . . . One thing is certain: if they are to do her any good, it will be in the next few days. Let nothing interfere in bringing them on."[62]

Nothing interfered, but Brown did not bring the guns. Neither did he attend the council meeting with the "Generals and Capts." He arrived three days after it met, on November 5, to be greeted by an exasperated Whitman.

Whitman had received five hundred dollars for Brown from George Luther Stearns, but—as usual—Brown said that was not enough. He needed tents and bedding, and left with these. Later Whitman claimed he didn't know where Brown was headed. But R. G. Elliott of Lawrence later said the free-staters' secret society had pledged to

'unman' the convention soon after its adjournment, a term of elastic definition, meaning anything from obtaining resignations of officials by persuasions to removing them by capital excision. Abduction was the method indicated at that juncture . . . John Brown had recently come from Tabor, Iowa, and was in the neighborhood in seclusion, was communicated with by William Hutchinson and expressed his readiness to execute the plans of the order but with the men exclusively of his own selection. To the fear expressed by Robinson that Brown would resort to bloodshed, Hutchinson gave assurance that Brown pledged his faith to be governed strictly by the expressed wishes of the order . . . he had surveyed the situation at Lecompton and said that he could seize Calhoun [the head of the Constitutional convention] and carry him to a

place within one hundred miles where he could hold him safely for three
months . . .[63]

That was unnecessary. Calhoun left the territory, unaware of the
plans against him. But, more important, the free-state settlers had won
the elections and held a majority of the seats in the new legislature.
Lane's fire-eating threats and the plot to hang or kidnap or threaten
men was all unnecessary. The new constitution was completed on
November 3 and sent to Congress, where it was debated for months.
But it was clear that despite the best wishes, or the worst wishes, of the
radicals, the worst of times was over.

George Luther Stearns decided to cancel the draft for seven thousand dollars that he had issued to Brown for a great Kansas war, and
wrote to him, ". . . in my opinion the Free-State party should wait for
the Border-ruffian moves, and checkmate them, as they are developed.
Don't attack *them,* but if they attack you, 'Give them Jesse' and Fremont
besides. You know how to do it . . ."[64]

Before that letter reached him John Brown had already assessed the
Kansas situation and started his new project. As soon as he reached
Whitman's home in Lawrence he sent for John E. Cook, one of his
original gang members, told him he was organizing an antislavery
force, and enlisted him.

Cook was short, twenty-seven years old, blond, handsome, and a
crack shot; he had ridden on raids in the summer of 1856 and lusted
for further adventures. He told Brown he thought he could gather
some more men; he had in mind Richard Hinton, correspondent for
the Boston *Traveller* and the Chicago *Tribune,* another newspaperman
named Richard Realf, and Luke F. Parsons.

These young men and Cook met with Brown on Sunday, November
8, 1857, and were encouraged to collect more recruits. Later Cook
received a note asking him to meet Brown at Mrs. Sheridan's, two miles
south of Topeka, and to bring his weapons, ammunition, and clothing.
He arrived alone at this rendezvous, but was soon joined by the renowned Captain Whipple—Aaron D. Stevens, the U.S. Army deserter
and murderer—Charles Moffet, and John H. Kagi. Kagi, a onetime
Yale student, was correspondent for the N.Y. *Post* and the Washington
National Era. He had already killed a man and gone to prison for his
share in Whipple's raids and crimes.

All these men were young adventurers for whom the violent days of
1856 had been heady, exciting, and rewarding, and to whom the coming of peace in Kansas, even with an antislavery victory, was far from
satisfactory. They longed for new fields, new efforts—and the fame of
which Captain John Brown was a living example.

Chapter 37

By the time Colonel Hugh Forbes knocked on the door of Frederick Douglass' home in Rochester, N.Y. he was dusty, dirty, travel-stained, probably lousy—and certainly in a towering rage. With only sixty dollars to enable him to get across the United States he had taken the cheapest and most uncomfortable stages and boats, stopped at flea-ridden hovels with crawling beds and ghastly meals. Throughout the entire trip his mind had been haunted by worries about his family in Paris, to whom he had not been able to send any money for the months he spent in Tabor with Brown, due, he was certain, to the callous indifference and neglect of Brown's financiers. No doubt Brown had given him that excuse. It filled Forbes with fury over the group he now persistently called the "humanitarians."

Douglass did not take him in, which speaks volumes for the colonel's condition, but he did put him up and pay his bill at a hotel. Douglass also contacted Miss Ottilia Assing, a German lady friend "with a deep interest in the John Brown scheme."[1] Miss Assing wrote a letter to persons in New York City, whom Douglass described as "several of my German friends," to introduce Forbes. These were, no doubt, German refugees from the revolution of 1848; it is interesting that they were in touch with Douglass and aware of Brown's activities. They found Forbes of little interest; his overriding need for money to send his family did not touch their sympathies.

Once in New York, Forbes burst in on Horace Greeley and delivered an impassioned report on how he had been "deceived, misled, swindled, beggared, his family in Paris turned into the streets to starve."[2] Greeley later claimed Forbes would not reveal the names of these monsters, but in view of the colonel's general loquacity, that is hard to believe.[3]

Then the colonel fell in with a group of black revolutionaries, formed

around a well-known physician of that race . . . who were notoriously at variance with the efforts and associations of many others of their race leaders. They held that it was the duty of all educated colored men to mould their people into separate and violent resistance . . . They wanted no help from white men, and some of them spent a good deal of intellectual effort in the endeavor to prove that somewhere in the historic past their race had been one of the ruling forces of the world. From such sources as these . . . Hugh Forbes received many hints of possible relations, which his imperfect conception of American affairs turned into remarks that . . . assumed a malignant aspect when put into letters to prominent men.[4]

255

That revelation provides an interesting peek at the seething under-currents clustered in New York City. Nevertheless, Forbes knew very well whom to write. His first letters were to Senator Charles Sumner, who had put him in touch with Higginson and—through the Worcester firebrand—with John Brown.[5]

The letter—in which Forbes said he had been badly treated by John Brown, who was plotting mischief with some Bostonians, including Frank Sanborn—came at a time when Sumner, whose eyes were apt to fix inward in fascination, was newly returned from a trip to Europe. Sumner's disabilities, presumably from the caning by Brooks, were peculiar enough to deserve a special niche in medical annals. He was healthy as a horse when it came to parties, tours, conversations, letters, and the routine of a rich life. But the thought of returning to the Senate routine and the scene of his humiliation prostrated him. He had also received a diagnosis—at a distance—from Queen Victoria's physician, who said ". . . if he returns to mental labor in less than a year . . . he will soon become a permanent invalid, if he does not lose his life."[6]

Losing the Senate would nearly be preferable to Sumner; by the time Forbes wrote him he was afflicted with prostatitis and found even appearances in the Senate chamber exhausting. Debates produced a "weight spreading over his brain."[7] The martyr, it was clear, was not ready to tackle new dragons or, for that matter, to remain to be drawn into revelations of conspiracies. He forwarded both of Forbes' letters to Frank Sanborn and retired to the life of a semi-invalid.

At this time, Sanborn was staring at a similar letter, which exuded hatred and demanded money. "You are at liberty to speak, write or publish what you please about me," Sanborn replied bravely, "only be careful to keep within the limits of your knowledge."[8] But he also enclosed ten dollars and explained this to the Parker as sympathy for Forbes' wife and children. No doubt he thought a little money would end the matter, but paying blackmailers never does that.

At Tabor, Captain Brown lectured nine recruits, one of whom was a fugitive slave named Richard Richardson. The recruits were to attend "military school" in order to prepare for an incursion somewhere into the South, where they would lead large numbers of slaves to safety in the mountains. The precise locations of these activities were not yet determined. Cook and some others protested; they had thought Brown had Kansas in mind, but Brown bore down as savagely as though they were all his sons. In a way, they were. He said they were to "agitate in Missouri, Arkansas, Indian Territory—perhaps even Louisiana." Kagi, besides being a gunfighter, was also an excellent newspaperman; he wrote fellow journalist Richard Hinton, then in Kansas, urging him to "investigate the road and conditions of the Southwest."[9] Hinton—considered a field member of the Brown army —traveled the Indian Territory, Missouri, Arkansas, and northern Texas and forwarded his descriptions to Kagi under the name of William Harrison.

By that time the party had loaded two wagons with the Sharp's rifles and ammunition and moved east. It was December and the winds were icy; they camped out of towns because the old man's funds were low. Around the evening fires the Hero delivered biblical exhortations about "purging the land with blood" that thrilled and enthused. In time, Virginia emerged as the "army's" staging area.

The leaders among the young men were not as interested in "Bible talk" as in the glory of their adventure: Stevens scorned religion but believed in "spiritualism," Kagi was an open skeptic, and Tidd was poorly educated. They were all accustomed to pious tags but most were also intellectual drifters, lost in a great and confusing world.

But as he had done years before in his Pennsylvania tannery, Brown encouraged debates and the young men began to enjoy themselves. Topics were posed. Who was the greatest general? How did civilization begin? That was lofty, high-sounding, significant. There is nothing like soaring conversation to overcome lowly surroundings; the nobility of an antislavery enterprise lent it the stature the old man fostered. The party stopped at Springdale, Iowa. In that Quaker village the name of John Brown impressed; arrangements were made to sell the team and wagon to farmer William Maxson. There was little cash; the Panic had ended but a slow depression had settled over the land. The men were boarded at Maxson's farm in lieu of payment. Brown saw them settled with copies of Colonel Forbes' manual; the "military school" had shriveled to their own efforts. The schoolhouse, however, was made available for debates, for drawing up a mock legislature and government for the phantom regime to come. Pretty Quaker farm girls in the vicinity were charmed by new young men from the fabled war of Kansas, who drilled with rifles and staged mock fights with wooden swords.

With his "army" of nine men established in winter quarters and cheerfully awaiting further instructions, Brown entrained for the east. His purpose, as always, was to raise money; it took more than peace in Kansas to destroy his abolition business.

His first stop was at Lindeville, Ohio, where John Brown, Jr. told him that Forbes was sending letters to all sorts of persons: an especially abusive message awaited the Hero himself. He dictated a reply in John junior's name saying the letter was too "offensive and insulting" to forward to his father, but hinting that he might send forty dollars—if the colonel stopped his campaign.

Then Brown appeared at Frederick Douglass' door in Rochester. When Douglass answered the knock, the old man said quickly, "I will not stay unless you allow me to pay board."[10] Trapped, Douglass stepped back, and the old man entered.

Once inside, the old man settled down, spending hours in his room planning his venture. Brown also asked for two smooth boards, which he used as a drawing table, on which he sketched—using a pair of dividers—a series of forts connected by secret passages through the mountains, with which he planned to hold off the slaveholders and the United States government. He also worked on a constitution; it was a document of constant conversation that "began to be a bore" for Douglass—although his children were far more interested and enthusiastic.[11]

This "Provisional Constitution" was a fascinating glimpse into Brown's mind. The preamble attacked slavery, sarcastically quoted from Taney's Dred Scott decision, and assumed that the Declaration of Independence was part of the legal structure of the United States. That was a persistent Brown illusion, though one he shared with many persons. The preamble was written in the name of "we, the citizens of the United States and the oppressed people."[12]

The governmental structure which followed this opening was rudimentary: a president and vice-president with unclear duties, a congress of between five and ten members, a judiciary of five—and a commander-in-chief with startling powers. Then followed forty-eight articles that ranged from a "constitutional" ban against "Profane swearing, indecent behavior, or indecent exposure, or intoxication or quarreling . . ." to the use of the death penalty for "deserters." Many of the articles were concerned with such matters as the division of confiscated property and the need to spare slaveholders who voluntarily released their slaves.[13]

The effect, overall, was far less impressive than the list of books Brown read; it revealed a paucity of general knowledge so pervasive as to be appalling. It is noteworthy that although Article XLII called for a Sabbath on "the first day of the week" and the creation of schools and churches,[14] it nowhere mentioned God. No greater evidence could be provided of the vast distance that separated Brown from any recognizable religion than his constitution, with its emphasis on punishments, trials, death, confiscations, divisions of spoils, weapons, and war. Amid this farrago, however, Article XLVI stood out as comically inconsistent: "The foregoing articles shall not be construed so as in any way to encourage the overthrow of any State government, or of the general government of the United States and look to no dissolution of the Union, but simply to amendment and repeal. And our flag shall be the same that our fathers fought under in the Revolution."[15]

It was only after this effort that Brown turned toward his letters, which he signed "Nelson Hawkins care of Wm Watkins Rochester." These came more easily; Brown's letter to Higginson implied, as he took care to hint to all his Boston supporters, that the clergyman was more serious than other men:

I now want to get for the *perfecting* of BY FAR the most *important* undertaking of my whole life; from $500 to $800, within the next Sixty days. I have written to Rev. Theodore Parker, George L. Stearns and F.B. Sanborn Esqur, on the subject; but do not know as either Mr. Stearns or Mr. Sanborn, are abolitionists I suppose they are. Can you be induced to operate at Worcester & elsewhere during that time to raise from *Anti-slavery men and women* (or any other parties) some part of that amount? . . . Hope this is my last effort in the begging line.[16]

To Parker he was more dignified, though equally conspiratorial, and described his venture as "an important measure in which the world has a deep interest, as well as Kansas, and only lack from five to eight hundred dollars to enable me to do so,—the same object for which I asked for secret-service money last fall."[17]

Brown also soothed Sanborn, who was upset by the Forbes letters, and succeeded in persuading him to help pressure Higginson for some of the three thousand dollars in Kansas Aid money that Higginson held in his keeping.

"He speaks of a plan but does not say what it is," Sanborn wrote to Higginson. "Still, I have confidence enough in him to trust him with the moderate sum he asks for—if I had it—without knowing his plan."[18]

Higginson was far more wary. "I am always willing to invest in treason," he wrote, "but at present have none to invest . . . But I'll raise *something* if only $5 and send it on. I may be able to persuade a Committee who have a trifling balance left."[19] To which Sanborn responded: "The Union is evidently on its last legs and Buchanan is laboring to tear it in pieces. Treason will not be treason much longer, but patriotism."[20]

Stearns, too, was apparently upset, writing Brown: "Colonel Forbes has written several abusive letters to Charles Sumner and Sanborn, claiming you had made a positive contract to pay him money, based on promises made to you by the New England men. Is it so?"[21] Stearns also suggested that Brown come to Boston, and offered to pay his expenses. He wanted a face-to-face explanation.

But the Hero had already drawn his plans; they centered around a meeting at Peterboro, under the luxurious ceilings of Gerrit Smith's mansion. He fired letters of invitation to all in his inner circle of New England financiers—Parker, Higginson, Sanborn, Stearns, and Howe —who had also received unsettling letters from Forbes. Higginson, whom Brown regarded as a key figure—perhaps because of the Kansas Aid Committee's three thousand dollars—received an urgent invitation, heavy with promise: "A Rail Road business on a *somewhat* extended scale is the *identical* object for which I am trying to get means," Brown wrote, ". . . I now have a measure on *foot* that I feel sure would awaken in you something more than a common interest . . ." If Higginson would meet with Brown and others, he "would never regret having been one of the council."[22]

In the end, only Sanborn answered the summons. He traveled to Peterboro, and arrived on February 22, 1858, Washington's Birthday. It was a time when that event was still heavy with patriotic sentiment; Brown had chosen the day deliberately. But with his usual attention to detail, he had arrived early, on February 18. Gerrit Smith wrote in his diary: "Our old and noble friend Captain John Brown of Kansas arrives this morning."[23]

The mansion at Peterboro was as busy as a hotel: guests were always arriving or departing, and the servants were skilled, experienced, and unseeing. The rooms were heated with great fireplaces and Sanborn had a Harvard friend—Edwin Morton—who was tutor to the Smith children. He was warmly greeted by his friend and by Gerrit Smith, portly and courteous, and shook hands with Captain Brown—who was older, greyer, more patriarchal.

The four went upstairs and sat in Morton's room while the Captain explained his plan of fortifications, his provisional constitution, and his great purpose. The others were taken aback: it was clear Brown was in earnest, and equally clear that his plan was—as Sanborn later admitted—"desperate in its character, wholly inadequate in its provisions . . . and of most uncertain results."[24]

Objections were raised, but Brown, his eyes gleaming, kept repeating, "If God is for us, who can be against us?"[25]

They talked late, and resumed the next day. One can visualize the interruptions, and the deliberate attempt to keep conversation on a social level during meals, when others were present. One of these guests was Charles Stuart, Theodore Weld's now elderly mentor, still in his tartans, still blazing against slavery, still pursuing the cause: still famous in the movement.

His presence at such a moment is startling. Sanborn later blandly omitted Stuart's name from any discussions or reviews of the Brown project, but the coincidence—like so many coincidences in the saga of the Secret Six and John Brown—is a little too much to accept. The whole network of radical abolitionists intertwined. Who knew what or when, and who did what where, and who told whom—these things will never be completely known.

All that is definite is that Sanborn and Smith—exhausted with heroics, tired of raising objections that were fiercely or biblically ridden down—took a walk together to consider the Captain's project. They left Brown "at home, by the fire, discussing points of theology with Charles Stuart." That alone is an interesting aside; neither Brown nor Stuart were students of theology; they were preachers of the new doctrine, in which their salvation was in punishing others for sinning.

"You see how it is," said the millionaire, whose immense wealth gave him the strength of ten, "our dear old friend has made up his mind to this course, and cannot be turned from it. We cannot give him up to die alone. I will raise so many hundred dollars for him; you must lay the case before your friends in Massachusetts, and ask them to do the same."[26]

"I had come," said Sanborn, "to the same conclusion, and by the same process of reasoning. It was done more for regard for the man than from hopes of immediate success."[27]

That was Sanborn's recollection years later, however, after Brown was encased in sermons and interred in textbooks. Even then it sounds strange. What sort of friends help a man commit suicide?

Sanborn, Brown's ardent disciple, was at first so enthused by the Peterboro discussions that he told his old college friend Morton that he had "a half a mind" to join Brown's expedition. Brown didn't learn that until Sanborn had already left for Boston, and when he himself was on the verge of leaving the mansion. He was thrilled at the thought: with someone of Sanborn's connections in his "army" he saw unsuspected vistas dawning. He dashed off the most effusive of his innumerable letters. "I greatly rejoice at this," he said in part, ". . . What an inconceivable amount of good you might so effect by your *counsel,* your *example,* your *encouragement,* your *natural and acquired ability* for active service!"[28]

But when it came to danger the huge, six-foot-four schoolmaster remained a clerk. His reason for not joining a venture he approved was that "the interests of other persons were then too much in my hands and in my thoughts to permit a change in the whole course of my life."[29]

So much for the noble agreement that Gerrit Smith and Sanborn had reached "as the sun was setting over the snowy hills" of Peterboro—that their "dear old friend" could not be allowed to "die alone."

On March 5, 1858, Brown was registered in room 126 of the American House in Boston under the name I. Smith. His supporters arrived individually: Sanborn, Parker, Stearns, Howe, and Higginson. Both Sanborn and Higginson, the two youngest, were very enthusiastic; Stearns radiated hope. Howe heard the plan and approved; it sounded reasonable to a veteran of the Greek war of independence who had no idea of the military changes that had taken place in thirty years. Parker was less optimistic, but he did believe Brown's project would have a great effect. That was relatively wan for Parker, but the famous polymath was in declining health. Though only forty-eight, he was working on his autobiography. His activities during the previous year had been prodigious: among other things, he had lectured seventy-three times. Many of these talks had been, à la Emerson, on greatness, with examples from American history.[30]

In Peterboro the New York member of the Secret Six, Gerrit Smith, had no doubt that Captain Brown's plans would, this time, succeed. "The slave," he wrote Representative Joshua R. Giddings, "will be delivered by the shedding of blood—and the signs are multiplying that this deliverance is at hand."[31]

All of the Secret Six—including Parker, who once argued that either war was right and Christianity wrong, or Christianity right and war *always* wrong; Smith, a former leader in the peace movement; Howe, who had plunged into the care of the handicapped and the ignorant; the impassive George Stearns; and the poetically inclined Sanborn—had grown absolutely bloodthirsty. Yet they knew, as did the nation, that the overwhelming majority of Southerners had no slaves. What was astonishing, therefore, about their enthusiasm, was that they cheerfully contemplated the shedding of innocent blood.

In the classic manner of terrorists, they concealed the grisly essence of their plans in abstract, semicoded language. Wrote Sanborn to Higginson on March 8: "$1,000 is the sum to be raised here—of which yourself, Dr. Parker, Dr. Howe, Mr. Stearns and myself are each assessed to raise $100 . . . of $500 we are sure . . . Hawkins goes to prepare agencies for his business near where he will begin operations. Dr. Cabot knows something of the speculation, but not the whole, not being quite prepared to take stock . . . G. R. Russell has been consulted."[32] The next Boston meeting was set for March 20, 1858.

Brown was off, then, to Philadelphia, leaving behind a note for Parker. He wanted the scholar to put his mighty pen to work "composing a substitute for an address you saw last season, directed to the officers and soldiers of the United States Army." He still harbored the thought that if he could get the right words on paper, he could lure deserters. Parker, however, was not to be directly employed by the likes of John Brown any more than he and his associates would enter the "army." He sent Brown a copy of General George B. McClellan's report on European armies.[33]

Brown was concerned about reading: he knew he had only a handful of turbulent young men waiting for him in Iowa, and asked Sanborn for some books. One was for "the best written" life of Napoleon.

At Philadelphia the Captain, flanked by John Brown, Jr.—snatched from domesticity to act as his father's clerk, liaison, and secretary—presented his plan to a group of substantial members of the free black community at the home of the Reverend Stephen Smith. Frederick Douglass was present, together with the Reverend Henry H. Garnett and William Still. Brown had already visited Brooklyn, where he explained his project to Dr. and Mrs. J. N. Gloucester, a wealthy black couple, and had also written a long letter to the black leader, J. W. Loguen, in Syracuse.[34]

The Philadelphia effort evoked praise but very little money, and no one offered to join the venture, though all agreed to help behind the scenes. Brown was undismayed: as in real estate and the wool business he had now created his master plan, and the reaction of others did not deter him. He wrote letters to North Elba, pleading with his daughter Ruth to release her husband, Henry Thompson, who had already been wounded in his service. Henry was not anxious for more adventure; he and Ruth had two children, and he had learned his lesson.

But Henry's two younger brothers read the biblical letters, replete with calls to sacrifice and glory, and decided to enlist. Watson Brown, twenty-two, and Oliver Brown, nineteen, also listened to their father when he raced up to North Elba, and decided to join their elder brother Owen—then in Iowa—in the venture. Orders, in the fashion they had known since childhood, poured over them all. John Brown, Jr. was to travel toward ". . . Chambersburg, Gettysburg and Uniontown—and Harper's Ferry," and "to explore roads and contact friendly families."[35]

Dr. Samuel Gridley Howe had earlier spoken to Julia about "a very remarkable man . . . who seemed to intend to devote his life to the redemption of the colored race from slavery, even as Christ had willingly offered his life for the salvation of mankind . . ." and then added, sternly, that she "should not mention to any one this confidential communication." To make sure she did not, Julia Ward Howe "allowed the whole matter to pass out of my thoughts."[36]

"It may have been a year or more later that Dr. Howe said to me: 'Do you remember that man of whom I spoke to you—the one who wished to be a saviour for the negro race?' "[37] She did.

"That man," said Howe, "will call here this afternoon. You will receive him. His name is John Brown." Julia, aware the visitor was important, opened the door herself—though that was a task highly placed ladies usually left to the servants.

"I beheld a middle-aged, middle-sized man, with hair and beard of amber color, streaked with gray. He looked a Puritan of the Puritans, forceful, concentrated and self-contained. We had a brief interview . . . I saw him once again at Dr. Howe's office, and then heard no more of him for some time."[38]

The above took place on March 20, 1858, the day of the meeting that revealed that the funds for the venture were still far from the one thousand dollars Brown needed. That was surprising, considering the wealth of the Six, but it must be remembered that John Brown was only one of their interests and activities. The modesty of their investment provides a measure of his actual importance to them.

Brown left Boston to dart, in his usual zigzag, shadowy manner, to several promising places: to New York City, where he saw the famed antislavery Quaker Gibbons and Hopper families, to Peterboro for another oblique assault on the treasures of Gerrit Smith, then to Rochester and the home of Frederick Douglass, and finally—accompanied by J. W. Loguen of Syracuse—across the border to Ste. Catharine, Canada. Here, he met Harriet Tubman, a justly famed guide for slaves escaping across the border. Brown was impressed; no doubt he hoped to obtain her knowledge of Appalachian routes, but the gnarled heroine was illiterate, and relied on a visual memory. Nevertheless the visit was helpful; Brown prowled restlessly and rapidly to Ingersoll, Hamilton, and Chatham—towns that harbored many free blacks and escaped fugitives making decent lives for themselves in a land with no slavery.

They also maintained, on both sides of the border, an underground organization called the League of Freedom—barred to all whites—and they had a knowledge of routes extending from the swamps of Florida to Virginia, and from there through the mountains to Canada. They knew many pockets where men could hide undiscovered for weeks, such as limestone caves in Kentucky as well as wild regions in the Mississippi Valley.³⁹ Brown had heard of this organization and its knowledge, and hoped to tap its membership for his following. That was a major factor in his plan.

There was another colony of escaped slaves at Buxton, near Lake Erie; this was not far from Chatham, home of a well-known black physician and black leader, Dr. Martin R. Delaney. Brown appeared at Delaney's door twice but he was not home; Brown left without leaving his name. That created some mystery; Delaney was intrigued enough when they finally met to follow Brown to a hotel room.

Repetition had polished Brown's persuasions: Delaney was first astonished, then intrigued, and finally cooperative. By the time they parted Delaney had agreed to help Brown stage a constitutional convention in Chatham; he would also attend himself, and bring as many others as possible.

The charade took place on May 8, 1858, in a frame schoolhouse, and was attended by twelve white and thirty-four black men. The whites did not include any of the Secret Six, nor Wendell Phillips, nor any other of the innumerable radicals to whom Brown had told his plans. The blacks were Dr. Delaney's contacts and friends, but did not include Frederick Douglass, Loguen, the Gloucesters, Stephen Smith or any other of the black leaders with whom Brown had toiled so long.

The old man looked impressive enough for a larger gathering: he had allowed a spectacular bushy white beard to appear; this—together with his gleaming eyes and "measured tread as he circulated about with his hands under his coat skirts of plain brown tweed"⁴⁰—made a formidable impression. That image of stern coherence vanished in the debates. According to correspondent-recruit Realf, Brown spoke for a long time about the wealth of research he had devoted to the antislavery and military situation; among other things, he claimed that he had developed "a fort so simple it could be built by twenty men in a day," that would "withstand all siege guns." After a time Dr. Delaney proposed that the constitution be examined.

A general discussion erupted. Someone said that blacks had no right to create a constitution in the United States, and Brown likened the blacks to Indians on a reservation, and to the Mormons. Someone else mentioned treason, and Brown pointed to the article that denied the sense of his undertaking. George J. Reynolds, a leader in the League of Freedom, rose to object to the flag of the United States, and said he would never swear allegiance to it. Brown replied that by ending slavery the flag would be restored to its original purity.

The sessions moved on to a Baptist church, then to an engine house. Finally, the men filed up and signed, to Brown's congratulations. On the evening of Monday, May 10, John Brown was elected commander-in-chief, Kagi secretary of war, Realf secretary of state, George Gill secretary of the treasury, Owen Brown treasurer, Osborne P. Anderson and Alfred Ellsworth members of congress. A number of blacks refused to serve as president or vice-president, and the majority of the men that Dr. Delaney had persuaded to attend vanished afterward— no doubt with relief.

The only tangible outcome of all this effort was that the old man was, once again, out of money.

Another problem took on the form of Colonel Hugh Forbes. The colonel had been eased out of Brown's abolition business at a time when New York City and most of the North was darkened by the depression. The former fencing master, translator, and military lecturer—who had lost his posts by joining Brown—tramped the streets at a time when his skills were no longer wanted. Horace Greeley's door was closed, the German refugee circles distrusted and disliked him, and he had lost what little security he held when he joined the conspiracy.

In early May 1858, when Brown was collecting his young men for the convention, Forbes wrote a hysterical, abusive letter to Howe. Its revelations appalled the physician, who contacted the rest of the Secret Six. Forbes threatened to sell his knowledge to the N.Y. *Herald*—a newspaper that had already called for an end to "Nigger Agitation" and to the use of the issue of "Bleeding Kansas."[41] What the Democrats could do with Forbes' revelations were enough to make the New Englanders quake.

A flurry of backstage notes were exchanged, while Howe sent a lofty letter to Forbes, saying that "he had confidence in Captain Brown— but . . . was not responsible for Captain Brown's acts." He pointed out the inconsistency of denouncing a project and demanding a leading role in it, and ended with the sort of noble apostrophe then current on the stage and in popular literature. "You, sir, are the guardian of your own honor! but I trust that for your children's sake at least you will never let your passions lead you to a course that might make them blush."[42]

Gerrit Smith now began to retreat as hastily as he had once rushed forward; he immediately said: "Brown must go no further—and so I write him." He added: "I never was convinced of the wisdom of his scheme. But as things now stand it seems to me it would be madness to attempt to execute it. Col. F. would make such an attempt a certain and most disastrous failure. I write Brown *this evening.*"[43]

Higginson was adamant at the opposite pole. He wished he had enough money to "buy out the other stockholders & tell the veteran to go on."[44] Sanborn thought Forbes was "either a madman or a villain," but George Luther Stearns, like his fellow businessman Gerrit Smith, counseled caution.

The argument was still raging when, on May 11, 1858, the day after Brown was elected commander-in-chief in Chatham, Howe entered his office to find a note on his desk. It had been written by the senior senator from Massachusetts.

Dear Sir:

———I write you to say that you had better talk with some few of our
friends who contributed money to aid old Brown to organize and arm
some force in Kansas for defense, about the policy of getting those arms
out of his hands and putting them in the hands of some reliable men in
that territory.

———*If they should be used for some other purposes, as rumor says they may be, it
might be of disadvantage to the men who were induced to contribute to that very
foolish movement.* If it can be done, get the arms out of his control and keep
clear of him at least for the present. This is in confidence.

Henry Wilson[45]

Had Colonel Forbes understood American politics there is little doubt
that the fears of the Secret Six would have been more than realized.
But Forbes went to men in Washington whose names were headlined
—in the radical newspapers he himself read—as the leading statesmen
of the land. Foolishly, therefore, Forbes approached the very people
most anxious not to provide the South with proofs of a Northern
conspiracy against the peace.

He went to Senator Henry Wilson, who had contributed to the
Kansas Aid Committees, appeared at their rallies, and was on close
friendly terms with Howe, Stearns, Higginson, and the others. He
also went to Senator William H. Seward of New York, noted for his
"higher-law" stand—and also for his loftiness regarding the sins of
Southerners, which enabled him to rise above his own role in the
noisome machine politics of New York.

Seward heard Forbes out, and then turned him out.[46] Wilson, whom
Forbes accosted on the floor of the Senate, heard him out too—and
warned the conspirators. Forbes did not approach the secretary of war
or any other authorized officials; his conspiratorial background made
that unthinkable. There is always the possibility that he thought Wilson and Seward were part of the grand design of Northern conspiracy
against the South. If so, their published attitudes made his selection
somewhat logical if he still hoped to obtain a place in the movement,
and to displace Old Brown.

A mystery remains regarding Sumner and his role in these backstage
movements. The Senator had called Forbes' name to Higginson's
attention, and was acquainted with revolutionary circles in Europe—
as well as with similarly minded refugee circles in the United States.
He was Howe's close personal friend, and not much less close to the
other members of the Secret Six. He supported the Kansas Aid Committee, and had made Kansas his personal issue to such an extent that
his "Crime Against Kansas" speech had led to the caning by Brooks.

Colonel Forbes sent Sumner at least two of his blackmailing letters.
Shortly afterwards, Sumner departed for Europe. His reasons were
announced as medical, but it is clear that his departure was opportune.
Out of sight, out of mind.

A copy of Senator Wilson's warning to the Secret Six was sent to Brown, together with a letter from Stearns, in his capacity as an official of the Kansas Aid Committee. Stearns wrote: "You will recollect that you have custody of the arms alluded to, to be used for the defense of Kansas . . . it becomes my duty to warn you not to use them for any other purpose, and to hold them subject to my order as chairman of said committee."[47]

Brown was equal to the occasion. He answered Stearns with a soothing letter, saying that "none of our friends need to have any fears in relation to hasty or rash steps being taken by us . . ." Amid the smooth assurances he also wrote: "We have those who are thoroughly posted up, to put on his track . . ." As usual, he cited his need for "two or three hundred dollars without delay" and cautioned against excitement, closing piously: "In all thy ways acknowledge *Him, and He* shall direct thy paths."[48]

By that time the Secret Six had decided that Brown's project had to be delayed until the alarm quieted. Higginson argued against the vote, but Parker toiled with him. "You are a better soldier than I," he said flatteringly, "but I think I'm right in the matter."[49]

Other efforts were made to calm the situation. Howe wrote to Senator Wilson saying: "I understand perfectly your meaning. No countenance has been given Brown for any operations outside of Kansas *by the Kansas Committee.*"[50]

That reassured Wilson. He would have been far less satisfied if he had known that the Kansas Committee had turned the guns over, in lieu of repayment of a loan, to George Luther Stearns—and that Stearns had already given them to John Brown. In fact, as these notes were being exchanged, the guns were in Ohio, in the keeping of John Brown, Jr.

With the Senator placated the Secret Six—or Secret Five, since Higginson, knowing the vote, refused to attend—met and decided to give Brown money, and to send him back to Kansas until the situation cooled.

That did not take long; all were busy men and their public activities continued as though nothing had happened backstage. Higginson gave a fiery speech to the American Antislavery Society and said, regarding slavery: "It is destined, as it began in blood, to so end."[51]

A fortnight later, in a speech to the American Peace Society, Gerrit Smith called for total disarmament and the abolition of all armies and navies. He said that "no Christian nation would ever attack an unresisting nation . . . Wars would cease if one nation" would completely disarm.[52]

But in the same speech Smith said settlers in Kansas needed Sharps rifles; he called nonresisters to slavery "pernicious," and wound up urging that an international court be established to settle disputes between nations. This jumble of contradictions, which mirrored the intellectual fantasies of Smith's audience, evoked such applause that the peace society had 280,000 copies printed and distributed.

In early June—after an interval of a month—the abolitionist financiers and propagandists summoned Brown to Boston, gave him five hundred dollars in gold, and told him to go back to Kansas until, in effect, further notice.

The old man was pleased; he was assured that in the fall or the following spring he would receive between two thousand and three thousand dollars, and could then launch his project to free the slaves of the South by force. In view of such a complete underwriting of his business, he could almost regard Colonel Forbes as having helped.

In conversations with Higginson, who was inclined to be disappointed, Brown radiated satisfaction. He assured the battle-hungry clergyman that he understood his attitude, and referred somewhat scornfully to the other members of the Secret Six as not being "men of action." This held Higginson's loyalty.

Then Brown went to Cleveland to give his orders to his army.

Some were to work through the autumn; he would keep in touch with them. Some were to join him in Kansas later. Cook was to go to Harper's Ferry, make a study of the roads and community, contact slaves, and wait for orders.

Richard Realf had an interesting assignment: he would go to New York City, search out Colonel Forbes, insinuate himself into his confidence, and steal whatever letters from John Brown the Colonel had in his possession.[53]

Not long afterward Realf walked the steaming streets of New York City in a state of indecision. He was a poet; it seemed to him that raiding was less dishonorable than an assignment to deliberately strike up a friendship in order to betray. Away from the hypnotic presence of John Brown and the encouragement of his fellow "army" members, Realf began to think of the entire project and its rationale as unreal.

He picked up a book by Dr. Francis Wayland, president of Brown University; it was entitled *Limitations of Human Responsibility.* Realf said later that he had been taught a lot about his responsibilities, but that the idea that they had a limit was new to him. He read Dr. Wayland, who argued that "there were certain things which I might thoroughly believe myself, but which I had no right to enforce *nolens volens* on my neighbor . . ."[54]

There was also, it seems, a girl, from whom Realf borrowed money.

Finally Realf wandered into the offices of the National Kansas Aid Committee, and had the remarkable good fortune to run into William F. M. Arny.

Arny had become a board member of the national committee when Abraham Lincoln refused to serve, and had gone to Kansas as general agent of the organization. He had known John Brown for many years, during which their paths kept intersecting, and he also knew Realf. Arny was surprised to see Realf in New York City, and listened sympathetically as his tale tumbled out. Realf was a waif lost in a great storm in a strange land—and Arny was no admirer of John Brown. He advised Realf—who had once lived in England—to forget about Brown, return to England, get married, and settle down. He gave Realf enough money to book passage[55] and, very probably, saved his life.

Chapter 38

There were worse summers than 1858, but not many. The Dred Scott decision had created an emotional hurricane. A wave of resistance against the Fugitive Slave Law swept across the North, while in the South demands to renew the importation of slaves were raised. Extremists were further apart than ever, and the moderate majority began to split—moving toward one or the other pole.

President Buchanan struggled to restore the balance. As before, Kansas was a key to the dispute. California's entry into the union as a free state had given the North the edge: sixteen free states to fifteen slave states. The bargain to bring Kansas in as a slave state was still, in Buchanan's opinion, the best of answers.

Therefore he insisted—despite every indication that the settlers of Kansas did not want slavery—on forcing upon that territory the Lecompton constitution, which included slavery clauses. In this, he was assisted by what people called "the directory"—the language of the French Revolution still being current. The "directory" consisted of three pro-Southern cabinet members: Cobb of Georgia, treasury; Thompson of Mississippi, Interior; and Jeremiah Black, attorney general. All three were assisted by the sly and unscrupulous Senator from Louisiana, John Slidell. The result was, according to Secretary of War Floyd, that a Cabinet meeting under Buchanan was like "Hamlet—with the part of Hamlet left out."[1]

The issue led to a meeting between the President and Senator Douglas. Greatly shaken by the Supreme Court's Dred Scott decision, Douglas was clinging, with some desperation, to the issue of local control over slavery. The legal argument was shaky but it was the only argument with which Douglas could retain both proslavery and antislavery votes in Illinois—whose own south was as distinct from its own north as were the two national regions.

Douglas called on the President in the autumn of 1857, to see if the Buchanan administration would allow the settlers of Kansas to decide on slavery for themselves, and in particular to wait three weeks until a referendum on the issue was over. Buchanan refused. At that Douglas' temper rose, and he spoke loudly. He would oppose the entry of

Kansas as a slave state. In response the President partially raised himself from his chair, and warned Douglas of the fates of Democratic Senators Tallmadge and William Rives, who had run afoul of Andrew Jackson. That was an error. No two men could be less similar than the fiery Jackson and the half-timid Buchanan.

Douglas walked to the door, turned, glared, and said, "Mr. President, I wish you to remember that General Jackson is dead."[2]

The struggle between the two men tore holes in the Democratic party —North and South. With Buchanan continuing to insist on the Lecompton Constitution into 1858, these grew larger. The dispute was marked by endless strategems and proposals; it retarded the creation of Kansas as a state. Conditions were calm in most regions of the territory, but violence erupted in the southeastern corner, especially in Linn and Bourbon counties, where Brown and others had committed so many crimes in 1856.

In May 1858, only a week after Senator Henry Wilson sent his warning to Dr. Howe, a ghastly event occurred in Kansas. Embittered over being driven from his claim by James Montgomery and his gang, a Southern settler—Charles Hamilton—led a Southern gang of thirty men from Missouri into a hamlet called Trading Post. Hamilton and his men snatched settlers from their fields and cabins, lined them up and shot them down. Five were killed at once; others were wounded.[3]

Governor Denver raced to the scene with troops and managed to restore order, though Montgomery, who had already burned and wasted much of the region, called for vengeance.

The Hamilton murders were part of a continuing miniwar between Hamilton and Montgomery, but held a larger significance. If the Pottawatomie murders introduced terrorism as a political tactic, the Hamilton murders could be said to mark the moment when Southerners followed suit in the same region, for the same purpose.

It was coincidental that Hamilton committed his murders at the same time that Colonel Forbes raised his own questions in Washington, and just as attention was being drawn toward the New England authors of Kansas violence. The atrocity was horridly fortuitous for the Secret Six: it brought focus—and placed new onus—on the South. It also marked another of the several eerie occasions when, as if through some malign force, a situation potentially perilous to John Brown was, once again, dwarfed by an outside event, to spare his activities the attention they deserved.

The newspapers seized on a name left behind by French *voyageurs* many years before—the Marais des Cygnes—to implant the massacre in the mind of the North. John Greenleaf Whittier, the political poet, wrote some of his most stirring verses for the *Atlantic Monthly*.[4] The memory of Pottawatomie was buried even deeper under an avalanche of anti-Southern reproaches.

The event added new flames to an already high political bonfire:

Senator Douglas was preparing to run for reelection in Illinois, and the popular Abraham Lincoln[5] was given a good chance to achieve an upset. With the undying, jealous hatred of President Buchanan and many factions in his own Democrat Party against him, Douglas had his hands full.

Lincoln made that clear in his opening salvo in June 1858, with his "House Divided" speech. The phrase came, of course, from the Bible, and had originally referred to true and false concepts of God. Lincoln used it politically, assuming very high ground indeed. The warning that the nation could not endure half-slave and half-free was hailed, then and since, as the acme of statesmanship.[6]

Douglas' reply was sharp. The nation, he said, had been half-slave and half-free from its inception, and the theory that a single system had to prevail would destroy the freedom to diversify upon which it was founded. Lincoln's doctrine, sáid Douglas, would set "section against section, and hammer a tyrannous, grinding uniformity of institutions . . . upon the variety of the American scene."[7]

That set the issues. Douglas was caustic about the Republican and Northern unwillingness to accept the Supreme Court decision on slavery, but Lincoln was vague on that, as on many other matters.

The drama of their confrontation was heightened by physical differences: Lincoln's tall homeliness, which endeared him to many, contrasted to Douglas' short, bulldog fearlessness. Lincoln was the more cautious; Douglas was like a miniature lion trailed by a pack of smaller enemies. Their clash lit the political landscape and provided a relief from the pettiness of Kansas difficulties, and from the carping, critical sectional and party newspapers. Much more than the Senate hinged on the outcome of the Lincoln-Douglas debates. Douglas was the only one of the two whose doctrines and following could unite the entire nation, but Lincoln was already political leader of the Illinois Republicans, and virtually the only antislavery spokesman who could moralize without being denunciatory. Both men were a credit to the nation, and so were their debates.

By that time John Brown was back in Kansas—calling himself Shubel Morgan—at the head of a gang of about fourteen men, some of them members of the Chatham meeting. The old man had grown to depend on Kagi, who was clever with words and a good companion.[8] Aaron D. Stevens, the erstwhile Captain Whipple, was with Brown, as were Gill and Tidd.

He headed to the region he knew best in the southeast. This region was also described by Governor Denver: "From Fort Scott to the crossing of the Osage river, or Marais des Cygnes as it is called there, a distance of about 30 miles, we passed through a country almost depopulated by the depredations of the predatory bands under Montgomery, presenting a scene of desolation such as I never expected to have witnessed in any country inhabited by American citizens . . ."[9]

Brown visited Montgomery, and judged him a splendid man: they thought alike.[10] He and his gang settled on the claim of a blacksmith, Eli Snyder, where he built a two-story "fort." There were no invaders to repel, but Brown was not convinced of that. In a matter of weeks, having undertaken the support of a gang of men and constructed an expensive headquarters, he was again short of money. That led to some night raids, pursuits, and nights spent cowering on the prairie. The Hero fell ill.

His sickness was probably malaria, and he was carried to the cabin of Reverend Adair, where his sister helped nurse him. Visitors were given excuses and false names; John Brown was far from being a popular man in Kansas, despite the lofty newspaper stature he enjoyed in the East.

By September 1858 the Captain was recovering and Kagi was in Lawrence trying to collect promissory notes, given to the Kansas Aid Committee by various settlers in exchange for food and help of various sorts in earlier periods. A large package of these, obtained by Stearns in payment for loans he had made to the Committee, had been sent to Brown. Brown chose to use them as bills due to him, and especially as part of the five thousand dollars voted to him by the New York committee in early 1856, and which he had never received.[11]

The Kansas Aid agents in Lawrence—Whitman, Conway and Arny —were miserably aware that Brown had connections more important than their own; they also knew his real reputation, and fended him to the best of their ability. But as soon as he could move around, the old man sent orders demanding that all monies collected by the committee be held for him, and an angry correspondence was pursued. Meanwhile Brown collected several hundred dollars; as usual when Brown was involved there were no records, no rendering, no statement, and no receipts—merely sums of money which he used for his own mysterious purposes—pouring from many hands into his.

During all this, the Captain was in and out of Lawrence, staying at the home of Augustus Wattles occasionally, still orating about his "mission." New York *Tribune* correspondent William A. Phillips listened to him predict war if the Republicans won the next Presidential election. That was not an unusual prediction: the entire South warned of that. More unusual was Brown's insistence that American slaves would fight. Phillips challenged that: he thought the blacks were a "peaceful, domestic, inoffensive race . . ." Brown said: "You have not studied them long enough. Human nature is the same everywhere."[12]

That delusion, which all the abolitionists shared, bound Brown to his New England supporters more than his plans, which had grown hazy and indeterminate. "I have great faith in the wisdom, integrity and bravery of Captain Brown," wrote Gerrit Smith to Sanborn that summer. "I have frequently given him money . . . in his contests with the slave-power. Whenever he shall embark on another of these contests I shall again stand ready to help him . . ." Then he added, piously: "I do not wish to know Captain Brown's plans. I hope he will keep them to himself."[13]

Meanwhile the skies slowly filled with the rising phenomenon of Donati's Comet, which became more visible from the end of August, until, by early October 1858, "it filled the western sky from the horizon nearly to the zenith. Its broad, scimitar-shaped tail was computed to be nearly eighty million miles" long;[14] the most impressive comet to appear since 1680. The phenomenon seemed to many in the United States that year a portent of the times; it was as though the nation was coming under the spell of immense, unknowable forces, subject to unpredictable, awesome events.

Forces of change were, in fact, collecting beneath the deceptively normal surface of the nation as the election campaigns wound toward the polls. The Lincoln-Douglas debates made Lincoln's name known in the North—except New England, where men were far too proud to believe that intelligence could exist elsewhere—and in the South, where plotters gathered.

Throughout 1858 the South boomed economically and seethed politically as the rhetoric of the campaign evoked fiercer Northern outcries—not simply against slavery—but against slaveholders. A peak was reached by the cold, selfish, and impulsive Seward of New York in September 1858, when he first discussed the "two radically different systems of labor, one slave and one free . . ." and said, "Shall I tell you what this collision means? . . . It is an irrepressible conflict between opposing and enduring forces . . . the United States will, sooner or later, either become a slaveholding nation or entirely a free-labor nation."[15] This was no more than Lincoln was saying, or other Republicans, or antislavery Democrats, but the phrase, "irrepressible conflict," fell into the mind of the nation like a glowing ember.

The South had its counterpart orators who called for the annexation of Cuba—a goal desired by Buchanan—and even of Mexico and all Central America; they spoke of a Caribbean slave empire free of Yankeedom, upon which a new planter aristocracy would rise. But these chimeras were, somehow, unable to take root with large numbers. It remained for Robert Barnwell Rhett, W. L. Yancey, and Edmund Ruffin—orators, journalists and agitators—to create an underground movement that paralleled the Secret Six. From 1858 forward, they worked for "secession," as the New Englanders had worked even longer, for "disunion."

In that gathering twilight of democracy, with extremists in both sections angrily opposing the idea that a single society could have two systems, and with only a few voices, like that of Douglas, able to argue in traditional terms and even with Douglas' argument poisoned by the slavery issue, which constricted every topic, the nation went to the polls. The results were catastrophic for the Democratic Party and President Buchanan.

Lincoln lost in Illinois, but the Republicans swept other parts of the North like a flame: Indiana, Ohio, all upper New England, New York —even Pennsylvania, Buchanan's home state. The "directory," that clutch of Southerners and pro-Southerners around Buchanan, had lost control of the House. Some newspapers blamed the debacle on the "Kansas swell"—the President's effort to force a proslavery constitution upon free-state settlers. Douglas, who had opposed that effort, was proved right. He and his supporters were nearly as jubilant as the Republicans; they thought it meant a change in the administration attitude.

Had that occurred it might have helped the situation. But James Buchanan could only read that Douglas had triumphed despite White House hostility: he resolved that the senator would never be president. The "directory" laughed off the results, analyzing them as the usual off-year injuries, and blamed the depression and business factors.

Meanwhile the political condition of the nation was growing incoherent. The Supreme Court had lost immense influence and prestige, the White House was occupied by a weakling, and Congress was divided. All three branches of the American government were in disarray, and talk of sectional war grew rampant.

In Kansas the Brown gang was split into smaller units of two or three; Kagi rode with Montgomery much of the time, and was in charge of the "fort" on the Snyder claim. Old Brown floated around the landscape, usually with two or more of his boys.

They lived off the settlers. The acting governor, Hugh S. Walsh, wrote to Secretary of State Lewis Cass, urging "a reward of $300 for Montgomery and $500 for old John Brown" to "break up their organization or drive them from the Territory."[16] Putting Brown's price higher than Montgomery gave proof he was considered the greater menace.

Cass did not respond to this suggestion and the Sheriff of Linn County, at the head of a large *posse comitatus*—citizens assembled for the purpose—surrounded Fort Snyder and demanded its capitulation. Stevens-Whipple shouted defiance and the sheriff, after learning the Captain was not inside, went away.

On December 6, 1858, the sheriff tried another tactic. A meeting of citizens in Linn County was called; Montgomery and Brown appeared, and a peace agreement was signed, in which all crimes—whether committed by Northern or Southern settlers—were forgiven, prisoners were to be released by the authorities, and further assaults, of any nature, to be ended. That was a sort of frontier solution, and would seem to have removed any possible excuse for violence, but neither Montgomery nor Brown were reasonable men. There was booty to be taken, and barely ten days after the "peace" Montgomery said a free-state prisoner, one Benjamin Rice, was still being held in Fort Scott. He swooped on that settlement at the head of a hundred men. Brown did not take part in the actual assault; he seldom did. It was his practice to send some of his men into the fray, while he waited, with the usual few who acted as his bodyguard, at a rendezvous.

The raiders broke down the door of the building where Rice was held, and released him. While they were thus occupied, a storekeeper named J. H. Little emerged across the street with a shotgun and fired both barrels. The charge of buckshot would have ended newspaper-man Kagi's career as a raider on the spot, had he not worn a heavy overcoat. Little was shot dead for his temerity, and his store was looted of seven thousand dollars worth of goods and articles. Then the noble antislavery forces rode away, taking one prisoner with them. Gill, one of Brown's ardent followers, later said the Old Man fiercely ubraided Montgomery for taking a prisoner alive, saying the man should have been shot.[17] Brown also wanted Fort Scott burned to the ground.[18] Acting Governor Walsh's estimate of the more dangerous of the two guerrilla leaders was accurate.

As usual, reports of the Fort Scott outrage traveled through the South in fairly accurate terms, Southern newspapers usually being factual regarding Northern crimes. But the New York *Tribune* later said the storekeeper Little had been a former deputy U.S. Marshall—a fact that was considered injurious—and was "hanged for being officious still in the matter of taking and holding Free State prisoners."[19] It is possible that Kagi, one of Little's murderers, may have written the article. He was, after all, still a newspaperman.

The southeastern section of Kansas flared again as a result of the Fort Scott raid. Southern settlers organized a new militia; official mes-sages were exchanged and propagandists on both sides prepared their versions of the incident. Captain Brown, meanwhile, prepared a coup of his own.

Assembling his men he divided them into two groups, keeping Gill, Jeremiah Anderson, a horse thief known only as Pickles, and four others. Captain Stevens-Whipple was put in charge of six men, includ-ing the mean-looking Albert Hazlett. On the chill evening of Monday, December 20, 1858, the combined force crossed into Missouri.

Soon afterward, Brown and his crew entered the Missouri home of Harvey G. Hicklan. They held the family at bay, ransacked the house, carrying out whatever they chose and stuffing their pockets with the men's watches and other valuables. Hicklan's horses were fastened to the Hicklan wagon; the five slaves of the household were told they were being liberated. Beds were stripped of blankets and linens that were thrown into the wagon; the blacks clambered in later. Hicklan and a house guest were tied and carried along; Brown thought hostages would cover his retreat.

Then Brown and his force clattered down the road a mile and stopped outside the home of John B. Larue. The Larue house was ransacked: stripped of valuables, food, clothing, and goods. A wagon and horses were hitched; five more slaves were taken along to liberty.

Meanwhile Stevens-Whipple and his men arrived at the home of David Cruise. Young Luther Cruise, thirteen, was asleep upstairs, but was awakened by the sound of his father's window being raised. Cruise asked the travelers their business and was told: "We're Missourians from Bates County. We've been to Fort Scott on business and are on our way home. We'll pay you if you let us sleep on the floor."

It was bitterly cold outside and Cruise observed he "couldn't turn a dog away on a night like this."[20] He started downstairs and his son joined him; both were in their nightshirts. They opened the door and seven roughly dressed men poured inside. Cruise walked over to the fireplace and turned around just as Hazlett shot him through the heart.

Young Luther watched his father die as the other men raced through the house looking for loot. In an upstairs bedroom one held a gun to Mrs. Cruise's head and forced her to open all the closets. Later, Stevens-Whipple took credit for killing Cruise, claiming self-defense. Then the band left, taking Cruise's horses, a wagon, jewelry, and one female slave. When they rejoined Captain Brown and the others Hazlett was riding a fine new horse.

A heavy snowstorm covered the trail of the raiders; their first stop on returning to Kansas was Augustus Wattles' home, then the settler Mendenhall's, and finally Reverend Adair's in Osawatomie—on Christmas Eve. By that time a hornet's nest had been raised, and not just in Missouri. Most Kansans were outraged and alarmed; Missouri put a price of $3,000 on Brown's head and from the White House the President added another $250.

The Captain, meanwhile expected the Missourians to invade and returned with some of his men to Captain Bain's settlement where he prepared some earthen breastworks. News came, however, that the armed men in search of him were Northern free-state settlers. He had made his last misjudgment in Kansas. Augustus Wattles told him the territory was "too harassed." Brown said, "I will draw the scene of the excitement to some other part of the country."[21] He had grown to speak as though he was a sovereign force in himself.

He was, in truth, taken aback by the storm rising around—and against—him. Jim Lane, who had turned peaceful, petitioned the governor for an official commission to capture both Brown and Montgomery. Even Montgomery tried to disassociate himself from Brown. "For Brown's doings in Kansas, I am not responsible," he said. "I know nothing of either his plans or his intentions. Brown keeps his own counsel and acts on his own responsibility."[22]

Not everyone turned against him, by any means. Wattles gave the Brown party shelter, even while disavowing Brown publicly. Montgomery was personally cordial. William Hutchinson, a newspaper correspondent for the *New York Times* talked to the Hero in Wattles' home and departed considering Brown's course "justified." The Northern press made the Missouri incursion a heroic rescue of slaves against great odds. And a legend, concocted by Brown, Kagi, and the others, soon softened the invasion of homes, the looting, and other unpleasant aspects of the raids. A poor slave, said the Captain, had been found weeping by one of his men. Questioned, he said he was to be sold and parted from his family. Brown led a raid into Missouri to prevent this tragedy. While in Wattles' home, Brown also drew up what he called his "parallels," in which the Hamilton murders were contrasted with his own heroic deed. Both the weeping slave and the "parallels" were heavily covered in the Northern and New England press, and helped his reputation.

"Do you hear the news from Kansas?" wrote Gerrit Smith. "Our dear John Brown is invading Missouri and pursuing the policy which he intended to pursue *elsewhere*. I have a handsome letter from his son John."[23]

As he made preparations to take his stolen horses, oxen, slaves, and goods out of the territory, the name of John Brown soared aloft—and the name of David Cruise, who "wouldn't turn away a dog on a night like this," vanished beneath the notice of idealists.

Chapter 39

In late January 1859, the Hero led his men, wagons, and liberated slaves across the Kansas plains and escaped his pursuers—according to his friends—through sheer heroism. His critics said he had the aid of abolitionists. Both were right.

On February 5, the Brown caravan reached safety in Tabor, Iowa. Captain Brown knew the town and its people well; but he forgot that it was a religious community. When he suggested a prayer of thanksgiving for himself and his men at Mr. Todd's church, it was not warmly received. The copastor, the Reverend Dr. King, said it was his view that "destroying life and stealing horses"[1] did not entitle anyone to public praise.

The statement created some division inside the congregation, as well as indignation in Captain Brown and his men. The following night a town meeting was held to discuss the issue, and the Captain was invited to rise and explain the matter. He started, and then stopped when he saw Dr. Brown, of St. Joseph, Missouri, enter and sit down. Dr. Brown owned slaves.

"One has just entered whom I prefer not to hear what I am going to say," said the Captain, apparently under the impression that even the right of listening to a public debate should not be granted the unworthy. "I respectfully request him to withdraw."[2]

The congregation disagreed, and men jumped up to say so. The outcome was predictable: with great dignity, Captain Brown walked out and, once outside, said to his men, *"Look to your arms."* Inside, the congregation passed an antislavery resolution, but also voiced opposition to taking "lives or property" in the antislavery cause. The members did not know all the facts, but they knew dangerous men when they met them.

From Tabor eastward, however, Brown and his men began to meet a far warmer and more cheering reception. They stopped at various hamlets and in Des Moines the editor of the *Register* welcomed Kagi, whom he knew, and paid the group's ferry fare across the Des Moines River. On February 25 they stopped at Grinnell, founded by Josiah Grinnell, a famed abolitionist, and received the hero's welcome for which they longed. The Captain was so pleased he wrote the details and sent it to the Tabor town fathers, as evidence of their poorer judgment.

From Grinnell on the party traveled slowly, like veterans of a great engagement, hailed by the folk at home. On March 10, they left West Liberty, Iowa, for Chicago, in a boxcar. The train was met by Allan Pinkerton, who raised the money to pay for its journey, and then sent the slaves on to Canada.

By that time Northern newspapers were fluttering in the wake of the Hero. In Cleveland he was interviewed by Charles F. Browne, writer for the *Plain Dealer,* who used the pen name Artemus Ward. Browne thought Kagi was "a melancholy brigand" and that John Brown could make a fortune "letting himself out as an Ice Cream Freezer."[3]

The Tabor reception had taught Brown to de-emphasize the bloodiness of his deeds; he now said he never killed anyone, and regarded "the enemy's arms, horses, etc., as legitimate booty." His act had grown polished, and gleamed well—away from Kansas.

As always, he had money on his mind. His white beard fluttering in the wind, he watched as an auctioneer put two of his horses and a mule up for sale. The Captain said they had been captured "in border fighting near Fort Scott." He described one horse and mule as "abolition stock. I converted 'em." He had grown very salty in such references, which were grimly amusing to the urban crowds.

He also attempted some lecturing, but the crowds were small. That was not due to any disfavor: the Cleveland section was well along in defiance of the Fugitive Slave Law. At this time, a number of Oberlin people—businessmen, professors, and students—were on trial for assisting escaped slaves. The press of the South raged; the press of the North hailed the prisoners; the trial was a farce. In the end the "Oberlin prisoners" were released with the assistance of Joshua Giddings and Ohio Governor Salmon Chase, and the Kentucky slave hunters barely escaped heavy local prison terms.[4]

With his usual uncanny luck Brown had arrived just in time for the Oberlin trial; Kagi was able to report it for Boston and New York newspapers. In the fevered climate it created, nobody was going to arrest the hero of Kansas. He walked past the President's "wanted" posters uncaring; it was no wonder he considered himself beyond ordinary rules, and above ordinary men.

Brown had seen Frederick Douglass in Cleveland but he stopped, again and as ever, at Rochester to tell and retell of his latest great project—though he left the specific location unmentioned. Douglass had heard it all before, many times. But a small, very black man, who acted as Douglass' servant and clothes cleaner, listened intently. Shields Green sometimes called himself Emperor Green. He was a fugitive from South Carolina—"a state," Douglass said, "from which a slave found it no easy matter to run away . . . He was a man of few words and his speech was singularly broken, but his courage and self-respect made him quite a dignified character." Brown saw the way Green listened as he talked about fighting slaveholders, and "Green promised to go with him whenever he should move."[5] But Frederick Douglass, the most important black leader, remained as smiling and elusive as ever.

"Mr. Smith spoke well; G.W. Putnam read a spirited poem and Mr. Brown was exceedingly interesting, once or twice was so eloquent that Mr. Smith and some others wept . . ."[6] So wrote tutor Edwin Morton at the Smith mansion to his old college chum Frank Sanborn, who was awaiting Brown's arrival in New England with palpitating heart.

The meeting Morton described was, of course, to help Brown. Gerrit Smith handed a paper around; he had started the subscription off with four hundred dollars. He also said: "If I were asked to point out—I will say it in his presence—to point out the man in all this world I think most truly a Christian, I would point to John Brown."[7]

Morton concluded in his letter: "I was once doubtful in my own mind as to Captain Brown's course. I now approve it heartily, having given my mind to it more of late."

If Morton, whose approval was unimportant, had turned a more admiring eye toward Brown, Higginson—who received a breathless note from Frank Sanborn on Brown's return—felt somewhat different. "It had all begun to seem to me somewhat chimerical," he said later.[8] His wife Mary's health was worse, and he had just completed an unsettling exchange with Lysander Spooner that cast Brown and his activities in a somewhat different light.

Spooner had approached Higginson and others with a suggestion that white Northerners should join the black slaves of the South in an attempt to join with Southern nonslaveholders, to overthrow the peculiar institution as individuals. He circulated that proposal, and Higginson in his response had then hinted of the Brown plan.

He was not the only one to respond. Lewis Tappan wrote Spooner in horror at the "use of any deadly weapons," and Hinton Helper, whose statistic-packed book, *The Impending Crisis,* intended to prove slavery was economically unfeasible, thought the Spooner plan would make matters worse. Wendell Phillips said he still believed in the Garrisonian principle of nonresistance; Theodore Parker thought Spooner impractical. For his part, Spooner was appalled at the Higginson-Brown plot, and wrote Gerrit Smith saying it was doomed to failure.[9]

Higginson disagreed; he believed in the Brown plan. But he was beginning to wonder if Brown would ever actually move. In response to Sanborn's plea he sent only twenty dollars, and wrote Brown saying he would assist once matters were under way.

The others were also in changed circumstances. The greatest change was that which overcame Theodore Parker. In declining health for several years, he had persisted in his endless preachings and sermonizing, his writings and his letters, but by early 1859 he was unable to fill his pulpit. "Consumption, having long since slain almost all my near kinsfolk, horsed on the north-wind, rode at me also, seeking my life."[10]

He left Boston, "in haste." The couple closest to him, Dr. Samuel Gridley Howe and Julia, sailed with him on the same boat to Cuba. The trip was rough; Julia was seasick and so was Parker—a "wretched sailor." None of them fit in the green island of Cuba; of all Bostonians they were among the most proper. Parker spent hours, as he had for years, bent over a desk, writing feverishly; he was doing his own biography in the form of a *Letter to the Congregation*—in which he looked back on himself and his struggles with deep self-pity. "With some justification one might say that in his search for greatness, Parker finally turned to himself."[11]

The Howes saw Parker and his wife off from Cuba for Europe; Julia Ward Howe said later: "I still carry in my mind the picture of his serious face, crowned with gray locks and a soft gray hat, as he looked over the side of the vessel and waved . . ."[12]

Bereft of the Parkers, the Howes met and became friendly with the Frank Hamptons of South Carolina. The two couples became so congenial that the Howes went to Charleston as house guests, and were also entertained at the pillared and gracious home of Wade Hampton, whose family was then away in Europe. Meeting the Southern planters in their homes, and being received as a gentleman, Howe was stricken to think that war could sweep down on such people—especially when Wade Hampton assured him, "We mean to fight for it."[13]

Brown was in Boston in early May 1859. He had visited North Elba and been intermittently troubled by his "ague" but he was still very much the man of business. His reception was mixed. Higginson, whose admiration for others was in proportion to their admiration for him, remained away in Worcester. Pressed by Sanborn to solicit funds for Brown in that city, he grew petulant. "I have drawn so largely on others . . ." he said, "it is hard for me to solicit money for another *retreat* . . ."[14]

Howe also balked. His objections were based on his meetings with Southerners. "It shocked him," said Sanborn, "to think he might be instrumental in giving up to flames and pillage their noble mansions."[15] Imbued with that belated pang of conscience, he debated the

propriety of looting and carrying off property with Captain Brown—
who was properly grim and warlike. Apparently the debate didn't last
long—after all, it was not Dr. Howe's property that was at stake—and
Howe not only allowed himself to be reconvinced, but introduced
Brown to substantial businessmen like railroad magnate John Murray
Forbes. Forbes thought he saw "a little touch of insanity" in Brown's
"glittering gray-blue eyes" but allowed him to spend the night and
made a donation.[16] That was, as always, the price for meeting John
Brown.

A. A. Lawrence, who had paid that price many times, was also honored by a call but on this occasion was not impressed. "He has been
stealing negroes and running them off from Missouri," he wrote in his
diary, ". . . and would be hanged if taken in a slave state. He has
allowed his beard to grow since I saw him last, which changes his
appearance entirely, as it is almost white and very long. He and his
companion (Jeremiah Anderson) both have the fever and ague, somewhat, probably a righteous visitation for their fanaticism."[17]

Others less familiar with the Captain were more taken with him.
George Luther Stearns, one of the Secret Six and the largest contributor to Brown's visit on this occasion, was impressed, on entering the
Bird Club, to find the Captain seated with Senator Henry Wilson and
other notables.[18]

Concord also was still admiring. Taken there to speak at the town
hall again by Frank Sanborn, Bronson Alcott said that the audience,
consisting "of the best people,"—Emerson, Thoreau, Judge Ebenea-
zor Hoar—listened respectfully and made up a collection.[19]

The Sage himself let the occasion pass without comment: years of
traveling in "uncomfortable trains, living in primitive hotels, lecturing
in ill-ventilated and poorly lighted halls in all sorts of weather" had
brought on signs of age.[20] His personal voice of conscience, the oc-
togenarian Aunt Mary, had finally grown too outspoken and quarrel-
some for Coolidge Castle, and had been packed off to spend her last
days on Long Island.

Emerson himself was now established in the American Pantheon as
the leading intellectual of New England. His income had risen to more
than four thousand dollars a year and was rolling in easily; his discontent with society had noticeably abated.

There was, in other words, a cooling in the upper reaches of New
England; as the antislavery cause had spread into widespread popularity its espousal was no longer as arresting, or as rewarding. The new
religion was now a mass movement, and new spokesmen were rising
on all sides.

Brown left New England determined to put his "mill" into opera-
tion. He stopped at Collinsville, Connecticut, and paid blacksmith
Blair his final, long delayed installment for the thousand "pikes,"
despite that man's astonishment and curiosity. "Kansas matters are
all settled," said Blair, "of what earthly use can they be to you

now?"²¹ But he was glad to get the money and get rid of the rusting, primitive spears.

From there the old man raced through his various contacts, leaving a trail of letters as he traveled. He talked, with reckless abandon, about his men, his arms, his plans, to many people—none of whom made any serious demurral or warned the authorities. His itinerary was confusing: Ohio . . . Pennsylvania . . . North Elba . . . back to Pennsylvania. John Brown, Jr., whose life, now and forever, was bound and linked to the old man's abolition business, made efforts to ready and ship the rifles, forward letters, run errands, relay orders. His position created "a profound depression" in him.

Brown was still making ready, in his own involved, curiously complex fashion. On intermittent trips to North Elba he argued with his sons: he wanted them all, but Salmon and Jason refused as did Henry Thompson. In the end he had his youngest son, Oliver, his third, Owen, and his fifth, Watson. Kagi, of course, was his right hand; Stevens-Whipple remained as though no other course was possible. John E. Cook was already at Harper's Ferry—where heedless of the future—he had married.

While traveling with Brown, Jerry Anderson wrote his brother, Dr. John B. Anderson:

> I wouldn't be surprised if you should hear of me being in some place before long. We are going to start from here next Monday (June 19th) for Cleveland, from there across Pennsylvania, on a *surveying expedition.* I think I shall write you from that region in a few weeks. You need not be uneasy about us *stealing niggers,* for that is not our business, but be patient. Our theory is new, but undoubtedly good, practicable and perfectly safe and simple, but I judge when we put it into practice, it will astonish the world and mankind, in general. We called on Fred Douglass again as we passed through Rochester; he is to be one of us.²²

But the weeks passed without the world hearing of any great novel theory being applied. The New Englanders had been told that the target date was July 4, 1859—a choice that Brown considered especially significant. That day passed calmly with no move made; Brown's preparations always took more time. By mid-August he and his men had been established for weeks not far from Harper's Ferry, Virginia, in a rented farmhouse owned by the heirs of a Dr. Kennedy.

Letters poured in and out, but the days were hot, stuffy, and boring. The men emerged only at night. They played checkers, read their few books, and argued in undertones. They wrote long, endless letters filled with noble denunciations of slavery and indiscreet hints. The Captain would sit apart in the kitchen, drinking tea, trying not to exacerbate sensitivities—and avoiding questions.

Despite Jerry Anderson's assurance to his brother that "Fred Douglass . . . is to be one of us," the famous black leader did not appear. Neither did any of the other blacks whom Brown had cultivated so carefully over the years. Brown chafed at that; it took many letters to get Douglass to agree to visit with him to discuss the project.

Their meeting place was an old quarry near Chambersburg, Pennsylvania. Douglass was told that Kagi, Brown's "secretary," would be present, that Brown's "mining tools" were in Chambersburg, and that Brown had to be there to remove and to bring money. En route, accompanied by Shields Green, Douglass visited the Reverend James Gloucester, told him he was meeting Brown, and obtained a contribution of ten dollars.

Douglass' appearance in Chambersburg excited the black community, which urged him to make a speech. He agreed, but also dropped in on Henry Watson, a black barber who knew about Captain Brown, and who gave him directions to the stone quarry. "I approached the old quarry very carefully," Douglass said, "for John Brown was generally well-armed, and regarded strangers with suspicion . . . He was passing under the name of John Smith."[23]

He found Brown carrying some fishing tackle. He wore an old, weatherbeaten hat, and his clothing was "about the color of the stone-quarry itself." Douglass thought the old man looked anxious and worn. The four men—Kagi, Shields Green, Brown, and Douglass—sat among the rocks while Brown revealed his final plan.

Douglass listened with shock and surprise as Brown outlined a completely new approach. Instead of running off slaves—the original plan —he was going to attack the federal arsenal at Harper's Ferry.

Douglass immediately objected that such an attack would be on the federal government and "array the whole country against us." Brown was not upset at that thought; he believed something startling was exactly what was needed. Then the two men argued for hours. Douglass was not arguing for himself: it was obvious he had no more intention of joining Brown's "army" than did other leaders of the black community. He argued against what he considered a dangerous, rash, and harmful project—and in that, he showed more conscience than the Secret Six. But, of course, Douglass was also thinking of the white reaction against his people.

Brown, however, had concentrated on his project. All his efforts had resulted in recruiting four blacks and twenty whites, not counting himself. All were young men; three were his sons. Those who had raided with him in Kansas were experienced to some extent. His money was, as always, running low: train trips and spears and shipments and food for his group cost a great deal. They were waiting for him in the old Kennedy farmhouse, hiding by day from the neighbors, fearful to go anywhere at night. He had his fifteen-year-old daughter Annie, and the seventeen-year-old wife of his youngest son, Oliver, doing the cooking, cleaning and washing. It was—and somewhere in his worried mind he knew—a pitiful handful with which to attack a strongly defended federal installation.

His new plan was to seize the arsenal by surprise, take a number of prominent and respectable citizens as hostages, and hold out indefinitely. If worse came to worst he could negotiate his freedom with the hostages. His occupation of the arsenal would serve "as a trumpet to rally" the slaves to his defense. Douglass shook his massive head and dropped all banter and patience. He knew his people: they had been kept in ignorance, without schooling, but they were not fools. He told Brown he was going into a "steel trap, and . . . would never get out alive."[24]

They spent the rest of Saturday and part of Sunday, August 21, in fruitless debate. No man had ever changed John Brown's mind, but Douglass tried more sincerely than any other. In the end Brown put his arm around him and said, "When I strike, the bees will begin to swarm, and I shall want you to help hive them." Douglass was touched but unconvinced. He started to leave, and looked at Green, the fugitive slave he had harbored so long. To his surprise Green said, "I b'leve I'll go wid de old man."[25]

The arsenal was located at the joining of the Potomac and Shenandoah rivers, fifty-seven miles by road from Washington, D.C., eighty by rail from Baltimore. The Baltimore & Ohio railroad crossing over the Potomac, through a covered bridge, ran along Potomac Street, its tracks on a bank forty feet above the river, in the town of Harper's Ferry. Another railroad joined the B&O at the bridge. The arsenal sat on the river side of the town's main street and was set off from the houses and shops on the land side by an iron fence and a gate. It consisted of a series of brick buildings, some of which held manufacturing facilities; others served as warehouses and offices. The surrounding mountains and the merging waters made a fine sight. The view from the bluff was magnificent. Houses dotted the hills above the arsenal.

Roughly thirty-five hundred "mechanics" were employed at the arsenal. They were largely from the North—the nation's repository of skilled workers—and earned about two dollars a day. That payroll supported a number of saloons, boardinghouses, and cheap restaurants, together with clothing stores and other outlets. Harper's Ferry was a good market for the neighboring farmers who sold their beef, eggs, milk, and vegetables at firm prices. The town's population in 1859 was about five thousand.

In no sense was Harper's Ferry a typical Virginia village. It was a small industrial town, somewhat drab and grimy, but set in a location noted for its scenic beauty, that General Washington had also surveyed and chosen as a site for an arms factory.

While Brown was taking Shields Green, instead of Frederick Douglass, back to his farmhouse hideout, the nation seemed to be recovering from the fevers of the previous year's election. Politicians began to angle for the presidency; in Congress at least eighteen Democrats alone wanted to replace Buchanan. In the Republican party, Lincoln was far down the list of likely nominees—though occasionally mentioned for the vice-presidency. Senator Seward seemed the favorite for the big prize.

Business was brisk, crops were good and prices high. In Kansas, at long last, peace had settled the territory, and men had begun to build genuine towns and livelihoods. In Medford, Massachusetts, George Luther Stearns and his family moved into a fine new home; Stearns took pleasure planting elms on the handsome avenue it fronted.

In Worcester Higginson lined up lecture appearances and wrote articles; he was a regular and well-known contributor to the *Atlantic Monthly* and other publications, where his views on the injustice with which women were treated, and the need for healthful exercise, intermingled with calls for courage in life, made him invigorating reading for many. Sanborn plagued him about Brown and his need for money. Higginson sent small, irregular sums.

Dr. Howe and Julia found it a pleasant summer; their trip to Cuba and the South had led her to write a travel article that appeared in the *Atlantic*. As was to be expected, it landed her in trouble with her husband, who tended to grow irritated with such efforts, and one sentence—in which she spoke of "the natural indolence of the negroes in tropical countries"—led to a stern lecture in *The Liberator*.[26] But as usual, Julia triumphed over all: she was asked to become a society writer for the Newport season by the New York *Tribune*.

At Peterboro the master of the mansion sent Brown two hundred dollars in June, and wrote: "You live in our hearts, and my prayer to God is that you may have strength to continue in your Kansas work. My wife joins in affectionate regard for you, dear John, whom we both hold in very high esteem . . ."[27] In August 1859, Smith sent Brown another hundred dollars.

An ailing Theodore Parker, pursued by an inability to come to terms with death, had gone to England and then to Paris, drawing up lists of the notables he met as he moved with his entourage. Famous, well-to-do, his mind still active, he found his declining powers difficult to accept. He moved on to Switzerland, then to Italy. From there he wrote to Dr. Howe: "What a pity that the map of our magnificent country should be destined to be so soon torn in two on account of the negro, that poorest of human creatures, satisfied, even in slavery, with sugar cane and a banjo."

Julia read that and turned to the Doctor. "This is poor dear Parker's foible," she said. "He always thinks he knows what will come to pass. How absurd this forecast of his!"

"I don't know about that," said Dr. Howe.[28]

On August 20, 1859 Secretary of War John B. Floyd received an anonymous letter, warning that "Old John Brown, late of Kansas" planned to strike against a federal armory in Maryland from Harper's Ferry. Floyd consulted his list, saw there was no federal armory in Maryland, and filed the letter at once.[29] All bureaucrats to whom an error in detail is more important than the body of any message would have applauded that reaction.

Inside the Kennedy farmhouse the men argued over their captain's plan. The proposed assault on the arsenal—located in the heart of town along the railroad tracks—was far from the mountain campaign they had been told to expect.[30] But Brown insisted the slaves would rise and receive guns, and that then the party could leave, with hostages, to launch its campaign. In the end Brown threatened to resign. That brought the others around. Then the Captain produced forms he had prepared; they were headed **Greetings,** in ornate letters. Below that, in black, impressive type, appeared **Head-Quarters War Department.** One by one, he called in his men to take oaths and receive commissions. His three sons were all captains. So were Stevens-Whipple, Tidd, Cook, William Thompson, and Jeremiah Anderson. The younger men—Edwin and Dauphine Thompson and Leeman, were made lieutenants. The black men—now numbering five, with Shields Green—were privates.

The pikes, Sharp's rifles, and two hundred revolvers were in hand. The two young girls had been sent back to North Elba. Farewell letters were written: the young Coppocs, who came from a Quaker home in Springdale, may have recalled their mother's grim words when she learned they had joined Captain Brown: "When thou gettest a halter round thy neck, wilt thou think of me?"[31]

Still the Captain lingered. The young men cooked themselves strange, scrambled meals while Brown, who had shaved away his white beard, brooded and drank tea. On October 15, the last recruit arrived. He was a scrawny young man named Francis Merriam. He had a spotty complexion, a glass eye, and six hundred in gold. He had come, by a complicated route, from Sanborn and Higginson.[32] He handed over his money; Brown took it, administered the oath, and added Merriam to the army. Now he had twenty-one men: sixteen white, five black.

Sunday, October 16, 1859, was cold and rainy. Brown liked Sabbaths; he conducted services. On this occasion he asked one of the black men to lead—a rare honor. After the service, he read his strange "provisional constitution," whose jumbled phrases sounded impressive to the young men. Then he had each recruit recite his oath to him as commander-in-chief once again, in unison. The men's hearts began to beat faster.

The heavy wagon was loaded with pikes and rifles and hitched to a team. More pikes and rifles were put in a smaller wagon. Merriam and the younger Coppoc were to move the heavy wagon to a schoolhouse in the area when they received word: the schoolhouse was the depot where Brown would arm the slaves he expected from the hills.

Then Brown clambered into the seat of the lighter wagon, picked up the reins, and clucked to the horses. Behind him nineteen men fell into an untidy double file, and started toward the ferry. They had nothing to say to one another; months of being penned together had exhausted their conversation. The rain continued to fall lightly; the old man, grim as death, drove the wagon, while the men trudged gloomily, their weapons hidden under greatcoats.

All Brown's papers were left behind in the farmhouse. Letters from the Secret Six, his Provisional Constitution, his "Headquarters, War Department" forms crammed inside a carpetbag that had been placed inside a large, conspicuous trunk.[33]

They entered Harper's Ferry without arousing any attention and even managed to seize several men who were—despite the inclement weather—walking the streets. They crossed the bridge to the main gate of the arsenal and captured an unresisting watchman. Then they moved amid the buildings of the giant installation, and captured a second watchman near the rifle works. Kagi and two of the black privates—Copeland and Leary—were left inside the rifle works with that hostage. Captain Brown took his remaining men and several hostages back and installed himself in the engine house. He directed Stevens-Whipple to take Cook and two others to the estate of one Lewis Washington, a descendant of George Washington. He looked about with satisfaction: his plan was moving well.

Washington opened his door to four armed men. They pushed him back to his bedroom and watched while he dressed. As he wondered about their intentions, Stevens said, "We have come for the purpose of liberating all the slaves of the South." Washington looked at him sharply, but remained silent.

Then Stevens helped himself to an antique pistol that had been given to George Washington by Lafayette, and to a glittering dress sword that had been a gift to the first president from Frederick the Great of Prussia. Both heirlooms had often been shown to visitors. Stevens now turned to Lewis Washington and asked, "Have you a watch?"

Washington looked at him with contempt. "You told me your purpose was philanthropic," he said, "you did not mention at the same time that it included robbery and rascality. I do not choose to surrender my watch. There are four of you here with guns, and you may take it—and my money—but I will not surrender it."[34]

Disconcerted, Stevens said, "I presume you have heard of Osawatomie Brown?"

Washington said he had not, and Stevens observed he didn't know much about Kansas. Washington said shortly he was disgusted with that subject, and never read about it.

"Well," said Stevens, "you will see him this morning." To his disappointment Washington did not seem impressed, and did not respond when one of the men came back and said, sarcastically, that Mr. Washington's carriage was waiting. Stevens pushed Washington outside with his Negro manservant, who took the reins of the carriage. Washington rode toward Harper's Ferry with his captors.

En route the raiders stopped at another house, broke down the door, and emerged with Mr. Allstadt and his eighteen-year-old son. Finally they clattered back to the arsenal, with Washington, the two Allstadts, and ten slaves in their custody.

Brown was pleased, and greeted Washington with pleasure. He also grasped the ceremonial sword with delight; Washington noted that Brown held this symbol tightly, and carried it about in his hand.

Then Cook was sent to instruct Owen, young Coppoc, and Merriam to take the heavy wagon to the schoolhouse. Brown expected thousands of escaping slaves to emerge from the hills as soon as news of their deliverance reached them.

Cook had barely disappeared into the dark when the express train from Baltimore arrived, at a little past 1:00 A.M. The train stopped to exchange passengers at Wager House—a combination train station and hotel at the other end of the bridge—and its conductor was amazed to learn the way ahead was blocked. He and the engineer walked forward to investigate, and were driven back by shots. Hayward Shepherd, the Negro baggagemaster at Harper's Ferry, ventured out, was shot, and hit. He cried out in surprise and pain, and several men rushed out to carry him inside the station. They sent for Dr. John D. Starry, who said Shepherd's wounds were fatal. The first casualty of John Brown's blow for black freedom was a free black man.

The train remained at the station and its passengers began to gather along the tracks and inside Wager House. The shots had aroused a number of people and they began to seek the source and cause of the disturbance. When dawn arrived a number were milling about in front of the arsenal but a shot from inside killed one, Thomas Boerly, a well-known resident. From the engine house, Brown sent out one of his hostages to declare the invaders wanted fifty hot breakfasts prepared and sent to them. After two senseless murders, the insolence of the request aroused a storm of helpless indignation.

Kagi, who watched the sun rise with trepidation, sent a note to Brown from his rifle works redoubt, advising a retreat to the hills. It is possible, though hardly likely, that the withdrawal might have been successful. The Captain snorted, and sent word that Kagi should "remain firm."

Dr. Starry, who had hesitated, finally mounted his horse and rode about giving the alarm. Messengers were sent to nearby towns. In Charleston, Virginia, the Jefferson Guards were roused and hastily began to assemble. Other volunteer and regular militia groups formed in Frederick, Maryland. Throughout the region surrounding Harper's Ferry farmers hitched their wagons, saddled their horses, and snatched their rifles.

Then Captain Brown decided to allow the train through. The whistle blew, passengers clambered back aboard, and the train huffed its way past the arsenal and down toward the Ohio Valley, as fast as its engineer and fireman could send it.

By 7:00 A.M. men collected around the arsenal in increasing numbers and began to fire at the invaders. Inside, the breakfasts remained untouched; the Captain had decided they might be poisoned.

The train Brown had allowed through finally reached Monacacy and its conductor ran into the telegraph office. His alarm reached the lower echelons in Baltimore and was received with incredulity. But when the message reached John W. Garrett, head of the B&O, he immediately informed the White House, the governor of Virginia, and the commander of the Maryland National Guard. Armed insurrection involving Negro slaves led by abolitionists was the most serious imaginable emergency.

Inside the arsenal John Brown listened to the sound of bells ringing and watched his men, pale and sweating, at their posts. Bullets pinged off their brick refuge. Brown was grim. Where were the slaves? He had expected hundreds to pour in, eagerly snatching at the guns and pikes he had waiting for them. Osborne P. Anderson, the black man who had come from Canada to help, said the Old Man seemed puzzled.

Brown saw men scramble down from the hills and climb into small boats that began to approach the arsenal from the river. He turned and said, with open relief, "Here come our men." Stevens had better eyesight. He shook his head. "I'm afraid those aren't our men, Captain."

By 11:00 A.M. the volunteer groups and militia around the arsenal prepared to make a sortie. Firing rapidly, they advanced across the bridge. Oliver Brown and William Thompson retreated from their guard posts; Dangerfield Newby also fell back, after exchanging shots with George Turner. Turner fell dead and Newby himself was then struck by a six-inch spike fired from a gun. It created a ghastly throat wound and he died almost immediately.

Then the Jefferson Guards poured onto the arsenal grounds. Hazlett and Osborne P. Anderson ran down the bank, hid in the bushes, and wondered if they would succeed in saving their lives. One of Brown's young men, Billy Leeman, twenty, became so frightened that he broke into the open and ran down to the river, where he was shot. His body remained in the shallows for some time. Kagi fled out the back way of one of the rifle works, went down the bank, tried to cross the river, and was shot dead. John P. Copeland, a black student who had left Oberlin College for this adventure, was wounded, shot and clubbed, and dragged back alive. His relative, Leary, was also wounded and captured.

Brown still had his hostages but a large part of his force was dead or captured. Inside the engine house he had chosen for his fortress, he determined to parley, and sent out a prisoner with William Thompson, one of his son-in-law's brothers, to discuss terms. Shots whizzed past both men and they halted. Thompson was taken prisoner, and held inside the railroad station.

Incredulous that other men would treat a white flag with his own irreverence, Brown sent out Stevens, his son Watson Brown, and another hostage. Both Stevens and Watson were shot at once. Watson

staggered back to his father's redoubt and one of the hostages ran out
and dragged Stevens back.

Then both sides settled down to snipe at one another, and the rain
resumed. The town continued to fill with volunteers, militia, and other
troops; the hills, too were dotted with men. In Baltimore, Washington,
New York, Boston, and other cities, newspaper extras appeared. "A
Slave Rebellion of Immense Size" had been mounted. The facts were
lurid enough; the dispatches worse.

President Buchanan and Secretary of War Floyd sent Brevet Colonel
Robert E. Lee and Lieutenant J.E.B. Stuart to Harper's Ferry. They
arrived at eleven o'clock that night and found the saloons doing a
roaring business. Men wandered around firing rifles into the air, or in
the general direction of the arsenal. Lee's first order was to close the
saloons and disperse the crowd. Then he sorted out the various militia
and national guard groups, and conferred with their officers. Terrible
incidents had taken place during the day. From inside the arsenal a
sniper had shot and killed the popular mayor of Harper's Ferry; in
retaliation the prisoner Thompson had been shot dead. Lee was told
that the mysterious leader inside the arsenal had demanded he be
allowed to leave with his hostages, and had ordered food, wagons, and
horses delivered for that purpose. Colonel Lee, in civilian clothes,
looked icily toward the arsenal.

Inside the redoubt, both Watson Brown and Oliver Brown lay mor-
tally wounded. The Captain was down to four men and his hostages.
Lee did not know how many men were inside; he decided to wait until
dawn to attack, and then to use bayonets. He did not want the hostages
injured in a crossfire.

Watson Brown, twenty-three years old, begged to be put out of his
misery. "Oh, you will get over it," his father said. "If you must die, die
like a man."[35]

Later the Captain remembered that his son Oliver was also gravely
wounded, and toward morning, stopped his restless pacing to call,
"Oliver. Oliver." There was no reply, and he said to the air, "I guess
he is dead."[36]

Then he swung around to his silent prisoners and said: "Gentlemen,
if you knew my history you would not blame me . . . I went to Kansas
a peaceable man and the proslavery people from Kentucky and Virginia hunted me down like a wolf. I lost one of my sons there . . ."[37]

At dawn Colonel Lee ordered all the men under arms to draw up in
formation. He talked to the various militia commanders, and finally
assigned marine Lieutenant Israel Green the honor—Lee, Green, and
Stuart considered it such—of leading the assault with a picked group
of twelve marines. Green thanked him. Lieutenant Stuart was ordered
to the door of the engine house, to make a final demand for surrender.
He was not to parley, but to leap aside if the men inside remained
adamant. He approached and the door of the engine house opened a

crack. Stuart handed over a note signed by Colonel Lee, calling for surrender. A gnarled hand emerged to take the message, and Stuart stared in surprise.

"Why, aren't you old Osawatomie Brown, whom I once held prisoner?" he asked.

"Yes, but you didn't keep me," Brown replied.[38] Then he began to repeat his demand that he be allowed to leave peacefully with his hostages. Stuart leaped to one side, waved his hat, and the marines charged.

While the defenders fired, the marines brought a heavy ladder against the door. They pushed and it buckled; they poured inside. Washington, calm amid disorder, pointed to a man kneeling behind a carbine and said, "This is Osawatomie."

Green rushed at the old man and thrust at him so forcefully that his light dress sword, stopped by a belt buckle, bent double. Brown staggered back, bent over, and Green pounded him unconscious with the sword handle. In the affray two marines were shot; Jeremiah Anderson was pinned, like a giant bug on a needle, by a bayonet that went through him and into a wall; and young Dauphine Thompson was bayoneted to death as he sought to crawl under a wagon. Only Edwin Coppoc and Shields Green, the fugitive slave, were taken alive and unharmed.

Brown's mill had been started and had run its bloody course in thirty-six hours.

Chapter 40

Telegraphs hummed and headlines shrieked Slave Insurrection! Descriptions of the movements of hundreds of blacks, directed by daring white generals—armed, fierce, and determined—followed. Higginson heard a neighbor shout, "Old Osawatomie Brown has got himself into a tight place at last." He ran to a newspaper, rushed home and read it with mounting excitement, and with envy.[1] The great blow had been struck—and he had been at home.

He wrote an excited letter to his mother: he was sure the effort would succeed against "all the force likely to be brought against them & can at least retreat to the mountains & establish a Maroon colony . . . like those in Jamaica & Guiana . . ."[2]

Dismay reigned at the mansion Peterboro. The New York *Herald* unearthed excerpts from a Gerrit Smith speech given two months before, in which the magnate had warned that insurrection could occur "any year, any month, any day . . ." That speech was printed alongside telegraph dispatches from Harper's Ferry, saying, "Is This the First Act?", and "Are those white abolitionists spoken of in our dispatches emissaries of the peaceful Gerrit?"[3] The magnate read the paper and flushed crimson. He rushed to his office. There he rummaged through his files, pulled out every letter he had ever received from John Brown, Sanborn, or Stearns, and threw them into the fire. The flames could not consume them too soon for Gerrit Smith; he was a lawyer and he knew the rules of evidence—and the laws against being an accessory to murder and treason.

In Concord, the schoolmaster Frank Sanborn, who had sworn to John Brown two years before that "I shall prize anything from you as a momento of the bravest and most earnest man it has ever been my fortune to meet,"[4] was following Smith's example. He burned every scrap that bound him to John Brown and his mill, and it was only much later—after the danger had passed and only the glory remained—that he said he had destroyed all the evidence lest it "compromise other persons."[5]

The news reached remote North Elba more slowly. The raid had started Sunday evening, October 16, 1859 and appeared in screaming headlines on Monday and Tuesday, creating fear and horror through the nation. Democratic newspapers thundered at this result of fanatic abolitionism; plantations tightened their security; Southern towns created local defense companies. Republican newspapers in the North were reserved, but at first a tidal wave of universal condemnation rolled from editorial desks.

A neighbor came by to tell the Brown clan, but its members were not sure until a three-day-old newspaper was brought to them on Friday, October 21. They crowded around to read of the capture of old John Brown, the wounded Stevens, Edwin Coppoc, John Copeland, Copeland's relative Leary, and Shields Green. Seventeen of the raiders had been killed: the authorities did not yet know how many had escaped capture. The Browns knew—though they may not have known about Merriam, who joined only on the eve of the raid.[6]

They knew that their father had led two more of his sons—Watson and Oliver—to their deaths, as well as the two young Thompson boys, brothers to Henry Thompson, who had married Ruth Brown. Years later, Annie Brown recalled them all huddled around the newspaper "struck dumb, horror-stricken with a grief too deep and hard to find expression in words, or even tears."[7] Young Martha Brewster Brown, the youthful widow of Oliver, who had cooked and cleaned at the Kennedy farmhouse for the raiders, was pregnant. She told Annie, in the days that followed, that only her baby kept alive a spark of life within her; otherwise she did not want to live.[8] The others hoped that the missing raiders would remain missing: they knew that Owen Brown was among them.

There were families other than the Browns and the Thompsons

grieving that week, and with fewer persons to mourn with them. Hayward Shepherd, the free black baggagemaster of Harper's Ferry, was dead and so was Mayor Fontaine Beckham, shot dead, though he had no gun, by one of the raiders. So was George W. Turner, a gentleman-farmer and friend of Colonel Washington; and the Irishman Thomas Boerley was gone. So, for that matter, was a young marine, who died in the final assault on the engine house. John Brown had led seventeen of his followers and five other men to their deaths and the toll was not yet over, but by the time his family read the accounts of his last exploit the scales of rationalization were already beginning to shift in his favor.

The first week after Harper's Ferry was one of confusion and dismay in New England. Gerrit Smith sent his son-in-law, Charles D. Miller, to Boston and then to the Ohio home of John Brown, Jr. to search out and destroy all Smith letters—and every other shred of evidence that might connect the Secret Six to the Hero. A stream of letters from various citizens began to pour into Peterboro, denouncing Smith. The New York *Herald* reported that letters and documents found in the carpetbag John Brown had left behind in the Kennedy farmhouse implicated Smith, Joshua R. Giddings and Frederick Douglass, and said that Smith had "supplied the sinews of war."[9] In the same issue the paper printed a fiery Smith speech calling for insurrection, and John Brown's "provisional constitution"—side by side.

The following day, October 21, 1859, the *Herald* printed Smith's "My dear Friend" letter to Brown, dated June 14, and ran an editorial charging Smith and Frederick Douglass were "accessories before the fact."[10] The millionaire was, by then, unable to sleep, unable to work, and running a fever.

Sanborn, Stearns, and Dr. Howe spent the same sort of week. Sanborn received an especially nasty shock when Francis Merriam, who had escaped from the raid, appeared in Concord. "I declined to see him," said Sanborn "out of regard for his safety."[11]

Only weeks before, the schoolmaster had taken Merriam in hand very cordially, and encouraged him to carry the remains of his small inheritance to Virginia and join the Captain's adventure, though he regarded the frail young man with thin contempt. " 'Tis a virtue posted in numbskulls, to give money freely," he wrote to Higginson with chilling cynicism, ". . . I consider him about as fit to be in this enterprise as the devil is to keep a powder house; but everything has its use & must be put to it if possible . . ."[12]

Usefulness over, Merriam in Concord was a hideous embarrassment. Sanborn sent Henry Thoreau—the erstwhile aloof observer of nature and governments—to handle the thin, nervous fugitive. Thoreau introduced himself as a Mr. Lockwood, and put the young man on the next northbound train, demolishing forever the image of his own aloofness from these shadowy and immoral activities. Sanborn, meanwhile, told his confederates that Merriam was "wholly crazy"—a necessary judgment, apparently, to relieve his conscience.[13] Years later he persisted in that door-shutting; Merriam was never allowed into the great Brown pantheon, though he had dared more than Sanborn or any of the Secret Six.

But Sanborn was, at the time Merriam appeared, a very busy and worried young man. He conferred with everyone, including Emerson and Thoreau.[14] Wendell Phillips, that famed nonresistor, who was not, obviously, shocked by the violence of the raid, was especially helpful. Sanborn, who had already decided to turn over his annual school chestnut hunt to someone else, drove to Boston in a chaise with George Luther Stearns, who preserved a gambler's mask, to consult with John A. Andrews, an ambitious abolitionist lawyer. Andrews gave his opinion that both men were liable to arrest and extradition to Virginia. Sanborn—carrying a small overnight bag for a hotel stay in Boston—bolted immediately. After a steamer trip to Portland, Maine, he dashed off a hurried note to Higginson in Worcester:

> Dear Friend: According to the advice of good friends and my own deliberate judgment I am going to try a change of air for my old complaint. By this means it is thought that others will benefit as well as I; whether my absence will be long or short will depend on circumstances. Yours of the 19th was rec'd yesterday before I left home. Should you have occasion to write me again I have a friend in Quebec named *Frederick Stanley* to whom you can write. Burn this.
>
> Yours ever[15]

Frederick Douglass was ahead of Sanborn: he had gone to Canada as soon as news of the raid appeared. He was under no illusions as to his fate if Virginia caught him, and the free black community of Canada provided a warm and welcoming shelter. Reading in the newspapers about incriminating documents left behind in Brown's carpetbag, the black leader decided it would be unsafe to return to the United States. He was joined in Canada, however, by Osborne P. Anderson, the free black from Canada who had taken part in the raid and who had escaped.

Anderson had fled through the darkness with Owen Brown, Cook, Tidd, Barclay Coppoc, and Merriam—the physical weakness of the last having slowed the others' pace. They wandered many miles out of their route before reaching Chambersburg, Pennsylvania, where they took trains and other routes north. Cook, who could neither believe in the seriousness of his situation nor forego food, wandered into capture quite soon. Hazlett was spotted and arrested in Pennsylvania, then returned to Virginia.

Anderson said Shields Green, Douglass' former servant, could have escaped with him, since both he and Green had been ordered by Brown to bring in slaves from the surrounding countryside soon after the arsenal was taken. "Why then did Shields not come with you?" Douglass asked. "Well," said Anderson, "I told him to come, that we could do nothing more, but he simply said he must go down to de ole man."[16]

Governor Henry A. Wise of Virginia was among many Democratic hopefuls contending for the presidency. That desire—and misjudgment of both his own abilities and his position—led him into the error of conducting the first Brown interrogation, before newspaper reporters and a collection of the curious, soon after the old man was captured.

Lieutenant Stuart identified the captive in the paymaster's office next to the engine room, to which he had been carried. Brown's head was bloody from the beating Lieutenant Green had given him.

"This is the celebrated John Brown of Kansas notoriety," said Stuart, "a man so infamous for his robberies and murders that if people here knew his antecedents he would not be permitted to live five minutes."[17]

Someone suggested the old man be cleaned and his scalp treated. Stevens, lying wounded nearby, said, "Yes, it is a shame that a man like that should be so maltreated and neglected, with no surgeon near him and no one to pay him the least attention."

"You son of a bitch!" Stuart said savagely, "You had better keep silent! Your treatment is that of men who are midnight thieves and murderers, not men taken in honorable warfare. If you came to make war, why didn't you bring a surgeon with you?"[18]

From the first the questioning of John Brown went oddly. He denied, despite the carpetbag with the "provisional constitution" and the letters about slave insurrection, that he intended to create a slave uprising. He denied he had received money and help from others—in the face of letters in the carpetbag. He claimed that the killing of innocent citizens of Harper's Ferry was done without his knowledge. He denied evidence, facts, truth, purpose, events, witnesses, and common sense. He did all this with the air of a man on a sacred mission; he was like an honest minister attempting to answer critics of his religion. He was shaky but self-possessed, certain of his virtue even while the air over the arsenal still reeked with blood.

Brown's first questioners were politicians, reporters, and bystanders. The politicians—Senator Mason of Virginia, Governor Wise, Representative Vallandigham—had the contents of the carpetbag and knew that Brown was a creature of the Emigrant Aid Society, of New England, of Ohio abolitionists, and of other Republicans. They sought to get him to admit these connections, and expose his sources of guns, spears, money, and men. Brown said he acted alone. But the South—and the nation—knew better.

Had the matter been simple the parties involved, including the intellectual authors, could have been held responsible. But John Brown had introduced into peaceful Virginia what he had earlier introduced into Kansas: the idea that killing innocent people is no crime in an effort to achieve a greater good. The new religion had started with arguments against such relatively harmless sins as smoking and drinking, had then grown to crusades denouncing and forbidding even commerce with persons whose morals were held to be invidious; it had expanded into antislavery as the answer to every ill of humanity; and it had finally come to full flower in the belief that killing anyone—innocent or guilty—was an act of righteousness for a new morality.

On his pallet the terrorist did not have the temerity to admit his purpose; he claimed his murders were accidental, his motives lofty. But the South was not deceived, any more than the settlers of Kansas had been. A great, bloody horror had risen to threaten their civilization and their lives; by contrast, the arguments of moderates everywhere were made to look foolish and inadequate.

The North could not admit what John Brown could not admit. As in the case of the Pottawatomie murders, Northern newspapers and their readers began to avert their eyes and to deny the evidence. After their joint initial reaction of shock and horror, the newspapers of both sections began to take divergent views of Harper's Ferry. The North started to play down the extent of the violence and the significance of twenty-two deaths, and to stress the glorious goals of John Brown. The South began to emphasize the threat of violence and the need to punish lawbreakers; Harper's Ferry was shown as proof of a widespread Northern desire to see the whites of the South massacred, if necessary, to impose a new morality.

October 25, 1859, only nine days after Brown opened his mill, he—together with the wounded Stevens, Coppoc, Shields Green, and Copeland—was marched from the jail, a former private home, to the white-pillared, red-brick courthouse of Charlestown. By coincidence—for once adverse to Brown—the circuit court was sitting, which meant proceedings could be quick. The Virginia authorities were intent upon remaining within the formal rules of law, but also intent upon punishing Brown and his followers without delay. They wanted to make it plain that such efforts as his would bring speedy punishment.

At the hearing, Brown did some preliminary shouting about "mock trials," which the Virginians were courteous enough to ignore. A grand jury returned four indictments, two involving slave insurrection and two for murder; separate trials were ordered to begin at once. Against the opinion of physicians, Brown claimed to be unable to stand or walk; he lay on a pallet and newspapermen packed the court as the case opened on October 27.

By then the Republican newspapers of the North had recovered their nerve, and it was obvious that a cause célèbre was under way.

The switch in Northern sentiment was reflected in a legal opinion, drawn by John A. Andrews for George Luther Stearns; its thrust was that even if Virginia indicted the Secret Six for treason, they would be tried in Massachusetts. That put a different face on matters, and Wendell Phillips sent a copy to Frank Sanborn in Quebec, saying—in effect

—"Come home; all is safe."[19] Sanborn then reappeared in Concord and began to posture in the sun of reflected glory.

Waldo Emerson had privately written his brother William immediately after Brown's raid: "We are all very well, in spite of the sad Harper's Ferry business, which interests us all who had Brown as our guest twice . . . He is a true hero but lost his head there."[20] Three days later, however, Emerson publicly told Sarah Swaine Forbes that "Brown was a hero of romance & seems to have made this fatal blunder only to bring out his virtues. I must hope for his escape at the last moment."[21]

In Ashtabula, Ohio, John Brown, Jr. had already been visited by Charles D. Miller, who was searching for Gerrit Smith letters to destroy. He found himself suddenly surrounded by protectors. Provided with a refuge in the editorial offices of the Ashtabula *Sentinel,* Brown was guarded from Southern authorities by members of the local League of Freedom,[22] wearing in their lapels the same black ribbons that had once marked a similar league, organized by Charles Robinson and involving Jim Lane, in Kansas.

Gerrit Smith, however, remained distraught, insomniac and fevered. He complained of "cold sweats" and called Dr. John McCall of Utica, who misunderstood the situation. Dr. McCall didn't credit the rumors that a man of Gerrit Smith's wealth and status would be involved "with such a notorious fringe character as John Brown," and, examining Smith with the objectivity of physical medicine, ascribed his symptoms to that horrendous condition—constipation. The doctor also innocently advised the magnate to "cultivate cheerfulness."[23]

Dr. Samuel Gridley Howe shared all Gerrit Smith's fears and sensations. According to Mrs. Stearns later, he appeared at the Stearns mansion in Medford in the grip "of a dread that threatened to overwhelm his reason."[24] Pacing the floor, he insisted to Stearns that they had no alternative but to flee the country at once. The manufacturer, behind his surface calm, was nearly as fearful, but Mrs. Stearns decided later that Stearns left with Howe only to help that harassed and frightened figure. In any event, the two fled to Canada on the same day that old Brown appeared in the Charlestown courthouse for his hearing.

The Rev. Thomas Wentworth Higginson did not run away and did not burn his letters. He longed to be called to testify, but the investigators ignored him. No punishment could have been as galling; Higginson was cheated of his hour in the John Brown drama, which he had helped to write. But if he did not take physical flight, he did shrink from admitting that he had deliberately assisted an effort designed to inspire a slave uprising[25] with bloody consequences for men of his own race. That admission required more moral candor than Higginson possessed.

As John Brown's trial raced toward its inevitable conclusion, the Northern press began an idealization unprecedented in the history of the nation. George Washington had never enjoyed such a press; Lincoln later would not be so well treated. Until Brown's time no American—including the heroes of the Revolution—had enjoyed such a steady series of admiring descriptions and slanted reportage as the terrorist received in the North—despite a steady stream of denigrations from the South.

All courtrooms stage dramas, but Brown's trial was melodramatic. On the second day of the proceedings—which were notably well conducted, with the defendant being allowed to interject his own comments at will—his appointed lawyers read aloud a telegram. It said that Brown's aunt and a first cousin had died insane and confined; that two children of an uncle had been temporarily confined for insanity; and that a third child was still under restraint. The lawyers then suggested that clemency for reasons of insanity be considered. That enraged Brown enough for him to forget his helplessness. He sat up like a jack-in-the-box and shook his fist in the air. "If the Court will allow me," he thundered in the voice that had silenced so many with whom he had disagreed. "I look upon this as a miserable artifice . . . the pretext of those who ought to take a different course . . ."[26]

The insanity issue was potentially embarrassing to Brown and his admirers. If he was mentally deranged, what of those who approved his actions? To lawyers, who take a cooler view than physicians of human behavior, the issue was legally even clearer. If Brown was insane so were similar political terrorists. To admit such an assumption would amount to creating a license to murder for all who opposed a political condition mandated by law. Eyes fixed upon Judge Parker, who calmly observed that a statement by a layman in Ohio did not constitute evidence, and ordered the trial to proceed. Both factions sighed with relief.

In the end it took the jury only forty-five minutes to find Brown guilty. On November 2, 1859, he was returned to Judge Parker for sentencing. The judge asked if he had anything to say for himself. He did, of course. This was John Brown's great moment and he rose like a man inspired. He began with some old lies: he had not intended to commit murder or treason, or to run off slaves. But his final burst sailed into the empyrean. Mentioning the New Testament—a book he never before recalled—he said: "I believe that to have interfered as I have done in behalf of His despised poor, is no wrong but right. Now, if it is deemed necessary that I should forfeit my life for the furtherance of the ends of justice, and mingle my blood with the blood of millions in this slave country whose rights are disregarded by wicked, cruel and unjust enactments, I say let it be done."[27]

Brown's words—with their stirring, evocative religious chords covering a tangle of lies and denials—were anticipated by Thoreau, who read aloud before an emotional crowd in Concord on October 30, and again in Boston on November 1, "A Plea for Captain John Brown."

"It was [Brown's] peculiar doctrine," said Thoreau, "that a man has a perfect right to interfere with force with the slaveholder, in order to rescue the slave. I agree with him . . . Some eighteen hundred years

ago Christ was crucified; this morning, perchance, Captain Brown was
hung. These are two ends of a chain which is not without its links. He
is not Old Brown any longer; he is an angel of light . . ."[28]

And, on that same November 1, Wendell Phillips, the great pacifist
and nonresistor of Boston, rose in Brooklyn to declaim: ". . . the lesson
of the hour is insurrection. Insurrection of thought always precedes
insurrection of arms. We seem to be entering on a new phase . . .
Virginia is a pirate ship and John Brown sails the seas as a Lord High
Admiral of the Almighty, with his commission to sink every pirate he
sees . . . Harper's Ferry is the Lexington of today . . ."[29]

The arguments of Thoreau and Phillips fit one another as precisely
as a mortise and tenon, but that was not surprising. Brown, Thoreau,
Phillips, Emerson, and their associates belonged to the same movement and responded to the same themes. The hero's courtroom statement, delivered a day after Thoreau's prediction of his martyrdom,
was hoisted by that movement as a banner. It was hailed in revolutionary circles in Europe as a masterpiece of liberty. Few recognized it as
a rationale for murder in the name of mercy. With its contrast of the
poor and the rich, the enslaved and the powerful, it fit into a dozen
causes, movements, plots, and purposes. That was predictable, but
what was far more remarkable was that the blasphemous essence of
Brown's oration was not immediately denounced by more of the clergy
of the North. Some of them were so deluded as to hail John Brown as
fervently as did revolutionists, though with far less appreciation of the
inherent bloodiness of his message.

Brown's hanging was set for December 2, 1859, a date that allowed the
abolitionists a full month in which to indulge in an orgy of propaganda.
The delay alarmed and further angered the South, where serious
efforts to organize secession sprouted like so many dragon seeds.

Oddly enough, the abolitionist campaign of justification did not
influence Gerrit Smith, whose worry over his personal situation
swelled into an obsession. His son-in-law Charles D. Miller, a Harvard
graduate and classmate of the poet Lowell, had been diligent in seeking to cover the magnate's tracks. He appeared at Frank Sanborn's
residence in Concord soon after the schoolmaster returned from Canada, to demand whatever Smith letters he held. Sanborn assured him
they had all been destroyed. In return Miller told Sanborn that his
letters to Edwin Morton, the Smith family tutor and another party to
the conspiracy, were "buried under a brick in the broad walk leading
to Mr. Smith's hall-door."[30]

By that time Morton himself was buried, as far as the authorities
were concerned, almost as deeply. Having gone to the powerful New
York politician Thurlow Weed for advice, and having been told to
leave the country,[31] Morton had gone first to Canada and then sailed
for Europe. He would remain there—all expenses paid—until all was
well.

Meanwhile the millionaire, whose incessant diatribes against a civilization, in which he so conspicuously prospered, had inspired widespread dislike, was harassed by the newspapers. A reporter from the New York *Herald* (Sanborn called this antiabolitionist newspaper the "Satanic Press") observed that Smith refused to answer questions. "I am going to be indicted, sir, indicted!" Smith said testily. "You must not talk to me about it."[32]

Smith's appearance, noted the reporter, was "far different from what he was . . . His calm, dignified, impressive bearing has given way to a hasty, nervous, agitation, as though some great fear was constantly before his imagination. His eye is bloodshot and restless as that of a startled horse. He has lost flesh . . ."

On November 11, a few days after Brown was sentenced to be hanged, the Buffalo *Gazette* reported that Gerrit Smith,

> . . . ex-Member of Congress, has been confined in the Lunatic Asylum here since Monday last . . . It was only by strategem that his friends succeeded in getting him here. He has been, ever since the arrest of Brown . . . haunted with the idea that he was culpably responsible for all the lives that have and will be sacrificed . . . and the fear of being called on to answer at the bar of justice preyed on him . . . that his mind, never exempt from a tendency to be unhinged, gave way . . . For some days . . . he manifested a most nervous anxiety to anticipate the requisition . . . and to proceed to Virginia and surrender himself . . . His friends pretended to chime in with his notion, and when he set out for Utica he was under the impression he was on his way to Richmond or Charlestown . . .
>
> I am assured that . . . he is in no way implicated . . . That Gerrit Smith's case is one of decided lunacy is certain. Still his friends consider it far from hopeless . . .

In Virginia Brown's financiers were named in a confession by young, blond, talkative John E. Cook. Captured and returned to the Charlestown jail, Cook no doubt hoped for mercy through cooperation. The newspapers blazoned the names of the Six—all of whom Cook had cited. That shook Dr. Howe, cowering in Quebec with George Luther Stearns, and he issued a "card" dated November 14, 1859, headed "Boston."

> Rumor has mingled my name with the events at Harper's Ferry. So long as it rested on such absurdities as letters written to me by Col. Forbes, or others, it was too idle for notice. But when complicity is distinctly charged by one of the parties engaged, my friends beseech me to define my position . . . As regards Mr. Cook . . . I never saw him . . . never even heard of him until the outbreak at Harper's Ferry. That event was unforeseen and unexpected by me; nor does all my previous knowledge of John Brown enable me to reconcile it with his characteristic prudence and reluctance to shed blood, or excite servile insurrection. It is still, to me, a mystery and a marvel.

After these blatant lies, which astonished his Boston admirers, Howe then assumed, as was customary with his coterie, the mantles of lofty virtue.

As to the heroic man who planned and led that forlorn drive, if ever my testimony as to his high qualities can be of use to him or his, it shall be forthcoming at a fitting time and place.[33]

Then he cited "certain deadly instruments" among the statutes of the union that upheld slavery, and said that "high legal authority" had told him that "each one must protect himself as best he can."

Boston was appalled, and the New Orleans *Daily Picayune* jeered: "At the indistinct vision of a possible rope . . . the eulogist of another man's treason absconds . . ."[34]

On the same day that Howe's handwashing statement appeared, the black leader Frederick Douglass sailed for England. He left behind a statement that the Baltimore *Sun,* described as "a curiosity, a rare specimen of craven impudence."

That was far more lofty than the circumstances warranted. Douglass had no illusions about his fate in Virginia, and good reason to believe that he would be treated with far less caution than the famous Dr. Howe, the wealthy Gerrit Smith or any of the others of the Secret Six. Even in Canada he feared being kidnapped. He said later: "Slavery seemed to be at the very top of its power; the national government, with all its power and appliances, was in its hands."[35]

England—where Douglass had been feted and could lecture—was a sensible destination, though he had to leave his family behind in Rochester, and feared he would never be able to return. Nevertheless, his sense of humor appeared in his parting letter. "I have always been more distinguished for running than fighting," he said, "and by the Harper's Ferry test, I am most miserably deficient in courage." But he added: "I am ever ready to write, speak, publish or organize, combine or even to conspire against slavery when there is a reasonable chance of success."[36]

Higginson watched these various reactions with open scorn. He was especially tart with Dr. Howe: ". . . since language was first invented to conceal thoughts," he wrote Howe, giving a novel theory in passing, "there has been no more skillful combination of words."[37] Wounded, Howe wrote back that he was only trying to support Brown's own claim that "he was not the agent or the ally of others, but an individual acting on his own responsibility."[38]

Sanborn added his own rationale: "It was important that the really small extent of our movement should be concealed and its reach and character exaggerated."[39] Higginson was not placated. "Is there no such thing as *honor* among confederates?" he asked.[40]

But these were backstage disputes. The soaring rhetoric of Brown's courtroom statement on being sentenced to hang, and the rush of well-known names to his defense were altering the situation, in terms of the movement, from a fiasco to a triumph. Journalist James Redpath, married and living in Boston, still ardent, was hastily writing a book on John Brown. He also, with nearly incredible diligence, wrote a series of articles in the Boston *Atlas & Daily Bee,* called "Notes on the Insurrection."

Redpath, who boasted of his intimacy with Brown in Kansas, and who had traveled to Haiti with Francis Merriam to explore the history of successful black revolutions, cheered the prospect of Brown's hanging. "Living bravely, dying, he will teach us courage. A Samson in his life, he will be a Samson in his death. Let cowards ridicule and denounce him; let snake-like journalists hiss at his holy failure—for one, I do not hesitate to say that I love him, admire him, and defend him. God Bless Him!"[41]

Similar sentiments came from Rome, Italy, where Theodore Parker —waiting "for the *coupe de grace* which ends all my earthly troubles" and drinking "tumblers of asses milk"—wrote: "A man held against his will as a slave has a natural right to kill every one who seeks to prevent his enjoyment of liberty . . . The freeman has a natural right to help the slaves recover their liberty . . . and as a means to that end, to aid them in killing all such as oppose . . ."[42]

To these arguments, which ignored Brown's murder of men who neither held slaves nor had opposed him, the dying minister, who once dreamed of being another Luther, added: "It is said in the Democratic newspapers that Captain Brown had many friends in the North who . . . furnished him with some $20,000 . . . I think much more is true of us" He also wrote: "All the great charters of Humanity have been writ in blood."[43]

Despite the rhetorical flourish—and even though he knew his own life was ebbing—Parker did not admit his actual function in the John Brown abolition mill. Nor did it occur to him to return home and take the stand in Virginia.

Meanwhile Higginson and some others had come to different conclusions. They thought Captain Brown ought to *escape.*

The first efforts centered around a plan to lease a yacht to carry Brown out of the country, after an assault on the Charlestown jail by Kansas toughs including James Montgomery. That was discarded because of expense, and a second plan was conceived, using German refugees from their own abortive revolution of 1848. The Germans asked only one hundred dollars a man, and were confident of success but when Sanborn learned that two thousand dollars or three thousand dollars would be needed, he said: "Object abandoned."[44]

The fact was that as the month of November lengthened, Brown himself provided such wonderful letters and statements from his cell in Charlestown that it became clear that his escape would injure, and not improve, the vision being mounted in the North and in Europe.

In Boston Emerson, standing erect as always, lectured a respectful audience on courage, and mentioned John Brown, predicting he would be a favorite with history. He referred to Brown as "The Saint, whose fate yet hangs in suspense, but whose martyrdom, if it shall be perfected, will make the gallows as glorious as the Cross."[45] That made the linkage nearly official.

Reading this in his cell at Charlestown, the prisoner was quick to pick the clue. "Remember, dear wife and children all," he wrote, "that Jesus of Nazareth suffered a most excruciating death on the cross as a felon, under most aggravating circumstances. Think also of the prophets and apostles and Christians . . . May God comfort all your hearts, and soon wipe away all tears from your eyes. To Him be endless praise!"[46]

That letter and others of a similar tone poured from Brown's pen, were reprinted all over the North, and helped build one of the most curious funeral pyres ever constructed—in which the condemned was both an architect and one of the most assiduous builders. Comparisons of John Brown with Jesus began to be made by many persons in many places; letters poured in to newspapers and to the condemned from Quakers, from ministers, from ordinary citizens, and celebrities. Judge and Mrs. Russell, who had harbored Brown in Boston, appeared in Charlestown to visit him in his cell; Lydia Maria Child announced she was writing a book about Brown, and a Boston sculptor, Edwin A. Brackett, appeared—commissioned to immortalize Brown with a Grecian-style bust.[47]

In their clumsy way, Brown's men sought to emulate his stance. All of them—including Stevens—wrote long letters about the nobility of the cause for which they would die. Only Hazlett, caught in Pennsylvania and returned, remained silent—except to insist his real name was Harrison, and that he was innocent.

For the rest, the legend built rapidly. By the end of November the stage was set for the last act—the claques in place, the scenario complete. In Brooklyn the Rev. Henry Ward Beecher rose in his pulpit to say: "Let no man pray that Brown be spared. Let Virginia make him a martyr. His soul was noble, his work miserable. *But a cord and gibbett will redeem all that* and round up Brown's failure with a heroic success."[48]

In his jail cell, where someone sent him a copy of Beecher's sermon, the old man wrote on the margin: "Good."[49]

One letter arrived that the newspapers did not print. It was from Mahala Doyle, who was living in poverty in Chattanooga, Tennessee.

John Brown: Sir,—Altho vengeance is not mine I confess that I do feel gratified to hear that you were stopped in your fiendish career at Harper's Ferry, with the loss of your two sons, you can now appreciate my distress in Kansas, when you then and there entered my house at midnight and arrested my Husband and two boys, and took them out of the yard and in cold blood shot them dead in my hearing, you cant say you done it to free slaves, we had none and never expected to own one, but has only made me a poor disconsolate widow with helpless children, while I feel for your folly I do hope and trust you will meet your just reward. Oh how it pained my heart to hear the dying groans of my Husband and children, if this scrawl gives you any consolation you are welcome to it.[50]

Brown, whose egotism had soared high enough to make him feel equal to God, kept that letter among the others.

Brown's wife—whom Higginson and others were already using at rallies, demonstrations, and meetings—waited in Baltimore to receive her husband's body after the execution. She was permitted a visit on the old man's next to last day. The Hero lost his temper when she was not permitted to spend the night.

On December 2, 1859, he rose after having slept, in a calm mood. He wrote a few last-minute letters and set aside his old, heavily marked Bible for an admirer. Long after the tumult and the speeches had ended, the Reverend Abner C. Hopkins, a West Virginia clergyman, carefully examined Brown's underlinings. "No pencil mark," he said, "distinguishes or emphasizes a single passage that is distinctly Christian. He was religious but not Christian; religion was the crutch on which his fanaticism walked."[51]

At the time Brown set the Bible aside, he sent for Virginia prosecutor Andrew Hunter. Hunter answered the summons, no doubt from curiosity, and Brown said he wanted to make his will. Hunter began to instruct him, but Brown said he hadn't time. The dignified lawyer sat down, took a pen, and did the old man a final favor.[52] (There was a gesture on Brown's part as well: he had drawn a will the previous day, in which he left fifty dollars to the New England Woolen Company, from which he had embezzled far more.)

Then Brown said goodbye to his men, excepting Hazlett, who was still maintaining his foolish pretense to be an unattached stranger. And, even on the verge of death, Brown did not forget to reproach Cook for having told the truth about the enterprise.

His executioners came at 11:00 A.M. and tied his elbows. He was wearing a black suit that had been donated by admirers, a slouch hat, a cotton shirt, white woolen socks, and red bedroom slippers. He was conveyed to a field outside Charlestown in an open wagon, seated on his own black walnut coffin. En route, he said: "This is a very beautiful country."

Simultaneously, rallies and meetings were being held in the North; church bells were tolling and cannons being fired to commemorate Brown's "martyrdom."

A special scaffold had been built. The rope was contributed by Kentucky, and had previously been on display. The field was bare, even of a tree, so that the spot could not be fixed later and used as a landmark. The South knew it was hanging a man the North was hoisting to sainthood.

The old man went up the steps quickly and was immediately hooded, to prevent a platform speech: Governor Wise had finally learned that Brown could use such opportunities to great effect. Hooded, with the rope around his neck, Brown was kept waiting for several minutes while troops maneuvered into position. They included cadets from the Virginia Military Academy, and one of the academy instructors, Professor Thomas J. (Stonewall) Jackson. John Wilkes Booth was among the militiamen from Richmond. Otherwise, none but special guests had been allowed near the scene, but people could be seen clustered in the distance.

The hatchet came down on the rope, the trap sprang, and John Brown dropped, then dangled—freed at last of his compulsions. In front of the scaffold, Colonel J.T.L. Preston shouted from his horse: "So perish all such enemies of Virginia! All such enemies of the Union! All such enemies of the human race!"

After a long wait the physicians made an examination and said the criminal was dead. Wrote Richard Hinton: "While the body was hanging David S. Strother, known as Porte Crayon of *Harper's Weekly* a member of Prosecutor Hunter's party, raised the cap from his [Brown's] face and took a sketch . . . He said that the celebrated Lydia Maria Child had published that she wanted a portrait or likeness of Brown in every condition of life to hang in her room and that he had taken this sketch to send her, that 'she might have him, too, when it was finished.' "[53]

Part V
CURTAIN CALL

Chapter 41

The horizon became alight with fire, and billowing clouds of hatred darkened the land. Nowhere were those fires and smoking pillars more searing and blacker than in the South. Its people were first amazed and then driven into fury by the Northern elevation of John Brown. Revelations that his raid had been incited, financed, and armed by famous persons in the North, and that other Northerners rose to praise the terror he created, imbued the people of the South with fear—and with a rising realization that something new and dangerous in racial conflicts was upon them.

"John Brown's effort was peculiar," said Abraham Lincoln. "It was not a slave insurrection. It was an attempt by white men to get a revolt among slaves . . ."[1]

It was that peculiarity the white Southerners found inexplicable and sinister. The idea that men of their own race would kill them on behalf of another had never really been credible to them, until Harper's Ferry. Until then they had scorned the Northern concern for black slaves as a cloak for political power. The abolitionist clergy and its attempt to paint all the people of the South as Christian pariahs had not shaken the Scotch-Irish inheritors of the faith of John Knox; they knew better. But when white men were shot dead in the streets of Harper's Ferry, and the murderers held aloft as examples of a higher law, the South felt itself at bay.

From rostrums and in editorials, in conversations and letters, the Southerners agreed that Harper's Ferry was merely a harbinger of more raids to come. Led by whites, financed and armed by the North, directed by men safe in Northern sanctuaries, these raids would strike against plantations and homes alike, to create a guerrilla war unpredictable in its pattern, perilous to the safety of all white Southerners.

The White House, Congress, and the Supreme Court had proved unable to prevent the rise of this threat; unable to deter such voices as those of Joshua Giddings, who had publicly looked forward to the time "when the torch of the incendiary shall light up the towns and cities of the South, and blot out the last vestiges of slavery";[2] unable to quiet the piercing shrieks of Garrison who had, at the time of the Kansas troubles, called for the shooting of all slaveholders, and said "Who will go for the arming of our slave population?"[3]

Seward's speech, and his comments on an irrepressible conflict; the

orations of Emerson and Thoreau, of Wendell Phillips, and Senator
Charles Sumner; the sermons and the tracts; the subsidized distribution of Helper's Book, *The Impending Crisis;* all these things were a
virtually unanswerable argument that the North was preparing to destroy the white South, in the name of the blacks.

In that climate, which resembled that of a separate nation threatened
with invasion from without and rebellion from within, Southerners
tightened their controls over slaves. They barred the movements of
free blacks. They censored the mails, and sought to drive all Northerners out of their midst. Harmless commercial travelers were forbidden
to continue their sales routes, transplanted Yankees were threatened,
ostracized, tarred and feathered, and jailed. The secessionist plotters
gloated in a turn of the tide that led toward their goals.

The Southern siege-moves seemed faint and distant to a world whose
attention was drawn toward the unprecedented display of grief
mounted in the North over John Brown's hanging. When the train
carrying his coffin arrived at Philadelphia it was met by a large, emotional crowd, including the congregation of the Shiloh Baptist Colored
Church. The mayor feared violence and told Mrs. Brown the body
should not be embalmed in his city. A hearse, in which a long covered
toolbox had been placed, drove away from the station and satisfied the
onlookers, while the real coffin was placed in a furniture van and driven
to a dock to be shipped to New York City by boat.[4]

In that city Brown's body was embalmed by McGraw & Taylor; the
Southern coffin was exchanged for one of Northern wood. A wake was
held, and attended by many prominent persons. Then the funeral
party traveled to Troy and more elegiac orgies, then to Rutland, Vermont, and across Lake Champlain, and, finally, to the bleak farmhouse
at North Elba where John Brown had foresightedly placed his grandfather's headstone.

For the duration of this long journey, the North indulged in a frenzy
of mourning far greater than any ever before seen. Its intensity rose
like a rocket on the day of Brown's hanging, and remained high over
the Northern skies for weeks. Buildings in Cleveland were draped in
black; black-bordered poems and elegies appeared in newspapers;
sermons were preached in hundreds of pulpits; rallies, demonstrations, and special prayer meetings were held. Echoes were heard in
Europe—from conspiratorial and liberal circles, from minorities in
empires, and from exiles. Victor Hugo, banished from France but
enjoying life on the island of Guernsey with three mistresses, sketched
an obscure, hanging figure meant to represent all the oppressed of the
world, and wrote a statement characterizing slavery as "a great crime
by a great people."[5]

In Concord, which repeated the mourning meetings held throughout small towns across the North, Emerson—flanked by Thoreau and
Alcott and respectfully followed by two or three lesser local celebrities
—presided over a ceremony in which poems and elegies were read,

and a dirge, composed by Sanborn, was sung by the citizens. In many places militia assembled to fire salutes into the air while church bells tolled, as though for the passing of a great and revered national leader.

Moderates, alarmed by the reaction of both North and South, hastily mounted demonstrations—"union" meetings—to recall and extoll the bonds that held the nation together. Organized and attended by businessmen and civic leaders, these were impressive on the surface. A massive meeting at Faneuil Hall was addressed by Caleb Cushing and Edward Everett; another was held in New York City, at which Mayor Tiemann, John A. Dix, and Washington Hunt spoke. But the South was not impressed. Those in the North who now deplored excess, and who had disregarded former President Pierce's warnings that Northern agitators harbored revolutionary purposes, had waited too long and said too little during thirty years of agitation.

And even as the civic leaders were belatedly speaking for national unity, a John Brown cult was rising as from the ground. No count can be made of the snippets of rope sold as part of the original used to hang the Hero—though the authorities had taken the precaution of burning the original against that very possibility. Splinters of wood, purportedly from the scaffold, were also sold—although the real timbers belonged to a Charlestown carpenter, who later used them to make a porch. Tracts describing the "Life and Trial of Captain Brown," transcripts of the examination and of interviews, lithographs, drawings, fables, recollections of associates and old friends—all these gushed in a manner remeniscent of the Middle Ages, its relics, charms and amulets. The Brown cult in fact manifested the spread of what intellectuals had earlier called the "New England Religion," which now reached the level of the common denominator, and was converting a host of followers—who came to regard antislavery as equal to salvation.

Their fervor created enormous clamor at a time when the Democratic newspapers nearly outshouted the Southerners in their effort to fasten the blame for Harper's Ferry upon the Republican Party. Lincoln kept saying "John Brown was not a Republican!"[6] But it was hard for the party to shake its connection with Joshua Giddings, Senator Seward, Sumner and all its other stentorian abolitionists. In the South there was no doubt of Republican responsibility for events: the term "Black Republican" entered the language as if by magic.

Three days after Brown was hanged, Congress met in a nearly revolutionary atmosphere. "A reign of terror opened on the lower South" according to a British consul.[7] While Southern meetings on secession were being held, abolitionism in the North was being carried beyond the hands of the coterie of the Secret Six, the Emigrant Aid organizers, Garrison, Phillips, and others—into the political arena. In the House the caustic Thaddeus Stevens poured acid into gaping Southern wounds, and tensions rose higher every day. Within the first weeks, the possibility of riot in both chambers loomed imminent. Senator Hammond said: "the only persons who do not have a revolver and a knife are those that have two revolvers."[8]

The Senate passed a motion to open an inquiry on Harper's Ferry and Dr. Samuel Gridley Howe—who had crept back to Boston the day of Brown's hanging—ran to Senator Sumner for advice. The Senator, whose silence did not wipe away his introduction of Colonel Forbes to Higginson, or his close relationship with the Secret Six, advised Howe he had nothing to worry about; "the Massachusetts Committee" would be protected.

In large measure that "protection" was provided by Republican politicians anxious to prove the party had nothing to do with John Brown. Great efforts were made to insist that Brown was a lone operator, a sort of holy confidence man whose uncanny powers of persuasion and patterns of secrecy misled substantial citizens who gave him money while ignorant of his real purposes. When the New York *Herald* printed letters from Forbes proving the opposite, a campaign was mounted to vilify Forbes as an unscrupulous, down-at-the-heels European adventurer. Back in Italy and in command of a fortress near Messina, Sicily, Forbes was so discredited by that barrage that his Italian comrades drew away from him.[9] He died soon afterwards.

Despite that formidable demonstration against Forbes, Frank Sanborn remained terrified of being called to testify. He threatened to expose Senator Wilson's knowledge of the Brown venture unless he was spared that ordeal.[10] He also wrote hysterical letters to Higginson, saying in part, "there are a thousand better ways of spending a year in warfare against Slavery than by lying in a Washington prison," and adding, "I hope you burn all my letters about these things."[11]

The Mason hearings began in mid-December 1859, and continued intermittently for nearly six months. The scope of the Inquiry was limited to the Harper's Ferry raid. The choice of witnesses was whimsical, for while George Luther Stearns and Dr. Samuel Gridley Howe were called to testify, Higginson—who thirsted for the honor—was ignored.

The former shadow "Governor" of Kansas, Charles Robinson, was also called. He discussed various conspiratorial and bloody events in the territory, but his testimony was largely stricken. Richard Reaf, the English poet, had been discovered in Texas; at the hearing he spoke at length about his membership in Brown's fantasy government. Augustus Wattles appeared, and so did Senators Wilson and Seward, who gave some guarded statements about Forbes' warnings and revelations. Nothing really new was unearthed, and much that was provocative was either stricken from the record or left unexplored. Howe and Stearns, both severely moralistic about other men, distinguished themselves by lying under oath. So did the highly placed Senators Wilson and Seward. So, for that matter, did most of the other witnesses, with the exceptions of the innocent Harper's Ferry witnesses and Richard Realf.

Gerrit Smith, secure inside the lunatic asylum—where he had been joined by his wife and enjoyed both carriage rides and gracious dinners with the administrators during his brief weeks of peril—was released as the hearings proceeded. He proudly announced his willingness to appear and testify—if his doctors approved. They did not.

By June 1860, when the Inquiry ended, it had succeeded in establishing the only event that could not be denied: the Harper's Ferry raid. The connections between Brown and the Secret Six were left as undisturbed as possible. The reasons did not lie so much in lack of intelligence on the part of Senator Mason and his Southern colleagues, so much as in the backdrop of the political maneuverings under way in the nation.

There was a presidential election due in November, and on its outcome hinged the fate of the nation. There were men in Congress and throughout the country who hoped for the best, while others not only prepared but planned for the worst. Some were sincere in their belief that the nation could not, as Lincoln had said, endure so divided. Others were intent upon proving that proposition.

Had it not been for President Buchanan and his cohorts in the Democratic party, there is a possibility that the crisis could have been delayed. The leading Democratic contender was Senator Stephen A. Douglas, and he was capable of accepting a diverse country, of fighting for local rights, and of rising above sectional and cultural disputes. With a Southern, slaveholding wife and a Northern background of his own, Douglas believed that the West and its golden opportunities would make slavery obsolete without effort, and would swing the nation into more productive and unified paths.

Therefore the Democratic secessionists of the South and the Democratic abolitionists of the North had to deny Douglas the nomination. A tide of bile rose against him; stronger even than the attacks on him during the tides of the Kansas troubles; it remains to stain his name and distort his position to this day. However, the Democratic party might have surmounted its extremists had not President Buchanan— who hated Douglas with the implacable and unreasoning hatred of a smaller man for a larger—thrown the weight of his interests and cohorts against the Illinois senator. In effect, the Douglas controversy split the Democratic party, and left the Republicans dominant in the North. From there the course of events in the summer of 1860 ran irresistibly toward war.

Long before that, and even before the Mason Hearings were concluded, the Rev. Theodore Parker had grown weary of the bickering in his apartment in Rome and climbing its one hundred twenty steps. He had grown to hate the Eternal City. Its recollections, inherent in its stones, of the mortality of individuals and the immense sweep of time, must have seemed nearly unendurable.

Still writing interminable letters almost to the end, and feverish for the war against slavery to occur, he moved to Florence in April 1860. "Out of the Papal States," he recorded.[12] Then he sank into melancholia. Great events were under way at home; a collision for which

Parker had grown to long was almost at hand but in May 1860 he died offstage.

Emerson was reluctant to speak at a Boston Memorial meeting for Parker. Nevertheless, he knew he was associated in the public mind with the famous minister, and he managed a few graceful, kindly phrases for his former brother in the clergy.

It was a summer whose beauty appeared more enchanting against the backdrop of sinister trends. Hawthorne returned from England, where he had read with horror of Emerson's having coupled the name of John Brown with that of Jesus. "Nobody," he said firmly, "was ever more justly hanged." Nevertheless he was served strawberries and cream in the luxuriant Emerson garden, with Thoreau and Alcott appearing to honor him.[13]

Emerson was beyond deigning to notice passing comments such as Hawthorne's, but they did not remain unobserved. Young William Dean Howells, arriving in Concord in August 1860 to pay homage, heard Emerson dismiss Hawthorne's *Marble Faun* as "mere mush," and call Edgar Allan Poe "the Jingle-Man."[14]

Emerson seemed to have the best of both worlds. His name was hailed on both sides of the Atlantic, and he had become a literary rarity, being esteemed even by the nonliterary world. When James Redpath produced his jumble of fables disguised as a biography of John Brown, he dedicated it to "Wendell Phillips, Ralph Waldo Emerson and Henry D. Thoreau, Members of the Faithful who, when the mob shouted Madman! said, Saint!"

Redpath was not wrong about his pantheon: he knew the movers. Lincoln's nomination was regarded by abolitionists as a defeat: they preferred Seward, whom they considered more ardent against slavery. Of Lincoln, Emerson asked icily: "Who is this country court advocate?" Wendell Phillips went further, and called Lincoln "The Slave-Hound of Illinois."

But by the time the election results arrived, Emerson decided they were "sublime." In the "secession winter" of 1860 he appeared at the Tremont Temple and disappointed the antislavery zealots, who wanted the South to secede, by speaking for the Union and for war. His instincts were, as always, nearly unerring: Emerson rode the tides and trends of his times as easily as a gull on the water.

Other and far more ardent workers, though much less celebrated, made the same easy, almost subconscious transition. Theodore Weld, his wife Angelina, and his sister-in-law Sarah had retired to their farm in New Jersey. From there, in the early 1850's they had joined a venture to create a model community, religious but nonsectarian, dedicated to self-support and education. Weld, who liked teaching, was to run the school, Eagleswood. (For a time he had William Ellery Channing's former secretary, Elizabeth Peabody, as his assistant.) Located at the conjoining of the Raritan river and bay, twenty-five miles from New York with a beautiful view of the water, Eagleswood boarded students of both sexes.

When the school met difficulties, Weld began to exchange notes with Adin Ballou, the Christian anarchist whose colony, Hopedale, was also having trouble. Both agreed—at last—that the communal principle, ideal in the abstract, was impossible in reality, for it always crashed on the selfishness and indolence of those who shirked their share.[15] Then Weld's school began to prosper independently. Gerrit Smith sent his son, who turned out to be a drinker. Augustus Wattles sent a daughter, Henry B. Stanton a son.

Through the 1850's his establishment became a weekend center. William Cullen Bryant, editor of the New York *Post* and Horace Greeley of the *Tribune* visited; so too did coveys of Unitarian clergy: Reverends James Freeman Clarke, William Henry Channing, Octavius B. Frothingham, Edwin Chapin, Reverend Beriah Green, and even Thoreau.[16] The school was influential and marked by a commingling of all the avant-garde ideas—women's suffrage, working rights, eradication of social illnesses, temperance, and, of course, antislavery. The Reverend William Ellery Channing, in whose Concord home Sanborn had lived, believed in complete equality of all people; the Reverend Henry Bellows, another regular, launched Antioch College and headed the U.S. Sanitary Commission—a forerunner of the Red Cross—in the Civil War. Bronson Alcott was a frequent visitor; these were Alcott's people—until his daughter wrote *Little Women* and finally made enough for the family to stop begging.

Eagleswood played a role behind the scenes during the fifties; it contributed money to Kansas and, more than money, inspiration. In March 1860, Mrs. Marcus Spring, wife of one of the founders of the establishment, went to see John Brown in his cell at Charlestown; there, she impulsively offered a burial place to Stevens, and to the murderer Hazlett.

All of the Welds suffered through the trial and execution of the Hero; Angelina was so stricken she took to her bed. But the elections roused them and by the time Lincoln took office and Fort Sumter was fired on, they were ardent for the Union, and the fight against white Southerners. Weld's great disappointment was that his son, Charles Stuart Weld, was a conscientious objector.

A similar transformation overtook Gerrit Smith, who had evaded the Mason Hearings through the intercession of his doctors. In the fall of 1860 some New York Democrats accused him of being a behind-the-scene conspirator of Harper's Ferry, and Smith hired Lysander Spooner to sue them. Spooner, who also had been privy to the plot, discovered the accusers were of only modest means and had no proof. He forced them to issue a retraction in newspapers across the country. In the eyes of Gerrit Smith, that amounted to a public exoneration.

He moved through the post-election glow, believed that the Republican President would immediately free all slaves and give them the plantations upon which they had once worked, and joined the radical abolitionist movement as a patriot.

In Medford, Massachusetts, George Luther Stearns, jubilant at passing through the Mason Hearings without injury—as he thought—plunged into politics with the other members of the Bird Club. The group promoted lawyer John A. Andrews for governor and he was elected. The Bird Club moved into importance; Stearns moved with it. During the "secession winter" he was in Washington, accompanied by Howe, to confer with Senators Wilson and Sumner. Theirs was now the war party, and Massachusetts made ready. In the fading days of Buchanan's administration, it appeared that a compromise might still be possible; this alarmed Stearns, and he sent a telegram to Sumner, opposing the "surrender of the North." Sumner's reply was *"No possible compromise or concession will be of the least avail."*[17] Their personal dangers over, they were bold as lions.

Howe crossed the meridian with more private anguish. His behavior following the Harper's Ferry raid had been inglorious, if not almost cowardly. His flight to Canada was only less widely noticed than was his "card" disavowing any connection with John Brown. That was hard to shake or explain. Howe found Higginson's scorn particularly painful to endure. All the Secret Six had agreed, when they sent Brown on his mission, that they would not deny their role, no matter what happened. All—except Parker, who was out of the country, and Higginson, who denied the purpose of the raid though not his support of it—had broken their word. Howe crept back to Boston on the day that John Brown was hanged. He met a cold wife, disappointed in his behavior, and his spirits were not notably improved by the immense eulogies and praise the North was showering on the Martyr. In December 1859, a letter arrived from Senator Wilson warning that a Senate subpoena had to be obeyed or arrest could follow. The doctor again bolted to Canada. There he compared the United States Senate to the Austrian police, but denied that he was again in flight. He was in Canada, he said, to speak to the Canadian Parliament on behalf of the blind.[18]

He did, however, appear before the Mason hearing and lied. The balance of the year 1860 was miserable for him. When Parker died in Italy and his brain was sent to him, Dr. Howe put it on the top shelf of a cupboard, where it remained for many years, as a sort of macabre memento.

During the "secession winter," after Lincoln's election, when the mass of people, even in Boston, had not yet been convinced the South was worth a war and Wendell Phillips was so often threatened that his safety was in danger, Howe served as part of the orator's volunteer bodyguard. By that time he was beginning to recover his nerve. His own days of danger appeared safely over, at least as far as John Brown was concerned. His views toward the South, which had warmed slightly after he and Julia visited Charleston, had returned to their original marble. By the beginning of 1861, like George Luther Stearns, Gerrit

Smith, Theodore Weld, and his other associates—especially in the Secret Six—Howe was all for war and the reduction of Southern whites at any cost.

Frank Sanborn reflected his older associates as accurately as a mirror. Returning from Canada after his first flight, he fled again when he heard about the Mason hearing. Coaxed to return, he threatened to publicize Senator Wilson's knowledge of the Harper's Ferry plot unless he was protected. Arrested in Concord by four bailiffs from Boston acting for the Senate in April 1860, he resisted. Being six feet four inches tall and athletically built, he could do so. Later, he said: "I placed my feet against the posts and delayed them. I did the same at the posts of veranda. Meanwhile the church bells were ringing a fire alarm and people gathering by the tens. At the stone posts of the gateway I checked their progress once more, and it was some minutes before they got me on the gravel walk at the foot of my stone steps. At the stone posts of the gateway I checked their progress once more, and again, when the four rascals lifted to insert me in their carriage . . ."[19] Meanwhile a crowd collected and the entire village of Concord rallied to Sanborn's side. Old Colonel Whiting appeared to beat the horses of the bailiff's carriage, and Miss Whiting began to drive the carriage off. A lawyer also appeared, then scurried off to Judge Hoar for a writ of habeas corpus, which was issued at once. A deputy sheriff, armed with the writ, secured Sanborn's release. When the bailiffs refused, the sheriff made everyone in the crowd part of his *posse comitatus* and Sanborn was forcibly rescued.

That lifted his status. Subsequent court arguments in Massachusetts ruled his arrest warrant was defective. By that time the danger from the larger issues of the Harper's Ferry incident had passed.

It was the Reverend Thomas Wentworth Higginson who courted such episodes, and who was neither sought nor summoned nor threatened. He beckoned danger, but it evaded him. On the occasion of the antislavery meeting in Tremont Temple in Boston, when Phillips had been subjected to catcalls and unable to speak, and Emerson himself had been similarly drowned out, Higginson managed to say a few words. He contributed toward the war effort by writing an article in praise of Vesey's rebellion of 1822; the magazine was reluctant to print it.

In April 1861, when war did break out, Higginson was jubilant. They were all jubilant: Gerrit Smith, Frank Sanborn, George Luther Stearns, Emerson, Thoreau, Garrison, Phillips, Weld, and the rest. Of course, they thought it would be short, and none of them—except Howe, in his early youth—had ever seen a war, or any real violence.

The legal case for slavery had been made, and the Supreme Court had agreed. In his inaugural remarks the new President said "if the policy of the Government, on the vital questions affecting the whole people, is to be irrevocably fixed by decisions of the Supreme Court, the instant they are made in ordinary litigation between parties in personal actions, the people will have ceased to be their own rulers, having to that extent practically resigned their Government into the hands of that eminent tribunal."[20]

Mr. Lincoln wrote his own speeches and chose his own words. The Chief Justice of the United States, Roger Brooke Taney, who had handed down the Dred Scott decision, soon learned what that meant. In May 1861, the President suspended writs of habeas corpus. The Supreme Court, ignoring that order, issued such a writ, commanding the appearance of John Merryman, a prominent Baltimorean, who was being held in Fort McHenry by General George Cadwalader.

The General refused to give up his prisoner; Taney issued an attachment against him for contempt, and sent a federal marshal to serve it. The marshal was not allowed inside Fort McHenry. He returned to the Court to report his failure, and found the frail, eighty-four-year-old Chief Justice "sitting on a bench surrounded by a group of interested auditors. The afternoon was a gloomy one and the voice of Taney could scarcely be heard, so that the listeners gathered closer and closer ..."[21] Taney said Merryman's imprisonment was unlawful, because the President had no authority under the Constitution to suspend habeas corpus, nor to authorize a military officer to arrest and detain a citizen not subject to the rules of war; it was the duty of such an officer to turn a prisoner over immediately to civil authorities. He said he would put that in writing, and he did. Lincoln—who Taney observed had not "bothered to give notice to the courts of justice, or to the public by proclamation or otherwise"—ignored the Court.

The Court continued to meet but its business was, clearly, minor. Its decisions could only be said to have been relevant if they supported the wartime government; otherwise they were disregarded. Taney grew thinner and more frail, and privately railed against the President. In 1864 he could no longer attend to his duties and sat in bed, smoking cigars, discussing events with clarity. He died that year, in October, eighty-seven years old, at a time when the dream of Washington and Jefferson was in tatters, unaware to the end that he had been one of the architects of its ruin.

The others proudly played their new roles. Higginson, who dropped his reverence before the war, finally entered the Union Army as Colonel of a black regiment.[22] Filling that roster was not easy; James Montgomery, the freebooter of Kansas, was also a colonel of black troops. Neither saw any memorable action but both were involved in various skirmishes. Dr. Howe helped create the U.S. Sanitary Commission whose other members included Wolcott Gibbs, a chemistry professor at Harvard, and Frederick Law Olmsted. He did well; it was the sort of work for which he was suited.

He took Julia to Washington; she was now adoring again and Howe himself was restored as manly and heroic. They were invited to a review, and on returning to the capital found their carriage surrounded by troops. To while away the time they sang songs, including

an old Methodist hymn to which the troops—somewhere, somehow—
had put words:

> John Brown's body lies a mouldering in the ground;
> His soul is marching on . . .

The Reverend James Freeman Clarke, ardent abolitionist and friend
of them all, said: "Mrs. Howe, why do you not write some good words
for that stirring tune?"[23]
That night she awoke in her hotel—it was sometime before dawn—
and the poem began to come to her. She waited until the stanzas were
finished, then got out of bed in her nightgown and "found in the
dimness an old stump of a pen and scrawled the verses almost without
looking at the paper;" this was a trick she had learned when her
children were infants and a light might have awakened them. Then she
went back to bed and fell asleep.
Later the poem appeared in *The Atlantic,* but attracted little notice.
Finally Chaplain McCabe, newly released from Libby Prison, told how
he and other prisoners had used Julia's words to that former hymn of
peace, and it began to travel through the land.
That was only right. Her words, which hailed the coming of war as
holy, recalled grapes of wrath, and equated the sacrifice of Jesus with
the fight against slavery, were a hymn for the New England religion of
which she, her husband, and their coterie were all faithful members.[24]

Lincoln echoed the same faith at Gettysburg, where he ascribed the
founding principles of the nation to the Declaration of Independence
—a product of wartime propaganda—and linked the ancient and awesome words "consecrate" and "hallow" and "new birth" to the political ideals of the movement.
These were warlike ideals dedicated to forcing all men into the same
mold. They carried the leaders of the movement upward during the
conflict. George Luther Stearns became politically important and
helped muster black troops. Jim Lane of Kansas became a U.S. senator.
John Brown's old comrade in raids, James Montgomery, committed
such atrocities as a colonel commanding black troops during the war
that his promotion to brigadier general, and Francis Merriam's promotion beyond captain, were withdrawn.
Frank Sanborn did not go to war. Instead he became editor of the
Springfield *Republican* and, through John A. Andrews, abolitionist wartime governor of Massachusetts. He was also secretary of the state
board of charities, from which post he helped plan the lives and conditions of orphans, the deaf, prisoners, and the insane.
Gerrit Smith, stridently patriotic during the war, helped organize
"Loyal Leagues" to "promote unconditional loyalty to the Govern-
ment of the United States."
Even the Sage of Concord found the drums of war to his liking. "If

it costs ten years, and ten to recover the general prosperity," he said, "the destruction of the South is worth so much." At an abolitionist meeting in Boston in early 1863 he recited a poem that presaged the radical Republican postwar policy.

> Pay ransom to the owner
> And fill the bag to the brim,
> Who is the owner? The slave is owner
> And ever was. Pay him. [25]

Emerson even joined the Union Club; all the "disunionists" were Unionists during the war. He disdained Lincoln. He thought the President should remember "that humanity in a ruler does not consist of running hither and thither to stop the execution of a deserter."[26]

For all his fabled intuition, the Sage did not see any connection between the introduction of terror as a political weapon by Brown and the Six, and the use of the same methods, though from a different vantage, by the terrorist John Wilkes Booth, the first man to murder an American president.

What the leaders of the movement did grasp and hoist aloft was the image of Lincoln as a martyr as shining as John Brown. At a commemorative meeting at Concord for the slain President, Emerson said the Gettysburg Address "will not easily be surpassed by words on any recorded occasion. This, and one other American speech, that of John Brown to the court that tried him, and a part of Kossuth's speech at Birmingham, can only be compared to each, and with no fourth."[27]

Placing Lincoln in the pantheon with the two revolutionaries, and especially beside John Brown, set a tone that was, ever after, faithfully followed.

A half-million dead and a million crippled was a heavy price, but the people paid even more. The South was in ruins and the relations between the races disrupted beyond words, while the voice of *The Liberator,* Garrison, said the antislavery cause was won. The other abolitionists, with the exception of Wendell Phillips, agreed. They had argued for a generation that the blacks needed only freedom to build their own lives as did other free men; for them that was enough.

But abolition was, despite the Reconstruction, only part of what the war had wrought. New England had lost the flower of its manhood, and its unique character, two hundred years in the making, lay in ruins less visible but no less real than the ruin of the South. Thousands of farms were masterless and "fifty thousand extra women in Massachusetts alone" would dominate New England culture for a generation.[28]

Immigrants had poured into the North all through the war; these tides rose to floods as victory led to an orgy of change at the top—an orgy marked by corruption. The vision of Stephen A. Douglas, who died in 1861, became a reality as the nation surged west to build cities connected by railroads, heavy with factories, peopled with every ethnic group from Europe.

The dominant spirit in this new social order was fierce competition; men drove for wealth, power, and prestige. Postwar disillusion ran deep and savage; noble sentiments became sentimental in women and a cause for laughter in men. Literature sank to the level of ladies' novels, to which Thomas Wentworth Higginson—now calling himself "colonel"—contributed. The stature of the others in the Secret Six similarly dwindled.

George Luther Stearns of the mighty beard and the open wallet died in 1867; Emerson appeared and contributed a few words: "He has done well; is that not saying all?"[29] Gerrit Smith, who prided his reputation above all, endured the humiliation of being exposed, at last, by the Chicago *Tribune,* not so much as a conspirator at Harper's Ferry —that was not held against him—but as a coward and a liar in the raid's aftermath.

The magnate continued, diminuendo, until 1874. In his last year he returned to the Methodist Church, but not to its teachings. As late as 1938, the pastor, Rev. David Keppell could still recall Smith's tall, portly, imposing presence with its aura of great power and wealth.

Higginson went on to write innumerable books; when his wife Mary Channing died, he happily remarried. For a time, he was held high as a literary critic and he made Henry James miserable with his carping imputation that James was not a true American. He thought Emily Dickinson a mediocre poet, altered her lines, and was appalled when this exposed his own deficiency of taste. He was active for the rights of women—though not of Blacks—and other causes until his death in 1911.

Frank Sanborn, whose books centered on those he knew from his brief days in the literary summer of New England, reminisced forever about Emerson, Hawthorne, Thoreau, and others—but especially about John Brown. He left a long and mendacious record about Brown, was notably malicious toward those with whom he differed, but drew some interesting portraits, done in loving colors, about those with whom he agreed. Up to his death in 1917, he was active on behalf of women's rights, prohibition, trade unionism, and allied causes.

By the time he was seventy, Dr. Samuel Gridley Howe stopped dyeing his beard and let his hair grow long. He abandoned the state charities to Sanborn, and sank toward helplessness. Julia tended him, though the task kept her tied down—a condition she never liked. In June 1876 with awesome appropriateness, he was stricken blind and dumb by a stroke that presaged his death.

In the end, as in the beginning, Emerson remained the totem of the coterie. But the war brought him down a considerable distance from his pedestal and even after its conclusion he found it hard to "get the hate out of his system."[30] He spoke for a savage peace, and contradicted the poses of a lifetime.

Elected a Harvard overseer, he could barely read from the podium and Leslie Stephens, hearing him for the first time, thought he was "rambling and incoherent." His eyes were going. God placed upon him a remarkable penalty: Emerson lost his memory, so slowly and so subtly that it was long before he realized the gravity of his condition. He accepted lecture dates but could no longer create new material; he delivered lines composed years earlier and pasted them together in new sequences, but his audiences had changed. In Chicago one listener described him as quaint: "dressed in clerical garb and wearing his hair long."[31]

He struggled feebly. His daughter thought to revive him abroad, but he knew better than to appear in quick-witted London. He chose Egypt instead, and thought he saw in brownness some special human qualities his own race lacked. The trip did not halt or slacken his decline; by 1881 he was on earth but no longer a reasoning part of humanity. The man who called himself "a transparent eyeball" in early manhood, and who longed to merge his soul with the physical world of his senses, at last got his wish. In 1882, alarming his family by aimless and lost walks, he wandered too long in the rain and contracted pneumonia, from which he died—still so restless he had to be heavily sedated to the end.

The movement continued. It had channeled all its reforming efforts before the war against slavery; afterward it branched into prohibition, trade unionism, socialism, anarchism, and other causes. The Secret Six had not been its originators but its followers. They represented its underside.

They were, of course, fools. Their rejection of the accumulated wisdom of the human race led them to repeat ancient follies, and to inspire others down grisly paths toward goals they considered noble. Their tactics were closely watched from Europe, and later emulated. Nietzsche would echo Emerson's comment that men without ethics behaved "as though God is dead," and Tolstoy would take his Christiantinged anarchism and communality from Adin Ballou's books on Hopedale,[32] the revolutionists of Europe would draw comfort from the efforts and results of John Brown. To them he became a sacred fool.

The movement for which he became a symbol has not yet ended; it continues to imperil religion and confuse millions. As in the case of John Brown and the Secret Six, its rhetoric is lofty and its methods base, but—despite noisy triumphs—its destiny is doomed by its dead fruit.

Notes

SECTION I

Chapter 1

1. Oswald Garrison Villard, *John Brown 1800–1859* (Boston: Houghton Mifflin, 1910), p. 154.
2. Ibid. p. 158.
3. Cf. Howard Report Appendix, *ex parte* testimony, 1193; Villard, op. cit. p. 159.
4. James C. Malin, *John Brown and the Legend of Fifty-Six* (Philadelphia: The American Philosophical Society, 1942), p. 385.
   Dr. Malin, who explored John Brown's career in Kansas with a thoroughness that has enraged propagandists, especially Marxists ones, quotes George Grant—a young settler who knew the Brown boys, saw them leave on their murder mission, and spoke to them afterward—as saying, "it was the current story that Brown shot Doyle but personally did nothing more . . ."

   In later letters and various contradictory statements the Brown sons did their best to exonerate their father and only reluctantly admitted even his presence at the murders. Salmon tried to throw the blame on Wiener, and Townsley sought to clear himself by saying he was forced to accompany the party but did not strike a blow. It is habitual for group murderers to blame one another. Somebody had to strike the first blow, and that is the leader's responsibility. In this instance "the current story" fits the personalities involved far more credibly than their lies and later attempts at cover-ups.
5. Cf. Howard Report Appendix, *ex parte* testimony, 1197–1198; Villard, op. cit. pp. 161–162.
6. Malin, op. cit. p. 675; and Villard, op. cit., pp. 162–164.
7. Malin, op. cit., pp. 674–678, covers a fascinating account of Glanville, who was later shot by free-staters, but recovered. The quote on p. 677, is from James Christian, a free-stater and lawyer, who was, for a time, a partner of James Lane.
8. Villard, op. cit., p. 164.

Chapter 2

1. Tilden G. Edelstein, *Strange Enthusiasm: A Life of Thomas Wentworth Higginson* (New Haven: Yale University Press, 1968), p. 155.
2. Oscar Sherwin, *Prophet of Liberty: The Life and Times of Wendell Phillips* (New York: Bookman Associates, 1958), p. 323.
3. Edelstein, op. cit. p. 155.
4. Ibid. p. 156.
5. Ibid. p. 157.
6. Sherwin, op, cit. p. 320. Cf. *The Liberator*, XXIV, June 2, 1854.
7. Sherwin, pp. 326–327.
8. Edelstein, op. cit. pp. 157–158.
9. Sherwin, op, cit. pp. 330–331.
10. Edelstein, op. cit. p. 161.
11. Ibid.
12. Henry Steele Commager, *Theodore Parker: Yankee Crusader* (Boston: The Beacon Press, 1962), p. 238.
13. Edelstein, op. cit. p. 160.
14. Ibid. pp. 163–164.
15. Ibid. p. 171.
16. Robert C. Albrecht, *Theodore Parker.* (New York: Twayne Publishers, 1971), p. 111.
17. Ibid. p. 115.
18. Tilden Edelstein, op. cit. p. 174.

Chapter 3

1. Andrew S. Berky and James P. Shenton, eds., *The Historian's History of the United States* (New York: G.P. Putnam's Sons, 1966), 2 Vols., Vol. I; P. Orman Ray, *The Repeal of the Missouri Compromise,* pp. 654–665.
2. Eli M. Thayer, *The New England Emigrant Aid Society* (Worcester, Mass.: Franklin P. Rice, 1887), passim.
3. Henry Steele Commager, *Theodore Parker* op. cit. pp. 206–207.
4. Ralph Volney Harlow, *Gerrit Smith: Philanthropist and Reformer* (New York: Russell & Russell, reissue 1972), pp. 3–4.
5. Ibid. p. 245.
6. Richard O. Boyer, *The Legend of John Brown: A Biography and a History* (New York: Alfred A. Knopf, 1973), p. 395.
7. Ibid. p. 400.
8. Ibid. pp. 400–401.
9. Richard Henry Dana, "How We Met John Brown" (*Atlantic Monthly,* July, 1871), pp. 1–9.

Chapter 4

1. James C. Malin, *John Brown and the Legend,* p. 3, summarizes Brown's business career to this point with a clarity that remains unsurpassed.

2. Oswald Garrison Villard, *John Brown,* p. 79.
3. Richard O. Boyer, *The Legend of John Brown,* p. 422.
4. Ibid. p. 455.
5. Ibid.
6. Ibid., p. 460.
7. Villard, op. cit. p. 84.

Chapter 5

1. James C. Malin, *John Brown and the Legend,* p. 525, makes the point that the most prominent free-state leaders in the Kansas Territory would not have been there at all had the New England Emigrant Aid Company not paid them salaries, expenses, sent them goods, and advised them. That lets a considerable amount of hot air out of the idealistic balloons they managed to float aloft.
2. Oswald Garrison Villard, *John Brown,* p. 82.
3. Ibid.
4. Malin, op. cit. pp. 16, 493, 494, 495, 497 probes incisively into the Brown locations, and disproves their legitimacy as claims.
5. Allan Nevins, *Ordeal of the Union* (New York: Charles Scribner's Sons, 1947) 2 vols; Vol. 1., pp 313–14.
6. Ibid.
7. Malin, op. cit. pp. 511–520. The majority even of the "free-state" settlers voted to exclude blacks, of any condition, from the territory—including the settlers at Osawatomie. This prejudice was so strong that Kansas exclusion laws remained for years; "even equality in public schools was not extended in practice," says Malin, "until 1870, not even in Lawrence, and the franchise was not granted until the fifteenth amendment to the federal constitution overrode the state constitution."

Chapter 6

1. Oscar Sherwin, *Prophet of Liberty,* op. cit. p. 341.
2. Robert C. Albrecht, *Theodore Parker,* op. cit. p. 106.
   In part this long anti-Spaniard diatribe was, it seems, inspired by Parker's burning jealousy of the great fame and acclaim accorded the nearly blind but brilliant historian William H. Prescott, whose histories of Spain and the New World conquests had created a deserved worldwide reputation. Parker sneered at Prescott's monumental and amazing labors, complained that he "described events and not causes," and said he wanted a historian who would "not only tell all, but judge all." It is clear he believed his description of Spanish New World influence did just that, though no effort was more naively revealing.
3. Ibid.

4. Allan Nevins, *The Ordeal of the Union,* op. cit. p. 386.
5. Ibid. p. 382.
6. Oswald Garrison Villard, *John Brown,* op. cit. pp. 83–84.
7. Ralph Volney Harlow, *Gerrit Smith,* op. cit. p. 341.
8. Ibid.
9. James C. Malin, *John Brown and the Legend,* op. cit. p. 9.
10. Robert Penn Warren, *John Brown: The Making of a Martyr* (New York: Payson & Clarke, 1929), p. 102.
11. Villard, op. cit. pp. 85–86.
12. Frank Preston Stearns, *The Life and Public Services of George Luther Stearns* (New York: J.P. Lippincott, 1907), pp. 112–113.
13. Ibid. p. 106.

Chapter 7

1. The role of American newspaper proprietors and journalists in helping to create a civil war in the United States has never been fully—or honestly—aired, discussed, analyzed, or reviewed.
2. Allan Nevins, *Ordeal of the Union,* p. 389.
3. Ibid. p. 383.
4. Richard O. Boyer, *The Legend of John Brown,* p. 566.
5. Nevins, op. cit. p. 392.
6. The Big Springs Convention, which Lane stampeded, created the Free State party. The second meeting, held in September 1855, was to create a free-state constitution movement.

Chapter 8

1. Oswald Garrison Villard, *John Brown,* pp. 89–90.
2. Villard, op. cit. p. 87.
3. Ibid. p. 88.
4. Ibid. p. 88.
5. Ibid. p. 112.
6. The only national figure who repeatedly drew attention to this was Senator Stephen Douglas who was hooted by extremists both North and South.
7. Robert Penn Warren, *John Brown,* p. 105.
8. Villard, op. cit. p. 89. The comment may have been in answer to complaints; Mrs. Brown and the young children were bereft in the "Frosty region."

Chapter 9

1. Frank Preston Stearns, *Life of George Luther Stearns,* p. 94.
2. James C. Malin, *John Brown and the Legend,* 521–23, and Robert Penn Warren, *John Brown,* pp. 107–109.
3. Ibid.

4. Oswald Garrison Villard, a pro-Brown biographer, repeated the canard, as have other pro-free-state writers. To do otherwise is to open a barrel of worms.
5. Malin, op. cit. p. 516.
6. Ibid. p. 523. Later Francis testified before a federal grand jury.
7. Robert Penn Warren, *John Brown*, p. 110.
8. The rationale for this was that the free-staters at Lawrence, although not associated with the rescue, would not be believed. Therefore, a defense was necessary—according to Oswald Garrison Villard (*John Brown*, pp. 113–14). He does not explain why those responsible for defying the sheriff and his posse, as well as the released prisoner, were not held for the authorities.
9. Warren, op. cit. p. 113.
10. Malin, op. cit. pp. 16–17.
11. Ibid. pp. 256–257. But this account by George Washington Brown, editor of the *Herald of Freedom*, was written on the heels of the Harper's Ferry raid, when G.W. Brown had grown disillusioned.
   At the time that old Brown and his sons appeared in Lawrence, the *Herald of Freedom* account, dated Dec. 7, 1855, was not only respectful but flattering—and has been endlessly repeated.
12. Malin, op. cit. pp. 20–21.
13. Allan Nevins, *Ordeal of the Union*, p. 411.
14. Malin, op. cit. p. 529.
15. Warren, op. cit. p. 138.
16. Ibid.

Chapter 10

1. *Herald of Freedom*, April 29, 1856.
2. James C. Malin, *John Brown and the Legend*, pp. 719–20. The Brown boys had staked their claims on the east side of Middle Creek, which was then part of the cattle range used by Dutch Henry Sherman. That may explain, says Malin, why they were so eager to find him on the night of Pottawatomie murders . . . and why they killed his brother, Dutch Bill.
3. Ibid. pp. 720–24.
4. Malin, op. cit. pp. 532–34, and Oswald Garrison Villard, *John Brown*, pp. 134–35. Malin explored White's background more thoroughly than Villard, and discovered it to be honest. A number of Brown biographers persist in portraying White as a villain, accepting the Brown clan version. A number of Brown biographers also place a "Rev." before White's name, though he does not appear to have been an ordained minister. The same writers, however, usually omit the "Rev." when mentioning such persons as Higginson and others who were ordained ministers, and whose conduct is portrayed admiringly. This curious inversion,

in which the title "Rev." is used only in an invidious context, reveals bias.
5. Ibid.
6. Malin, op. cit. p. 533. Villard does not mention that this was a rump meeting.
7. Ibid.

Chapter 11

1. Allan Nevins, *Ordeal of the Union,* p. 420.
2. James C. Malin, *John Brown and the Legend,* p. 536.
3. Robert Penn Warren, *John Brown,* p. 146. Warren says the Sheriff was slapped in the face.
4. Malin, op. cit. p. 45.
5. Ibid. p. 46.
6. Ibid. pp. 537–50.
7. Oswald Garrison Villard, *John Brown,* pp. 135–36.
8. Malin, op. cit. p. 549.
9. *Herald of Freedom,* April 29, 1856.
10. Villard, op. cit. p. 136.
11. Ibid., p. 136, n. 84 says it was James N. Filer, a young New Yorker who returned to that State soon afterward, leaving the suspicion to fall on Charles Lenhart, a printer.
12. Malin, op. cit. p. 79.
13. Nevins, op. cit. pp. 430–31.
14. F.B. Sanborn, *Recollections of Seventy Years* (Boston: The Gorham Press, 1909), p. 51.

Chapter 12

1. Allan Nevins, *Ordeal of the Union,* p. 434.
2. James C. Malin, *John Brown and the Legend,* p. 240.
3. Presidential Proclamation, February 11, 1856.
4. Oswald Garrison Villard, *John Brown,* pp. 142–43.
5. Ibid.

Chapter 13

1. Allan Nevins, *Ordeal of the Union,* p. 439.
2. Dumas Malone, ed., *The Dictionary of American Biography,* p. 210.
3. Ibid.
4. Nevins, op. cit. pp. 441–43.
5. Ibid. 445–46.
6. David Donald, *Charles Sumner and the Coming of the Civil War* (New York: Alfred A. Knopf, 1960), p. 291.
7. Ibid., pp. 296, 297, 303, 308. Within a few minutes Representative Brooks and a South Carolina colleague were walking to-

gether down the street. Later, Brooks was fined for assault. Senator Sumner lay unconscious for several minutes, bleeding heavily. He was taken home in a carriage by Senator Wilson. As Sumner was sinking "into a dazed sleep," he murmured, "I could not believe a thing like this was possible."

Chapter 14

1. Oswald Garrison Villard, *John Brown*, p. 149.
2. James C. Malin, *John Brown and the Legend*, pp. 317, 389.
3. Ibid. p. 562.
4. Villard, op. cit. p. 153.
5. Malin, op. cit. pp. 563, 565.
6. Ibid., pp. 53, 54, 564, 565, and Villard, op. cit. pp 150–51.
7. Villard, op. cit. p. 150.
8. Ibid. p. 151.
9. Malin, op. cit. p. 567.

SECTION II

Chapter 15

1. Tilden G. Edelstein, *Strange Enthusiasm*, p. 151.
2. Ibid.
3. Ibid. p. 176.
4. Ibid. p. 181.
5. Richard O. Boyer, *The Legend of John Brown*, p. 553.
6. Robert C. Albrecht, *Theodore Parker*, p. 72.
7. Boyer, op. cit. p. 545.
8. Frank Preston Stearns, *Cambridge Essays* (Freeport, N.Y.: Books for Libraries, repr. 1968), pp. 218–19.
9. Ibid. p. 91.
10. Louise Hall Tharp, *Three Saints and a Sinner: Julia Ward Howe, Luisa, Annie and Sam Ward* (Boston: Little, Brown and Company, 1956), p. 179.
11. Ibid., pp. 314–15.
12. Frank Preston Stearns, *The Life and Public Services of George Luther Stearns*, pp. 91–92.
13. Franklin Benjamin Sanborn, *Recollections of Seventy Years* (Boston: The Gorham Press, 1909), 2 vols., Vol. II, pp. 268–94.
14. Ibid. p. 315.
15. Ralph Volney Harlow, *Gerrit Smith* (New York: Russell & Russell, reissue 1972), p. 333.
16. Ibid. p. 345.
17. Ibid. p. 349.
18. Ibid. p. 345.

19. Ibid.
20. Syracuse *Journal,* May 31, 1856.
21. Ralph Volney Harlow, *Gerrit Smith,* pp. 345–6.

Chapter 16

1. Van Wyck Brooks, *The Flowering of New England 1815–1865* (New York: E.P. Dutton & Company, 1936), pp. 107–109.
2. David P. Edgell, *William Ellery Channing: An Intellectual Portrait* (Boston: The Beacon Press, 1955), p. 28.
3. Ralph L. Rusk, *The Life of Ralph Waldo Emerson* (New York: Columbia University Press, 1949), p. 101.
4. Ibid. p. 100.
5. Ibid. pp. 105–107.
6. Finney was actually licensed to preach by the Presbyterian Synod at St. Lawrence in 1823, after being converted and sponsored by Reverend George Washington Gale.
7. Gilbert Hobbs Barnes, *The Antislavery Impulse, 1830–1844* (New York: Harcourt, Brace & World, 1964, paperback), p. 12.
8. Benjamin P. Thomas, *Theodore Weld: Crusader for Freedom* (New Brunswick, N.J.: Rutgers University Press, 1950), p. 14.
9. Ibid., pp. 11, 201.
10. Gilbert Hobbs Barnes, *The Antislavery Impulse,* op. cit., p. 9.
11. Ibid., pp. 10–11.
12. Ibid.
13. Owen Brown was the son of Captain John Brown, of the Eighteenth Connecticut, who died of malaria or a similar outbreak during the Revolutionary War, leaving a wife, ten children, a farm, and livestock. The widow could not handle the property without help; without it, said Owen years later, "we lost our crops, then our cattle, and so became poor." He was six years old, and had to struggle hard; he became an apprentice and later a shoemaker, then a tanner and farmer. He prospered eventually, married, moved several times, and had, from two wives, ten sons and six daughters. His son John was born in Torrington, Connecticut in 1800, and his father helped him for many years, in addition to teaching him the tannery and farming business.
14. Edgell, op. cit. pp. 205–09.
15. In 1798 James Robison authored a book entitled *Proofs of a Conspiracy against all Religions and Governments of Europe, carried on In The Secret Meetings of Freemasons, Illuminati and Reading Societies.* It created a sensation, since it paralleled many rumors of Masonic entanglement in the French Revolution, that influenced the passage of the Alien & Sedition Act in the U.S.
16. Whitney R. Cross, *The Burned-over District: The Social and Intellectual*

History of Enthusiastic Religion in Western New York 1800–1850 (New York: Harper Torchbooks, 1965, paperback), pp. 114–16.
17. Oswald Garrison Villard, *John Brown,* p. 26.

Chapter 17

1. Benjamin P. Thomas, *Theodore Weld,* p. 18. The Oneida approach, begun in Switzerland and other European countries, was especially helpful for poorly financed seminaries. Others sprang up quickly in Andover, Maine; Wesleyan, Ohio; Auburn, New York; Wilmington, Delaware; Maryville, Tennessee; and other places. But labor was mandatory only at Oneida.
2. Ralph L. Rusk, *The Life of Ralph Waldo Emerson,* pp. 117–18.
3. Ibid., pp. 134–40.
4. Ibid., pp. 139–40.
5. Ibid.
6. Ibid. p. 150.
7. Thomas, op. cit. p. 28.

Chapter 18

1. Dumas Malone, *Dictionary of American Biography.*
2. Ralph Volney Harlow, *Gerrit Smith,* p. 50.
3. Benjamin P. Thomas, *Theodore Weld,* p. 30.
4. Gilbert Hobbs Barnes, *The Antislavery Impulse,* p. 43, n. 10.
5. Thomas, op. cit. p. 63.
6. Gordon Carruth, ed., *The Dictionary of American Facts and Dates* (New York: Thomas Y. Crowell Company, 1966), p. 174.

Chapter 19

1. David P. Edgell, *William Ellery Channing,* pp. 211–12.
2. Ibid. p. 213.
3. Ibid. p. 66.
4. Ibid. p. 96.
5. Ibid. p. 99.
6. Ibid. p. 95.
7. Benjamin P. Thomas, *Theodore Weld,* pp. 39–40.
8. Richard O. Boyer, *Legend of John Brown,* pp. 231–34.
9. Gilbert Hobbs Barnes, *The Antislavery Impulse,* p. 34.
10. Thomas, op. cit. p. 49.
11. Barnes, op. cit. pp. 54–56.
12. Ibid., p. 56.

Chapter 20

1. Ralph L. Rusk, *Life of Ralph Waldo Emerson,* pp. 159–60.
2. Ibid. p. 163
3. Ibid. pp. 164–65.
4. Ibid. p. 167.
5. Ibid. pp. 176–77.
6. Ibid. p. 187.
7. Ibid. pp. 187–89.
8. Ibid. pp. 191–93.
9. Ibid. p. 195.
10. Gilbert Hobbs Barnes, *The Antislavery Impulse,* pp. 64–66. Benjamin P. Thomas, *Theodore Weld,* pp. 71–72.
11. Edward S. Corwin, *The Higher Law Background of American Constitutional Law* (Ithaca, New York: Cornell University Press, 1961), p. 87.
12. Thomas Sowell, *Race and Economics* (New York: David McKay Company, 1975), pp. 99–101. Dr. Sowell also remarks on the decline in efficiency of the sugar islands after emancipation, and discusses some of the complex reasons for this.
13. U.S. Bureau of the Census, *The Statistical History of the United States* (New York: Basic Books, 1976), pp. 8, 14.
14. "Christianity is part of the Common Law of England," wrote Sir Matthew Hale in 1736, in *Historia Placitorum Coronae.* and a similarly definitive statement is found in Blackstone's *Commentaries on the Laws of England,* Vol. IV, in 1765.
15. Corwin, op. cit. passim.
16. Whitney R. Cross, *The Burned-over District,* p. 202: "Most people, like Gerrit Smith, fell easily and thoughtlessly into the common modes of religious terminology . . . as a matter of course."
17. Stanley Elkins, *Slavery: A Problem in American Institutional and Intellectual Life,* cf *The Abolitionists: Immediatism and the Question of Means* (Boston: D.C. Heath, 1964), pp. 90–91.
18. Lewis Perry, *Radical Abolitionism: Anarchy and the Government of God in Antislavery Thought* (Ithaca, N.Y.: 1973), p. 39, cites Mather creating "Reforming Societies," or "Societies for the Suppression of Disorders" outside but close to the church.
19. Rousas J. Rushdoony, *Revolt Against Maturity,* (Fairfax, Va.: Thoburn Press, 1977), p. 208.
20. Ibid.
21. Corwin, op. cit.; p. 88, n 135.
22. G. Edward White, *The American Judicial Tradition: Profiles of Leading American Judges* (New York: Oxford University Press, 1976) describes, somewhat naively, how American law is whatever the Supreme Court decides.
23. Rushdoony, op. cit. pp. 129–30.
24. Nothing could better illustrate the unworldliness of Weld & Co. than their indifference to the fact that the nation had just nar-

rowly averted civil war over the tariff. That crisis, ended by compromise in early 1833, had led Calhoun and South Carolina to threaten secession, President Jackson to threaten to hang Calhoun—and other, equally melodramatic confrontations.
25. Rushdoony, op. cit. pp. 129–30.

Chapter 21

1. Richard O. Boyer, *The Legend of John Brown,* pp. 251–52.
2. Ibid.
3. Benjamin P. Thomas, *Theodore Weld,* p. 75.
4. Ibid. p. 76.
5. Ibid. p. 77.
6. Ibid. p. 78.
7. John L. Thomas, *The Liberator: William Lloyd Garrison* (Boston: Little, Brown and Company, 1963), pp. 182–84.
8. Bernard C. Steiner, *The Life of Roger Brooke Taney* (Baltimore, Md.: William & Wilkins Company, 1922), p. 87.
9. Ibid. Steiner notes that this campaign—instituted at a time when all the rest of the Cabinet was in favor of renewing the bank charter—started with a fifty-four page letter urging a veto. He describes this as "a demogogic letter, not legally sound, specious, abounding in logical fallacies and special pleading."
10. That move backfired when its president, Thomas Ellicott, a friend of Taney's who was considered a pillar of Quaker rectitude, immediately cashed large drafts on the Bank of the United States, in violation of understandings, and used the money to speculate in stocks.
11. Most Whigs, as well as many Democrats, considered Taney an obsequious instrument of President Jackson's—an unconscious tribute to Taney's skill in appearing modest, unassuming, and harmless.
12. Steiner, op. cit. p. 167.
13. John L. Thomas, op. cit. p. 173.
14. Gilbert Hobbs Barnes, *The Antislavery Impulse,* p. 72.
15. Ibid.
16. Ralph L. Rusk, *Ralph Waldo Emerson,* pp. 199–200.
17. Ibid.
18. Ibid. pp. 206–209.
19. Barnes, op. cit. pp. 74–76.
20. Benjamin P. Thomas, *Theodore Weld,* pp. 97–98.
21. John L. Thomas, op. cit. p. 195.
22. Ibid. p. 197.
23. Ibid. p. 185.
24. Ibid. p. 186.
25. David P. Edgell, *William Ellery Channing,* p. 44.
26. Ibid.

27. John L. Thomas, op. cit. p. 201.
28. Ibid., pp. 202–205.
29. Edgell, op. cit. p. 45.

Chapter 22

1. Oswald Garrison Villard, *John Brown*, pp. 43–44.
2. Ibid. p. 26.
3. Richard O. Boyer, *Legend of John Brown*, pp. 266–267.
4. Villard, op. cit. p. 28.
5. Ralph Volney Harlow, *Gerrit Smith*, p. 35.
6. Ibid. p. 117.
7. Ibid. p. 124.
8. Gilbert Hobbs Barnes, *The Antislavery Impulse*, p. 93.
9. Ibid. p. 95.
10. Ibid. p. 98.
11. Harlow, op. cit. p. 126.
12. Boyer, op. cit. p. 270.
13. Villard, op. cit. p. 37.
14. Herbert Agar, *The Price of Union* (Boston-Houghton Mifflin Company, 1966), p. 258.

Chapter 23

1. Ralph L. Rusk, *Ralph Waldo Emerson*, pp. 229–30.
2. Ibid. p. 230.
3. Perry Miller, *The Transcendentalists: An Anthology*, (Cambridge, Mass.: Harvard University Press, 1971), p. 151.
4. Ibid. p. 331.
5. Rusk, op. cit. p. 240.
6. Ibid. p. 241.
7. David P. Edgell, *William Ellery Channing*, p. 45.
8. Conrad Wright, *The Liberal Christians: Essays on American Unitarian History*, (Boston: The Beacon Press, 1970), *Emerson, Barzillai Frost and the Divinity School Address*, p. 45.
9. Ibid. p. 43.
10. Ibid. p. 46.
11. Ibid. p. 47.
12. Ibid. p. 53.
13. Rusk, op. cit. pp. 268–69.
14. Ibid. p. 269.

SECTION III

Chapter 24

1. Agar, op. cit. pp. 279–80.
2. Richard O. Boyer, *Legend of John Brown*, pp. 317–18.
3. Oswald Garrison Villard, *John Brown*, p. 47.
4. Ibid. p. 30.
5. Boyer, op. cit. pp. 326–27.
6. Ibid. p. 327.
7. Villard, op. cit. p. 38.
8. Gilbert Hobbs Barnes, *The Antislavery Impulse*, p. 124.
9. Ibid. p. 134.
10. Ibid.
11. Benjamin P. Thomas, *Theodore Weld*, pp. 162–64.
12. Ralph L. Rusk, *Ralph Waldo Emerson*, pp. 245–47.
13. John L. Thomas, *The Liberator*, pp. 258–60.
14. Whitney R. Cross, *The Burned-Over District*, pp. 287–92.
15. Ibid. p. 204.

Chapter 25

1. Oswald Garrison Villard, *John Brown*, pp. 31–32.
2. Ibid. pp. 38–41. Villard, Boyer, and other Brown apologists go to extraordinary efforts to depict Brown's behavior in a reasonable light—and fail.
3. Ibid. pp. 32–33.
4. Sylvester Graham, who issued "The Graham Journal of Health and Longevity" from Boston, was leader of what was called Physiological Reform, which included not only his famous biscuits, but also a regimen of cold water baths, loose clothing, exercise, and hard mattresses to promote good health and keep "amative instincts" under control.
5. Benjamin P. Thomas, *Theodore Weld*, pp. 168–69.
6. Arthur and Lewis Tappan, the supporters of these and other societies, were bankrupt, shriveled, and no longer unquestioned leaders.
7. Thomas, op. cit. pp. 169–72.
8. Robert C. Albrecht, *Theodore Parker*, pp. 24–25.
9. Ibid. pp. 29–33.
10. Ralph L. Rusk, *Ralph Waldo Emerson*, pp. 275–77.
11. Perry Miller, *The Transcendentalists*, p. 438.
12. Herbert Agar, *The Price of Union*, p. 285.
13. Ibid. p. 286.
14. David P. Edgell, *William Ellery Channing*, p. 49.

Chapter 26

1. David Donald, *Charles Sumner and the Coming of the Civil War*, p. 71.
2. Ibid.
3. Sir William Blackstone had classified blind, deaf mutes in the same category as idiots, since they were "bereft of those senses which furnish the human mind with ideas."
4. Donald, op. cit. p. 86.
5. Ibid. p. 87.
6. Julia Ward Howe, *Reminiscences 1819–1899* (Boston: Houghton Mifflin and Company, 1900), p. 82.
7. Donald, op. cit. p. 89.
8. David P. Edgell, *William Ellery Channing*, pp. 144–45.
9. Ibid. p. 115.
10. Everett Webber, *Escape to Utopia: The Communal Movement in America* (New York: Hastings House, 1959), p. 173.
11. Robert C. Albrecht, *Theodore Parker*, p. 39.
12. John L. Thomas, *The Liberator*, p. 301.
13. Perry Miller, *The Transcendentalists*, p. 465.
14. Ralph L. Rusk, *Ralph Waldo Emerson*, p. 289.
15. Gilbert Hobbs Barnes, *The Antislavery Impulse*, pp. 179–81.
16. Ibid. p. 185.
17. Van Wyck Brooks, *The Flowering of New England*, pp. 323–24.
18. Edgell, op. cit. pp. 61–62.
19. Richard O. Boyer, *Legend of John Brown*, p. 341.
20. These references, contrary to accepted myth, are not complimentary to humanity. See: R. J. Rushdoony, *Revolt Against Maturity*, pp. 291–97.

Chapter 27

1. Benjamin P. Thomas, *Theodore Weld*, p. 198.
2. Whitney R. Cross, *The Burned-over District*, p. 283.
3. Thomas, op. cit. p. 217.
4. Everett Webber, *Escape to Utopia*, p. 177.
5. Ralph L. Rusk, *Ralph Waldo Emerson*, p. 291.
6. Robert C. Albrecht, *Theodore Parker*, pp. 53–56.
7. Mark Foster ed. *Harmonium Man: Selected Writings of Charles Fourier*, (New York: Doubleday, 1971, paperback), passim.
8. It was called the Alphadelphia Phalanx. Gordon Carruth, ed., *Encyclopedia of American Facts and Dates*, p. 209.
9. Robert O. Boyer, *Legend of John Brown*, pp. 347–48.
10. Ibid.
11. Louisa May Alcott, *Transcendental Wild Oats* (Boston: Houghton Mifflin Company, 1915).
12. Clara Endicott Sears, *Bronson Alcott's Fruitlands* (Boston: Houghton Mifflin Company, 1915), p. 173.

Chapter 28

1. Oscar Sherwin, *Prophet of Liberty,* p. 138.
2. John L. Thomas, *The Liberator,* p. 325.
3. Ibid. p. 322.
4. Sherwin, op. cit. p. 141.
5. Thomas, op. cit. p. 330.
6. Herbert Agar, *The Price of Union,* pp. 307–308.
7. Robert C. Albrecht, *Theodore Parker,* p. 64.
8. Ibid. p. 69.
9. Ralph L. Rusk, *Ralph Waldo Emerson,* p. 306.
10. Ibid. p. 307.
11. David Donald, *Charles Sumner,* p. 108.
12. Ibid. p. 109–110.
13. Harold Schwartz, *Samuel Gridley Howe, 1801–1876* (Cambridge, Mass.: Harvard University Press, 1976), pp. 123–25.
14. Donald, op. cit. pp. 112–14.
15. Bernard deVoto, *Year of Decision*, Cf. Andrew S. Berky & James P. Shenton, *The Historian's History of the United States,* (New York: G. P. Putnam's Sons, 1966), 2 vols. p. 583.
16. K. Jack Bauer, *The Mexican War, 1846–1848* (New York: Macmillan, 1974), pp. 47, 49.

Chapter 29

1. Richard O. Boyer, *Legend of John Brown,* p. 362.
2. Stephen B. Oates, *To Purge This Land with Blood: A Biography of John Brown* (New York: Harper & Row, 1970), p. 57.
3. Boyer, op. cit. p. 362.
4. Oates cites the recollections of Aaron Erickson, veteran wool dealer, who tried to explain Brown's foolishness to him, and who also tested his "grades" and discovered them to be capricious and inaccurate; op. cit. p. 57, n. 10.
5. Justin H. Smith, *The War With Mexico.* Cf. Andrew S. Berky & James P. Shenton, *The Historian's History of the United States,* pp. 559–572.
6. Bernard deVoto, *The Year of Decision,* Cf. Berky & Shenton, op. cit. pp. 590–594.
7. Ralph L. Rusk, *Ralph Waldo Emerson,* p. 311.
8. Robert C. Albrecht, *Theodore Parker,* p. 75.
9. David Donald, *Charles Sumner,* p. 146.
10. Oswald Garrison Villard, *John Brown,* p. 50.
11. Frederick Douglass, *Life and Times of Frederick Douglass* (New York: Crowell-Collier, paperback, 1962), pp. 263–67.
12. Ibid. The interview and following quotes are summarized from pp. 271–75. Douglass, who lost his records of the period in a fire in 1872, here displays consummate tact and manages to give a realistic portrait of John Brown while avoiding offense to the "martyr's" followers.

13. In 1850, Parker said, "The man who attacks me to reduce me to slavery, in that moment of attack alienates his right to life . . ." Albrecht, op. cit. p. 101.
14. Douglass, op. cit. p. 275.

Chapter 30

1. Tilden G. Edelstein, *Strange Enthusiasm*, pp. 75–76.
2. Ibid. pp. 71–74.
3. Ibid. pp. 78–84.
4. Ralph Volney Harlow, *Gerrit Smith*, pp. 40–41.
5. "This is the last of earth—I am content."
6. The angry charge that the South deliberately fostered the Mexican War to expand slavery was maintained by Northern historians for a long time, until Justin H. Smith's examination of the record proved this view to be simplistic and erroneous. The facts are that border disputes, in which the claims of both nations were cloudy, were in existence long before Texas was occupied, rebelled, and gained independence. The fixed animosity of Mexico toward the United States in the nineteenth century led its leaders into serious miscalculations of Mexican strength and American weakness. War was threatened and started by Mexico itself; it reaped the rewards of recklessness. From a larger historical viewpoint, regrets by some contemporary Americans that the territory was acquired in war seem peculiar in the light of the high standard on which these lands support millions of people.
7. Ralph L. Rusk, *Ralph Waldo Emerson*, p. 337–42.
8. Ibid. p. 353.
9. Harold Schwartz, *Samuel Gridley Howe*, p. 140.
10. Ibid. p. 141.
11. Tilden G. Edelstein, *Strange Enthusiasm*, pp. 85–86.
12. David Donald, *Charles Sumner*, p. 173.
13. Ibid. pp. 180–181.
14. Richard O. Boyer, *Legend of John Brown*, p. 396.
15. Ibid. p. 411.
16. Ibid. p. 416.

Chapter 31

1. Tilden G. Edelstein, *Strange Enthusiasm*, pp. 96–97.
2. Ibid. pp. 91–92.
3. Robert C. Albrecht, *Theodore Parker*, p. 27.
4. Allan Nevins, *Ordeal of the Union*, Vol. I, p. 222.
5. Ibid. p. 225.
6. Oscar Sherwin, *Prophet of Liberty*, p. 187.
7. Nevins, op. cit. pp. 280–83.
8. Ibid. pp. 288–91.

9. Albrecht, op. cit. p. 99.
10. Nevins, op. cit. pp. 291–92.
11. Edelstein, op. cit. p. 2.
12. Nevins, op. cit. p. 301.
13. Oswald Garrison Villard, *John Brown,* pp. 64–66.
14. Edelstein, op. cit. p. 105.
15. Henry Steele Commager, *Theodore Parker,* p. 205.
16. Ibid. p. 208.
17. Albrecht, op. cit. p. 101.
18. Richard O. Boyer, *Legend of John Brown,* pp. 436–38.
19. Edelstein, op. cit. p. 113.
20. David Donald, *Charles Sumner,* p. 197.
21. Ralph L. Rusk, *Ralph Waldo Emerson,* p. 367.
22. Ibid.

SECTION IV

Chapter 32

1. Oswald Garrison Villard, *John Brown,* p. 165.
2. Ibid. pp. 165–66.
3. Ibid. 166.
4. Ibid.
5. James C. Malin, *John Brown and the Legend,* p. 571.
6. Ibid. pp. 576–77.
7. Ibid. p. 580. None of these indictments were ever actually pressed against any of the Browns, although, as noted, Jason and John Jr. were, for a period, in custody. Equally remarkable is the fact that the Brown family, from the father down, has ever after been pitied, though certainly at least part of the clan got away with murder for a time, and some of them for all time.
8. There is good reason to believe, as his sister, Annie Brown Adams wrote Hinton in 1894, that John Brown, Jr.'s "mind has always been more or less affected by the excitement and trouble in Kansas . . ." Cf. Malin, op. cit. p. 14.
9. Villard, op. cit. p. 194–95.
10. Much was later made of this though prisoners in the United States are still shackled.
11. Stephen B. Oates, *To Purge This Land,* pp. 147–48.
12. Ibid. p. 149.
13. Allan Nevins, *Ordeal of the Union,* Vol. II, pp. 449–50.
14. Villard, op. cit. p. 169.
15. It is interesting that virtually all Brown biographers, while admitting Redpath was incapable of the truth, could not resist copious quotes from this implausible idyll.
16. A little over a year later Redpath was editor of a newspaper in Doniphan owned by Lane. Richard Realf, a Brown gang member

and poet, was a contributor to the paper, as was William A. Phillips, correspondent for the N.Y. *Tribune*. After Dutch Henry was murdered in March 1857, the name of the Crossing and its settlement was changed to Lane. Cf. Malin, op. cit. pp. 709, 159.

17. Oates, op. cit. pp. 153–154
18. Malin, op. cit. pp. 590–91.
19. Hinton was also correspondent for The Boston *Traveler*.
20. Malin, op. cit. pp. 99–100.

Chapter 33

1. Frank Preston Stearns, *George Luther Stearns,* p. 114.
2. David Donald, *Charles Sumner* p. 300; also Allan Nevins, *Ordeal of the Union,* Vol. II, p. 448.
3. David Donald, *Charles Sumner,* p. 301.
4. A "free" Church meant a church without rented and exclusive pews, with no controlling membership, open to anyone—with no special doctrine.
5. Tilden G. Edelstein, *Strange Enthusiasm,* pp. 184–85.
6. Ralph Volney Harlow, *Gerrit Smith,* p. 350.
7. Stephen B. Oates, *To Purge This Land,* p. 158.
8. Ralph L. Rusk, *Ralph Waldo Emerson,* p. 390.
9. James C. Malin, *John Brown and the Legend,* p. 101.
10. Published in Boston, the book was titled *The Conquest of Kansas by Missouri and Her Allies*. Phillips' description of Brown as mystic, hero, and Cromwell *redux* provided a portrait being repeated to this day.
11. Oates, op. cit. p. 160.
12. Malin, op. cit. p. 350.
13. Ibid. Walker also wrote that once in Lawrence Brown asked him to take a letter to John Brown, Jr., saying he would rescue him, and that John junior said he wanted his father to stay away; that he wanted nothing to do with him, and that his father was responsible for his being in prison. That constitutes about the only genuinely human passage regarding John Brown, Jr. and his father in the thousands of pages written.
14. Jules Abels, *Man on Fire: John Brown and the Cause of Liberty* (New York: The Macmillan Company, 1971), pp. 96–97.
15. Malin, op. cit. p. 233.
16. Abels, op. cit. p. 97.
17. Edelstein, op. cit. p. 187.
18. Ibid. pp. 187–88.
19. Oswald Garrison Villard, *John Brown,* p. 228.
20. Ibid. p. 232.
21. Malin, op. cit. pp. 612–13.
22. Abels, op. cit. p. 99.
23. Edelstein, op. cit. p. 191.

24. Villard, op. cit. pp. 661–664.
25. Malin, op. cit. pp. 613–14.
26. Villard, op. cit. p. 241.
27. Oates, op. cit. p. 170.
28. Villard, op. cit. p. 246.
29. Malin, op. cit. p. 219.
30. Ibid. p. 626.
31. Villard, op. cit. p. 253.
32. Ibid., p. 248.
33. Abels, op. cit. p. 103.
34. Malin, op. cit. p. 627.
35. Oates, op. cit. pp. 172–73.
36. Malin, op. cit. p. 627.
37. Franklin B. Sanborn, *Recollections of Seventy Years,* Vol. I, p. 54.
38. Ibid.
39. Ibid. p. 52.
40. Ibid. p. 68.
41. Edelstein, op. cit. p. 190.

Chapter 34

1. Allan Nevins, *Ordeal of the Union,* Vol. II, p. 492.
2. Stephen B. Oates, *To Purge This Land,* p. 174.
3. Ibid.
4. Villard repeats mythical speeches made by Brown to the people of Lawrence; others have described his activities in defense of the town. Redpath later wrote lengthy imaginary accounts of a fierce battle that never took place.
5. Jules Abels, *Man on Fire,* p. 109.
6. Oates, op. cit. p. 176.
7. James C. Malin, *John Brown and the Legend,* p. 634.
8. Ibid. p. 635.
9. Tilden G. Edelstein, *Strange Enthusiasm,* p. 195.
10. Ralph Volney Harlow, *Gerrit Smith,* p. 355.
11. Ibid. p. 356.
12. Robert C. Albrecht, *Theodore Parker,* p. 121.
13. Ibid. p. 119.
14. Malin, op. cit. p. 637.
15. Oswald Garrison Villard, *John Brown,* op. cit. p. 258.
16. James C. Malin, *John Brown and the Legend,* p. 651. While in charge of the Brown gang, Holmes received about a dozen revolvers around November, 1856.
17. Ibid., pp. 735–36.
18. Ibid.
19. Oates, op. cit. p. 177.
20. Villard, op. cit. p. 262.
21. Malin, op. cit. p. 638.

22. Ibid. p. 639.
23. Villard, op. cit. pp. 267–69.
24. Ibid. p. 269.
25. Ibid.
26. Malin, op. cit. pp. 677–80.
27. Ibid.
28. In a fascinating note, Malin says W. H. Gibbons found a broken stone fragment in an empty lot in Kansas City that read: "To the Memory of Jerome H. Glanville; born 1825; murdered by four Yankee Abolitionists on Bull Creek, in . . ." That seems, considering the multiple coincidental factors, proof enough. Malin, op. cit. pp. 677–78.

Chapter 35

1. James C. Malin, *John Brown and the Legend*, pp. 698–99.
2. Tilden G. Edelstein, *Strange Enthusiasm*, p. 193.
3. Ibid.
4. Ralph Volney Harlow, *Gerrit Smith*, p. 357.
5. Ibid. p. 358.
6. Oswald Garrison Villard, *John Brown*, p. 270.
7. Jules Abels, *Man on Fire*, p. 127.
8. Ibid. pp. 127–28.
9. Malin, op. cit. pp. 699–700.
10. Ibid.
11. Ibid. p. 672.
12. Ibid.
13. Villard, op. cit. p. 674.
14. John Brown, Jr. later said Robinson not only knew, but asked John Brown to undertake further work of that kind when he called him to Lawrence. Malin, op. cit. pp. 415–16.
15. Higginson not only knew, but was belligerent about his knowledge. *He approved.* In 1898 he was still insisting that "I heard of no one who did not approve the act, and its beneficial effects were universally asserted . . . Governor Robinson himself fully endorsing it to me."
16. Harlow, op. cit. p. 392.
17. Malin, op. cit. p. 434.
18. Ibid. p. 684.
19. Ibid.
20. One curious feature of this treatment was that Julia Ward Howe, considered the epitome of the independent woman, adored her husband and faithfully obeyed him all their married life.
21. Villard, op. cit. p. 272.
22. Ibid.
23. David Donald, *Charles Sumner*, p. 350.
24. Frank Preston Stearns, *George Luther Stearns*, p. 133.

25. Robert C. Albrecht, *Theodore Parker,* p. 119; Edelstein, op. cit. p. 198.
26. Oscar Sherwin, *Prophet of Liberty,* p. 365.
27. Edelstein, op. cit. p. 199.
28. Donald, op. cit. p. 350.
29. Villard, op. cit. p. 275.
30. Ibid.
31. Ibid. pp. 276–77.
32. Robert Penn Warren, *John Brown,* p. 232.
33. Ibid.
34. Abels, op. cit. pp. 135–36.
35. Allan Nevins, *The Emergence of Lincoln* (New York: Charles Scribner's Sons), 2 vols; Vol I. pp. 15–16.
36. Malin, op. cit. p. 736–37.
37. Ibid. p. 737, n 41.
38. Ibid.
39. Ibid.
40. Ibid. pp. 738–46.
41. *Herald of Freedom,* May 9, 1857. Cf. Malin, op. cit. p. 748.
42. Franklin B. Sanborn, *Recollections,* pp. 102–103.
43. Ibid. pp. 104–105.
44. Gilman M. Ostrander, "Emerson, Thoreau and John Brown," Mississippi Valley Historical Review, Vol. XXXIX, No. 4 (March 1953), p. 720.
45. Ibid.
46. Ibid.
47. Malin, op. cit. p. 239.

Chapter 36

1. Bernard C. Steiner, *Life of Roger Brooke Taney,* p. 342.
2. Ibid. p. 340.
3. Ibid. p. 335.
4. Ibid. p. 341.
5. Ibid. p. 343.
6. Ibid. p. 65.
7. Ibid. pp. 344–48.
8. Ralph Volney Harlow, *Gerrit Smith,* pp. 392–93.
9. Ibid.
10. Jules Abels, *Man on Fire,* pp. 145–146.
11. Stephen B. Oates, *To Purge This Land,* pp. 202–203.
12. Oswald Garrison Villard, *John Brown,* p. 288.
13. Abels, op. cit. p. 140.
14. Oates, op. cit. p. 204.
15. Abels, op. cit. p. 140.
16. Ibid. p. 201.
17. Abels, op. cit. p. 141.

18. George W. Van Vleck, *The Panic of 1857* (New York: Columbia University Press, 1943), pp. 43–53.
19. Tilden G. Edelstein, *Strange Enthusiasm*, p. 204.
20. Ibid. p. 205.
21. Ibid.
22. James C. Malin, *John Brown and the Legend*, p. 691.
23. Ibid. p. 692.
24. Ibid. pp. 695–96.
25. Allan Nevins, *The Emergence of Lincoln*, pp. 157–61.
26. Van Vleck, op. cit. pp. 64–68.
27. Ralph Volney Harlow, *Gerrit Smith*, p. 394.
28. Abels, op. cit. pp. 141–42.
29. Villard, op. cit. pp. 292–93.
30. He later became involved in the settlement of Dutch Henry's estate. Malin, op. cit. p. 744.
31. He lost money on this ambitious project.
32. So charged G. W. Brown, a newspaperman himself. Malin, op. cit. p. 258.
33. Abels, op. cit. p. 154.
34. Ibid. p. 150.
35. Van Vleck, op. cit. pp. 64–72, 83.
36. Malin, op. cit. p. 705.
37. Villard, op. cit. p. 292.
38. Frank Preston Stearns, *George Luther Stearns*, p. 141.
39. Abels, op. cit. p. 154.
40. Villard, op. cit. p. 300.
41. Ibid. pp. 300–301.
42. Abels, op. cit. p. 155. Brown's disappointment did not compare with Lane's: he wanted those Sharp's rifles very badly.
43. Ibid., pp. 155–56. Whitman and the Kansas Aid Committee also wanted the rifles. The situation was ironic; they belonged to the committee in the first place but Brown had managed—through Stearns—to get them all, and was trying to use them to lure recruits to his side in Tabor. The radicals in Kansas, however, had other plans, in which Brown did not figure, excepting on the periphery.
44. This embarrassing rambling document, which sought to define the basis of sovereign authority, and cited ancient republics, "princes of antiquity, etc." was credited to Forbes by Brown admirers later. It was, more probably, a joint effort, with Brown adding his interjections. The result is foolish.
45. Oates, op. cit. pp. 211–212.
46. Ibid.
47. Malin, op. cit. p. 257–58.
48. Van Vleck, op. cit. pp. 73–76.
49. Ibid. p. 75.
50. Ibid.
51. Oates, op. cit. p. 212.

52. Ibid. p. 218.
53. Villard, op. cit. pp. 298–99.
54. Lewis Perry, *Radical Abolitionism:* cf. Richard Hildreth, p. 186.
55. Ibid. pp. 194–95. Spooner expressed these and similar ideas in a two-part essay, published in 1845 and 1846, and his reasoning permeated radical abolitionist circles. *Id est,* "natural laws" forbid slavery. The sources are pagan, though pre-christians had slaves.
56. Villard, op. cit. p. 301.
57. Malin, op. cit. pp. 705–706.
58. Ibid., 706.
59. Ibid., 707.
60. Ibid., 258.
61. Villard, op. cit. p. 304.
62. Ibid.
63. Ibid. p. 307.
64. Stearns, op. cit. p. 144.

Chapter 37

1. Frederick Douglass, *Life and Times,* p. 317.
2. Jules Abels, *Man on Fire,* p. 163.
3. Douglass told Brown that Forbes told Greeley all he knew.
4. Richard Josiah Hinton, *John Brown and His Men, With some account of the roads they traveled to reach Harper's Ferry* (New York: Funk & Wagnall's, 1894), pp. 162–163.
5. David Donald, *Charles Sumner,* p. 350. Dr. Donald, Sumner's latest biographer, glides very rapidly over Sumner's involvement—which was close and continuous—with the members of the Secret Six, but he does mention that the Senator recommended Colonel Forbes to Higginson when he was drawing up a list for his Disunion convention. Numerous persons testified that Brown was introduced to Forbes by Reverend Joshua Leavitt of the N.Y. *Independent.* But Forbes may have feared attacking a United States senator so firmly held aloft by so many, and there is reason to believe that two or even more parties brought the two men together. The coincidence of the Disunion convention remains the most persuasive as the earliest contact.
6. Ibid. pp. 327–29.
7. Ibid. p. 331.
8. Franklin B. Sanborn, *Recollections,* pp. 135–36.
9. Hinton, op. cit. pp. 157–58.
10. Douglass, whose irrepressible sense of humor wells from his recital, is careful to add—after Brown was sanctified—that he was "desirous of retaining him under my roof." Since Brown was dangerous and Forbes was loose and babbling, that ranks as one of the more disingenuous of many such statements in Douglass' reminiscences; op. cit. p. 315.

11. Douglass, op. cit. p. 316.
12. Robert M. Fogelson and Richard E. Rubenstein, eds, *Mass Violence in America: Invasion at Harper's Ferry* (New York: Arno Press & The New York Times, 1969), pp. 40–59. The "provisional constitution," with its biblical phrases and paragraphs suggestive of the higher-law philosophy, echoed the pietistic fashion of Brown's times, especially on lower levels of education. It is difficult, however, to understand how this mangled document can still be condoned by respectable writers today, when it so obviously consists of transparent rationalizations for terrorism.
13. Ibid.
14. Ibid.
15. Ibid.
16. Oswald Garrison Villard, *John Brown*, p. 320.
17. Frank Preston Stearns, *George Luther Stearns*, op. cit., p. 161.
18. Tilden G. Edelstein, *Strange Enthusiasm*, p. 208.
19. Ibid.
20. Ibid. p. 209.
21. Stearns, op. cit. p. 162.
22. Edelstein, op. cit. p. 209.
23. Villard, op. cit. p. 320.
24. Sanborn, op. cit. p. 145.
25. Ibid. p. 146.
26. Ibid. p. 147.
27. Ibid.
28. Villard, op. cit. p. 322.
29. Sanborn, op. cit. p. 151.
30. Notes biographer Robert C. Albrecht: "With some justification one might say that in his search for greatness, Parker finally turned to himself." Robert C. Albrecht, *Theodore Parker*, p. 129.
31. Ralph Volney Harlow, *Gerrit Smith*, p. 399.
32. Villard, op. cit. p. 325.
33. Abels, op. cit. pp. 174–75.
34. Villard, op. cit. p. 323.
35. Ibid.
36. Julia Ward Howe, *Reminiscences*, op. cit., pp. 253–54.
37. Ibid. p. 254.
38. Ibid.
39. Hinton, op. cit. pp. 172, 173.
40. Ibid. p. 176.
41. George W. Van Vleck, *The Panic of 1857*, pp. 91–92; Stephen B. Oates, *To Purge This Land*, pp. 248–249.
42. Abels, op. cit. p. 197.
43. Harlow, op. cit. p. 400.
44. Edelstein, op. cit. p. 210.
45. Villard, op. cit. p. 339.
46. Fogelson and Rubenstein, op. cit. pp. 253–55. In this testimony before the Mason Hearings in the Senate, Senator Seward denied

he was told about a slave insurrection, insisted Forbes discussed only Kansas, and said he listened as an act of charity to a man in distress, but heard nothing to warrant charity. His statement remains a cool example of mendacity, incredible especially because Forbes knew nothing of Kansas intrigues and everything about the Secret Six and Brown's plans.

47. Oates, op. cit. p. 249.
48. Edelstein, op. cit. p. 212.
49. Ibid. p. 293
50. Villard, op. cit. p. 341.
51. Edelstein, op. cit. p. 211.
52. Harlow, op. cit. p. 401.
53. Fogelson and Rubenstein, op. cit. p. 104 (Realf's testimony before the Mason hearing).
54. Ibid. p. 105.
55. Ibid. p. 71 (Arny's testimony before the Mason Hearing).

Chapter 38

1. Damon Wells, *Stephen Douglas: The Last Years, 1857–1861* (Austin, Tex.: University of Texas Press, 1971), p. 8.
2. Allan Nevins, *The Emergence of Lincoln,* Vol. II, p. 253.
3. Oswald Garrison Villard, *John Brown,* op. cit., pp. 187–88.
4. Suitably titled "La Marais du Cygne," *Atlantic Monthly,* 1858.
5. Lincoln was not, however, well-known outside his own state.
6. That bold bugle call was not followed by a bold development of the thesis, however, Lincoln dithered into a prediction of slavery's "ultimate extinction." He also got involved in a conspiracy theory, charging that Chief Justice Roger Taney, former President Franklin Pierce, sitting President James Buchanan and Senator Douglas were involved in a plot to extend slavery.
7. Nevins, op. cit., Vol. II, pp. 364–65. Douglas' argument, in the light of what the antislavery cause actually produced, deserves more respectful treatment than it has received. Accusations that he lacked a moral sense sound strange from those willing to condone force in the name of freedom, and conformity in the name of progress.
8. Brown referred to Kagi, of whose allegiance he was proud, as "our Horace Greeley."
9. Villard, op. cit. p. 351.
10. Ibid. p. 350. Villard quotes a letter from the N.Y. *Evening Post* describing Montgomery as a "cultivated, educated gentleman."
11. Ibid. p. 359.
12. Stephen B. Oates, *To Purge This Land,* p. 260. Not only Brown but Parker, Higginson, and the other members of the Secret Six held this idea aloft as though it meant that the black slaves were to be assessed in the same light as free white men. It did not occur to

them that the slaves—uneducated, unarmed, unorganized, without money, land, or leaders—were at least sensible enough to keep from committing mass suicide. What the Six could not realize was that their knowledge of the black race was minimal and was, at once too lofty and too impractical—and too stereotyped. None of them ever took the trouble to get to know the people about whom they orated so much.

13. Ralph Volney Harlow, *Gerrit Smith*, pp. 402–403. There is no way of knowing whether Gerrit Smith was serious in adding this pious wish to remain ignorant, or whether it was part of the constant cryptic codes the conspirators used even in their interchanges with each other.
14. Frank Preston Stearns, *George Luther Stearns*, p. 178.
15. Allan Nevins, op. cit. Vol. I, p. 409.
16. Jules Abels, *Man on Fire*, p. 214.
17. Ibid. p. 215.
18. Villard, op. cit. p. 367.
19. Jules Abels, op. cit. p. 215.
20. Ibid. pp. 216–18. Oates glides rather swiftly over this expedition, as he does over all Brown's crimes. Villard covers the event more honestly. Abels is blunt and candid: he compares Brown's attitude toward people as similar to that of Stalin and Hitler, who used terror and the murder of innocent people deliberately, although he is confused by Brown's use of religious rhetoric.
21. Villard, op. cit. p. 375.
22. Ibid. p. 377.
23. Harlow, op. cit. p. 403.

Chapter 39

1. Oswald Garrison Villard, *John Brown*, p. 385.
2. Ibid.
3. Ibid. p. 392.
4. Nothing could better illustrate the feeble grasp of the federal government than this defiant attitude toward national law, reflected in the South as well as the North.
5. Frederick Douglass, *Life and Times*, p. 317.
6. Ralph Volney Harlow, *Gerrit Smith*, p. 403.
7. Ibid.
8. Stephen B. Oates, *To Purge This Land*, p. 270.
9. Lewis Perry, *Radical Abolitionism*, pp. 194, 204–206.
10. Robert C. Albrecht, *Theodore Parker*, p. 130.
11. Ibid. p. 129.
12. Julia Ward Howe, *Reminiscences*, p. 233.
13. Ibid. p. 235.
14. Tilden G. Edelstein, *Strange Enthusiasm*, pp. 217–18.
15. Oates, op. cit. p. 270.

16. Villard, op. cit. p. 398.
17. Ibid. pp. 399–400.
18. Frank Preston Stearns, *George Luther Stearns,* p. 181.
19. Alcott said he "impressed me as a person of surpassing sense, courage, and religious earnestness." Cf Villard, op. cit. p. 398.
20. Ralph L. Rusk, *Ralph Waldo Emerson,* p. 398.
21. Jules Abels, *Man on Fire,* p. 240.
22. Richard J. Hinton, *John Brown,* p. 239.
23. Douglass, op. cit. p. 318.
24. Ibid. p. 319.
25. Ibid. p. 320.
26. Howe, op. cit. p. 236.
27. Harlow, op. cit. p. 404.
28. Howe, op. cit. pp. 242–43.
29. The letter was explicit and, with the exception of the error regarding Maryland, factually accurate. It is reproduced in full in the files of the Mason hearing, pp. 250–252, and in Robert M. Fogelson and Richard E. Rubenstein, *Mass Violence in America: Invasion at Harper's Ferry,* pp. 250–52.
    The writer was David J. Gue, who learned of Brown's plan from a Quaker, Moses Varney, in Springdale. Varney believed it would be disastrous and thought someone should warn the authorities to prevent a suicidal venture.
30. Only the superb historian Allan Nevins has pointed out that Brown located his effort in a region densely settled, with numerous good roads. It had no "chasms, swamps, no unknown caverns; troops could move through it at will," and Brown did not even bother to survey the area for escape routes, for places to lead the slaves he expected to free, did not stock or fortify any future station, but planned to put extra weapons only a mile above the town—in its schoolhouse. He did, Nevins points out, inform himself about antislavery families in nearby towns: perhaps he expected help from these. But the signs add up to a raid, using hostages to escape, and later fundraising attempts. In other words, to do in Virginia what he did in Kansas.
31. Villard, op. cit. p. 571.
32. Edelstein, op. cit. pp. 219–20. Both these men knew Brown was at Harper's Ferry and his plan; they knew where to send Merriam. "Higginson," says one biographer, "found the one-eyed, frail Merriam to be either mentally unbalanced or severely retarded" —which made him doubtful about the success of the enterprise. *But he sent him along.*
33. Oates, op. cit. p. 287.
34. Fogelson and Rubenstein, op. cit. p. 32.
35. Villard, op. cit. p. 448.
36. Ibid.
37. Ibid.
38. Robert Penn Warren, *John Brown,* p. 378.

Chapter 40

1. Tilden G. Edelstein, *Strange Enthusiasm,* op. cit., p. 221.
2. Ibid.
3. Ralph Volney Harlow, *Gerrit Smith,* p. 407.
4. James C. Malin, *John Brown and the Legend,* p. 345, carries the entire pledge of eternal loyalty.
5. Franklin B. Sanborn, *Recollections,* Vol. I, p. 187.
6. Richard J. Hinton, *John Brown,* p. 332.
7. Stephen B. Oates, *To Purge This Land,* p. 317.
8. The baby was still-born; Martha died soon after.
9. Harlow, op. cit. p. 407.
10. Ibid.
11. Sanborn, op. cit. Vol. I., p. 204.
12. Edelstein, op. cit. p. 220.
13. Ibid. p. 222.
14. The extent to which Sanborn confided in Emerson and Thoreau has never been examined; yet these three were very close. No explanations seemed to have been necessary when Sanborn fled to Canada: Wendell Phillips wrote the fugitive schoolmaster on October 22, 1859—while news of Harper's Ferry was still reverberating—that he had conferred with lawyer Andrews, Higginson, and Emerson. That does not indicate aloofness.
15. Oswald Garrison Villard, *John Brown,* p. 530.
16. Frederick Douglass, *Life and Times,* pp. 320–21.
17. Jules Abels, *Man on Fire,* p. 298.
18. Ibid. p. 299.
19. Sanborn, op. cit. Vol. I, pp. 191–96. Ellen Emerson, the Sage's daughter, helped at Sanborn's school; Emerson also conferred with George Luther Stearns, and talked to Judge Hoar.
20. Ralph Rusk, *Ralph Waldo Emerson,* p. 401.
21. Ibid. Emerson never commented on the innocent dead at Harper's Ferry.
22. Oates, op. cit. p. 316.
23. Harlow, op. cit. p. 409.
24. Oates, op. cit. p. 313.
25. Edelstein, op. cit. p. 224. Edelstein makes the point that Higginson, like Brown, and the others of the Secret Six, denied they intended to provoke a slave uprising, but he does not point out the deracinated nature of their goal.
26. Villard, op. cit. p. 507.
27. Ibid. pp. 498–499.
28. Edward Stone, ed., *Incident at Harper's Ferry* (Englewood Cliffs, N.J.: Prentice-Hall, 1956), pp. 190–191.
29. Ibid. p. 188.
30. Sanborn, op. cit. Vol. I., p. 196.
31. Ibid. p. 197.

32. Harlow, op. cit. p. 410.
33. Villard, op. cit. p. 531.
34. Abels, op. cit. p. 339.
35. Douglass, op. cit. p. 321.
36. Allan Nevins, *The Emergence of Lincoln,* Vol. II, p. 95; and Edward Stone, op. cit. p. 94.
37. Abels, op. cit. p. 339.
38. Ibid.
39. Ibid.
40. Edelstein, op. cit. p. 226.
41. Ibid.
42. Robert C. Albrecht, *Theodore Parker,* p. 134. Parker overlooked, rather cavalierly, that John Brown was not assisting slaves to fight, but was asking slaves to assist him.
43. That exaggeration, which relegated civilization and all the arts of reasonable persuasion to limbo, was neither true nor Christian, but Parker was fading.
44. Edelstein, op. cit. p. 230.
45. Gilman M. Ostrander, "Emerson, Thoreau and John Brown," p. 723.
46. Villard, op. cit. p. 541.
47. Brackett was also supposed to size up the chances for a rescue.
48. Abels, op. cit. p. 342. Abels is unique among Brown biographers in being disgusted with this transparent campaign to insist upon Brown's martyrdom by men safe from personal danger.
49. Ibid. Abels says this appeared in the New York *Herald* and is false.
50. Villard, op. cit. p. 164. This letter is usually included in Brown biographies with the comment that Mrs. Doyle could not have written it, because she was illiterate. The only proof of that charge is that it was made by a Kansan anxious to play down the Pottawatomie murders. Malin cites proof that Mrs. Doyle could write for herself, when he mentions she conducted a correspondence with Reverend David Utter years afterward. Other proof seems evident: anyone familiar with the stilted letters that persons are apt to write for illiterates would recognize that Mrs. Doyle's letter to John Brown is not of that category: it glows with truth.
51. Robert Penn Warren, *John Brown,* p. 434. Numerous biographers have displayed their ignorance regarding John Brown and Christianity. One of the latest of these dwells, time and again, on Brown's purported Calvinism. But neither Calvin nor Presbyterians, nor any of the branches of Christianity favor, directly or indirectly, murder as a means of salvation. To imply otherwise is to traduce great religious movements and their spiritual leaders, and to misrepresent their principles. Brown, like the Secret Six, was far from any recognizable Christianity.

52. Hinton, op. cit. p. 389.
53. Ibid. p. 393. "If he sent it," Hunter added, "she has the best portrait of Brown ever taken."

SECTION V

Chapter 41

1. Roy P. Basler, ed, *The Collected Works of Abraham Lincoln* (New Brunswick, N.J.: Rutgers University Press, 1953), 8 Vols., Vol. III, p. 541.
2. Allan Nevins, *The Emergence of Lincoln*, Vol. IV, p. 104.
3. Ibid. pp. 103–104.
4. Oswald Garrison Villard, *John Brown*, p. 561.
5. Hugo suggested an epitaph: "Pro Christo sicut Christus."
6. He stressed the point in virtually every speech during this period.
7. Nevins, op. cit. Vol. IV, p. 108.
8. Ibid. p. 121.
9. Richard J. Hinton, *John Brown*, p. 152.
10. Tilden G. Edelstein, *Strange Enthusiasm*, p. 232.
11. Ibid.
12. Henry Steele Commager, *Theodore Parker*, p. 304.
13. Ralph L. Rusk, *Ralph Waldo Emerson*, p. 404.
14. Ibid. p. 405.
15. Benjamin P. Thomas, *Theodore Weld*, pp. 227, 229.
16. Ibid. pp. 231–33. Thoreau thought they were all very queer.
17. Frank Preston Stearns, *George Luther Stearns*, p. 241.
18. Harold Schwartz, *Samuel Gridley Howe*, pp. 244–46. Schwartz describes Howe's behavior as "hysterical."
19. Franklin B. Sanborn, *Recollections*, Vol. I, p. 209.
20. Basler, op. cit. Vol. IV, p. 268.
21. Bernard C. Steiner, *Life of Taney*, pp. 489–93.
22. He later wrote a book about the experience.
23. Julia Ward Howe, *Reminiscences*, pp. 274–275.
24. I am indebted to Mel Bradford for this insight: Mel Bradford, "Lincoln & the Rhetoric of Revolution," *Triumph* magazine, Vol. VI, Nos. 5 & 6, May and June 1971.
25. Rusk, op. cit. pp. 416, 418.
26. Ibid. p. 419.
27. Gilman M. Ostrander, "Emerson, Thoreau and John Brown," p. 726.
28. Van Wyck Brooks, *New England: Indian Summer 1865–1915*, (New York: E. P. Dutton, 1940), p. 99. Brooks describes the "glorious phalanx of old maids" left to dominate New England literature; he considers this the beginning of what would be two or more generations of the feminizing of American writing—while the men turned toward business and anti-intellectualism. He traced

these currents through a rejection of tradition in colleges in favor of engineering, a coarsening of national tone, and a reduction of vision.

29. Stearns, op. cit. pp. 383–385.
30. Rusk, op. cit. p. 428.
31. Ibid. 449.
32. See: Lewis Perry, *Radical Abolitionism,* passim.

Bibliography

Abels, Jules. *Man on Fire: John Brown and the Cause of Liberty.* New York: The Macmillan Company, 1971.

Adams, James Truslow. *America's Tragedy.* New York: Charles Scribner's Sons, 1934.

Agar, Herbert. *The Price of Union.* Boston: Houghton Mifflin Company, 1966.

Albrecht, Robert C. *Theodore Parker.* New York: Twayne Publishers, 1971.

Alcott, Louisa May. *Transcendental Wild Oats.* Boston: Houghton Mifflin Company, 1915.

Auchampaugh, Philip Gerald. *James Buchanan and His Cabinet on the Eve of Secession.* Boston: J.S. Canner and Co., 1956.

Barnes, Gilbert Hobbes. *The Antislavery Impulse: 1830–1844* New York: Harcourt, Brace & World, 1964.'

Basher, Roy P., ed. *The Collected Works of Abraham Lincoln.* New Brunswick, N.J.: Rutgers University Press, 1953, 8 vols.

Bauer, Jack K. *The Mexican War 1846–1848.* New York: Macmillan Publishing Co., 1974.

Beals, Carleton. *Brass Knuckle Crusade: The Great Know-Nothing Conspiracy, 1820–1860.* New York: Hastings House, 1960.

Bercovitch, Sacvan. *The American Puritan Imagination: Essays in Revaluation.* New York: Cambridge University Press, 1974.

Berky, Andrew S. and Shenton, James P. *The Historian's History of the United States.* New York: G.P. Putnam's Sons, 1966, 2 vols.

Boller, Paul F. *American Transcendentalism: An Intellectual Inquiry.* New York: G.P. Putnam's Sons, 1974.

Boston Courier for 1858, Radicalism in Religion, Philosophy and Social Life. Freeport, New York: Books for Libraries Press, repr. 1972.

Boyer, Richard O. *The Legend of John Brown: A Biography and a History,* New York: Alfred A. Knopf, 1973.

Bridenbaugh, Carl. *Mitre and Sceptre: Transatlantic Faiths, Ideas, Personalities and Politics, 1689–1775.* New York: Oxford University Press, 1962.

Brooks, Van Wyck. *The Flowering of New England 1815–1865.* New York: Random House, 1936. *New England: Indian Summer 1865–1915.* New York: E.P. Dutton Co., 1940.

Brown, Arthur W. *William Ellery Channing.* New York: Twayne Publishers, 1961.

Butterfield, Roger. *The American Past.* New York: Simon and Schuster, 1947.

Carlyle, Thomas. *Works,* New York: John W. Lovell Company, 1869, 10 vols.

Cash, W.J. *The Mind of the South.* London: Thames and Hudson, 1971.

Clive, John and Bailyn, Bernard. "England's Cultural Provinces: Scotland and America." *William and Mary Quarterly,* XI, (1954), pp. 200–213.

Coles, Harry L. *The War of 1812.* Chicago: University of Chicago Press, 1965.

Commager, Henry Steele. *Theodore Parker: Yankee Crusader.* Boston: Beacon Press, 1960.

Connelley, William Elsey. *John Brown.* Topeka, Kans.: Crane & Company, 1900.

Corwin, Edward S. *The "Higher Law" Background of American Constitutional Law.* rpr. Harvard Law Review XLII—1928–29 by Cornell University Press, Ithaca, N.Y., 1961.

Craton, Michael. *Sinews of Empire: A Short History of British Slavery.* New York: Doubleday, 1974, paperback.

Cross, Whitney R. *The Burned-over District: The Social and Intellectual History of Enthusiastic Religion in Western New York, 1800–1850.* New York: Harper & Row, 1965, paperback.

Cunliffe, Marcus. *The Nation Takes Shape: 1789–1837.* Chicago: University of Chicago Press, 1967.

Current, Richard N. *Daniel Webster and the Rise of National Conservatism.* Boston: Little, Brown and Company, 1955.

Curry, Richard O., ed. *The Abolitionists: Reformers or Fanatics?* New York: Holt, Rinehart and Winston, 1965.

Dalzell, Robert F. Jr. *Daniel Webster and the Trial of American Nationalism.* Boston: Houghton Mifflin Company, 1973.

Dodds, John W. *The Age of Paradox: A Biography of England 1841–1851.* New York: Rinehart & Company, 1952.

Donald, David. *Charles Sumner and the Coming of the Civil War.* New York: Alfred A. Knopf, 1960.

Douglass, Frederick. *Life and Times of Frederick Douglass: His Early Life as A Slave, His Escape from Bondage, and His Complete History.* London: Collier-Macmillan, 1962, Collier Books, paperback.

Durden, Robert F. *The Gray and the Black.* Baton Rouge, La.: Louisiana State University Press, 1972.

Edelstein, Tilden G. *Strange Enthusiasm: A Life of Thomas Wentworth Higginson.* New Haven, Conn.: Yale University Press, 1968.

Edgell, David P. *William Ellery Channing: An Intellectual Portrait.* Boston: Beacon Press, 1955.

Edwards, Jonathan. *Images or Shadows of Divine Things,* ed. Perry Miller. New Haven, Conn.: Yale University Press, 1948.

Eisenschiml, Otto. *Why Was Lincoln Murdered?* Boston: Little Brown and Company, 1950.

Elkins, Stanley. *Slavery: A Problem in American Institutional and Intellectual Life,* cf *The Abolitionists: Immediatism and the Question of Means.* Boston: D.C. Heath, 1964.

Emerson, Ralph Waldo. *English Traits.* Cambridge, Mass.: Harvard University Press, 1966. *Emerson's Essays.* London: J. M. Dent & Sons, 1906.

Ernst, Robert. *Immigrant Life in New York City, 1825–1863.* Port Washington, N.Y.: Ira J. Friedman Inc., 1965, reissue.

Fogelson, Robert M. and Rubenstein, Richard, eds. *Mass Violence in America: Invasion at Harper's Ferry.* New York: Arno Press & New York Times, 1969.

Freehling, William C. *Prelude to the Civil War: The Nullification Controversy in South Carolina 1816–1836.* New York: Harper & Row, 1965.

Gabriel, Ralph Henry. *Religion and Learning at Yale: The Church of Christ in the*

College and University 1757–1957. New Haven, Conn.: Yale University Press, 1958.

Gray, Henry David. *Emerson: A Statement of New England Transcendentalism in the Philosophy of its Chief Exponent.* New York: Frederick Ungar Publishing Co., 1965.

Hall, Thomas Cuming. *The Religious Background of American Culture.* Boston: Little, Brown and Co., 1930.

Harazti, Roger. *John Adams & The Prophets of Liberty.* Cambridge, Mass.: Harvard University Press, 1952.

Harlow, Ralph Volney. *Gerrit Smith, Philanthropist and Reformer.* NY: Russell & Russell div. of Atheneum, rpr. 1972.

Hawkins, Hugh, ed. *The Abolitionists: Immediatism and the Question of Means.* Boston: D.C. Heath, 1964. *The Abolitionists: Means, Ends and Motivations* Boston: D.C. Heath, 1972.

Hayek, F.A., ed. *Capitalism and the Historians.* Chicago: University of Chicago Press, 1974.

Heimart, Alan. *Religion and the American Mind: From the Great Awakening to the Revolution.* Cambridge, Mass.: Harvard University Press, 1968.

Hertz, Emanuel. *The Hidden Lincoln: From the Letters and Papers of William H. Herndon.* Garden City, N.Y.: Blue Ribbon Books, 1940.

Hibben, Paxton. *Henry Ward Beecher: An American Portrait.* New York: Press of the Reader's Club, 1942.

Hinton, Richard J. *John Brown and His Men.* NY: Funk & Wagnalls, 1894.

Hobsawm, E.J. *The Age of Revolution, 1789–1848.* New York: New American Library, 1962.

Hollis, Christopher. *The American Heresy.* London: Sheed and Ward, 1927.

Howe, Daniel Walker. *The Unitarian Conscience: Harvard Moral Philosophy 1805–1861.* Cambridge, Mass.: Harvard University Press, 1970.

Howe, Julia Ward. *Reminiscences 1819–1899.* Boston: Houghton Mifflin, 1900.

Hutchison, William R. *The Transcendental Ministers: Church Reform in the New England Renaissance.* New Haven, Conn.: Yale University Press, 1959.

Isely, Jeter Allen. *Horace Greeley and the Republican Party, 1853–1861.* Princeton, N.J.: Princeton University Press, 1947.

Jones, Maldwyn Allen. *American Immigration,* Chicago: University of Chicago Press, 1960.

Keonig, Louis W. *The Invisible Presidency.* New York: Rinehart & Company, 1960.

Kilby, Clyde S. *Minority of One: The Biography of Jonathan Blanchard.* Grand Rapids, Mich.: Wm. B. Eerdmans Publishing, 1959.

Kraus, Michael. *The United States to 1865.* Ann Arbor, Mich.: University of Michigan Press, 1959.

Ladies of the Mission. *The Old Brewery and the New Mission House at Five Points.* New York: Arno Press, 1970, reissue.

Leighton, Walter L. *French Philosophers and New England Transcendentalism.* New York: Greenwood Press, 1968.

Lerner, Gerda. *The Grimké Sisters from South Carolina: Rebels against Slavery.* Boston: Houghton Mifflin Company, 1967.

Main, Jackson Turner. *The Anti-Federalists: Critics of the Constitution 1781–1788.*
New York: W.W. Norton, 1974, paperback.

Malin, James C. *John Brown and the Legend of Fifty-Six.* Philadelphia: American
Philosophical Society, 1942.

The Contriving Brain and the Skillful Hand in the United States. Ann Arbor, Mich.:
Edwards Brothers, 1955.

Mathews, Donald G. *Agitation for Freedom: The Abolitionist Movement.* NY: John
Wiley & Sons, 1972.

May, Henry F. *Protestant Churches and Industrial America.* New York: Octagon
Books, 1963.

The Enlightenment in America. New York: Oxford University Press, 1976.

McClure, Alexander K. *Recollections of Half a Century.* Salem, Mass.: Salem
Press, 1902.

Meredith, Roy. *Mr. Lincoln's Contemporaries: An Album of Portraits by Mathew S.
Brady.* (NY: Charles Scribner's Sons, 1951).

Meyer, D. H. *The Instructed Conscience: The Shaping of the American National Ethic.*
Philadelphia: University of Pennsylvania Press, 1972.

Miller, Perry. *The New England Mind: From Colony to Province.* Cambridge, Mass.:
Harvard University Press, 1953.

The New England Mind: The Seventeenth Century. Cambridge, Mass.: 1954.

The Life of the Mind in America: From the Revolution to the Civil War. NY:
Harcourt, Brace & World, 1965, Books 1 through 3.

The Transcendentalists: An Anthology. Cambridge, Mass.: Harvard University
Press, 1971.

Milton, George Fort. *The Eve of Conflict: Stephen A. Douglas and the Needless War.*
New York: Octagon Books, 1963.

Morrow, Glenn R. *The Ethical and Economic Theories of Adam Smith.* New York:
Augustus M. Kelly Publishers, 1969 repr.

Nevins, Allan. *Ordeal of the Union.* New York: Charles Scribner's Sons 1947–
1971, 2 vols. *The Emergence of Lincoln.* NY: Charles Scribner's Sons, 1950, 2
vols.

Nichols, Alice. *Bleeding Kansas.* New York: Oxford University Press, 1954.

Nichols, Roy F. *The Stakes of Power 1845–1877.* New York: Hill and Wang, 1961.

Nye, Russell Blaine. *The Cultural Life of the New Nation 1776–1830.* New York:
Harper & Row, 1963, Harper Torchbook, paperback.

Oates, Stephen, B. *To Purge This Land With Blood: A Biography of John Brown.* New
York: Harper & Row, 1970.

Ostrander, Gilman M. "Emerson, Thoreau and John Brown." *Mississippi Valley
Historical Review,* vol. 4 (March, 1953), pp. 713–726.

Perry, Lewis. *Radical Abolitionism: Anarchy and the Government of God in Antislavery
Thought.* Ithaca, NY: Cornell University Press, 1973.

Philipson, N.T. and Mitchison, Rosalind. *Scotland in the Age of Improvement:
Essays in Scottish History in the Eighteenth Century.* Edinburgh: University Press,
1970.

Poster, Mark. *The Harmonium Man: Selected Writings of Charles Fourier.* New York:
Doubleday & Co., 1971, Anchor Books, paperback.

Quarles, Benjamin, ed. *Blacks on John Brown.* Urbana, Ill.: University of Illinois
Press, 1972.

Allies for Freedom: Blacks and John Brown. New York: Oxford University Press, 1974.

Robinson, Charles. *The Kansas Conflict.* New York: Harper & Brothers, 1882.

Ruchames, Louis. *A John Brown Reader.* New York: Abelard-Schuman, 1959.

Rushdoony, Rousas J. *The Nature of the American System.* Nutley, N.J.: Craig Press, 1965.

    The Messianic Character of American Education: Studies in the History of the Philosophy of Education. Nutley, N.J.: Craig Press, 1972.

    This Independent Republic. Nutley, N.J.: Craig Press, 1973.

    The Flight from Humanity: A Study of the Effect of Neoplatonism on Christianity. Nutley, N.J.: Craig Press, 1973.

    The Myth of Overpopulation. Nutley, N.J.: Craig Press, 1969.

    Revolt Against Maturity. Fairfax, Va.: Thoburn Press, 1977.

Rusk, Ralph L. *The Life of Ralph Waldo Emerson.* New York: Columbia University Press, 1949.

Sanborn, Franklin Benjamin. *Recollections of Seventy Years.* Boston: Gorham Press, 1909, 2 vols.

Scheidenhelm, Richard, ed. *The Response to John Brown.* Belmont, Cal: Wadsworth Publishing, 1972.

Schwartz, Harold. *Samuel Gridley Howe 1801–1876.* Cambridge, Mass.: Harvard University Press, 1976.

Sears, Clara Endicott, and Alcott, Louisa May. *Bronson Alcott's Fruitlands, with Wild Oats.* Boston: Houghton Mifflin Company, 1915.

Seldes, Gilbert. *The Stammering Century.* New York: Harper & Row, 1965, Harper Colophon Books, paperback.

Semple, Ellen Churchill. *American History and its Geographic Conditions.* Boston: Houghton Mifflin Company, 1903.

Sherwin, Oscar. *Prophet of Liberty: The Life and Times of Wendell Phillips.* New York: Bookman Associates, 1958.

Singletary, Otis, A. *The Mexican War.* Chicago: University of Chicago Press, 1960.

Smith, Chard Powers. *Yankees and God.* New York: Hermitage House, 1954.

Sowell, Thomas. *Race and Economics.* New York: David McKay Company, 1975, paperback.

Smith, Elbert D. *The Death of Slavery: The United States 1837–65.* Chicago: University of Chicago Press, 1967.

Stearns, Frank Preston. *Cambridge Essays.* Freeport, N.Y.: Books for Libraries Press, repr. 1968.

    The Life and Public Services of George Luther Stearns. Philadelphia: J.B. Lippincott, repr. Krause, New York 1969.

Steiner, Bernard C. *Life of Roger Brooke Taney, Chief Justice of the United States Supreme Court.* Westport, Conn.: Greenwood Press, repr. 1970.

Stone, Edward, ed. *Incident at Harper's Ferry.* Englewood Cliffs, N.J.: Prentice-Hall, 1956.

Tansill, Charles Callan, ed. *The Making of the American Republic: The Great Documents, 1774–1789.* New Rochelle, N.Y.: Arlington House, n.d.

Tharp, Louise Hall. *Three Saints and a Sinner: Julia Ward Howe, Louisa, Anne and Sam Ward.* Boston: Little, Brown and Company, 1956.

The Peabody Sisters of Boston. Boston: Little, Brown and Company, 1950.

Thayer, Eli M. *The New England Emigrant Aid Society.* Worcester, Mass.: Franklin P. Rice, pub., 1887.

The Journal of Christian Reconstruction. "Symposium on Christianity and the American Revolution." Vallecito, Cal: Chalcedon, 1976, Vol. III, No. 1.

Thomas, Benjamin P. *Theodore Weld: Crusader for Freedom.* New Brunswick, N.J.: Rutgers University Press, 1950.

Thomas, John L. *The Liberator: William Lloyd Garrison, A Biography.* Boston: Little, Brown and Company, 1963.

Villard, Oswald Garrison. *John Brown 1800–1859: A Biography Fifty Years After.* Gloucester, Mass.: Peter Smith, repr., 1966.

van Vleck, George W. *The Panic of 1857: An Analytical Study.* New York: Columbia University Press, 1943; AMS Press, 1967.

Warren, Robert Penn. *John Brown: The Making of a Martyr.* New York: Payson & Clarke, 1929.

Waugh, Alec. *A History of the West Indies from 1492 to 1898.* Garden City, N.Y.: Doubleday and Company, 1964.

Webber, Everett. *Escape to Utopia: The Communal Movement in America.* New York: Hastings House, 1952.

Wells, Damon. *Stephen Douglas: The Last Years, 1857–1861.* Austin, Tex: University of Texas Press, 1971.

Welter, Ruch. *The Mind of America, 1820–1860.* New York: Columbia University Press, 1975.

Weyl, Nathaniel, and Marina, William. *American Statesmen on Slavery and the Negro.* New Rochelle, N.Y., Arlington House, 1971.

White, Edward G. *The American Judicial Tradition.* New York: Oxford University Press, 1976.

Williams, George H. *Wilderness and Paradise in Christian Thought: The Biblical Experience & the Paradise Theme in the Theological Idea of the University.* New York: Harper & Row, 1962.

Wilson, Don W. *Governor Charles Robinson of Kansas.* Wichita, Kans.: University of Kansas Press, 1975.

Winks, Robin W., ed. *The Historian as Detective: Essays on Evidence.* New York: Harper & Row, 1968.

Wright, Conrad. *The Liberal Christians: Essays on American Unitarian Thought.* Boston: Beacon Press, 1970.

Wright, Conrad, intro. *Three Prophets of Religious Liberalism: Channing-Emerson-Parker.* Boston: Beacon Press, 1961.

Zornow, William Frank. *Kansas: A History of the Jayhawk State.* Norman, Okla: University of Oklahoma Press, 1957.

Index

361

Index

365

365

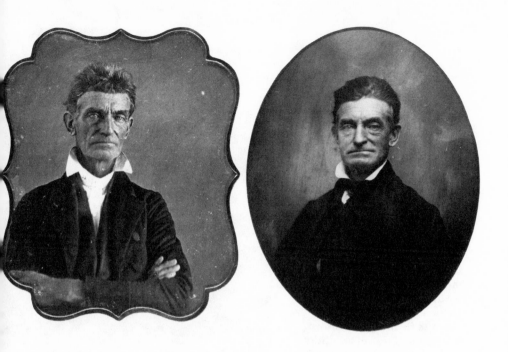

UPPER LEFT:
Daguerreotype of a desperate-looking John Brown in Kansas, 1856.
Boston Athenaeum

UPPER RIGHT:
John Brown in the late 1840s.
Boston Athenaeum

LOWER RIGHT:
John Brown, wearing a beard as a disguise, in May, 1859, just before his assault on Harper's Ferry Arsenal.
Boston Athenaeum

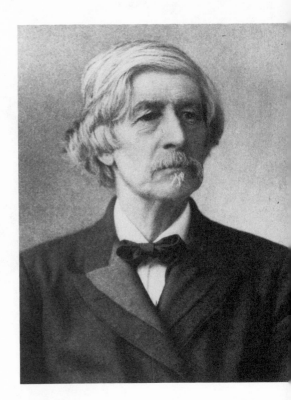

Outwardly staid, inwardly mercurial, George Luther Stearns, wealthy Boston manufacturer (1809-1867), helped arm and finance John Brown. After the outbreak of hostilities he helped provoke, he joined the Union army as a major.
Boston Athenaeum

Six foot three schoolteacher Franklin B. Sanborn (1831-1917) married an invalid heiress and inherited her fortune, helped arm and finance John Brown. Sanborn later became a powerful governmental official in Massachusetts, promoting State control of education and philanthropy.
Boston Athenaeum

Gerrit Smith (1797-1874) inherited vast holdings from his father, who had been a partner of John Jacob Astor. Smith helped arm and finance John Brown. When Brown was arrested for murder and treason, Smith fled and feigned insanity.
Boston Athenaeum

Reverend Thomas Wentworth Higginson (1823-1911) rejected Christianity in favor of Unitarianism, helped arm and finance John Brown. As a later literary critic he altered Emily Dickinson's poems "to make them suitable for publication," became an advocate of women's rights, Prohibition and Socialism.
Boston Athenaeum

Dr. Samuel Gridley Howe (1801-1876), a famous physician and hero of the Greek War of Independence, helped arm and finance John Brown. His wife, Julia Ward Howe, later became even more famous for creating the words to The Battle Hymn of the Republic.
Boston Athenaeum

Reverend Theodore Parker (1810-1860), the most famous preacher of his day, turned against Christianity in favor of Unitarianism, helped arm and finance John Brown. He died in Rome, Italy of tuberculosis after the Raid on Harper's Ferry Arsenal, but before the outbreak of war.
Boston Athenaeum

BROWN COUNTRY — KANSAS TERRITORY, 1856

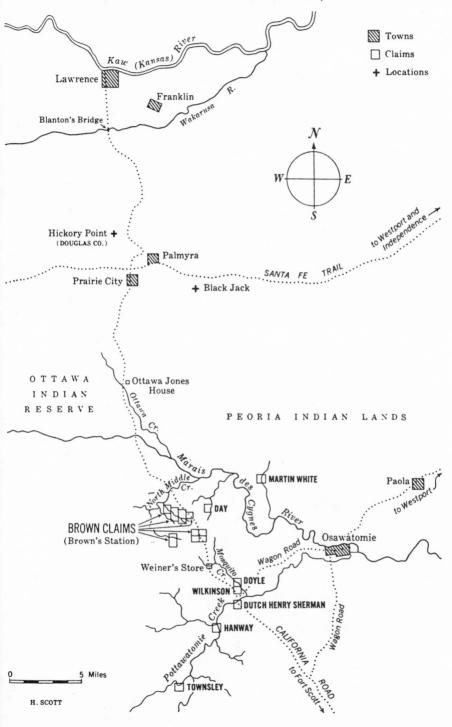

Towns
Claims
+ Locations

Kaw (Kansas) River

Lawrence

Franklin

Wakarusa R.

Blanton's Bridge

N
W—E
S

Hickory Point +
(DOUGLAS CO.)

Palmyra

to Westport and Independence

Prairie City

Black Jack

SANTA FE TRAIL

OTTAWA
INDIAN
RESERVE

Ottawa Jones
House

Ottawa Cr.

PEORIA INDIAN LANDS

Marais des Cygnes River

North Middle Cr.

MARTIN WHITE

Paola

to Westport

DAY

BROWN CLAIMS
(Brown's Station)

Osawatomie

Wagon Road

Weiner's Store

Mosquito Cr.

DOYLE

WILKINSON

DUTCH HENRY SHERMAN

Wagon Road

HANWAY

Pottawatomie Creek

CALIFORNIA ROAD

to Fort Scott

0   5 Miles

TOWNSLEY

H. SCOTT

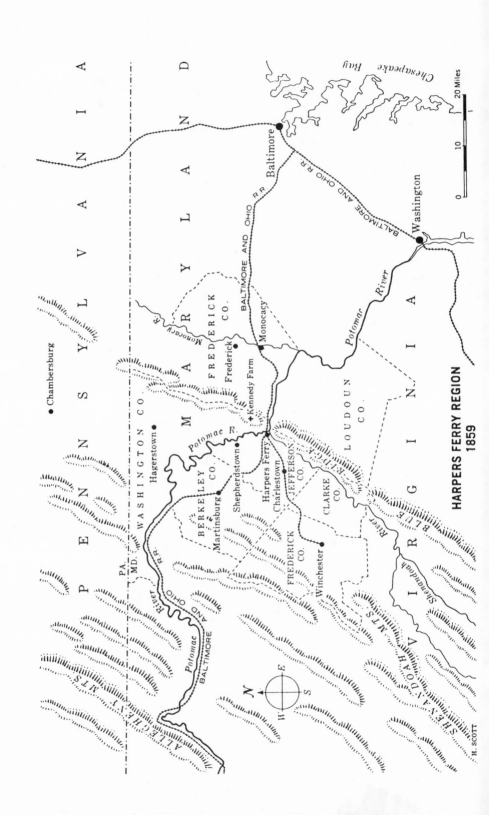

HARPERS FERRY REGION
1859

PENNSYLVANIA

MARYLAND

VIRGINIA

Chesapeake Bay

Baltimore

Washington

BALTIMORE AND OHIO R.R.

Potomac River

Monocacy

FREDERICK CO.

Frederick

Kennedy Farm

BALTIMORE AND OHIO R.R.

Monocacy R.

LOUDOUN CO.

Chambersburg

WASHINGTON CO.

Hagerstown

Potomac R.

BERKELEY CO.

Martinsburg

Shepherdstown

Harpers Ferry

Charlestown

JEFFERSON CO.

CLARKE CO.

FREDERICK CO.

Winchester

BLUE RIDGE

Shenandoah River

SHENANDOAH MTS.

ALLEGHENY MTS.

PA.
MD.

BALTIMORE AND OHIO R.R.

Potomac River

BALTIMORE

N
E
S
W

20 Miles

10

0

H. SCOTT